DEVELOPING

A GODLY

ENVIRONMENT

Volume Three

By

Rayola Kelley

Hidden Manna Publications

DEVELOPING A GODLY ENVIRONMENT

Volume Three
Copyright © 2010 & 2023 by Rayola Kelley

ISBN: 978-0-9891683-3-5

Except where otherwise indicated, all Scripture quotations in this book are taken from the King James Version of the Bible.

Featuring the Following Books:
Godly Discipline
Prayer and Worship
Don't Touch That Dial
Face of Thankfulness
ABCs of Christianity

The letters *SC* stands for information taken from *Strong's Exhaustive Concordance of the Bible,* while the letters *WD* identifies information taken from the *Webster's New Collegiate Dictionary.*

You can obtain a study reference book to complement your studies of this volume at Gentle Shepherd Ministries' website at www.gentleshepherd.com.

Hidden Manna Publications
P.O. Box 3572
Oldtown, ID. 83822
www.gentleshepherd.com

Facebook:
https://www.facebook.com/HiddenMannaPublications/

MEMORIAL
AND
ACKNOWLEDGMENT

In Loving Memory Of:

Lorrie Anderson Jones
Carol Sue Haskins
Betty Swinford
Vickie Brown
Elaine Johnson
Rolland Danielson
Frances Binam
LeNita Binam
Muriel Payton

Special Acknowledgment:

I want to acknowledge the
editing works of Jo Reaves and Crystal Garvin.
I also want to thank all of those
who have proofread these books through the years.

Contents

INTRODUCTION

Developing a Godly Environment is third in a series of seven volumes that are a combination of books of various themes of the Christian life. Each volume was assembled to harmonize with the Gentle Shepherd Ministries Discipleship Course.

Volume Three addresses the type of inward environment that must be present to ensure spiritual growth. Spiritual growth can only occur when godliness is being established in the Christian life. A godly environment includes uprightness, righteous prayer, Spirit-inspired worship, the attitude of thankfulness, and godly conduct.

Personal discipline is a necessary characteristic to ensure the proper inward environment of the Christian. The first book in this volume *Godly Discipline* explains not only how such discipline is developed, but how it will express itself, as well as how this discipline is often an omitted component in many Christians.

The present day presentation of Christianity makes the Christian life appear as if it is simply a matter of praying, going to church, and reading the Bible. However, to develop godliness in our spiritual lives requires inward discipline. The Apostle Paul refers to the Christian life as a race and a battle. Whether you are a runner or a soldier, discipline is a must in order to endure the challenges, fight the battles, and finish the course. This book reveals the disciplines of the Christian life that will produce character, godliness and endurance in the Christian walk.

There is no life in God without prayer and worship. *Prayer and Worship* is a candid book about the true reasons for praying to God and worshipping Him. Genuine prayer and worship are disciplines. One disciplines the soul, while the other disciplines the spirit. Although these subjects are popular, many believers still do not comprehend what it means to have a powerful prayer life, and to come to a place of worship that is acceptable to God. This book challenges popular perceptions about these two subjects. The author tears down formulas and misconceptions to reveal the simplicity of powerful prayer, and the beauty of pure and acceptable worship.

The third book in this volume is about hearing God's voice. To know the voice of God demands discipline, which ensures spiritual growth. *Don't Touch That Dial* discusses the many different voices that are vying for man's attention. The many misconceptions concerning the voice of God have caused much confusion. He is speaking today, but few know how to discern between God's voice and the myriad of other voices. It takes a certain type of discipline to learn how to wade through the various voices to be able to recognize the voice of God. This small book addresses the misconceptions and challenges that people encounter when they are seeking to know God's will. Ultimately, this book will bring understanding as to how God's voice manifests itself to His people.

The attitude of thankfulness is absent in many Christians. Drowned out by various demands of the world, Christians have lost sight of their incredible blessings. As a result, their attitude towards God has drifted from the boundaries that are able to discipline it. One of those boundaries that clearly discipline attitudes is thankfulness. *The Face of Thankfulness* considers the real blessings of the Christian life in light of three unlikely examples. It reveals how thankfulness disciplines not only the attitude, but inspires people's actions.

As you consider each example in this book, you will begin to realize why blood-bought saints are the most blessed people in the world, and should serve as living expressions of thankfulness in regards to God. Each of these examples not only reveals the blessings of encountering Jesus, but unveils the discipline of how the face of thankfulness will manifest itself in each person who responds to the incredible virtues of Christ, the Son of the Living God.

ABC's of the Christian Life summarizes what it takes for the Christian to have a victorious life. By using the English alphabet, priceless nuggets of this incredible walk are outlined. The book presents different truths, experiences, and disciplines of the Christian walk. The goal of this small book is to help Christians to understand what it means to graduate from the infant stages to the mature Christian stage. It is in the mature stage that a believer can be assured that his or her inward environment is conducive for him or her to discover the reality of God in an intimate relationship of agreement, worship, and service.

Each book in Volume Three will clearly challenge the environment of the reader's inner man. Therefore, it is important for each person to take to heart the themes of these books as he or she examines, accepts the challenge, and embraces the way of a disciplined, godly life.

Book One

GODLY DISCIPLINE

INTRODUCTION

You may be surprised that a simple subject such as discipline could comprise an entire book. After all, you are either disciplined in a matter or you are not. Surprisingly, discipline can be a very intense subject. Godly discipline has been one of the virtues I have struggled with in my own life. I have learned that nothing gets accomplished without some form of discipline. In fact, the opposite of discipline is laziness, slothfulness, and irresponsibility.

In ministering to people, I have discovered that godly discipline is one quality that is often missing in their lives. It is as though many people are waiting for something to happen, or something to be handed to them without any action on their part. These individuals eventually become frustrated, disillusioned, angry, and bitter.

I have come to realize that discipline involves both attitude and action. Without the attitude, there will be no action. And, without the application, there will be no establishment of character and results.

The contemporary Church often overlooks godly discipline. Because of its absence, I believe this book is vital. The Christian life is a disciplined life, and without the application of this excellent virtue, one will not finish the course set before him or her. God has provided the tools to ensure godly discipline. These simple tools are generally overlooked or ignored in the modern Church. The content of this book is basic Christianity, but it will probably not be popular in the midst of "easy believism" and all the different heretical teachings that are invading and challenging the Church today.

If you study the life of Jesus Christ and the saints, godly discipline is quite evident. In fact, the price these individuals paid in order to establish and maintain this virtue is evident. You will also see why it is important. If it is missing, the Christian life will prove to be more difficult, and the struggles and challenges will bring an individual closer to defeat and destruction.

The question is, do you have godly discipline or is it greatly missing in your life? This book will help you not only discover what constitutes discipline, but what it will take for it to be established in your life.

1

THE PURPOSE OF DISCIPLINE

Chaos at any level is an open door to the kingdom of darkness. 1 Corinthians 14:33 tells us God is not a God of confusion or chaos. It is on the shirttails of confusion that the seeds of discord or division are sown in relationships, families, and churches. Confusion always clouds the real issues in a matter, and causes people to focus or blame such confusion on issues that are symptoms of the problem, but not the core of it. This is why Jesus' warning was given in Matthew 12:25, "...Every kingdom divided against itself is brought to desolation; and every city or house divided against itself shall not stand."

Obviously, there must be order to establish an environment in which there is clarity, agreement and resolution. Today many people live in an environment where unresolved issues fester and grow into fear, anger, and bitterness. However, to gain order in our lives, homes, and churches, all things must be brought to the light and brought into line with God's Word.[1] Order of any type requires discipline. Such a prospect brings us to the purpose of godly discipline: To enable us to partake of holiness. The writer of Hebrews made this statement, "For they verily for a few days chastened us after their own pleasure, but he for our profit, that we might be partakers of his holiness" (Hebrews 12:10).

Chaos comes through three avenues, Satan, rebellion, and insecurity. Although Satan always looks for open doors, he is able to take territory because there is no real authority or power present to expose his work, stop his advances, and drive him back. Rebellion exists because there is no order. There must be order to stop any type of rebellion in its momentum. Insecurity is present because there are no sure boundaries that serve as checks and balances to attitudes and behaviors. In other words, anything goes. The results are obvious. Satan creates oppression in the environment, rebellion produces fear, and insecurity will express itself in anger.

People must have boundaries in order to know where they fit and what is expected of them. Such an environment ensures that they will be receptive to receive instructions. It will bring temperance to their attitude, and bring their behavior under control, making them open to instruction. Otherwise, they will fight against, ignore, shun, mock, and reject any instruction. If order is missing, a person will not have the means or ability to properly receive. Chaos causes torment, insecurity, and anger. Hence,

---

[1] Ephesians 4:17-5:13

enters the terrible reality behind confusion. Confusion blinds people to the truth, putting their souls in harm's way and their feet on the path of sin and death.[2]

Obviously, order must not only be prevalent in the physical environment, but in the inward disposition of the person as well. In fact, physical environment reveals much about the inward environment. For example, when I was around 11 or 12 years of age, I used to watch five children for friends who lived across the street from us. Since my parents were across the street, I knew I had some muscle behind me. These children ranged in age from two years older than me to two years younger, filtering down to age three.

The first thing I did when I walked into their door was to establish a working order to clean the house. Our friend liked cats and housed anywhere from 10 to 26 cats indoors. These cats rarely used the litter box. Their favorite place was the laundry room where they would find the right spot in all the piles of dirty clothes. I knew there was no order in the environment to begin with, so how could I maintain discipline unless the environment was first brought into order? Needless to say, cleaning the house always proved to be a challenge.

There must be order in an environment to establish order among those who occupy that environment. It takes discipline in both arenas to ensure harmony. It only takes one individual out of order to create chaos. After all, one bad apple will taint the rest of the apples unless it is separated.

As we will see throughout this book, discipline ensures order. It challenges wrong behavioral patterns as a means to confront wrong attitudes. When wrong attitudes change, behavioral patterns will follow suit.

In this present age of "tolerance," people are struggling with the concept of discipline. They view it as harsh, rather than as a means that ensures order. Such people do not see the need for order because their way of thinking is out of order. And, the only time such people get excited about chaos is when it dares to intrude into their personal world. Such intrusion will cause them to react.

What most people fail to realize is that order establishes authority. Discipline simply confirms authority. Without authority there is no respect. Without respect, individuals have no power to speak into a person's life about matters that could determine a person's well-being or spiritual destination. It is vital to understand that people who are properly being confronted with fair discipline do not line up to the discipline. Rather, they line up to the quality of authority that is being upheld through discipline. As a leader of people, I have often been able to keep order because people respect me. However, I have also had people test my authority. The disciplinary measures I take will cause those who are

---

[2] John 8:32-36; Romans 8:2; 2 Corinthians 4:3-6

teachable to adjust their attitudes and behavior to the authority that is being upheld.

Authority is tried three ways, through opposition, testing, or challenge. The foremost ones who oppose godly authority are those who serve the kingdom of darkness. In some cases, these people will vehemently oppose a believer in every way. Clearly, such people hate the truth, as well as prove to be fools at heart.

Some people will test your authority. These people want to see whether you mean what you say. I remember being tested by one of our friends' children I previously made reference to who I babysat. He was only two years younger than me. You need to keep in mind that I played with these children. However, as the babysitter, I was in a position of authority regardless of my age and the fact that he was the same height as I was, and stronger. To make a long story short, the confrontation started in the living room of the house and ended on the front lawn, with both of us rolling on the ground. Eventually, I got him in a leg lock and used all my weigh to press him against the ground. In the end, my authority held, and he never tested me again.

Other people will challenge your authority. Such challenges point to rebellion. Rebellion's main goal is to come out on top. Challenges of such nature basically mock your authority. This is where clear discipline must be executed to ensure both order and respect. Once again, respect is necessary to not only ensure order, but to be able to speak into a person's life. For the Christian, it is a life-and-death matter in light of preaching the Gospel and sharing his or her testimony about Jesus' redemption.

The big challenge for many people in regards to authority is that many who are in authority lack personal discipline. Authority that exists outside of the basis of proper discipline can prove to be a hard pill to swallow. Such authority undermines all authority to those who do not see or possess the consistent discipline to back it up.

For example, some people mishandle authority. This proves they are inexperienced; therefore, they lack wisdom and are hypocritical. Other people abuse authority. Such abuse finds its source in arrogance, and will always cause division. There are those who neglect their authority. These are people who fail to take responsibility for their position. They become indifferent to their reality and their position. Finally, you have those who overstep their authority. These types of people do not really recognize or respect any authority. It is their way of getting around authority or defying it.

This brings us to the core of the problem with all people as far as order and discipline. It is called foolishness. Foolishness must be confronted. It can prove to be unteachable and destructive. According to a word study on becoming a fool by Os Hillman, dated February 11, 2006, there are four types of fools. One is the simple fool. This is the person who makes a mistake due to foolishness, but learns the lesson. A good example of this type of fool is King David.

The second type of fool is the hardened fool. This is a person who never learns the lessons, because he or she will not listen to the experience of wisdom and godly instruction. Such people continue to commit the same error, eventually tasting the bitterness of judgment. Foolishness of this nature can be observed in the life of King Saul.

The third type of fool is the mocking fool. This is an individual who scoffs at the things of God. This type of person is cynical towards His truths, and takes pride in exalting his or her "so-called" wisdom over God's unchangeable wisdom. Ultimately, such a person will disregard anything that is of God, from God, and because of God.

The fourth level that a person can reach in foolishness can be found in the life of Nabal.[3] The likes of Nabal blatantly reject or deny God. They are wicked people, who bring disgrace upon that which is true and righteous, while despising holiness.

We all start out being foolish. We make foolish decisions, until life brings a harsh reality that produces a reality check through some form of discipline. If a person learns, he or she will become wise, but if a person holds on to his or her right to be foolish, such a person will become a fool in his or her ways and decisions.

Foolishness is always surrounded by chaos. It brings upheaval to the environment, torment to the soul, and despair to the spirit. It is only through discipline that the proper order and wisdom can be brought to a person's life. However, it will be the person's choice as to how he or she will respond to the challenge of discipline. Such a choice will be determined by the attitude of the person.

Godly discipline serves as personal points of authority and godliness. Without discipline we remain foolish in our notions and a fool in our practices. Without discipline, we will lack authority, walk in hypocrisy, and will prove to be ineffective in our lives.

The question is do you possess such discipline? As you consider the rest of the chapters in this book, carefully examine your attitude, character and conduct. Make sure that godly discipline is tempering every area of your spirit, soul and body.

---

[3] 1 Samuel 25:2-38

2

TYPES OF DISCIPLINE

What do you think of when you hear or read the word "discipline"? You might think chastisement. Granted, this is a form of discipline, but it does not encompass the complete idea of discipline. There is so much more to it. According to the *Webster's New Collegiate Dictionary*, it is a form of chastisement, but it also points to training or development through instruction and exercise. In addition, it entails both self-control and being under control

There are three types of discipline. They are physical, mental, and spiritual discipline. Any athlete has knowledge about the necessity for developing physical discipline. This is where a person trains his or her body to function at its peak. This involves building up muscles and strengthening one's endurance level. An athlete has to be in shape in order for his or her body to rise up to meet the challenge. A person who is not physically prepared is most likely to suffer injury and defeat.

Mental discipline is a necessity for all discipline. People have to mentally discipline themselves before they can physically meet the challenge. Without the mental discipline, the body will always find excuses as to why it will not discipline itself. This is where the thought process takes place. The body is quick to tell the mind that it prefers to sleep in instead of train. Therefore, thought patterns and approaches must be changed in order to challenge body, mind, and spirit. Unless individuals are prepared to ignore the excuses, and simply do what is necessary, the physical training will never occur. Athletes know that the majority of the battle is fought in the mind. The body will always give in to excuses or preferences. And, the only means by which the mind can be brought under control is by the will.

The will of man points to determination. There must be a determination to discipline the body. Determination requires establishing a goal. It is not enough to desire or want discipline in an area. This usually means the emotions are at a fever pitch. Emotions may display zeal to see something happen, but the zealous feeling is temporary. Such zeal gives way to complacency. Complacency always deals in the future, never the present. In other words, I have already blown it; therefore, I might as well start tomorrow, but meanwhile, I might just as well enjoy myself. Sound familiar?

Emotions represent good intentions, but these intentions lack endurance. This zeal will only last as long as the emotional momentum is present. The reality of life is that everyone must land. Once that happens, reality sets in. The desire to discipline an area is gone, and now the person has to face the emptiness of his or her intentions.

Such people may have desired the benefits of discipline, but they did not have the determination to pay the price. The reason they did not have the determination to discipline themselves is because they have not yet counted the cost. Discipline involves a cost. Jesus understood this. He counted the cost and set out to pay the price. In fact, it became His whole focus. The key to paying the price is making the end results your whole focus. Zeal without knowledge or the willingness to pay the price simply means there is no real, set goal that is worth going the necessary distance in order to get the desired results.[1]

The lack of focus implies a lack of vision.[2] Vision points to something outside of self. In other words, if your idea of discipline is about how something will make you feel or make you appear, it will not be enough. Vision comes down to the way something will be. It is beyond self. It may mean gaining some kind of prize, accomplishing some kind of feat, or establishing some type of result or effect. Nevertheless, the vision must be bigger than self before it can get past personal emotions and intentions. Jesus proved this in His own life. Luke 9:51 says, "And it came to pass, when the time was come that he should be received up, he steadfastly set his face to go to Jerusalem." Jerusalem was not about Jesus, but about the salvation of souls.

Spiritual discipline entails disciplining the inner man. People can take credit for physical discipline. Some individuals have even developed tremendous mental discipline, but spiritual discipline has to do with submission more than personal temperance. This is brought out in the fruit of the Spirit.[3] Before temperance or self-control, there must be meekness. Meekness implies strength under control. Meekness points to the type of attitude that will be developed in the person. In the kingdom of God, a person must come under the control of the Spirit before there can be temperance or godly conduct. The Apostle Paul confirmed this when he stated, "This I say then, walk in the Spirit, and ye shall not fulfil the lust of the flesh" (Galatians 5:16). In order for a person to come under control, he or she must submit to the Holy Ghost.

Once a person is practicing temperance, testing will follow to establish an attitude of meekness in greater measure. It is at this point that character is established. Jesus proved this order. He first came to the Jordan River where the Holy Ghost came upon Him. This represented not only His anointing, but He now was under the Spirit.[4] Luke 4:1 tells us what happened after His baptism, "And Jesus being full of the Holy Ghost returned from Jordan, and was led by the Spirit into the wilderness."

---

[1] Luke 14:28-32; Romans 10:2-3

[2] Proverbs 29:18

[3] Galatians 5:22-23

[4] Matthew 3:13-4:1; Romans 5:1-5; James 1:2-4

Jesus was anointed, prepared and led to the wilderness where He was tested by the devil. There, He stood and withstood the temptation of Satan. After His ordeal, Jesus returned in the power of the Spirit. There, His reputation went out into the entire region.[5]

The work of the Spirit is to anoint, prepare, lead, and empower us into a powerful life, which points to a disciplined life. As you study the Christian life, you begin to realize that every aspect of it is disciplined by submitting to the work of the Spirit. For example, if a person is walking after the Spirit, there will be no condemnation. The Apostle Paul stated that the righteousness of the Law would be fulfilled in us if we walk in the Spirit.

Other benefits of walking in the Spirit are that we will mind the things of the Spirit, righteousness will be evident, and we will become the sons of God.[6] He summarized the end results of walking in the Spirit in Romans 8:13, "For if ye live after the flesh, ye shall die: but if ye through the Spirit do mortify the deeds of the body, ye shall live."

By walking in the Spirit, the flesh will be subdued. The Bible talks about those things that must be disciplined to ensure the quality of our spiritual lives. Keep in mind that there cannot be discipline until one is under the control of the Spirit. Anything that is disciplined outside of the Spirit of God will develop an improper attitude. Instead of the person realizing that it is the power and sanctifying work of the Spirit that keeps discipline in a proper light, he or she will take credit for it. This means that the person will touch God's glory with vainglory. According to the Apostle Paul, there will be no vainglory taking credit for the work of God. Godly discipline finds its source, power, and determination in the Holy Ghost. Therefore, all godly discipline will be for the glory of God.

The Apostle Paul gives us the insight to the first point of discipline in 1 Corinthians 9:27, "But I keep under my body, and bring it into subjection: lest that by any means, when I have preached to others, I myself should be a castaway." "Castaway" means rejected, worthless, or reprobate.[7] The body is the temple of God. We are warned that if we destroy this temple, God will destroy us. The Apostle Paul kept his body or conduct in subjection, so he would not be a hypocrite. In order to do this, Paul would only render his body in ways that made him an instrument of righteousness.[8]

Excusing ourselves from our responsibility to discipline our body robs us of credibility. If you fail to keep your body in subjection, not only are you a hypocrite, but you are also a liar. You do not believe what you proclaim. Such hypocrisy brings a reproach on the Gospel.

---

[5] Luke 4:14

[6] Romans 8:1-2, 4-5, 10, 14; 1 Corinthians 3:16-17; 6:17-20

[7] Strong's Exhaustive Concordance; #96

[8] Romans 6:12-13

Next, the area in our lives that must come under control is our thought-life. It is up to each of us to bring our bodies into subjection. But, when it comes to mental discipline, we must come to terms with how much our mental functioning and conclusions are undisciplined. The only way we can do this is by agreeing with God's evaluation. Our thoughts are different, contrary, and base when compared to God's thoughts. Our thoughts must be brought from the base level of vanity, perversion, and selfishness to embrace the higher thoughts and ways of God. In order to bring them from the depths of foolishness, they must first be brought under control. The Apostle Paul tells us that we must bring them into obedience to Christ. This means we must line all of our thoughts up to the Person, teachings, and examples of Jesus.[9]

The Apostle Paul instructs believers as to what to think upon in Philippians 4:8. When you consider what a person is to think upon, you can clearly see that these virtues summarize the very Person of Jesus. Paul goes on to instruct that those things people have learned, received, heard, and seen in regard to their spiritual lives must be applied to their walk. If they do, the God of peace will be with them. After all, the mind that stays on God will have peace.[10]

To line up one's thoughts to the obedience of Christ is not only a mental discipline, but it ensures that the mind will not erect another god through vain imaginations and speculations.[11] This is what happens when people have failed to come to terms with the real God of the Bible, and line up to His character and ways in their way of thinking and doing.

The next area that must be controlled is the tongue. James tells us that we must bridle the tongue, for no man can truly tame it. "Bridle" means to curb the activities of the tongue.[12] This means to restrain or rein in the tongue. Sadly, many people just let their tongue flap, without realizing its evilness or poison. The tongue is usually the last member of the body to come under control. It enjoys freedom without any restraint. What many do not realize is that the tongue exposes the heart.[13]

A person once told me that he thought he had the right to say what he wanted. After all, he was simply expressing his personality, and if people did not like it, so what. I agreed that he could say whatever he wanted, but he also had to accept the consequences that often come with an undisciplined tongue.

As Christians, we do not have the right to express anything other than edification.[14] Edification can entail encouragement, warning, rebuke, or exhortation. In other words, edification is not simply encouragement,

---

[9] Isaiah 55:8-9; 2 Corinthians 10:3-5
[10] Isaiah 26:3; 2 Corinthians 10:5; Philippians 4:9
[11] 2 Corinthians 10:5
[12] Strong's Exhaustive Concordance; #5469
[13] Matthew 15:17-19; James 3:2, 8
[14] Ephesians 4:25, 29-30; James 3:13

19

or a legalized way of flattering someone. It is a means to build someone up in the knowledge of Christ, based on his or her spiritual condition.

The tongue will also reveal much about a person's spiritual life. It is the cause of most of the problems in our lives. Proverbs 21:23 states, "Whoso keepeth his mouth and tongue keepeth his soul from troubles."

James tells us that those who do not control their tongues cause their religion to become vain, especially to others. In other words, religion will become useless. It will mean nothing to those who know that it is all words without action or life to back it up. Ultimately, your tongue will either confirm your proclamations about Jesus, or expose you to be a hypocrite. It will either show you to be wise, or a fool who slanders, gossips, and flatters for personal reasons.

The next area that needs to be disciplined is our vision. The body must be brought into subjection, the thoughts must be lined up to Jesus, and the tongue's activities must be reined in. These three areas show some type of restraint on our part, but when it comes to vision, aggression is required. The Apostle Paul brought this out in Philippians 3:14, "I press towards the mark for the prize of the high calling of God in Christ Jesus." Paul was pressing forward. It was as if he was travailing. This implies that he was willing to lose it all in the process, to gain the prize.

Restraint forces certain areas into a place of order, but aggression of this type creates adversity in order to define purpose and result. This also produces discipline. For example, the more Paul pressed towards the prize, the more focused he became on his goal.

Vision forces this type of discipline because it requires a person to get past self. Such discipline is not easy for those who are self-centered. This is why vision is vital for discipline. It gives people a mark to aim for. The more focused they become the more discipline is developed in their lives.

A pastor gave the three ingredients for disciplining the body, soul, and spirit. Fasting is one means of disciplining the body. Fasting has to do with restraining our body from partaking. Personally, I cannot fast unless God calls me into it because of my blood sugar levels. Over the years, I have refrained from certain foods that are unhealthy for me. This has not been easy because my taste buds relish certain unhealthy foods. However, my body has responded quite nicely. Surprisingly, I no longer miss these foods; therefore, it is not a matter of fasting, but a lifestyle.

For our society of abundance, I believe the real key to properly disciplining our bodies is something called moderation.[15] Moderation is a discipline in itself. We are a society that heaps upon our flesh all the lusts we can grab a hold of. We hoard, justify, and hold these pursuits up as God honoring us. These fleshly pursuits are nothing more than self-serving indulgences that reveal we are a gluttonous society that is not

---

[15] Philippians 4:5

only idolatrous, but (in such gluttony) we oppress others with our selfishness. I fear for our society. In order to learn what is important, we may have to lose it all. In order to learn moderation, we may have to partake of the cup of leanness. In order to recognize our many worldly idols, God will have to probably bring them down to the dust in utter defeat.

We can discipline the soul by meditating on the Word. The Word keeps us from sinning, cleanses us from the unholy, and reveals our spiritual condition. It serves as both our milk and meat.[16] As you can see, the Word feeds, cleanses, and renews the soul.

The way that we discipline the spirit is to pray in the spirit. We know that when we pray in the spirit, it personally edifies us.[17] It is the way to keep the channel open to God, and the Rivers of Living Water flowing freely through our lives.

Are you disciplined in your Christian life? Perhaps you are disciplined in some areas, but not in others. Ask the Lord to show you where discipline is lacking, and to help you establish the determination to ensure the necessary discipline. After all, we do not want to be a castaway because of our body, idolatrous due to our thoughts, have our religion considered vain because of our tongues, or perish because we have no vision. Obviously, there is only one choice. Either I choose the way of discipline, or become defeated because there will be no order, reality, credibility, or purpose in my Christian life.

---

[16] Psalm 119:9-16; I Corinthians 3:2-3; Ephesians 5:26; Hebrews 4:12; 5:12-14
[17] Romans 14:15; 1 Corinthians 14:15; Ephesians 6:18

3

DISCIPLINE VS. CONTROL

The Christian life is a disciplined life. Jesus called his followers to this disciplined life when He told them to follow Him. This means they were to follow Him in His teachings, examples, and ways. His followers were being asked to abandon the life they presently knew, in order to follow Jesus into a new, unknown life. This abandonment is known as consecration.

Consecration is necessary for separation from the world and its various entanglements. Without this separation, Christians can never be followers of Jesus because they will constantly play the harlot with the world.[1] This agreement will keep these individuals operating from a carnal level; ultimately preventing godly discipline from being formed in them.

The followers of Jesus left families and homes to follow Him into a new life. They left their careers behind to take on new positions. They left behind personal dreams and hopes, to consider possibilities that would exceed their imaginations. Ultimately, they were flinging themselves upon the Master, to do His bidding.[2]

Consecration is total abandonment from one's present life. This involves subjecting the will, mind, and emotions to the master. Abandonment of this nature points to a person becoming a disciple. Disciple points to a student, but the involvement the student has with the teacher has a greater implication. For a disciple, it is not just a matter of learning, but also a matter of being. Disciples leave behind the old to take on the new. However, a disciple's goal does not stop with taking on the new way. It goes beyond simply being a disciple to training others in the same way. This was clearly brought out in Jesus' initial invitation to His followers, "...Follow me, and I will make you fishers of men" (Matthew 4:19). Jesus was not just calling these men to follow Him so they could learn and witness great things, but to be trained to continue the work of attracting others to this new life.

Jesus reaffirmed this call for true discipleship before His ascension in Matthew 28:19-20, "Go ye therefore, and teach all nations, baptizing them in the name of the Father, and of the Son, and of the Holy ghost: Teaching them to observe all things whatsoever I have commanded you: and, lo, I am with you always, even unto the end of the world." Therefore,

---

[1] James 4:4
[2] Matthew 19:27-29

most disciples point others to the leader, teaching, or belief. As Christians, we not only point people to Jesus and His teachings, but to eternal life, a lasting hope, and an everlasting kingdom. We point people to a way of life that is expressed in everlasting love, unfeigned faith, and unwavering hope.

Jesus called His disciples to personally experience and taste this life. The Apostle John confirmed this in 1 John 1:1, "That which was from the beginning, which we have heard, which we have seen with our eyes, which we have looked upon, and our hands have handled, of the word of life."

This brings us the word "disciple." It comes from the word discipline. To be a disciple, you must come into the disciplined lifestyle that is being advocated by the leader. Otherwise, any teaching remains an intellectual concept that turns into complacency, self-righteousness, or emotional zeal with a cause. Such zeal is nothing more than good intentions that prove to be empty. Such teachings will result in the person parroting Jesus in His wisdom or trying to imitate His righteous example, but not someone who has power and authority because he or she has partaken of this life.[3]

Today, we have many parrots and imitators of Jesus in the kingdom of God, but few who have been prepared to continue to train people to be followers of Him. Disciples are the people who actually experience the heavenly life because they have partaken of it. After all, teachers cannot take others any further than they have come in their own personal life. Some have never gotten past the intellectual level. These people make Christianity a matter of facts and concepts, while it remains dead letter to the students.[4]

Others have kept Christianity on an emotional level. On good days, they are flying high in their feelings for Jesus, but eventually they land. When they land, they display the epitome of despondency, despair, and unbelief. As you study these three states, they take you back to pride. Despondency is often wounded pride, while despair is a manifestation of pride that has been let down by life. Unbelief is pride that has been hardened towards truth or disappointed because God has not lived up to its expectations.

Peter displayed these states in his emotional roller coaster ride as Jesus' disciple. In his zeal, he declared he would die for Christ. In his self-confidence, he took up the sword for Him. However, Jesus' words caused him to crash land. When Peter realized that Jesus was not going to subdue His enemies, he went into fear and confusion. These two reactions produced unbelief. In his state of unbelief, he denied Jesus. Jesus' warning that he would end up denying Him brought a harsh reality check to his zeal. Peter's zeal was temporary, and could not withstand

---

[3] 2 Timothy 3:5 & 7
[4] Romans 7:6; 2 Corinthians 3:6

the real test. The reality of his failure in his emotional weakness to stand caused Peter to fall into utter despondency and despair.[5]

There are some people who get caught up with the supernatural when it comes to their Christian life. How many people do you know that act "super spiritual" but they are unable to connect to the reality around them? Christianity simply becomes a platform where spiritual experiences or enlightenment are pursued without the keen awareness of Jesus. Jesus remains a concept to these individuals who stand on the outskirts of what is real. This causes the Christian life to operate in some kind of spiritual fantasy, while ignoring the practicality of Christianity that must be applied on a daily basis. Such a scenario keeps Christianity limited to one spiritual experience after another, rather than a relationship with God through Jesus Christ.

How can Christians simply settle for being parrots or imitators of Christ? Sadly, it comes down to something called delusion. People actually deceive themselves about what is going on in their lives. They relate knowledge to truth, emotional feelings to reality, and spirituality to superiority in God.

As you wade through their delusion, you will find one common denominator: control. Knowledge, emotional zeal, and spirituality give people a sense of personal control. Behind this control is pride. Pride operates in the disguises of understanding, self-sufficiency, and a false light of self-righteousness. Personal understanding is the way of controlling knowledge about God. Self-sufficiency towards the matters of God serves as a pseudo-faith in self, while the false light serves as a point of spiritual elitism. No matter how you cut it, these three avenues serve as points of control.

The reality is that no one is in control of his or her world. Due to arrogance, we can perceive ourselves as being in control of our lives, our homes, and our worlds. This arrogance or pride is expressed in looks and attitudes. There are five main looks that harbor different attitudes of pride. They are the rebellious look, smug look, blank stare, look of self-pity, and anger.

The rebellious look is a way of mocking that which challenges the foolishness of pride. Such a look keeps people from facing reality. The smug look hides skepticism and unbelief towards truth, so that truth can be disregarded or considered inferior. The blank stare hides self-exaltation, as it appears to remain clueless or indifferent to reality, allowing the individual who owns it to ignore or deny what is really happening. Self-pity is a way of downplaying personal consequences by becoming noble in its sufferings. This fake nobility is the means of getting relief from the pressure of being made accountable, while being exalted. Anger is often a form of self-righteousness that comes out of offense and jealousy. It declares that it has been unjustly treated or is not being

---

[5] Matthew 26:33-35, 75; Romans 10:2

treated in the fashion it deserves. Therefore, it has the right to respond in ungodly ways.

Eventually, life reveals our pride and proves that our conclusion about controlling our reality is foolish. Present reality has a way of mocking theories, shooting holes through our unrealistic emotions, and insulting our spiritual elitism. It constantly reveals that we are not in control.

Sadly, we all start out in this delusion. We believe that even though different elements challenge our control, we perceive ourselves as holding the winning card. Since we hold the right card, it is a matter of waiting to play our hand at the right time to gain the desired control.

Such games manifest themselves in various ways. People are forever trying to get others to accept their presentation of reality in order to maintain their delusion about themselves and the world that they long for. I am sure you have seen these people. They play games of flattery to give the impression that they are on your side. However, their real motive is to win your confidence in order to seduce you into their desired reality.

There are mind games where people can play games with other people's minds. They know how these individuals think on an emotional level. By using logic against emotional insecurities, they make the other person think it is all his or her fault and he or she must adjust to the other person's idea of reality to make things right. There was a man who constantly used his intelligence to twist his wife's emotions. She felt like she was a pretzel that was trying to maintain some point of sanity as she waded through her emotional chaos.

There are those who withhold affections to get others to adjust to their desired world. In other words, they make them pay until they are ready to concede. You can see this with married couples.

Other games consist of people running others around in their ridiculous reality. These people never land to face the real world. Their goal is to either talk present reality away or persuade others to see their reality and adjust. These games all hide the treachery of pride.

Obviously, when the time arrives where people actually reveal their card by playing their whole hand, they are shocked to find it is not good enough to win the game. This causes confusion as these individuals scramble back to the drawing broad. Up until this time, they felt they were in control because they held the winning card. Once the hand is revealed, and it falls short, people can no longer live in such delusion.

Aaron and Miriam and those of the tribe of Korah had to face this in the wilderness. They thought themselves to be better leaders than Moses. Either they perceived God agreed with them or they never thought about His perspective. It matters little how we perceive others or ourselves if God is not in agreement with our conclusions. God did not agree with these people's conclusions. As a result, Miriam became a leper for seven days. She had to taste the bitterness of separation from the life she knew. Those of the tribe of Korah were actually swallowed up by the earth, tasting death, the ultimate consequence for their rebellion.[6]

Instead of facing delusion, people retreat to figure out a new game plan. We see this scenario in the life of Simon the Sorcerer. He bewitched the people of Samaria with occult powers. When Philip preached the things concerning the kingdom of God, many believed him, including Simon. However, Simon did not give up his personal agendas. He still wanted the people's adoration. He followed Philip and beheld miracles and signs.[7]

One day, Simon witnessed the Holy Ghost coming upon people. When Simon saw the Holy Spirit come down when the apostles laid hands on people, he played his card by offering money for this gift of God. The Apostle Peter rebuked him with these strong words in Acts 8:20, "Thy money perish with thee, because thou hast thought that the gift of God may be purchased with money." Peter proceeded to tell him that his heart was not right, and that he was full of bitterness, and enslaved to iniquity.

Simon thought he could buy God's favor and His gifts. Others think they can con or flatter Him. Some believe that they can impress Him. When you consider these delusional attitudes about God, you realize such people do not know Him nor do they believe Him.

All of these attempts speak of some form of control. People do desire to control their worlds, but this requires them to control God and life. The practice of attempting to control God or believing that they can control God speaks of immaturity, foolishness, and unbelief. Sadly, this is how many of us walk out our lives before Him.

This brings us to true discipline. Many people mistake controlling their worlds with disciplining their lives. To control our world, we must keep people ignorant or off guard. Such attempts create façades or appearances of control. In other words, these individuals want to control their world, in order to appear as if they are disciplined. As long as their world is in line with their notion of what is right and wrong, all will be well.

The truth is people operate in extremes. Even though people may appear calm on the outside, much is going on behind the scenes. Extremes always imply one's world is out of control or in chaos in some way. Discipline points to bringing something into balance, so it can reach its potential. The only balance is when Jesus is in His rightful place in a person's life.

Where did man get the idea that he must control his world? Perhaps, it came from the Garden of Eden. Adam was given dominion over the garden. Dominion in this text means to prevail against, reign, or rule over.[8] When Adam sinned, he turned this dominion over to Satan

---

[6] Numbers 12; 16; 26:10

[7] Acts 8:9-24

[8] Strong's Exhaustive Concordance, #7287

who is now the god of this world. This is why Satan could offer Jesus all the kingdoms of the world when tempting Him. They all belong to him. [9]

Man lost his right to rule over his world in the first garden. Even in his fallen state, the concept of rule has been perverted. To rule over something does not necessarily mean controlling a person's world, thoughts, or personality. Rule means a prescribed guide for conduct or action.[10] Control beyond godly conduct and action becomes oppressive tyranny.

It is vital that we test the spirit behind our disposition. Are we seeking personal discipline or are we trying to control our world, to establish order in our lives? Let's consider the difference between these two approaches.

Control demands perfection from without, especially from the people who are in our world. This results in putting the burden of change or order on others, while we remain out of control. In fact, if you observe people who insist on order in their world, you will see that they have no personal discipline. Since their lives are out of control, they want everyone else to display restraint in order to bring some order to their out-of-control lives.

Godly discipline produces transformation from within.[11] This transformation changes a person's way of developing inward discipline. It enlarges perceptions and radically changes lifestyles, as each aspect of a person's life comes under the work and guidance of the Holy Ghost.

Control demands that you control your world. Therefore, people must see it your way and do it your way. Such control causes resentment and oppression, as others are always being made accountable for how your world functions.

Godly discipline brings everything that has to do with personal conduct under the control of the Spirit. Since disposition has to do with discipline, this means a person's ways are lined up to God, his or her thoughts brought into order with the Person of Jesus, and his or her body into subjection to godliness.

The pursuit of control causes people to operate according to their own point of view. This is darkness that points to delusion. Spiritual darkness enslaves people to what they can perceive. There is no eternal perspective, and no way in which character can be established. Darkness of this nature prevents individuals from growing up in the knowledge of Jesus, which results in spiritual maturity.

Godly discipline produces liberty in the Spirit. It allows people to find their place in the kingdom of heaven, and to reach their potential. They

---

[9] Genesis 1:26, 28; Matthew 4:8-10; John 16:11; 2 Corinthians 4:3-4; Ephesians 2:2

[10] Webster's New Collegiate Dictionary, © 1976 by G. & C. Merriam Co.

[11] Romans 12:2

are able to get beyond self to consider the spiritual possibilities, and to seek God's eternal perspective about matters.

Control gives in to the flesh, while discipline gives way to the Spirit. Control finds its origins in tyrannical pride, while godly discipline obtains its liberty, authority, and power in discovering and doing it according to God's way.

Is your life out of control or under control? A good way to discern is if you are trying to control your world or struggling to come under control. Are you manipulating and pushing others, or are you holding yourself accountable for your own attitudes? Your fruits will tell on you.[12]

---

[12] Matthew 7:20

4

INITIAL DISCIPLINE

I am going to make a statement about discipline that is vital to this subject. Only discipline can produce discipline. Whenever you give in to self, there will be no discipline. If you give way to your thinking, feelings, needs, and fleshly desires, discipline will be missing. At points where personal discipline is missing, chaos will reign.

Therefore, to establish discipline, there must be discipline present. It is easy for those who are out of control to talk about discipline, dream about it, and wish for it, but fail to do anything about it, because they have no basis of discipline in which to develop it.

To develop discipline, one must establish what I call initial discipline. Initial discipline is the base or foundation of all discipline. It is at this point that godly discipline can be established and brought forth. Before I can explain how this base discipline is established, we must understand that no one is born with discipline. Our natural preference is to go with whatever is comfortable or convenient.

Discipline is contrary to our natural tendencies; therefore, it has to be formed in us. It is established when you go against the grain of what is natural and what would represent the path of least resistance. In other words, true discipline is not forced; rather it becomes a personal choice. Its goal is about changing how you think, as well as putting into perspective how you feel. This will bring into balance your needs and change your priorities. Sadly, many people just want to receive personal discipline in some magic way, rather than take the necessary steps to establish it in their personal lives.

The main opposition to discipline is the old man. The Apostle Paul talks about the old man in Galatians 5:17-21, Ephesians 4:17-29 and Colossians 3:5-17. The old man is the base disposition of the fallen, sinful condition of man. The old man is fleshly. This means that he only does that which feels good, seems beneficial, and appears acceptable or successful to others. The old man will not do something unless it serves his purpose. He does everything to get around unpleasant responsibility or taking accountability for his way of thinking and doing. The old man explains away responsibilities, excuses away wrong doings, and justifies irresponsibility. Ultimately, he must be pampered, exalted, and considered. He must be treated as God.

This brings us to the base nature of the fallen disposition. It is pride. Pride is the predominate idol of mankind. This idol demands to be God. It wants to be served because it believes itself to be superior in knowledge, right in its knowledge and logical conclusions, and capable in abilities. As a result, this pride produces a self-serving mentality that produces behavioral patterns. Behavioral patterns will determine our attitude towards life. Attitudes can develop mindsets that play an important part in defining lifestyle patterns. As people give in to the worship and pampering of the old man, habits are cemented into people's way of doing and thinking. These habits reveal a person's general attitude towards life and God.

Since the mentality of the old man is that he deserves to be served, this automatically demotes others to an inferior position. Underneath the arrogance of the old man's pride and fleshly preference for lust rests complacency, laziness, apathy, and insensitivity. These lackadaisical responses are a product of the state or attitude of slothfulness.

I had to realize that it takes genuine humility to face the reality of my true environment. I have to take some drastic and contrary steps to address the ways of the old environment. For example, I had to do what I do not want to do, to not only give myself a reality check about my own attitude, but to change it in a constructive way. I had to go against the grain of the slothfulness of the old man in me, to let him know that he will not reign in my life. I had to fight the harsh reality that death works in my body, and that I must discipline it to spiritually live and overcome the destructive designs of the old man.

Let us consider the attitude of slothfulness. The first reality about slothfulness is that it is the sin of selfishness and unacceptable to God no matter what form it may manifest itself. The second fact about slothfulness is that it is the opposite of personal discipline. Therefore, to have discipline, you must develop the opposite state of slothfulness. Slothfulness is the natural state of the old man, while discipline is a choice. Slothfulness travels the road of least resistance, while discipline chooses the straight, narrow path to bring about change or results.

The book of Proverbs describes the attitude of slothfulness. The reason this book of the Bible points out this state is because it is the state of those who are unwise or foolish. Proverbs is a book of wisdom. In fact, it describes every aspect of wisdom from its attitude down to its fruits. The next time you read or study Proverbs, do it from the basis of it revealing the essence of godly wisdom in every way.

Proverbs 26:13-15 summarizes slothfulness. The first Scripture states, "The slothful man saith, There is a lion in the way; a lion is in the streets." In other words, slothful people always have an excuse as to why they fail to do what is *necessary*. They do not take care of needed responsibilities to properly function in their worlds. Therefore, nothing ever gets done. The lives of the slothful are cluttered with unresolved issues and unfinished responsibilities. There is no real order or reasoning to their lives.

Proverbs 15:19 says, "The way of the slothful man is an hedge of thorns..." This means slothful people box themselves in with excuses and faulty reasoning, producing justifiable procrastination. Procrastination is comprised of vain excuses, but it is obstinate because it has no intention of doing anything that will cause any real inconvenience. People who procrastinate may delude themselves as to why they are failing to do that which is responsible. Therefore, the mental excuses create a smoke screen to cover up the sinister way of this attitude. It is also the means by which to appear noble for being slothful. The truth is that nothing will ever be accomplished unless circumstances force it. Most of the time, someone else ends up carrying the burden.

Proverbs 26:14, says, "As the door turneth upon his hinges, so doth the slothful upon his bed." These people have an uncanny way of ignoring the reality around them. In a way, they turn their backs on it if it gets a little too uncomfortable. They may not be proud of their environment, but they have no initiative to change it. They may cry about it and complain about it, but they will not lift a hand to make it different.

In fact, one of the fruits of slothfulness is the unwillingness to take care of details. Details are often inconvenient and bring little recognition because they seem insignificant in light of the bigger plan. These details often create drudgery that can be overwhelming. Eventually, these unresolved details develop into an emotional tidal wave that results in greater chaos and ruin to their already cluttered pigpens.

Fenelon talked about the unwillingness of those who ignore or refuse to take care of details. He stated that it offends family and those who work with such individuals. If you are lax in small ways, you will fail to be sacrificial in big things. When you cause undue burdens for others, they have a hard time believing you really love God.[1]

Proverbs 26:15 says, "The slothful hideth his hand in his bosom; it grieveth him to bring it again to his mouth." Here again, we see the intention of those who are slothful. They ignore what has to be done, and even if it would benefit them, they will not move their hand. As a result, their desire to avoid any real work or labor will end in destroying them in the long run.[2]

Solomon also made this statement about the slothful in Proverbs 18:9, "He also that is slothful in his work is brother to him that is a great waster." These people will waste more time trying to get out of a project, than if they would just do it. They may take a couple of steps forward to do something, but will take ten steps backwards, because they complicate all matters in order to avoid any inconvenience. As a result, they end up doing things wrong, because their intention is never to do right, but only to do that which will serve their purpose. If they manage to do something, it generally has to be redone, because they took

---

[1] The Seeking Heart, Fenelon, © 1992 by Christian Book Publishing House
[2] Proverbs 19:25

shortcuts, or they will become bored or impatient with projects that fail to serve their purposes. Therefore, these people continually drop the ball of doing right, forcing other people to pick it up. Eventually, these slothful people become users, because they begin to expect or assume other people will pick up where they left off as a means to prevent total ruin. Such users suck the life out of those around them.

As you consider slothfulness, you can only conclude that it wears blinders. Although, slothful people may not be happy with their worlds, they refuse to do anything about them. Even though their worlds drain the life out of them, and create depression, they expect others to deliver them from their terrible plight. After all, they are mentally incapacitated, because they have been wronged or they perceive that their world is too depressing. As you study these people's mentality and habits, you begin to realize that these blinders serve their purpose quite well.

Slothfulness represents the road of least resistance and fleshly pursuits. Solomon instructs us to learn well from the examples of the slothful in Proverbs 24:30-34. Consider the work of these people. Look upon their environment, and receive instruction. Where will the excuses of slothfulness bring you? What will the idle hands of the slothful accomplish? The fruits of slothfulness are summarized in one word: poverty.

Slothfulness brings disgrace to the Gospel. It shows disobedience and unbelief. It can be mocking towards those who refuse to enable it. It will be jealous towards those who are disciplined. It will be condescending towards those who will not play the game. If you are slothful, you are in trouble. You are on the comfortable path of ruin. There is no one who can save you from destruction, unless you are willing to repent and change your way of thinking and doing.

It is important to understand that there are three levels of discipline. The first level begins at the point of taking personal responsibility. For example, are those your clothes lying around? Quit being a sluggard, pick them up and put them where they belong. Is that your dirty plate? Unless you have a slave, or two broken arms, put it in the sink or dishwasher. Is that your tool or instrument? Be a good steward of both time and money by putting it in the proper place so you and others can easily find it the next time there is a project that requires its use. Is that your messy space? Be mature and clean it up.

Initial discipline starts at the point of training yourself by taking personal responsibility for what you have been entrusted with. When you fail to take the necessary initiative to become responsible in these simple ways, you will unfairly put the burden on another. Paul's instruction in the area of personal responsibility is very clear in Galatians 6:5, "For every man shall bear his own burden." Each person must assume responsibility for his or her own personal burdens, and not expect others, who are carrying their own load, to carry his or her load as well. This is irresponsible and unfair.

Christians have been entrusted with their lives, families, homes, and jobs. They must be responsible to take care of what belongs to them, to do their best in whatever position they have been placed, and be honorable in their homes and jobs. Dropping the ball is unacceptable. Causing others to deal with irresponsibility that puts undue burdens on them robs them of time and energy. This causes frustration and the additional burden. Sadly, when slothful people are confronted, they are unteachable and will consider any requests or demands to pick up the ball of responsibility and finish the course as being rude and unfair.

Taking responsibility for what has been entrusted to us will establish the base from which godly discipline will be developed. Without taking responsibility, all discipline will be forced rather than developed. For example, some people are forced to work to live; otherwise, they would have no initiative to do so. Others are forced to alter lifestyle habits through illnesses or circumstances. The problem with forced discipline is that the mentality remains in place.

When discipline is forced on people with a slothful mentality, they resort to game playing in order to get around any inconvenience. They will act like they are doing something. However, when you examine their activities, you realize these people are doing only what they want to do. If they are forced to do something, they usually do it with a bad attitude or the martyr syndrome. If they do something that seems considerate, it is for some type of response or recognition. This becomes obvious, because when they fail to get the desired response, they become insulted or moody. In fact, they remind you of little children who are waiting around for some type of approval.

The second stage of discipline is what we call reasonable service. The Apostle Paul made this statement in Romans 12:1, "I beseech you therefore, brethren, by the mercies of God, that ye present your bodies a living sacrifice, holy, acceptable unto God, which is your reasonable service." Reasonable service comes down to what is right before God. This means doing right by others. What does this mean in a practical sense?

To do reasonable service, you first must get past self. This is why we are to present our bodies up front as believers. If we never get past ourselves, we will never be sensitive enough to recognize our reasonable service. The Apostle Paul gives us insight into this aspect of this type of discipline in Galatians 6:2, "Bear ye one another's burdens, and so fulfill the law of Christ."[3]

The problem with the old man is that everything must serve his purpose. Slothfulness is not only arrogant, but it refuses to step past its self-serving comfort zones to see the burdens of others. People who never get past themselves to see the struggles of others will fail to do right, committing the sin of omission. (See James 4:17.)

---

[3] Refer also to Romans 8:4

Righteousness is an attitude that sets up the disposition. At this stage, the blinders are taken off and the person's perception is enlarged to see the plight of others. It is motivated to lift the burdens of others and fulfill the Law of Christ. How does this translate in a practical way?

Let's imagine that you are walking into the living room and someone has left an article lying on the floor. Obviously, it does not belong there. What will you do? The old man will say, "I didn't leave it there; therefore, it is no concern of mine." Slothfulness will act as if the article is invisible, so it does not have to contend with such an insignificant detail. However, what will righteousness say? "This article is out of place. I have two hands and the means to do something about it. If I don't pick it up, then it will become someone else's burden."

Righteousness is humble. Humility does not hold onto personal rights. It will always consider what is right in regards to others. It will recognize the opportunity to lift the burdens of others in practical ways. It will always go the extra mile without expecting recognition.[4] Without this humility, one will never move to the next stage of discipline: that of sacrifice.

Sacrifice is beyond responsibility and reasonable service. Responsibility is upholding personal burdens to ensure you are not burdening others. Reasonable service is doing that which is right. This means you will lift or share in the burdens of others. Sacrifice is when it personally costs you. It is beyond the ten percent and the extra mile. It is when it is not a matter of what is appropriate and right, but it truly becomes a sacrifice worthy of God's approval and acceptance.

We see this in the life of David's three brave men who broke through the battle line to bring him a cup of water from Bethlehem's well. The widow who gave her last two mites represents the epitome of this sacrifice, because Jesus noticed it and commented on it. It can be observed in Mary's example, the sister of Lazarus, when she anointed Jesus for His burial with expensive ointment.[5] Ultimately, it will bring glory to God. This is when self is out of the way, and everything is done for the sole purpose of pleasing and exalting God, regardless of the sacrifice.

There are two major requirements for the first two stages of discipline. In order to carry out personal responsibility, a person must stir up self. This means the person has to ignore the old man's excuses and reach down for inspiration. People do different things to inspire themselves.

I personally talk to myself about what is going on in my world. For example, I just used the last of the water in the pitcher; therefore, I need to refill it. I just used the last part of the juice, and I need to replace it. In order to complete various unpleasant projects, I do the one I least like

---

[4] Matthew 5:41
[5] 1 Chronicles 11:16-19; Mark 12:41-44; John 12:3-8

first in order to get over the initial hump of reluctance. My co-laborer, Jeannette, rewards herself after she finishes so many projects. It is up to each individual to figure out how to inspire themselves, and to successfully confront unpleasant projects.

The second aspect of discipline is diligence. We must be diligent in doing right. This requires us to be sensitive and aware of what is going on around us. We must be diligent to seek God's heart about matters. Proverbs 12:24 states, "The hand of the diligent shall bear rule: but the slothful shall be under tribute". In other words, the slothful are never diligent in fulfilling their obligations and find themselves becoming subject to others.

Proverbs 12:27 states, "The slothful man roasteth not that which he took in hunting: but the substance of a diligent man is precious." The slothful person always benefits from other people's labor. However, the labor of those who are diligent is precious to the Lord, because it is pure in motive, righteous in disposition, and godly in conduct. Paul stated that Christians must not be slothful in business, but fervent in spirit in their service to God.[6]

Hebrews 11:6 says, "But without faith it is impossible to please him: for he that cometh to God must believe that he is, and that he is a rewarder of them that diligently seek him." Diligence is a must in the Christian walk. Without it, people will fail to seek God in the way that they are able to find Him.

Do you have the initial discipline to be established in a greater measure of discipline in your life? Or are you still giving in to the rebellious base, selfish disposition of your old man? Are you being responsible or slothful? Are you helping others carry burdens, or ignoring the world around you, as you only do what is convenient or self-serving? Keep in mind, there can be no discipline without first establishing a foundation of discipline.

---

[6] Romans 12:11

5

FORCED DISCIPLINE

Discipline is a narrow path. It is meant to alleviate, rearrange, and change who we are, along with our lifestyles. Without this change, we would fail miserably to finish the course. After all, we are running a race. Any runner will tell you that it takes immense discipline to train your body to endure the rigorous demands of pushing it beyond its limits.[1]

Such discipline is not accomplished overnight. You must gradually build up your strength and stamina. The key to building up your endurance level in any area is to push yourself beyond comfort zones.[2] This is true for any discipline. You must be righteous in attitude and humble in disposition. This will allow you to go against the grain of what is acceptable, comfortable, or tolerable. You must push past the point of where you stopped last time. You must pass previous limitations to enlarge your abilities and to endure more.

This is true for any area of our lives. We must push past our present accomplishments to reach our maximum potential. Until we are willing to test and be tested, there will be no discipline. Discipline must be forced upon each of us before we will find out what we are made of, and what we are capable of overcoming and accomplishing in God's kingdom.

The problem is that certain forms of discipline must come from the outside. It is discipline that we will not have control over. Ultimately, it will force us out of comfort zones. Granted, we may train ourselves in certain areas, but we will do anything to avoid the inevitable goal of discipline: That of inward enlargement and change. We must be enlarged to discover what we can do, and what we must change in order to carry it out. As you consider God's way of doing, He actually uses different means to force discipline upon us. Each type of discipline tests different aspects of our lives. However, the goal of each discipline is to produce spiritual growth.

The truth about humanity is that we do not want to grow up. We want to be treated as adults, but we do not want the responsibilities that maturity requires. We want the respect, but we do not want to earn it by showing ourselves honorable in all that we do. We want people to acknowledge us, but we do not want to pay the price to be exalted by God in His kingdom.

---

[1] 1 Corinthians 9:24-26; Hebrews 12:1
[2] James 1:3-4

God brings about these forced disciplines for a couple of reasons. The first reason is to save our souls. Without some of these disciplines, people would not even consider God and embrace His salvation. Another reason is to bring us to our potential. Without these disciplines, none of us would ever reach our potential in His kingdom. Such discipline must come from the outside to test and enlarge our very being, because we do not have the capacity to discipline and enlarge ourselves. A good example is an athlete.

In the mind of athletes, they are striving to be the best. Until they are actually tested on the field in competition, they will never know if they are the best. Therefore, the real test will come from outside of their personal discipline. Often, competition will prove they are not the best. This not only gives them a reality check, but it gives them a goal of striving beyond their present state to become the best.

It seems that Christians ignore or forget that they are running a race. The Apostle Paul gave us insight into gaining the prize of Jesus. He talked about pressing forward to apprehend Him. Sadly, some Christians are content to be bystanders, while others are in the race, but have no intention of really running it or completing it. In their mind, they already have the race in the bag and do not have to be serious about training for it or running the course set before them. However, God's Word is clear that we are in a race and we must complete the course to gain our prize. The end of this course is heaven.[3]

There are four means by which God tests our character. It is His way of forcing maturity in our lives. The initial test of each discipline will usually reveal that we have not reached our potential. The goal is to enlarge our vision as to the prize that awaits us, so we can accept each discipline in the right way. However, the right way means lining up to God's righteous ways.

The first discipline is found in Hebrews 12:5-12. It is chastisement. Chastisement is God's means of addressing the flesh in our life. It is a way of testing the spirit behind us. Are we teachable and can we be corrected? If God loves us, He will correct us to teach us His ways. His ways are the ways of holiness. Through this type of discipline, He is trying to establish the state of holiness in our lives. It is not necessarily a matter of what we do, but a matter of what our inward state is in our approach to life.

There was an incident where God chastised both my co-laborer Jeannette and me. We had ignored warnings about a preacher and his wife. Eventually, the matter became serious in the church the pastor was overseeing. The Lord allowed us to see how the sheep were mistreated, while we remained unwilling to face and confront the truth about the spiritual condition of the pastor and his wife. God started to chastise us

---

[3] 1 Corinthians 9:24-27; Philippians 3:12-13; 2 Timothy 4:7; Hebrews 12:1

for failing to confront sin in the camp. For three days, we sat silently before Him, as He corrected our attitude and response.

The goal of discipline is to change the inward man, by clarifying what is holy and what is profane. It is vital that a person learn the lesson in order to change attitude, conduct, and lifestyle. It will create hatred for sin, and the necessary discernment to avoid temptation and resist evil. It will hate every false way, insist on righteousness, and follow after peace that can only come when a person's relationship is right with God.[4]

The second type of forced discipline is that of circumstances. Circumstances reveal our perception about life and God. Our perception is exposed through our reactions towards the circumstances. Ultimately, circumstances test our faith. What we often have to face in trying circumstances is the fact that self is very much alive, demanding to have its way and to be worshipped.

This is brought out in the incident with Jesus' disciples in the boat, during their encounter with a contrary wind in Mark 6:34-52. They had just witnessed the miracle of the feeding of the five thousand. Jesus separated Himself from them in order to pray. They got into the boat to row to the other side of the lake. It was during this time that they encountered a contrary wind.

Unpleasant circumstances often serve as contrary winds that run across our bow. They reveal that man is not in control of his life. When this revelation becomes a reality, one discovers where his or her dependency rests, in the area of the flesh or God.

Although putting confidence in the flesh is idolatrous and brings people under a curse, many continue to put their confidence in personal abilities.[5] They almost have to become tired and weak before they will realize that they cannot change the wind or determine the outcome. It is at this point that fear makes an entrance.

Fear is another test. Will individuals look beyond fear to gain God's perspective or will they succumb to it? If people give in to fear, there is no power to overcome, no confidence in God's love, and there will be confusion and instability.[6]

Jesus walked on the water towards His struggling disciples. Even though the disciples had just witnessed the miraculous, they still debated about whether it was Jesus coming towards them. Such a trial brings us to the harsh reality that circumstances test our level of faith. The more we choose to believe God in circumstances, the more enlarged our faith becomes to embrace more of God. This is what it means to have our faith tested. When you consider such a test, it is circumstances that serve as the fiery testing oven for our faith.[7]

---

[4] Psalm 119:104, 128; 1 Timothy 6:11; 2 Timothy 2:22
[5] Jeremiah 17:5-7
[6] 2 Timothy 1:7; James 1:8; 1 John 4:18
[7] 1 Peter 1:6-9

The more we debate about the character, truth, and ways of God, the harder our heart becomes towards Him. The Bible identified this type of response in Jesus' disciples as being unbelief, "For they considered not the miracles of the loaves; for their heart was hardened" (Mark 6:52).

Unpleasant circumstances will force me to choose to believe God or I will simply give way to my self-sufficiency and the situation. I will choose to believe the Word about His character or I will concede that circumstances dictate the quality of my life. I will overcome the circumstances with my faith in God or I will be overcome by my circumstances and live in despair. It is my choice. It is your choice.

The third type of discipline comes by way of enemies. Enemies of the soul challenge the children of God. They cause the currents of life to go against any progression the saint has made in the kingdom of God. Saints may go a couple of steps forward in their life in God and be knocked backwards ten feet. This is a tough test, for it reveals a person's heart condition concerning God.

It is easy to talk about faith until it is tested. It is inspiring to talk about our love and devotion to God until the enemies of our soul challenge it. Will I continue on, regardless of how much I am buffeted, or will I give up and give way to self-pity? After all, various thoughts are running rampant in my mind. "I love God, but, He apparently does not love me because look at what He is allowing in my life. This ought not to be! You would think God would make it easy, since I belong to Him."

The real goal of God is not to just have servants who will do His bidding, but servants who choose to possess hearts that will trust Him regardless of the situation. Such trust will bring Him glory. People think that if they do good works, God will be glorified. The truth is God wants to do a work in us, so He can be glorified in and through us. Glory has to do with majesty, not works. God wants to express His majesty in and through His people. Jesus talked about the Father being glorified in Him. Then, He talked about being glorified in His followers, "And all mine are thine, and thine are mine; and I am glorified in them" (John 17:10).

Chastisement changes attitudes; circumstances enlarge a person to be receptive to God, while being buffeted establishes character. You must learn endurance when all seems lost. You must have patience when the challenge drags on. And, you must cling to God when there is nothing but darkness that engulfs you.

We can see this in the case of Job. God allowed Satan to not only buffet Job, but he also brought him close to utter destruction. Job may have questioned God through his ordeal, but he still held firm to what he understood about the character of God. As a result, greater character or depth was established in Job.

Christians can talk about going deeper in God, but they do not realize that unless they are willing to be challenged through persecution, misunderstanding, and what seems like abandonment on God's part, this depth will be nothing more than a concept. Devotion to God can only grow sweeter during this time. He becomes precious to a person who through faith discovers Him in the midst of these grave struggles.

In such times, people will encounter the dark night of their soul. They cling to the unseen character of God and His promises. Through the process of humiliation, God goes deeper into the person's very being. Needless to say, individuals are not aware of His work, because they are wrestling before, and clinging to what they know in their heart about Him.

It is during this struggle that inward character is developed, refined, and brought forth in humility. This character will come out as a fragrance to the Church and the world.[8] It will edify the Church and cause uneasiness on the part of the unsaved.

The Bible is clear that true followers of God will suffer persecution. Persecution comes from our enemies. However, it is in persecution that the light or glory of Christ can come forth in a living testimony to the lost. As you can see, it costs to experience the depth in God that so many are clamoring for, but few are willing and ready to pay the price.

The final discipline is consequences. Consequences expose people's true disposition. They serve as points of judgment. Within the heart of every individual is foolishness. Proverbs 22:15 states, "Foolishness is bound in the heart of a child, but the rod of correction shall drive it far from him." At the core of foolishness is an unwillingness to grow up. We forever want to remain silly and immature. It takes consequences to give us a reality check.

One of the follies of sin is that it deems consequences as unjust. Personally, I have never paid a consequence I did not deserve. But I am also quite aware of the fact that I have never paid in full for my attitudes and deeds. The Apostle Paul understood the extent of his sin when he referred to himself as chief of sinners. His awareness of his spiritual condition made him receptive towards the salvation of Jesus.[9]

Regardless of our high opinion of who we think we are in the scheme of things, each of us deserves hell.[10] Regardless of the mercy that is shown each of us, many resent paying the consequences for personal foolishness. Such people resort to self-pity. The reason there is self-pity is because there is nothing honorable in paying consequences for personal deviations. This is when the old man will become a victim.

Arrogant humanity refuses to accept the fact that there are right and wrong ways according to our Creator. There are also acceptable and unacceptable ways of behaving. If we fail to do right, we will reap the consequences for our foolishness. This is one of the basic principles that rules life. The Apostle Paul confirms this, "Be not deceived, God is not mocked: for whatsoever a man soweth, that shall he also reap. For he that soweth to his flesh shall of the flesh reap corruption; but he that

---

[8] 2 Corinthians 2:15-16
[9] 1 Timothy 1:14-16
[10] Romans 12:3

soweth to the Spirit shall of the Spirit reap life everlasting" (Galatians 6:7-8).

Arrogance convinces us that we can handle anything that comes our way. Slothfulness declares that it does not matter what happens, while rebellion maintains that it does not care; therefore, it will not respond to rules or authority. This is the essence of foolishness. Due to its unbelief, slothfulness, and rebellion, it will deny there is a God in attitude and conduct. If there is no God, there are no sins or consequences, and the cross of Jesus was a product of a religious, misguided fanatic.

Consequences create sobriety in people and give them a reality check that proves no one is able to ignore or withstand a barrage of consequences. The price becomes too high, bitter, and counterproductive. This is when rebellious individuals can decide to care. It is at the point of caring that fear or respect is developed towards those who have authority. Proper respect for authority or laws will prove to be very healthy and productive.

To me, the hardest thing to witness is parents who will not make their children learn the valuable principle of reaping and sowing. In fact, such parents do not have a healthy love for their children or they would address the foolishness in their children with effective consequences. God's Word calls it a rod of correction. This rod varies according to the child, but it is obvious that proper discipline will confront such foolish attitudes and behaviors.[11]

This is an important principle for young people to remember. The longer you put off facing, confronting, and disciplining the old man's mentality, the more set you will be in the ways of sin and death.[12] You will blindly heap judgment upon yourself, as you give way to slothfulness and walk in the ways of rebellion.

Irresponsibility will be brought into your adult relationships. Eventually, life will bring you to a point of decision. If you marry a person who is responsible, it will cause problems down the line. You will lose the respect of your spouse. At this point, your spouse will become critical and mocking of your irresponsibility. This will bring you to a point of crisis in your relationship. You will either be forced to come to terms with your irresponsibility, or you will become belligerent about it.

Belligerence refuses to be moved, regardless of Scriptural and moral responsibility. It hides its face behind various games as it justifies it obstinacy. The more people give way to their belligerence, the harder it becomes for others to contend for their souls. Eventually, their justification will turn into delusion. This is when they will perceive any form of chastisement as being personally "picked on". They will see circumstances as unfair and consequences as being unjust, while blaming their condition and environment on others and Satan. In the end,

---

[11] Proverbs 13:24; 19:18; 22:15; 23:13, 14; 29:15
[12] Romans 8:2

these people cement themselves in their box of rebellion to the point that no one is able to contend for them. People eventually throw their hands up in despair, because the person is foolishly insisting on being a loser rather than an overcomer. The younger you are when you properly confront this selfish mentality, the less hardship you will have in your life.

Perhaps you are an adult who maintains foolishness in your own heart. You play games by throwing pathetic crumbs of fickle promises and fleeting intentions at people, rather than paying the price to know God. You have gotten away with a rebellious attitude, inconsiderate ways, and ungodly conduct, but it has cost you credibility in your relationships. You need to know that the consequences are being heaped upon you. Eventually, you will reap in full what you have sown. You may not care now, or maybe you are presently deluding yourself, but you will care on judgment day when the blinders are taken off, and you are facing Jesus. However, it will be too late to rectify your rebellion.

Consequences have a way of forcing us to face reality; therefore, embrace your consequences with a contrite spirit. Learn the lessons to develop wisdom. Such discipline brings each of us to a place of decision. Either we will face reality or reap horrible consequences down the line.

If you are truly walking the Christian life, you will encounter these four forced disciplines in your life at different times. They are all necessary to work holiness, faith, character, and sobriety in the lives of God's people. The question is, will you humble yourself and allow each discipline to have its way as the life of Jesus is worked in you, or will you heap destructive consequences upon your head?

6

GETTING A HOLD OF THE MIND

Discipline begins with the mind. As a minister of the Gospel, one of the things I remind people is that you must get a hold of the person's mind, before God can get a hold of his or her heart. This was brought out in my military experiences.

Boot camp is the initial introduction into the military. The main goal of boot camp is to take spoiled rotten, self-centered, immature Americans and get a hold of their minds. The purpose for this process is to change attitude and behavioral patterns. It takes extreme disciplinary measures to create the change of attitude and behavior that will be able to function within the working of the military system. This discipline starts when the person enters boot camp. The person has to be removed from comfortable environments.

By taking people out of their comfort zones, they are made vulnerable. Vulnerability is vital when changing people's attitudes and behavioral patterns. This vulnerability makes a person both dependent and receptive, because his or her surroundings are uncertain.

I can still remember my first night at boot camp. New recruits were bused in from the airport, where we had to be assigned to barracks. It was not only strange, but also frightening. I was out of my league, and I had no idea what was going to happen. It was not until midnight that I was finally in my bunk. I had very little sleep. Early in the morning, we were mustered out of our bunks to be officially introduced to military life. From that point on, our civilian mentality with its various attitudes was challenged with instructions that required personal discipline.

I did not understand the logistics behind the training in boot camp until years later. I viewed much of their requirements as petty. I never realized that those petty demands were setting up the basis for being a regimented soldier. Such pettiness clearly challenged the self-sufficient, independent mentality of the American mindset that was engraved upon my worldview. It was a means of breaking down the mentality with the intent of establishing the right attitude. Without the proper foundation, soldiers would not be able to function in a constructive way on the battlefields of the world. Instead of being capable of fighting a battle, they would be offered up as mere sacrifices, to make a patriotic statement, rather than winning a war.

Although I did not initially understand the full significance that boot camp played in my life, God was able to take the experience and help me understand the Christian life in light of it. The Christian life is a walk that involves a race and a battle. Therefore, we are inspired to gain the prize, as well as commanded to be effective soldiers in the kingdom of God.[1] I did not relate to the athletic part of it, but I could relate to the position of the soldier.

It was during this time that the Lord began to reveal to me the significance of boot camp. It was not just a matter of instructing us to recognize ranks or teach us to march. This initial introduction into military life was a means to get a hold of our minds for the purpose of obedience. It was vital that, as soldiers, our activities could be controlled, and our conduct lined up to the strategic points of the military in attitudes and actions.

Eventually, God revealed to me how our attitudes and conduct responded according to our mentality. The civilian mentality runs contrary to the military mentality. The civilian mentality encourages independent thinking. It promotes personal ambition and self-serving aggression. The military mindset must change the independent thinking and challenge all ambitions that are outside of the goal of the military. In fact, these ambitions must come into agreement with military supervisors and instructions. The military must also channel any aggression to express itself according to the mission that is before it.

As I compared the military mentality with Christianity, I began to understand what had to take place in my mentality to be a Christian. To understand the need for God to get a hold of our minds as Christians, we must come to terms with the type of mentality that exists in all men. This mentality is the expression of the old man. The old man's mentality can be summarized in one word: obstinate.

Obstinacy is the quality or state of being difficult when it comes to remedying a solution and subduing personal preferences. This means people will be contrary in considering that which opposes their opinions, purpose, or course, regardless of the reason, the arguments, or the persuasion of what is right or appropriate. People in this state are not pliable, and when confronted, will not be moved from their position. After confrontation, these people will maintain the same position, opinion, and attitude.

The old man's mentality of obstinacy is what hinders God's work. Behind obstinacy is pride; therefore, this mentality is nothing but an expression of pride. It refuses to be pliable because it insists that everything must adjust and agree with it. It may outwardly comply, but inwardly, it always maintains its present position.

The attitude of this mentality was described by Isaiah 14:13-14, "For thou hast said in thine heart, I will ascend into heaven, I will exalt my throne above the stars of God: I will sit also upon the mount of the congregation, in the sides of the north: I will ascend above the heights of

---

[1] 1 Corinthians 9:24-26; Colossians 3:14; 2 Timothy 2:2-4; Hebrews 12:1

the clouds; I will be like the Most High." This mentality is boastful. It refuses to allow itself to care, thereby maintaining an indifference to how it affects others. Such a mentality cleverly plays the game to control its world. It not only makes boastful declarations, but it manifests itself in looks. There are five different looks that express each of these declarations in Isaiah 14:13-14. We have already considered these looks in chapter 2. However, these looks and declarations are backed up by games.

The first expression we will consider in light of the arrogant declarations is that of rebellion. It controls with attitude. The people who operate in this mentality are not open to change. Rebellion is very mocking towards those who challenge its activities. It declares that it has rights; therefore, *it will ascend above those who dare challenge it, and rule from the heights of its arrogance.* As the Apostle Paul tells us, we must not think highly of ourselves, but instead to think soberly about our own spiritual condition.[2] In other words, get off your high horse, and deal with what is really going on in your present reality.

The second expression of obstinacy is that of being smug. This is where supremacy is ruling due to judgmentalism and skepticism. This type of person perceives him or herself as being superior; therefore, he or she has the right to judge you as inferior. These individuals use words to make their point of superiority. Since you are considered beneath them, they can be skeptical and suspicious of everything you say. In their arrogance, they will automatically dismiss you and regard your opinions as silly, stupid, and ridiculous even if you are right. Ultimately, they will declare that, in the end, they will *be exalted above your limited, silly world.* The Apostle Paul instructed us to not mind high things about ourselves, but to condescend to men of low estate.[3] In other words, who do you really think you are in your arrogance?

The next expression of obstinacy is that of the blank stare. This stare basically states that you have been shut off, and the person you are speaking to is now indifferent to you. This is a way of playing mind games with you. You are now at a disadvantage. You do not know if you have made a point or if the person is placating you with his or her silence. The truth is that behind this non-committal stare is the attitude that you really do not understand. In fact, you are not only ignorant about the situation in question, but your very opinions will be considered stupid and of no significance in light of the wise conclusions the person is diplomatically maintaining behind the stare. Such a mentality will not be moved from its high position. In fact, it declares that it will not humble itself, and *will remain sitting in the congregation of importance* because of its incredible wisdom. In the mind of such people, they believe if they remain quiet, eventually you will be proven wrong, and brought low at their feet, in absolute adoration and exaltation of their wisdom. Proverbs

[2] Romans 12:3
[3] Romans 12:16

3:7 states, "Be not wise in thine own eyes: fear the LORD, and depart from evil." As you consider these words, not only is this mentality foolish and lacking in fear of God, but it is evil.

The fourth expression of this mentality is that of self-pity. Self-pity is the essence of worldly sorrow that the old man always expresses when he gets called to accountability, or when he is trying to throw people off track concerning his wickedness.[4] Needless to say, it plays the martyrdom game. Self-pity declares that the demands are unfair, and the instructions cannot possibly be carried out. Ultimately, God is deemed as being unfair and a liar. Since the demand is considered terribly unfair by this person, and he or she so desires to appear quite noble in his or her state, he or she ultimately becomes a suffering martyr.

Martyrdom of this nature will exalt the person above the unfair demands of the circumstances and the people. It declares that in the end, *it will ascend above the heights* of the unfair circumstances, and be vindicated. The Apostle Paul put this attitude into perspective in Galatians 6:3, "For if a man think himself to be something, when he is nothing, he deceiveth himself." These people must deceive themselves in order to call God a liar and as being unfair, while justifying their rebellious attitude.

The final expression of the mentality of the old man is anger. Anger in this text is a determination to be right, no matter how wrong a person is. Ungodly anger is the unhindered manifestation of pride. It refuses to be wrong. In the Christian realm, it is good at playing the religious game, where all means are appropriated to prove a point. These people who hide their anger behind religious piousness must be proven right, and the offending culprit must be made to look like a fool, because he or she dared to question them. In these people's minds, *they will be exalted as God* when the situation is brought forth. Eventually, these people will become greatly insulted by any legitimate challenge, and show their true colors by becoming offended and vengeful. It would be wise for them to consider the Apostle Paul's warning to take heed when you think you stand, because you will eventually fall.[5]

The revelation of the obstinate mentality of the old man helped answer a question that had been filed away in my mind. Proverbs 6:16-19 tells us there are seven things that God hates. One of the things His hatred is directed towards is a proud look. This used to puzzle me. Why would God hate a simple look? As I considered the expressions of the obstinate mentality, I realized why God hates a proud look. A proud look not only expresses obstinacy of the heart, but it is also silently making a willful declaration to God that in the end, it will be exalted over His way, will, and position.

---

[4] 2 Corinthians 7:10
[5] 1 Corinthians 10:12 refer to Proverbs 16:18

Many people are making a lot of declarations, and playing the games to ensure the outcome of their worlds. They are declaring that they will be justified, vindicated, confirmed as being right, successful, happy, honored, recognized, rich, etc. They are maintaining that, in the end, people will realize that they are who they maintain they are, and that their present presentation of self and reality is true. Every time such a declaration is proclaimed or maintained, it reveals the obstinacy of man to be his own god, call his own shots, and determine his own reality. Somehow, he ends up perceiving himself as being exalted as God.

Declarations such as these indicate determinations. Determinations come back to exercising the will. When people make determinations, it is for the purpose of personal discipline or controlling their world. Sadly, most people make determinations in order to rule their worlds, rather than institute discipline so that their disposition, attitudes, and conduct will change.

In the kingdom of God, the declaration of "I am" is the same as making something a present reality. "I will" is the same as making a vow or commitment that is certain, and will determine future reality. As a result, Jesus instructed people to avoid making vows.[6] The reason for this is that people do not always have the means or power to make such vows a reality. Of course, this is not true of God. When He says, "I Am," He is determining the present truth. When He says, "I will," you already know it is a reality that will be brought forth by His power. God not only has the power to bring forth something, but He does not conveniently forget His claims, as many people do.

There are only two claims that a Christian can and must make. Job 13:15 gives us a clear insight, "Though he slay me, yet will I trust in him: but I will maintain mine own ways before him." The first claim is trust. You must choose or determine in the will area to trust God. This determination can be found throughout the Psalms. Such a choice will be a heart matter.[7]

Two words are associated with the concept of choosing to trust God. They are "put" and "shall."[8] Both of these words require personal discipline. You must put or place your trust in Him.[9] In order to place your trust in Him, you must not give way to the obstinate mentality of the old man. You must go against the grain of the old man, to develop a new perspective.

The word "shall" is an actual determination. In other words, you will put your trust in God. There is no debate or logic that will deter you from what you must do. In order to make trust a determination, you must focus

---

[6] Matthew 5:33-37

[7] Psalms 18:2; 55:23; 56:3; 61:4: 91:2; Proverbs 3:5

[8] Psalms 2:12; 4:5; 5:4; 64:10

[9] Strong's Exhaustive Concordance; #7760

on the goal of possessing God, to ensure that He becomes a reality and does not remain just a simple idea or concept.

The final determination has to do with responsibility. It is your responsibility to maintain your ways before God on a consistent basis, regardless of the circumstances. The word "maintain" means to chasten, correct or rebuke. The word "way" has to do with a person's way of thinking, feeling, and being. It represents the mode, quality, and manner of life.

The natural preference of people is that they want to control their worlds, but not maintain their ways. They perceive their way of being as right, but when it comes to being responsible for the consequences of their way, they quickly shift the blame towards others. These people may want others to adjust their world around them, but they do not want to be responsible for the way they are. Is it any wonder that very little gets accomplished or solved when it comes to personal discipline or relationships?

Obviously, God must somehow address this mentality before He can change a person's heart. There are four main sources He uses to get a hold of our mind. He uses man, circumstances, His Word, and the Holy Spirit. It is important to realize how He uses each source. For example, He will use man to warn us, circumstances to cause us to examine ourselves, His Word to penetrate our hearts, and His Spirit to bring us to a place of judgment or separation. Usually, man is God's hardest instrument for others to adhere to, but he can prove to be the most effective, as far as saving us some unnecessary problems. The reason I say this is because, to receive from man, you do have to humble yourself. After man's attempts fail to get a hold of the mind, even more trying challenges follow. Circumstances can break you; the Word can expose you, and the Holy Spirit can cause a tormenting struggle in the soul area.

It is also interesting to watch how man responds to these different sources. For example, people play the game with man, ignore circumstances, adjust the Word to their reality, and give way to a substitute spirit such as a religious or self-righteous spirit to maintain their delusion.

How much does the old man's mentality reign in your life? It does not matter what you proclaim about Christ if the old man is still calling the shots. You may be talking the talk, but you will not be walking the walk. If the obstinate mentality is still in place, you need to turn and face God. Let Him address this mentality, so He can begin to renew a right spirit within you and change your heart.

7

THE CALL

It is hard for people to realize that their unregenerate disposition is in total rebellion or opposition to God. Rather than submit to God, this disposition prefers to play the game. Rather than humble self, it simply conforms to some type of religious image. Rather than give way to what is acceptable, reasonable, and sacrificial it will cast crumbs at the feet of Jesus. These pathetic crumbs will replace the crowns that have been tried in the fires of adversity.

Obviously, unless the disposition of the old self-life is addressed, it remains in perpetual rebellion towards God. In its rebellion it can cleverly give the impression of compliance to spiritual matters, but it will never adhere to what is right. Without adherence to the transforming work of the Holy Spirit, there will be no loyalty, consistency, or faithfulness present for the inner man to get past personal preferences to do what is reasonable, let alone sacrificial.

This unregenerate disposition is often expressed by its mentality. This mentality walks in delusion, as it ignores or denies personal sin. It lacks initiative to do right and the inclination to respond. It insists on remaining clueless, so it never has to be emotionally involved. It continues to be indifferent to reality, harsh towards that which does not serve its purpose, and superior towards those who fail to properly worship it.

How do you deal with a mentality that is contrary to God in every way? After all, rebellion is nothing more than a lack of personal restraint or discipline in regard to authority and responsibility. For most people they still prefer the way of the unregenerate man. The only way for the fleshly man to deal with this mentality of misery is introspection. Introspection is an attempt to understand and control matters. However, the person's focus is still totally on self. Self with its pride is what is in total opposition to God. Therefore, in its rebellious state, self cannot sincerely respond to any authority. It can only continue to oppose or resist authority, even if it meant that the person could be helped. This can be clearly observed in children who are in rebellion. You cannot reason with them as long as they resist your authority. You must somehow get a hold of their mind to cause them to look outside of themselves.

The military had their way of getting a hold of the new recruit's mind in order to address the civilian mentality. As stated in the last chapter, there was a state of vulnerability created up front in new recruits in order to establish dependency. This implied that due to uncertainty of the unknown a person's resolve was down, therefore, he or she was receptive to change. The first stage is to make a person receptive to change that might be contrary to what he or she is used to.

The next stage of discipline the military used was actually accomplished through the exercise of marching. Marching, first, requires personal discipline. People must concentrate on the present to become aware of those around them, while being attentive to what is being said and done. Marching not only was a means to get new recruits past themselves, but it forged teamwork among them. Teamwork is vital in the military, but also effective in getting people to cease to focus on self, and think about, as well as regard others in their company.

In order to teach us to march, the military had to establish boundaries. These boundaries were developed by verbal commands. The first command taught and given was--Attention! The command of attention was a way of getting a hold of the mind. In fact, every sense in your body becomes focused and fine-tuned to the next instruction that follows.

To obtain this attention, we were taught how to stand at attention. Standing at attention was very important because it pointed to a state of readiness to respond. In other words, you could go forward, to the side or even do an about-face to go in the opposite direction when standing at attention. This state was also a means to narrow all outside influences and distractions, so that one could clearly hear the next command. Attention was a way to alleviate confusion and possible debate.

Is there something that is capable of creating a similar state of attention in Christians? First of all, in our initial stages of Christianity, we are made vulnerable by our understanding of our sinful condition and our need for salvation. True salvation will make a person receptive and open to Jesus. It is also in our initial response to the cross of Jesus that we are left with a sense of dependency upon Him as our Savior and Lord. However, the next stage for the followers of Jesus is the call. Most Christians associate the call to their position in Christ. The truth is that the initial call that goes out to all Christians is the same. It is the call to follow Him.

Jesus initially called His disciples to follow Him.[1] He called these men from the normalcy of the life they lived and were accustomed to. When you consider the implications of normalcy, you realize that Jesus was calling them into a life that was contrary to their present life. Even though these men had been somewhat exposed to or made aware of Jesus, they still had to possess a certain amount of uncertainty of where this Man would lead them. They were putting their total trust in a man who simply called them to a different life. Jesus was not calling them to a life of luxury, success, or ease. He was calling them to a life that would

---

[1] Matthew 4:19

equip them to carry on His work. However, these men only had the initial initiative to follow Him.

Personal initiative brings us to another point of the disciplined life. Jesus actually chose these men to follow Him.[2] The reason He could call them is because they were already in a state of readiness or a state of being able to respond. In the military, we would refer to that state as standing at attention. Because these men were in a state of preparedness, they could actually hear Jesus' call, and be ready to respond.

For example, Peter and his brother Andrew were casting their fishing nets into the sea, when Jesus called them. Busy people are paying attention to the task. Paying attention requires individuals to be sensitive to what is going on around them. James and John were mending nets. They were constructively doing something with their hands. People who constructively use their hands often prove to have initiative and flexibility.[3]

Levi, also known as Matthew, was collecting taxes. Although this was an unpopular occupation for a Jewish man, Matthew displayed the willingness to work in an unpleasant situation.[4] Due to the fact that Jesus chose him, we would have to conclude that he was a fair tax collector. This would reveal that he was a man of character. It was also in this position that he was obligated to interact with people.

Jesus found Philip and called him to follow Him. Philip in turn found Nathanael and encouraged him to follow Jesus. Philip was a man who believed Jesus, and had the initiative and inspiration to seek out Nathanael. Nathanael proved to be skeptical of Jesus, but in spite of it, he followed Philip to Jesus. Did Nathanael possess the necessary curiosity to find out if Philip's conclusion had some merit to it?

We do not know Nathanael's reason for following Philip, but Jesus gave us insight into his character. He was a man without guile or deceit. Perhaps in his sincerity he followed Philip to see if his conclusion was true about Christ. Jesus addressed his skepticism by sharing how He saw him under the tree before following Philip. This implied that Nathanael was a man who meditated or considered the world around him. Nathanael was surprised. He was sincere enough to recognize Jesus, and open enough to follow Him. In the first three Gospels, Nathanael is referred to as Barthlomew.[5] John is the only one who called him Nathanael. "Nathanael" means gift of God, while "Bartholomew" means Son of Tomai.[6]

---

[2] John 15:16
[3] Matthew 4:19-22
[4] Matthew 9:9; Luke 5:27-29
[5] Matthew 10:3; Mark 3:18; Luke 6:14; John 1:47-51
[6] Smith's Bible Dictionary

There is also Simon the Zealot. He belonged to a group that believed in adhering to the Mosaic ritual. In fact, they were fiercely devoted to it. Simon's name means hearing.[7] Obviously, this man heard Jesus' call, and redirected his devotion to Jesus with the same intensity, because he is also mentioned in Acts 1:13.[8]

We all know about Judas Iscariot, but what about the other Judas? This particular Judas was also known as Jude, Lebbeus, and Thaddeus.[9] He was the brother of James, and the half-brother of Jesus. He was the only sibling who actually followed Jesus in His ministry. He wrote the epistle Jude, but past these points, very little is known about him. Perhaps, his name will give us insight into the type of man he was. "Judas" refers to the name of Judah, which means "praise," while the name "Lebbeus" means man of heart. The meaning of these two names points to association and condition. We know this man was definitely associated with Jesus, the Lion of Judah, and that he must have had a strong, receptive heart of praise and gratitude towards Him to follow Him into service, and past the cross, to Pentecost.

There was Thomas, also known as Didymus.[10] Most associate this disciple with doubt, because he was the one who verbally doubted that Jesus had risen from the grave, in spite of the fact that there were various witnesses to attest to it. However, this popular name for Thomas is not a fair assumption of him. Thomas displayed boldness when it came to following Jesus when He had just spoken of His death after Lazarus' death. He then proceeded towards Jerusalem to raise Lazarus from the dead. At this point, Thomas said to the other disciples, "...Let us also go, that we may die with him" (John 11:16).

These eleven men had different backgrounds. They left all behind to follow Jesus when He called them. Although these men were very human, they were the ones who finished the course. They were all persecuted for their faith, and all but John was believed to have die a martyr's death.

Do you see a picture emerging concerning these men? They had initiative, flexibility, willingness, inspiration, and they were open. One was without guile and the other ones apparently had receptive hearts towards Jesus. As you consider these men, you realize their backgrounds, occupations and lifestyles varied. How could these men learn to march together? After all, to march together means getting into step with one another. It means functioning as a living organism. This type of unusual organism must learn to come together in agreement, in order to get something accomplished. For Christians, this agreement will come at the point of Jesus.

---

[7] Ibid
[8] Matthew 10:4; Mark 3:18; Luke 6:13-15
[9] Matthew 10:3; Mark 3:18; Luke 6:16; John 14:22; Acts 1:13
[10] John 11:16

I encountered women from all over the United States when I was in boot camp. We all had different backgrounds, ideas, dreams, and agendas. It was only as we marched together, that we began to get outside of ourselves, so that we could live together.

In marching, you must get in step with everyone else. This is contrary to the independent way of thinking and doing. In our independence, we expect those in our world to adjust to our drumbeat. We become upset and angry when others do not adjust.

It is very hard for independent people to realize that they are not the center of the world. Sadly, it takes other people to test and reveal a person's real character. As long as an individual can remain an island unto his or herself, he or she can live in a world of ignorant bliss. However, such a world is quickly shaken by the intrusion of others who do not walk according to this person's drumbeat.

This is a big problem in homes, organizations, and the Church. Most people are walking to their own drumbeat. They refuse to get past me, myself, and I. They will not change focus, and adhere to what is right by exalting the only one that can serve as the true head and leader of this living organism: Jesus Christ.[11]

It is only at the point of Jesus that His people can come to a place of agreement and function as His Body. It is only as Jesus becomes the main focus outside of self that those in His Body are able to become aware of those around them. It is only as each believer strives to possess Jesus that His Body will become effective in His kingdom.

When I marched in my company, I had to be aware of the person next to me to keep in step. The minute I considered myself, I would lose step, which potentially could throw the whole company off course. This was serious because the company was judged according to how it marched. The idea that it only took one self-centered person to be out of step brought a reality check as to how each person had to work together.

As people get into selfisms, they become a hindrance to the healthy function of the organism. Each person in the company was responsible to ensure the healthy function of the whole company. We had to not only march together, we had to work and live together. When a person became indifferent to others, it affected the morale of the whole company.

There was a recruit who was transferred to our company due to personality conflicts. Later, we discovered the problem. Her personal hygiene was intolerable. It finally got so bad that one night, some of the women ganged up on her, bodily carried her into the shower facilities, and put her in a bathtub of water. There they proceeded to scrub on her until she conceded to properly do it herself. From that point on, she kept up her personal hygiene.

---

[11] Colossians 1:15-18

Obstinacy is the manifestation of selfism. This attitude has no regards about how personal actions affect others. It is rude and disrespectful. Obviously, people must pass the various aspects of selfishness, so they can properly function as a team.

People who have the "I" problem walk according to their own personal drumbeat and have no regard for those who are involved with their lives. As people go in different directions, there is strife and contention. Those who walk to their own drumbeat inevitably lack personal discipline. They have no vision past themselves. They either play games to manipulate, or they become belligerent in trying to get their way.

Jesus dealt with those who were not ready to respond. The first indication that a person is not ready to respond is that he or she has excuses. These excuses seem logical enough, but they reveal that the person is not ready to adhere to Jesus' calling. The major reason is that these people's vision is not on the heavenly plane, but on the earthly plane. This means their priorities and values are wrong. In Luke 9:59, a man initially put off Jesus' invitation to first go bury his father. Another one asked Him to let him go home and bid farewell to his family. When Jesus calls, it is meant for the present time. You must be in the state of readiness or you will be left behind.

We see this same scenario in the parable of the wedding supper in Luke 14:16-24. The first individual declared that he had bought a piece of ground that he needed to see. This man either was a bad businessman for buying a piece of property he never set eyes on, or he was lying. The next individual excused himself in the same matter. Apparently, he bought five oxen he had not yet proven. The last man pulled a classic. He claimed he was married; therefore, he had no liberty to accept the invitation. It is not unusual to blame our spouse for a lack of commitment or readiness before God.

In Matthew's version of the parable, Jesus gives the attitude behind these excuses. They did not fear the king, and were being flippant.[12] In fact, those who excused themselves were making light of the invitation, as they went their way. Sadly, others persecuted those who would dare to invite them to the wedding supper of the king. This not only showed pride, but obstinacy towards the rule and authority of God. This parable revealed the king's response towards those who refused His invitation. They were destroyed.

Christians must give up all their selfisms to put into practice the Christian life. Each place where the Christian life is practiced, godly discipline will develop. This is vital because discipline serves as a catalyst that brings the Christian's virtues together to form godly character.

---

[12] Matthew 22:2-14

Has Jesus got your attention? Are you in a state of readiness, prepared to receive your next instruction, or are you excusing yourself from accepting Jesus' invitation or call? The invitation is for those who have not embraced Jesus' salvation, but the call is for those who need to embrace His life. Due to the fact that these people tasted the sweetness of His salvation, they should already be following Jesus out of love, faith, and hope.

8

SEEKING GOD

One of the greatest disciplines in our lives has to do with our spiritual life. Oswald Chamber tells us that Christians are being disciplined to know God.[1] There is only one way to develop this discipline, and it is summarized in Jeremiah 29:13, "And ye shall seek me, and find me, when ye shall search for me with all your heart." The word "seek" is the discipline that allows a person to discover God.

Seek means to strive after, ask, beg, beseech, desire, crave, and demand.[2] To seek something requires our complete attention and commitment. Jesus brought this out in the parables in Luke 15:3-9, of the one lost sheep and the lost coin. The sheep and the coin both held value, and both were lost. The one who lost these valuables dropped all to search for them.

Is God lost or missing? No, but we can easily become lost in our life before God. The demands of the world and life can cause us to lose track of God, making Him obscure to us. As we become consumed by the demands of life, we cease to be aware that we have become lost in our spiritual lives in the midst of all of our activities.

This is what married couples experience as they end up running different races and courses in their lives. Walls begin to develop between husband and wife as the communion that breathes life into their relationship lessens. They begin to think independently of each other, causing frustration and suspicion to develop. Eventually, they realize they are lonely. They feel separated from their spouse. This creates an emotional leanness. Ultimately, these two individuals must find each other, but it will require them to strive beyond the walls to silence the suspicion, and bring their emotions into proper perspective. This usually requires both people to battle it out with one another, until they can subdue suspicion.

Suspicion is nothing more than vain imaginations. These vain imaginations not only create a false, lop-sided reality, but they create distrust and discord. There can be no communion or agreement until these suspicions are rooted out, exposed for the culprits they are, and placed in the proper light. Once these suspicions are out of the way and the channels of communication open, peace will return.

---

[1] So Send I You /Workman of God; pg. 28
[2] Strong's Exhaustive Concordance #1245, 8548, 1875

Regardless of how lost believers may become in the midst of demands, God is never far away from those who belong to Him. Granted, He is far from the wicked, but when it comes to His people, He stands as the immovable Rock that never moves from His position and commitment. However, many things can subtly crowd in between God and His people. These barriers cause His people to lose direction and become lost in the maze of demands. As first, these believers do not recognize what is happening. As demands start sucking the life out of them, eventually they begin to sense that something is missing. Spiritual leanness begins to invade their souls.[3] Leanness can cause both desperation and confusion. The solution to this problem eludes most people because they are not aware that God is missing. After all, they are busy doing all of the normal, religious activities; therefore, they do not perceive that God is absent.

Out of this confusion comes frustration and anger. Nothing is pleasing or satisfying. In fact, all seems useless and unproductive. There is a restlessness growing that cannot be silenced. After hitting various walls and coming to dead ends, it begins to dawn on those who love God that their perception is wrong. The frustration they are feeling has nothing to do with activities, but is due to the fact that God has been crowded out of their daily living by useless demands.

At this point, people will begin to seek after God, although some might wonder why they should seek after God, especially in the light of "easy believism." After all, grace is supposedly handed to every person who has "accepted" Jesus Christ. However, if God is missing, it is up to the individual to seek God, to ensure their quality of life.

The prophet, Amos instructed the people to seek God and they would live.[4] The truth is we are all seeking some type of life. We may be looking to the world, education, religion, or relationships to discover the purpose and meaning of life. Each of these searches are worldly and will leave people disillusioned, confused, empty, and depressed.

The Bible is clear that there is only one source that can bring meaning and purpose to life, and that is Jesus Christ. In fact, He is life.[5] Therefore, we must seek the reality of God to discover life that has purpose or meaning. The Apostle Paul brought this out in Acts 17:27-28, "That they should seek the Lord, if haply they might feel after him, and find him, though he be not far from everyone of us: For in him we live, and move, and have our being; as certain also of your own poets have said, For we are also his offspring."

In most cases, people think they know God; therefore, they believe something else must be missing from their life. They often begin feeling after something that is vague and illusive. As they blindly search for this

---

[3] Psalm 27:5-7; 73:27; 91:1-2; Proverbs 15:29
[4] Amos 5:4, 6, 14
[5] John 14:6

missing ingredient, they haphazardly encounter the true God. It is not that these people found God by chance; it is that He finds them in their search, and they stumble over Him. Sadly, the natural tendency for most people is to seek life in the things that feed their flesh, stroke their ego, and satisfy the old man in them. They become dull towards God's overtures and continue on in their blindness.

Finding God involves every aspect of a person's being. To truly seek after God, a person must first prepare his or her heart to seek God.[6] This means setting his or her heart on God. Set implies fixing or fastening on the source. Setting is another discipline, and can be found throughout the Word of God.

To set the heart involves getting a hold of one's affections and directing them towards God. The Apostle Paul confirmed this in Colossians 3:2, "Set your affections on things above, not on things on the earth." To bring affections under control, people must reevaluate what is important. Without changing that which is valued on an earthly level to that which is heavenly, people will never be inclined towards the eternal. Ultimately, they will fail to seek those things which can only be found in Jesus Christ.[7]

The next area that must be disciplined in seeking God is the soul. To prepare the heart to seek the Lord means to change the inclination. To set the heart means to fix it on a goal. With the focus of the heart fixed, the person now is ready to seek for and find God. In summation, the heart is now ready to recognize God. Once the heart is prepared to seek for God with everything within it, the soul must then be prepared to seek after God. In fact, it must also be set like the heart to discover God.[8]

Isaiah 26:9 talks about the soul desiring God in the night. This prepares the spirit to seek God in the morning. Therefore, what does it mean to prepare the soul to seek God? It involves the will. In order for discipline to be exercised, it must graduate from the mind, and take root in the will area. Therefore, the will of a person must be set to find God.

The intellect must then give way to the mind of Christ. Psalm 10:4 tells us that the wicked will not seek God, since God is not in their thoughts. This is why the Apostle Paul instructs believers to cast down all vain imaginations, and bring their entire thoughts captive to the obedience of Christ.[9] Thoughts that are in obedience to Jesus will not only seek God, but will quickly adjust to what is righteous.

Emotions must line up to the Word of God before they can perceive spiritual truths and properly receive from God. Once the inclination is towards God, the heart fixed, the will set, the intellect giving way to the right mentality, and the emotions in line with God's Word, the strength to

---

[6] 2 Chronicles 12:14; 15:2, 12-13; 19:3; 30:19; Psalms 119:2

[7] Philippians 2:21; Colossians 3:1

[8] 1 Chronicles 22:19

[9] 2 Corinthians 10:5: Philippians 2:5

seek after God will be tempered in order to be brought into a place of meekness before the Spirit of God.

It is easy to talk about disciplining the body, but to discipline the soul involves the strength of God. Ezra 8:21 tells us that it is important to seek God in the right way. The main ingredient in seeking God is the Spirit of God. He is the only One who can lead a person to all truth concerning Jesus.[10] It is the Spirit of God who not only enables a person to pursue after God, and to guide him or her to places in God, but to endure the search.

Simple submission to the Holy Spirit is the key to finding God. Once again, men complicate their search because it becomes a search of the mind or flesh, instead of giving way to the Holy Ghost. Zechariah 4:6 confirms this, "...Not by might, nor by power, but by my spirit, saith the LORD of hosts."

Once the Holy Ghost is present, the heart fixed and the soul prepared, it is now time to carry it out. In other words, it is time to seek the Lord. One of the keys to daily seeking God is to do so early before activities begin to crowd out time with Him. It is when all is still and the soul is fresh from rest that one is prepared to seek God and find Him. In fact, such a person will take delight in approaching God, knowing He will meet with him or her.[11]

Seeking God should be our main priority each new day and in each new challenge to ensure the continuation of a satisfying life. Knowing His heart should be our desire. Gaining His perspective should be our goal. Communing with Him should serve as our bread. Worshipping Him should be our breath, doing His will should be our meat, and loving Him should be our heartbeat. After all, this privilege to seek out and find God was wrought on the cross of Jesus. Such a search will end in peace. One must keep in mind that it is a privilege to pursue after God as well as a point of grace, and this privilege must not be taken for granted or abused.

It is important to not forget the warning of Luke 13:24, "Strive to enter in at the strait gate: for many, I say unto you, will seek to enter in, and shall not be able." Genesis 6:3 warns that God's Spirit will not always strive with people. Isaiah 55:6 instructs us to seek after the Lord while He may be found. Many people will seek to enter into the kingdom of God, but will fail to enter for different reasons.

One of the main reasons that people will fail to enter in is due to sin. Sin separates people from God; therefore, some, no matter how hard they seek will not find God. Another reason is personal agendas. People with personal agendas will miss God as they insist that He adjust to their way of thinking. Others walk in delusion about their spiritual condition before God. Although they perceive themselves as being on the right

---

[10] John 16:13
[11] Psalm 63:1; Isaiah 58:2

path, the false religious light that is within them blinds them to their false way.[12]

All spiritual discipline originates with seeking and finding God. There is no real spiritual discipline outside of finding God, and establishing a relationship with Him. Any attempts outside of this main discipline will remain attempts that will have no power or effect.

How do you start each day? Do you immediately discipline your spiritual life by first seeking God and gaining His perspective? Without this discipline there will be no strength to endure and overcome any unsuspected challenges that life may bring.

---

[12] Proverbs 14:12; Isaiah 55:8-9; Matthew 6:22-23

9

THE ATTITUDE

We have considered the mentality of the old man. It is nothing more than arrogance in many disguises and activities. This unregenerate mentality produces a disposition that expresses itself in ungodly attitudes of superiority. This brings us to the disposition that will produce a godly attitude.

The Apostle Paul discussed the proper disposition in Philippians 2:1-11, by describing Jesus' mentality. Jesus' mentality was the opposite of arrogance. In fact, He separated Himself from that which would have deserved or demanded exaltation. He took on an attitude that expressed humility and came into subjection to another authority.[1] Ultimately, His attitude displayed submission that gave way to something greater as He conducted Himself as a servant. As a result, Paul instructed believers to actually take on the mind of Jesus in Philippians 2:5, "Let this mind be in you, which was also in Christ Jesus."

In essence, believers are being told to take on the mentality of the new man which is opposite of the old man's mentality.[2] The question is how can this mentality be developed in each of us? The first requirement is to let the mind of Christ be in you. The word "let" is a discipline. It requires letting go of what you now value, in order to give way to what is acceptable and true to God.

Giving way means bringing our thoughts into line with the Person of Jesus, and applying His attitude to our lives. As truths are applied by faith, the Holy Spirit begins to transform our minds, our way of thinking, to the character of Jesus Christ.[3] Applying the mind of Christ to the way we think produces a correct attitude towards God. When you take the ingredients of godly humility, submission, and subjection, you will develop the appropriate attitude towards God, that being the fear of God.

What is the fear of God? Some Christians have a watered-down version of this fear. However, there is one attribute of God that can clearly put this attitude in the right perspective: holiness. The fear of God comes out of a sense of God's holy character. In fact, this attitude will line you up to God's character by ensuring that you approach Him in a way that honors who He is.

---

[1] Matthew 11:28-29
[2] Romans 6:4-6
[3] Romans 12:2

Fear of the Lord is the opposite of being high-minded. Most people think of themselves as being superior. They judge according to personal opinions and prejudices. This superiority exists because they do not really know the character of God. In fact, in their delusion, their character outshines God, and makes them an exception in the midst of pathetic humanity. It is only in light of God's holy character that the fear of God can be formed. The writer in 2 Chronicles 19:7 made this statement, "Wherefore now let the fear of the LORD be upon you; take heed and do it: for there is no iniquity with the LORD our God, nor respect of persons, nor taking of gifts." God has no iniquity in His character. This is what constitutes His holiness. His holiness demands that His followers be holy as well.[4]

Once this attitude of godly fear is formed, it will bring much needed discipline in the person's life as it perfects holiness within his or her character. The Apostle Paul confirmed this in 2 Corinthians 7:1, "Having therefore these promises, dearly beloved, let us cleanse ourselves from all filthiness of the flesh and spirit, perfecting holiness in the fear of God."

Obviously, fearing God would be for our benefit. Deuteronomy 6:24 confirms this, "And the LORD commanded us to do all these statutes, to fear the LORD our God, for our good always, that he might preserve us alive, as it is at this day." This attitude will actually preserve us, and as Deuteronomy 6:25 points out, it shall be righteousness unto us.

The fear of the Lord will cause us to insist on personal holiness. Holiness is a state that hates sin, avoids evil, and will not tolerate wickedness. It points to sobriety that is full of integrity, and will be serious about dealing with personal sin. It is aggressive in confronting offenses against God, and is motivated by a fierceness that will not be subdued until personal wickedness is overcome. When you consider sobriety, aggression, and fierceness in this context, it also points to the fear of God.

What does it mean to fear God? Most people associate fear with awe, honor, and respect. It is true that the fear of God entails awe that is expressed in humility and will produce worship. Honor points to submission that gives way to something that is worthy, while respect has to do with recognizing authority and the rights of someone else. However, the fear of the Lord is so much more. It involves a dread about facing God in a displeasing state or manner. It is not conceited or deluded. As a result, the fear of the Lord assures purity in motives, attitudes, and conduct.[5] In fact, it must be present in every aspect of our Christian conduct. As a result, it proves to be a powerful discipline.

As you study the fear of the Lord, you can see why it brings godly discipline. This fear actually establishes sound boundaries that encourage discipline in various areas of a person's life. We find these

---

[4] Romans 11:20; 1 Peter 1:15-16
[5] Psalm 19:9

boundaries in God's commandments. Deuteronomy 5:29 states, "Oh that there were such an heart in them, that they would fear me, and keep all my commandments always, that it might be well with them, and with their children for ever!"

God's people can only serve Him in the boundaries of this healthy fear. Psalm 2:11 tells us, "Serve the LORD with fear, and rejoice with trembling." The reason this attitude is necessary in service is that individuals will keep in mind whom they are serving. Most religious people are serving according to their own perception of goodness and charity. As a result, they are making statements about their personal piety, rather than God's goodness and incredible commitment to the salvation of men's souls. Therefore, their focus is not singular, lacking sure purpose and direction. The Apostle Paul takes us one step further concerning this subject, by instructing believers to be obedient servants with fear and trembling, in singleness of heart, as unto Christ.[6]

The fear of God must be present to effectively worship God. Without this attitude, there will be no awe or realization of who God is. The Psalmist acknowledges this reality in Psalm 5:7, "But as for me, I will come unto thy house in the multitude of thy mercy: and in thy fear will I worship toward thy holy temple."

Fear of God leads to salvation. Psalm 85:9 confirms that salvation is near to those who fear Him. The Apostle Paul instructs believers to work out their salvation in fear and trembling.[7] Once again, the fear of the Lord reminds us who saved us. Obviously, if God stepped out of heaven to become a man, in order to secure redemption, we must make sure that we respond to His redemption in an honorable, respectful way.

This leads us to the subject of presumption. The fear of the Lord is the opposite of presumption. Due to its sobriety, the fear of the Lord does not make foolish assumptions about God. It carefully considers all things in the light of the character and ways of God, to ensure integrity of conduct. Ultimately, the fear of the Lord leads to wisdom.[8]

Wisdom is the opposite of foolishness. Foolishness lives without any regard to God. It is undisciplined, selfish, jealous, and rebellious. It refuses to be humbled, corrected, or open and teachable. It demands its own way. The book of Proverbs talks a lot about foolishness. It summarizes the difference between the wise and the foolish in Proverbs 14:24, "The crown of the wise is their riches: but the foolishness of fools is folly."

The fear of the Lord will produce strong confidence and a fountain of life as it inspires us to depart from that which produces death, while it prepares us to meet God in His holiness. On the other hand, foolishness will produce fools who become reprobates. These reprobates no longer

---

[6] Ephesians 6:6
[7] Philippians 2:12
[8] Deuteronomy 17:13; Psalm 111:10

retain the knowledge of God.[9] They have been turned over to the folly of their own personal reality.

Most people go on to be fools because they do not love God with everything in them. Love is the motivation behind this healthy fear, but sadly, love is being presented in an unholy manner. The love of God that is being upheld today is a sappy, sick type of love. It has no substance.

I have discovered that those who talk the most about God's love are actually insecure about His commitment to them. This insecurity often exists because these people are erecting or exalting another god that serves their particular lifestyle. Yet, underneath it all, they still have an inward knowledge of His holiness that they can never shake. Hence, enters the erroneous indoctrination about the love of God. This erroneous indoctrination declares that because of love, God will overlook sin. He will understand perversion, and He will tolerate inconsistencies in people's character. Therefore, to overcompensate for their lack of love and godliness, these people will keep speaking of His love to drown out the gnawing reality of His holiness, and the fact that they are insecure about meeting Him on judgment day because they have no real inner witness of salvation.

It is true that God loves people, but it can only be realized at the point of Jesus, and what He secured on that cross for each of us. In fact, God's love makes us all equal at the cross. This love has to do with forgiveness and reconciliation, and not overlooking defilement. His love never rejoices in iniquity, but only in the truth.[10] Therefore, His love does not serve as a license to live according to convenience of the flesh and the arrogance of pride.

People can only understand, know, and receive God's love in light of His character. God's love becomes a platform upon which His followers are encouraged to grow and develop. After all, it is not meant to be a means of hiding irresponsibility in order to live in a state of defilement. Its ultimate goal is to inspire His followers to become who they can be in His kingdom.

Personally, I know God's love in light of who He is. For example, I understand God's love in light of His holiness, because it results in chastisement. Such chastisement will enable me to partake of His holiness. I know God's love in light of His judgments because they remind me of consequences He wants me to avoid. I recognize God's love in His wrath, because He will not accept me on any other terms but the redemption of Jesus. Through the years, I have recognized that these aspects of God's love are always calling me higher, beyond the cross of Christ, to heavenly places that have been established in Him.[11]

---

[9] Proverbs 14:26-27; Romans 1:28

[10] 1 Corinthians 13:6

[11] Ephesians 2:6

This understanding has brought a healthy perception of fearing God. Fear of God is not being afraid of God, because one knows His commitment to ensure salvation. Rather, it is a matter of fearing Him because of who He is and what He is capable of doing. As Matthew 10:28 says, "And fear not them which kill the body, but are not able to kill the soul: but rather fear him which is able to destroy both soul and body in hell." His character demands holiness from each of His followers, as well as demands righteous conduct from them. God cannot cease to be God, but we can cease to be foolish, by choosing to love God, believe Him, and submit to the working of His Spirit.

A healthy fear of God makes us submissive. We are called to be submissive in three areas: To God, His Word, and other believers. People must have both the fear and love of God before they are able to come into proper submission. This is also true when it comes to obedience to His Word, and coming into unity with other believers to accomplish God's bidding and work in the great harvest field of humanity.

Due to the fact that people do not fear God, they do not fear His Word. Although many Christians claim to believe that the Word of God is the final authority, their lives clearly stipulate that it does not serve as their personal final authority. They may use the Word on others to correct them, but the Word is never allowed to line them up in spirit and truth. These people look to the Word to confirm their doctrines, but not to be tested by it. Their doctrines are what define, twist, and adjust the Word according to their personal opinions, prejudices, and preferences.

Such a self-serving attitude towards the Word reveals that these people do not tremble at God's Word. Ezra 10:3 makes reference to people who tremble at God's commandments. Isaiah 66:2 talks about those who tremble at His word. "For all those things hath mine hand made, and all those things have been, saith the LORD: but to this man will I look, even to him that is poor and of a contrite spirit, and trembleth at my word." The reason people do not tremble at God's Word is because they do not believe it is true.

If people believed the Word was true, they would be seriously applying all of its various warnings about arrogance, sin, and defilement. They would be confronting unholy attitudes, unrighteous conduct, and unacceptable pursuits and priorities in their lives. In essence, they would believe the Word, apply it to their lives, and walk it out in sobriety and humility.

Ephesians 5:21 instructs believers, "Submitting yourselves one to another in the fear of God." Obviously, we cannot properly honor others, until we exalt God in His proper place in our lives. Until this holy fear is in its proper place, people's typical response to others is to oppress those who are considered lesser with burdens and demands. This is why it is difficult to prefer others to ourselves, unless we have an awareness of the forgiveness God has displayed towards our own personal plight.[12] This preference not only puts people on an equal footing with us by properly honoring them, but it also exalts their needs as a preference above personal needs. Such preference will automatically make them a potential ministry.

Forgiveness is a necessity in light of His holiness. It allows Him to restore us out of love. It is because of God's love that He provided the means of satisfying the different aspects of His holiness. His heart's desire is to do all He can to bring each of us to forgiveness and reconciliation. This is where mercy and grace enter the scene. It is His commitment to display mercy when we deserve judgment, and pour out His grace when we deserve nothing for our ways. Keep in mind; our best attempts to please Him are considered filthy rags to Him.[13]

It is within the boundaries of God's holiness that we must and will submit to one another for His purpose and glory. We must submit or give way to something greater than ourselves. In this case, it means giving in to God's plan for His Body, the Church. Godly submission allows people to come together in unity of the Spirit at the point of Jesus' work, for the purpose of edification of the whole Body.[14]

How do we develop this fear of God? Deuteronomy 4:10b gives us this insight, "...when the LORD said unto me, Gather me the people together, and I will make them hear my words, that they may learn to fear me all the days that they shall live upon the earth, and that they may teach their children." We must learn to fear the Lord. Learning has to do with developing proper attitudes, patterns, or skills to execute something.[15] This type of learning is accomplished through application and example.

Most people have been conditioned by ungodly, pagan societies.[16] They have been taught the ways of these societies. When it comes to the things of God, there is no way for such people to discern the holy from the unholy. Therefore, individuals must unlearn these unholy attitudes and practices. The way people unlearn attitudes is to expose themselves to the environment that will challenge their present way of thinking. While in this environment, they must inundate themselves with the reality of the new lifestyle they are pursuing.

Attitudes must change before new practices can have an effect. For example, a person's attitude towards God must change before godly practices will have meaning or serve any real purpose. People must expose themselves to the environment of holiness before they can discern the holy from the profane. As they expose themselves to

---

[12] Romans 12:9-10

[13] Isaiah 64:6

[14] Ephesians 2:18-22; 4:12-16

[15] See Strong's Exhaustive Concordance, #3925

[16] Deuteronomy 18:9

holiness, they must begin to obey God's Word by applying it to their lives as truth, and walking it out on a daily basis. Application of God's ways to a situation will begin to reveal His character. As individuals learn more of God's character in a personal way, they will develop greater clarity as to what is acceptable and what is unacceptable to God. This is how each of us learns to fear God and develop spiritual discernment.

Fearing God will ensure that you will live a life of quality and meaning. Life can only be realized when people are walking in the ways of God. The fear of God encourages obedience and will result in deliverance. Obedience will bring confidence, because the person can be assured of abiding in the Rock of Ages.[17]

Fear of the Lord is not optional. This attitude is a must if believers are to properly function in their life and conduct before God. Sadly, this fear is missing in much of the Church. Many Christians are hiding behind sappy love, abused grace, and unholy experiences. All of these avenues may delude people, but they will never develop a fear of God or bring a person to the state of holiness.

Do you properly fear God or have you deluded yourself about His character? If you are flippant about God's character, His Word and His servants, take heed to the sobering words of Hebrews 12:28-29, "Wherefore we receiving a kingdom which cannot be moved, let us have grace, whereby we may serve God acceptably with reverence and godly fear: For our God is a consuming fire."

---

[17] Deuteronomy 6:2; Proverbs 14:26; 2 Kings 17:28, 39

10

THE PLACE

The greatest struggle in the kingdom of God is for people to get past their need to remain independent from God. Independence may tack Jesus on, but it reserves the right to determine personal pursuits and beliefs. Sadly, these people who see themselves as independent thinkers will be quick to surrender or fling their minds toward worldly and demonic beliefs in order to find something they can believe in outside of self. After all, people need some basis or foundation upon which to build their conclusions. The Prophet Isaiah gave a good description of humanity in Isaiah 53:6, "All we like sheep have gone astray; we have turned every one to his own way; and the LORD hath laid on him the iniquity of us all."

Due to independence, man is on the path of destruction. This independence expresses itself in rebellion. Although independence may comply to religious codes outwardly, it remains rebellious or indifferent to God's reign and rule. In his independence, man is holding onto the fantasy that he can determine his own identity. He believes that if he maintains the right to experience and explore the world as he so desires, he will discover who he is. Eventually, this pursuit not only proves to be futile, but it leaves him lost and empty. It is at this point that some discover that the most valuable truth is that there is no life or purpose outside of Jesus Christ.

Independence represents a life out of control because it has no real boundaries or purposes outside of personal preferences. This brings us to godly discipline. Godly discipline entails coming into a place of rest, confidence, service, and communion with God. In order to come into this place, you must seek for it. Interestingly, this place is not a physical location, but a Person. In other words, we must come to the place of God.

The word "place" implies a spot, space, occupancy, and position.[1] The Word of God uses nouns to describe the place God is to occupy in our lives. King David refers to God as his fortress, rock, high tower, and refuge.[2] Psalms 91 speaks of God being a secret place, and that one can abide under His shadow. This particular psalm also makes reference to Him being a habitation. These are all stable, immovable places.

---

[1] Strong's Exhaustive Concordance, #5117
[2] 2 Samuel 22:2-3

Jesus said in John 14:1-3 that He must go and prepare a place for us. As you study the relationship that Christians are to have in Jesus, you will discover that Jesus is the actual place each of His believers must reside in. Jesus said of His relationship with His followers, that He is the Vine and they are the branches. They must abide in Him to ensure both life and fruit. The Apostle Paul tells us that our life is hid in Christ.[3] Ephesians 2:6 states, "And hath raised us up together, and made us sit together in heavenly places in Christ Jesus."

What does it mean for God to be our place? Acts 17:28a summarizes it best, "For in him we live, and move and have our being." The important word is the word "in." This word implies inclusion, location, or position within limits.[4] It often determines purpose and authority. As you consider this small word, it points to boundaries that will create order and discipline. The New Testament uses this word numerous times to describe believers' relationship with Jesus. He is in them and they are in Him. This relationship carries significance, purpose, and authority.

When you consider that we live, move, and have our being or hope in God through the Person of Jesus Christ, you begin to realize that He is the only place of identification. Without this identity, a person will have no history, the present will be uncertain, and there will be no purpose to guide his or her future. Such a person will be tossed to and fro in the midst of ailing, hopeless humanity.

Identity establishes the environment in which we function. Environment is influenced by the choices we make in regards to God and His Word. It is obvious that the environment in which we live, or what influences us the most, will determine our attitude about the issues regarding God and life. It will determine the incline or direction of our preferences and priorities. As a result, we will naturally make choices according to what is being established as reality in our environment.

Choices will determine the type of personality that will be developed and expressed to others. Personality consists of the quality of character. Character will determine our attitude towards life and how we interact with others. As you can see, our personality will define our reality.

I know of young people who have learned to play games by conning the people around them with their personality. However, they are struggling with their own personal identity. After all, the con game has no real substance behind it.

For Christians, identity in Christ provides them with the freedom for their personality to be established. Since the Christian finds this identity in Christ, the truth and example that the Person of Jesus left, serve as the boundaries within which each believer is to operate. This produces discipline.

---

[3] John 15:1-8; Colossians 3:3
[4] Webster's New Collegiate Dictionary.

Identity also gives us a history or beginning in which we have a stake to keep us in the right path. This stake is the cross of Jesus. It points us heavenward where we can begin to realize that we now have a purpose, to possess the treasure of heaven, the Alpha and Omega, Jesus Christ.[5] Within these two limits believers can know how to live according to the cross, and move in light of their glorious future in Christ. Between these two boundaries, they will possess their very being, or hope, as they discover who they are in Christ.

Identification brings us to the other point of discipline in God's kingdom: that of position. It is vital that Christians find their position in Christ. In fact, position determines a person's place in the scheme of things more than any other source.

For example, consider the family. Usually there are children in the family. Due to their family associations, they have identity that gives them a history and a place of belonging. However, they are in a position of submission. Immediately, this determines their position in the family as to their order and function. This is especially true for the Body of Christ. The purpose for establishing each member's position in the Body is to train them how to live, and move, and have their being in Christ. As each member reaches maturity, each of their positions will change according to their responsibilities.

Although positions do not define a person's personality, they do discipline how that personality will be expressed. For example, a husband's personality will express itself through godly love and leadership in the family, while the wife's personality will be expressed through godly submission.[6]

Identification may establish our place, but position clearly defines responsibilities. Once again, these boundaries bring discipline. This is brought out through the example of servitude. All Christians have been placed in the position of servants. This clearly defines their responsibilities to the Lord of lords. The Apostle Paul explained the responsibilities of God's servants who function in the world. They must be obedient in the attitude of fear and trembling. Their hearts must be single in purpose as unto Christ. They must not be men-pleasers, but doing the will of God from the heart.[7]

As you can see, the concept of place has the ability to establish discipline at various levels of the Christian life. However, few understand their place in Christ. Since they do not know their place, they have no identity, making them lost and uncertain in the scheme of things. Without identity, there is no purpose or position to fulfill. A person who operates in this reality will discover that there is little hope, as their world

---

[5] Revelation 1:8, 11, 18
[6] Ephesians 5:22-26
[7] Matthew 20:25-27; Ephesians 6:5-7

spins out of control since there are no boundaries. Without boundaries, there will be no discipline.

The beauty about having our place in Jesus is that there are clear boundaries. It does not matter from which angle you consider Jesus, you will find both identity and position in Him. Identity determines position, while position upholds identity and establishes responsibilities. Christians who operate within these boundaries find liberty, confidence, and authority.

Let's consider some of the other aspects of our place in Christ. When we consider the Christian walk, Jesus gave us two examples: Servitude and suffering. Servitude points to the position of the servant that identifies us to Jesus through the attitude of humility. Suffering reminds us of the identification that comes through sacrifice. It points to the yoke that places us beside Jesus Christ in the great harvest field of humanity. This yoke speaks of submission or coming into agreement with our Lord.[8]

When we consider our place as the servant, Jesus provided us with boundaries through His example of servitude. He actually took on the position of a servant when He gave up His sovereignty as God and was fashioned in the form of a man. This allowed Him to become identified with each of us.[9]

As servant, Jesus' main goal was to do the will of the Father. As man, His ultimate focus was to be offered up as the Lamb of God. As servant, He came into submission to the Father, and as man, He was obedient even to the death on the cross. As servant, He denied self, and as man, He died on the cross.[10]

As you can see, Jesus' example serves as a powerful witness to His followers. As His followers, we have to give up our rights to the way we perceive life to become identified with Jesus. We must begin to do the will of the Father. The will of the Father is to believe upon Jesus with the intent of obeying Him, so that He can raise each of us up in the last day. To believe in Christ not only means that you look to Him for your salvation, but you believe Him as to His identity. To know Jesus is to love Him. If you love Him, you will obey Him. [11]

As obedient servants of God, Jesus once again provides important boundaries in which we are to operate. These boundaries have to do with the Law and righteousness. Jesus shows us our responsibility towards the Law, so that righteousness can be established in our lives.

Jesus said this about the Law in Matthew 5:17, "Think not that I am come to destroy the law, or the prophets: I am not come to destroy, but

---

[8] Matthew 11:28-30; John 13:13-16; 1 Peter 2:21-24
[9] Philippians 2:6-7
[10] Matthew 26:38-44; John 5:30; Philippians 2:8
[11] John 6:38-40; 15:10-17

fulfill." As man, Jesus did not simply obey the Law, He fulfilled the spirit and the intent of the Law.

The Apostle Paul makes this statement in Romans 10:4, "For Christ is the end of the law for righteousness to everyone who believeth." Christ is the end of the Law and the beginning of righteousness. These two boundaries again become points of discipline. In order to be victorious Christians, we must fulfill the Law to establish uprightness in our lives. In fact, righteousness begins where the Law ceases to be effective, which serves as a point of salvation. The Law cannot save us, but righteousness imputed to us will ensure us of salvation.[12]

The Apostle Paul tells us how to fulfill the Law in Romans 8:4 and 13:8-10. There is one word that ensures a right spirit, and that is love. There is only one way to bring forth the righteousness of the Law in our lives, and that is by walking after the Spirit in faith in the Son of God. Love compels us to obey Christ. We will not only be right before God, but we will do right by others. This will uphold the real purpose and intent of the Law.

Faith is the product of godly love.[13] Faith chooses to believe the character of God, and walk this life out in spirit and truth. This brings a person under the guidance of the Holy Ghost. It is at the point of active faith that God is able to meet the person, and reckon or count him or her as being righteous.

This brings us to the next two boundaries: that of grace and faith. The Apostle Paul made this statement in Romans 5:2, "By whom also we have access by faith into this grace wherein we stand, and rejoice in hope of the glory of God." Many Christians do not understand grace. Most believe that grace itself is a gift of God. This is not true. Grace is both an attribute and an act of God, by which He gives a person the gift of eternal life. According to Romans 5:20, grace reigns through righteousness unto eternal life, while sin always reigns unto death. Sadly, many people mistake grace with mercy and longsuffering. They actually think that grace is what causes God to overlook or tolerate sin in their lives. Grace has nothing to do with how God perceives our sin. Do not deceive yourself. God does not overlook sin. He displays longsuffering to the sinner and mercy to those who are seeking forgiveness. For example, mercy takes place when God refrains from showing deserved judgment upon those seeking forgiveness. Longsuffering is a characteristic of God that is displayed when He is giving man space to repent, while grace is God's means of giving man the life that He clearly does not deserve. However, man cannot receive this life until he believes God about sin and His provision of deliverance or salvation.

---

[12] Romans 4:2-6, 13-25
[13] Galatians 5:6

The problem is that many religious people do not strictly consider grace in light of repentance and forgiven sin. Rather, people hide behind a concept of grace to avoid facing the seriousness of their sin. They convince themselves that God's love and grace will cause Him to understand and overlook their sin. This is a blatant slap against His grace. As the Apostle Paul pointed out, faith serves as an access into this place of grace in God. We are saved by the grace of God that is shown to us by the gift of eternal life. However, this gift is only realized through active faith.[14] Faith, therefore, identifies us to God's work of grace, which ensures us of our position in the kingdom of God.

The question is, have you discovered the godly discipline that can only be discovered and established in Christ? If you have not, your spiritual life is not only out of order, but most likely you are also lost, struggling with sin, and depressed over character deviation and hopelessness that is invading the empty vacuum of your soul.

---

[14] Ephesians 2:8-9

11

DISOWNING SELF

One of the biggest struggles in the spiritual realm is not Satan, but self. A pastor once commented that people want deliverance from self or the old man. This is true. People are forever running to religious leaders or groups, looking for relief or deliverance from self. They have high expectations as they are taken through some type of religious exercise, and come away with high hopes. By the next day, their high hopes are usually dashed, as the realization that self is very much alive and well kicks in. At this time it becomes apparent that these high hopes are nothing more than zeal that is based on emotional fervor.

Self is the ultimate idol of man. In fact, people who are caught up with self chase after anything that will bow down and pamper them. In their mind, self has rights to pursue all that it desires and perceives will make it happy. Their attention, priorities, and lifestyles are established around the idea and pursuits of this one purpose, to satisfy self. The freedom and attention that these people often clamor for on behalf of self has nothing to do with what is right or honorable, but rather with the right to appease every aspect of self-gratification without paying the consequences.

One of the main reasons that self freely reigns is because people refuse to grow up and take responsibility for their sinful attitudes and ways. In fact, self always believes it is an exception to the rule. The harsh reality is that the more an individual is full of self, the more clueless he or she is about reality around him or her. Self also refuses personal discipline. Self wants to think according to its lusts. If individuals are thinking in this manner, they are not really thinking, but reacting according to their preferences and personal reality.

Self wants to declare and give way to personal rights without being responsible for the results. The selfishness of man does not want to discipline desire; therefore, self gives way to impulses and whims. Self often replaces reality with emotional sentimentality or intellectual conclusions. However, emotional sentimentality is fickle and changes with roving moods, while proving to be hypocritical and operating within fantasy. Intellectual conclusions are often divorced from reality. These self-serving conclusions remain indifferent to reality, as they exalt themselves to deem all reality outside of their perception as being silly, foolish, or insignificant.

This brings us to the subject of disciplining self. It is important to realize that discipline is not the means of dealing with self. Discipline may civilize self or keep it under some semblance of control. However, the real purpose of godly discipline is to form character. In fact, wherever self reigns, there is idolatry and opposition to all that would stipulate honorable character. Granted, self may conform outwardly by putting on a cloak, it may perform in a religious setting to throw up a smoke screen, and it may reform its speech and some of its lifestyle, but it is still reigning.

Self constantly plays the game by adjusting. It produces an outward impression that keeps others from suspecting its sinister, self-serving rule. It avoids being exposed and challenged. It conforms, performs, and reforms outwardly, but it will not give up its rights and come into submission to God. However, self will overplay its hand to reveal its hypocritical fruits. It will always sacrifice others to maintain dignity, while appearing noble.

Fake nobility is probably one of the greatest fruits of self. It not only gives a false impression of self-centered motives, but it looks so glorious in its personal exaltation. As a result, it can deceive the individual who is operating in it to think of self as being wise, caring, and honorable.

This is why nobility is not mentioned in Scripture. There is no true nobility where self is concerned. The Apostle Paul brings this harsh reality out in Romans 3. He makes it very clear that there is no righteousness in man. He lacks spiritual understanding, and insists on going his own way. Everything he does is unprofitable, because it is out of a wrong motive. Therefore, Paul's conclusion in Romans 3:12 to the matter was simple, "...there is none that doeth good, no, not one." Sadly, the hardest people to evangelize are those who think themselves to be good outside of Jesus. They see no need for Jesus, as they remain content to think of themselves as okay and acceptable.

In order to address fake nobility, God calls His people to be honorable. Honorable means a person of superior standing. Standing has to do with how one conducts self. Conduct is based on attitude towards something. In the case of Christians, it comes down to their attitude towards God.

Excellent standing in the kingdom of God involves integrity. The extent of integrity is determined by the quality of character. You cannot have character without discipline. You cannot have discipline without going against the grain of self. This means stepping outside of comfort zones, going against natural inclinations, and not allowing the natural tendency to operate by justifying ungodly actions and attitudes.

It is important to understand the difference between the nobility of self and honor or righteousness according to godliness. Most people can be quite noble, but few ever become honorable. After all, it is our natural tendency to think highly of ourselves, but it takes being honorable to be honest about ourselves, and face sin and moral deviation in our character. Honor in God's kingdom also means doing something about moral deviation through repentance and personal discipline.

The greatest point of moral deviation is our pride. Pride is what deceives us about the reality and consequences of sin. It convinces us that we have the right to experience something, regardless of whether it is contrary to God or not. This is when we will begin to toy with the idea of what this experience will add to our lives. Needless to say, the imagination usually turns out to be greater than the experience. Meanwhile, as we toy with it in our vain imaginations, we convince ourselves that we are either willing to pay the consequences, or we do not care about the consequences. Either conclusion throws out all boundaries, and from that point on, iniquity is manifested in the pursuit and practice of the desire.

The reason self claims nobility is that it refrains from doing that which does not matter to its pursuits or desires. This allows nobility to point out how pious it is because it does not, for example, murder, use drugs, or commit fornication. However, this pious individual may lie, cheat, and sacrifice others to maintain his or her level of arrogance and dignity. Actually, in the mind of such individuals, after weighing out personal sins in light of what they consider are greater sins, any minor discrepancies of character do not count. Needless to say, such fake nobility produces self-righteousness. It allows the person to focus on the sliver in his or her brother's eye, while maintaining the beam in his or her own character.[1] Self-righteousness in this text will sacrifice those with the sliver, so it can maintain its exaltation and self-delusion.

There was a woman who displayed a very critical spirit towards those who did not help her in her plight. She perceived that Christians had a responsibility to serve or take care of her regardless of the undue burden she put on them. In reality, this woman did not really want to work. She felt she had worked hard enough and it was time for her to benefit from the hard work of others. In the end, this woman compromised with wickedness in order to "survive." Even in compromise, this woman was freely judging others for failing to display the caliber of what she perceived to be Christianity.

Being honorable in God's kingdom is the opposite of fake nobility. Honor in God's kingdom is a product of His righteousness that is evident because it desires to please Him out of love and devotion. To be honorable, you must first face self and recognize personal depravity. The reason for this is because the delusion of self will keep a person from doing that which is right if it is not put in its proper perspective.

Keep in mind, wherever self reigns, there is idolatry. This means something is more important than God. Ultimately, every idol will be exposed and shaken by God. If a person is not honorable, he or she will go with the tendency to justify away righteousness in order to maintain self.

---

[1] Matthew 7:1-6

When a person is honorable, he or she will go against the grain of self in order to do right according to God. Such an individual must first deny self in order to neglect pride. This allows the person to humble self before the living God of heaven, to do what is right and acceptable. Honor of this nature means a person will do his or her reasonable service in a matter.[2] After all, reasonable service is beyond self, and in line with God's righteousness.

One of the greatest examples of honor in Scripture has to do with the type of conduct Christians are to display towards a weaker brother. This can be found in 1 Corinthians 8. A weaker brother is someone who is weak in character concerning a matter. Since character has not yet been properly developed in this area, this person will run what he or she considers deviant behavior through his or her mentality that has not yet been transformed by the Holy Spirit. This will taint the person's conclusion, preventing him or her from righteously judging the matter.[3] Tainted conclusions can result in disillusionment, betrayal, skepticism towards God, and loss of respect. Such conclusions will become a stumbling block to the weaker Christian, as they can hinder, cripple, or devastate a person's walk before the Lord.

Christianity presents many liberties, but these liberties must not be used, abused, or flaunted before those who are struggling in their spiritual life. Certain conduct may not pose a problem to you, but if it is wrong to a weaker brother or undermines the testimony of another, it must be wrong for you to do it in front of him or her.

I have discovered an interesting principle. It there is a flaw in our character, a weaker brother who has the same flaw will not only test our character at that particular point, but he or she will expose the flaw. In cases where such flaws have not honestly been faced, the idol still remains, and any exposure of the flaw will often produce rebellion and resentment.

For example, one of the controversial practices concerns the issue of drinking wine. There are certain cultures that drink wine as a normal, social practice. It is also obvious that people drank wine in the Bible for different reasons, such as a little wine for the stomach does not hurt a person. We are told to do everything in moderation. For some people they have made peace with this issue, but for others it is something that greatly weighs on their conscience. If a person with a tender conscience sees someone whom he or she considers a more spiritual Christian partaking of a bit of wine, it could become a stumbling block. If the more mature Christian becomes angry or resentful towards the idea that he or she cannot occasionally enjoy wine due to the weak conscience of a fellow Christian, then this individual's attitude towards wine is improper, and he or she needs to examine it to make sure a personal right or the actual activity is not being improperly exalted.

---

[2] Romans 12:1-2
[3] John 7:24

It is important to point out that the issues concerning weaker brothers are issues of the flesh. Not anything of a fleshly nature must hold more value than our relationship with God and our responsibilities to others. If it does, not only will it prove to be idolatrous and dishonorable, but it also will make people treacherous. Treachery becomes obvious as individuals scramble to justify fleshly preferences, while they refuse to deny self to do that which is righteous before God and towards others.

Confronting self was the first aspect of discipleship that Jesus clearly addressed. These are the qualifications He gave to establish this disciplined life, "...deny himself, and take up his cross, and follow me."[4]

People who sit under my teaching will tell you that my main emphasis is that people need to have a relationship with God. However, what follows behind the emphasis of relationship with God is what it will take to have this fellowship. Each person must deny self in order to discover the depths and lengths of God. Self will limit God from revealing Himself to the person. Therefore, for people to have a relationship with God, self must be out of the way.

The reason self must be dealt with is because it taints the truths of God and defiles His work. Jesus said that self must be denied. When you look up the word "deny," it means to disown or abstain from any involvement with self.[5] How do you cut off all identification with yourself? It comes down to making a willful decision to not give self any audience. We so love ourselves that we are compelled to listen, agree, sympathize, and perceive ourselves to be right, wise, practical, logical, and factual. Although self will cause us to feel condemned about certain matters, it will eventually let us off the hook, by either justifying or making it right at the expense of others.

Once we make a willful decision to divorce ourselves from the reasoning, feelings, and conclusions of self, we can begin to ignore claims of self. By ignoring the claims that self puts on your life, you will neglect the pride of life. As stated, pride serves as the point of moral deviation. When we give way to pride, it is a matter of time before we are set up to fall into sin, exposing the deviation that is ready to taint our character and undermine our faith and testimony. Since pride is deceptive and biased towards others, it makes us clueless about our spiritual condition. Behind this attitude are complacency, laziness, and apathy. The more ignorant we remain about our condition, the more we can justify giving way to self.

Pride always brings up our rights and encourages us to consider the actions of others. We will either use the actions of others to justify our selfish preferences or to exalt ourselves because we are not as bad as those around us. In fact, pride keeps us on a pedestal that is forever

---

[4] Matthew 16:24; Mark 8:34; Luke 9:23-24
[5] Strong's *Exhaustive Concordance,* #533

looking downward, rather than upward. It is forever judging others, while failing to honestly examine self.

Once pride is neglected, you will silence the main voice of self. Keep in mind that self must survive at any cost. In fact, it must and will survive, for it has rights to pursue all of its desires. As Christians, we must put down this right to pursue life according to self or the world, in order to find real life. The life that self offers has nothing to do with eternal matters. It is not only fleshly and unrealistic, but also temporary. Therefore, self must be denied its right to pursue or demand its personal concept of life.

As you study Jesus' instruction, you will see that each aspect of the disciplined life addresses the different claims of self. For example, denying self up front is to give notice to your pride that it will no longer have a say in the matter, regardless of what self may think, perceive, or feel is right. In fact, reality exposes the wickedness and treachery of pride. Therefore, it does not matter what self thinks, for it clearly opposes God and His righteousness. The next step of the disciplined life actually takes care of the lusts that motivate the many pursuits of self. Each step is designed to take away the power and influence of self to freely reign in our lives.

Denying self is also necessary when it comes to humbling self. Self is not only on the throne, but it is quite exalted in a person's way of thinking. To deny self, it must not only cease to reign, but its pride must also be removed from the pedestal. This often means a person must give up his or her dignity or need to come out appearing noble. True humility is devoid of any exaltation. It perceives itself as worthless and in need of intervention outside of self. Once self is clearly denied through the expression of true humility, the individual is prepared to receive from God without tainting or defiling it.

As people give way to God in this manner, they will begin to experience real life that is contrary to the survival mode of self. When people are in a survival mode, they merely fight to survive. Survival means people are trying to maintain life as they know it. This life may have some pleasurable experiences and temporary satisfactions, but otherwise, it exists in the midst of misery, uncertainties, anger, and delusions.

Regardless of the pathetic state, it strives to maintain its identity. It erects various walls and safeguards to keep its identity and sustain its rule. Each barricade makes it harder for truth to penetrate. Each wall ensures delusion. Each safeguard hinders God's work, and will avoid complete surrender as all costs. Self is bent on surviving, and will remain so until either heaven touches a desperate, seeking heart with truth, or the fires of damnation mock its arrogance in the bowels of hell.

Disowning self is the beginning of establishing godly discipline. It is where a person goes against the very essence of self. In doing this, he or she will find real life. This real life will be motivated by love, inspired by faith, and reasonable in service. Such a life is counted righteous or honorable before God.

Clearly, this shows us that an honorable person is minus the attitude and reign of self. Righteousness goes against the rule of self, causing resentment in those who refuse to give way to God. Today, people are putting a cloak over self to make it appear noble, but underneath, there is a wrong spirit that expresses itself through indifference, self-righteousness, jealousies, anger, self-pity, and resentment.

Denying self is the first act of consecration or total abandonment from that which brings defilement. This consecration is a must. Without this initial separation, godly discipline will never be developed. Without the necessary character, people will not be able to stand for truth or withstand the attack of the enemy. Their lives will be full of inconsistencies and hypocrisies. They cannot be fully trusted because they will operate in a mixed spirit. One minute, they may be open to God, and the next, they will be walking in accordance with their old way of thinking. The problem with this type of scenario is, not only do such people operate with a mixed spirit because their heart is divided and their faith weak, but they will be lukewarm and ineffective for God's kingdom.

Christianity is not simply a practice that you can put aside when you want to heap onto your flesh. It is a life and attitude that must penetrate every aspect of each of our lives. Sadly, people reserve certain aspects of their life to do as they please, without any consideration of God or others.

What about you? Have you denied self or are you justifying its influence in your life? If you have not contended with self, you are not only fleshly, but you are untrustworthy and ineffective in the kingdom of God.

12

THE DOOR TO LIFE

The next part of the disciplined Christian life is death. Self-denial subdues the deviant part of man by neglecting pride. Pride is neglected when personal rights are denied an audience. Once the right to the self-life is denied, the next step is crucifixion. Crucifixion of this nature means nailing the flesh to the cross. The flesh serves as the door between the world and pride.

Once the connection between pride and the world is broken, pride no longer has a platform. After all, pride justifies the appetites of the flesh to pursue after those things of the world that appeal, appease, and give temporary satisfaction. As long as the flesh is partaking of the world, it is temporarily satisfied. But, once it is no longer feeding on the lusts of the world, it leaves a great vacuum in the soul area, where guilt and desire war against each other. This creates emptiness, torment, and obsession. The Apostle Paul put the influence of the world in this perspective in Galatians 6:14, "But God forbid that I should glory, save in the cross of our Lord Jesus Christ, by whom the world is crucified unto me, and I unto the world."

Crucifying the flesh daily causes the world with all of its enticements and entanglements to become as if dead to me. My affections are unresponsive to the world's seduction. It no longer has the power to influence my way of thinking. Since the right to myself is being denied, sentenced, and put to death through the flesh, the world has no way to attract me to the promises of false happiness and security. Due to the fact that the connection with the world is being broken by the application of the cross to the flesh, the world is unable to offer pride a stage upon which it can freely operate and exalt itself over righteousness. Now that the world has lost access to my life, rebellion with its insatiable search for individuality, purpose, and recognition can be subdued. Since the rebel within me is no longer causing me to oppose authority, I can now discover who I am in Christ.

The cross has always gripped my heart. My first encounter with it was the altar on which the sacrificial Lamb of God was offered up on my behalf.[1] I gladly faced this altar as I realized my sin would be dealt with, bringing hope to my wretched soul. My second encounter with the cross was when I adhered to Jesus to pick up my personal cross to follow Him.

---

[1] John 1:29

At first, I was excited about this cross that had been specifically prepared for me. However, this excitement was the product of having romantic notions about the Christian life. In light of Jesus, the cross appeared noble, but there is a tendency to think of it simply in terms of an incredible sacrifice. Jesus' sacrifice exalted Him to a place of greatness that established an eternal legacy for those who would come to His altar, in need of mercy, forgiveness, and deliverance. However, the disciple's personal cross is opposite of such a noteworthy sacrifice.

In my immaturity, I did not have a proper perspective of my personal cross. The personal cross of the Christian is not about sacrifice, but death and discipline. Later, I learned that reasonable service and sacrifice actually occur beyond the Christian's personal cross, rather than being part of it.

As I faced my personal cross, I realized that there was nothing romantic about it. It actually presented a harsh reality, as I had to face the depravity of self. This cross revealed how self-absorbed I was. As the cross was applied, my pride declared the cross as being unfair. My flesh resisted and screamed foul. It took three years before pride lost its foothold and the flesh ceased to be a constant revolving door between my pride and the world. Needless to say, in this ordeal, a war between the flesh and the Spirit occurred. Even though the old man was greatly subdued, the war was far from being over. Carnality still desired to reign. There will always be the potential for the war to break out again, because if I do not keep my guard up, my pride can sneak in and my flesh can be resurrected.

My personal cross began to reveal an aspect of Jesus' cross that can be clouded by religious formulas and activities. His cross was all about my sin. He became sin or the sin offering on my behalf, so that I could be spared from judgment and receive eternal life. Christ's cross dealt with my sins, but my cross addresses the disposition of sin in me. This reign of sin in me had to be put to death to ensure that I did not walk under the harsh yoke of a death sentence. Just as the cross of Christ served as a door to eternal life, I realized that my cross served as the door to the abundant life that can only be found in Christ.[2]

My life in Christ was beyond the cross. It was beyond the pride that constantly sought ways to undermine this life. It was past the flesh that showed contempt towards God's character, and beyond the attractive life the world promised. In order to acquire the abundant life, I had to get beyond my personal cross.

Getting beyond my personal cross required me to taste certain aspects of death. Death is separation. I had to be separated from the influence of the old man. I also recognized that the death of this entity could not have any residue of personal nobility attached to it. In other words, I could not let the old man become a suffering martyr that could

---

[2] John 10:10; 2 Corinthians 5:21

be raised up in a heroic light to receive a stay of execution. This meant that the old man could not be left with any honor or dignity in his demise. He had to be exposed for the reprobate coward and infidel that he was.

Jesus instructed us to deny self and pick up our cross. As I considered His instruction, I could see the wisdom behind it. By first disowning self, I would not only strip the nobility away from the old man, but I would also ensure that he would die a dishonorable, unattractive death. In other words, he would die his deserved death: that of a coward.

Self-denial is a form of consecration, but the application of the cross represents the beginning of the work of sanctification. As long as self is alive and well, the Holy Spirit is limited in His work. In fact, there is a war raging in the soul area. This war is the flesh resisting any work of the Spirit.

The goal of the Spirit is to transform the inner man of each saint, so that he or she can be offered up as a living sacrifice for the purpose and glory of God. It is only when self is out of the way that the Living Water of the soul can begin to flow. As this Water flows through the receptive soul of the believer, it will wash away points of self-will. It will cleanse areas where self has subtly defiled what was pure, bogging the person down in the miry clay of indifference. As the water of the Holy Spirit cleanses, purges, and quickens the soul, He also will apply grace in weak areas, and humility in place of a person's strong points. In the end, He will revolutionize the way the believer will look at the life God has for each saint.[3]

The personal cross helped me discover real life. In fact, we can only choose how we die by how we live. As long as we are striving to maintain our old life, we will never discover the life we have in God.[4] It is important to realize that the old man is under a death sentence. It is a matter of time before this death sentence will be executed in the courts of heaven. Since the old man is already judged and condemned, he has no rights, claims, or privileges in regards to the present life.

As Christians, we must carry out the death sentence in regard to the old man in us, in order to discover the life that is beyond the cross. The question is, how do we carry out the death sentence? We must know that the old man is already dead, and must reckon it as a fact, so that we can live unto God. The more we know that the self-life is dead, the more the old man will be crucified through acts of righteousness. By choosing to live for Christ, we can choose to die to the old self-life. Each time self loses in the life of a believer, he or she gains a greater measure of his or her life in Christ.[5]

I watched a television program about the Jews in Warsaw, Poland during the Nazi invasion. Many of the Jews were driven into the ghettos

---

[3] John 6:37-39; Romans 12:1-2; Galatians 5:16-18
[4] Matthew 16:25
[5] Romans 6

of Warsaw. Once they were centralized, the Nazis began to ship them off to the camps where most of them died. In the midst of these Jews were a few rebels who knew what was happening. They tried to gather a resistance group against the Germans. This small band of rebels accomplished an incredible feat, as they stifled the advancement of the Germans into the ghetto. In my mind, these people were heroes. If you could talk to them today, they would not consider themselves heroes. In their eyes, they were already dead. It was only a matter of time before they would be shipped off either to some camp or shot. Since they regarded themselves as already being dead, they had the liberty to live life as they chose. As they lived life in reckless abandonment to the cause, they were also free to choose their martyrdom or death. Many sacrificed their lives for others.

These Jews were not extraordinary people, but they were living in extraordinary times that required them to get past the idea of life as they knew it, in order to face the reality of death that hung over them like a dark, foreboding curtain. As a result, they discovered life with dignity and purpose. In the end, they put up a resistance that even shocked the superior German army.

The difference between a coward and a hero is the matter of doing what needs to be done, regardless of circumstances or preferences. The preference of the cowardly old man is to preserve his idea of life. Therefore, the difference between heroes and cowards is that the heroes know that life has no purpose, unless one is willing to risk it for the sake of something that is worthy or greater. Heroes will tell you they were just doing their job. To these Jews, it was not a matter of being noble or sacrificial. It was simply a matter of doing what they had to do in light of the times they lived in.

Those who are victorious in the Christian life are those who do what is necessary and right in light of the situation. There is nothing clever about doing that which is necessary, nor is something made noble by doing what is right. Granted, it is honorable to do what is right, but ultimately, it is nothing more than our reasonable service. As you study the lives of God's servants, they were often persecuted and rejected. They accomplished some incredible feats because of their lives in God, but these servants never thought of themselves as being heroes. They were simply doing what God requested. At times, they were even reluctant, but their love and respect for God overshadowed any doubts or resistance. As a result, many of these servants even passed the hero status, and became people of whom the world was not worthy to know or witness their lives. Even though some of these people never saw the promises fulfilled in their lifetime, they knew that God was providing a better life for them. As the writer of Hebrews pointed out, some went gladly through their ordeal to obtain a better resurrection.[6]

---

[6] Hebrews 11

The cross marks the former life. This life ceases, so the new man or the life of Jesus can come forth in glory and power. Since the old man has been put into the grave, the person now becomes the reflection of the new man. This is the sanctified life where Jesus is being lifted up in wisdom, righteousness, sanctification, and redemption.[7]

I have struggled with my personal cross. The old man has proven time and again that he is the worse type of coward. He refuses to be offered up in order to give way to something greater. He is rebellious, as he insists on his way of doing, in spite of the destruction his ways wreak. He will conform, perform, and try to reform himself, because he has no intention of giving way to what is honorable. He wants to live, in spite of the fact that he is already a condemned man who is on borrowed time, enslaved in a prison of death, and chained to hopelessness. In spite of this death sentence, the old man still wants to put off the inevitable, so that he can develop some scheme to avoid execution. In the end, he brings worse judgment upon the person who harbors him.

Have you applied the cross to your life? There must be death before there can be godly discipline. Without this death, you will live the life of a coward. You will avoid death by crying, scheming, and becoming treacherous, as you sacrifice others in your place. You will justify your sins, excuse away your iniquity, and cover your transgressions. You may conform outwardly, perform with religious zeal, and reform your actions in certain questionable areas, but the disposition of the old man will remain alive and active in you. This old man will maintain the rebellious heart behind a religious cloak, mock the things of God with his arrogant look, and resent godly authority and instruction as he adjusts outward actions to maintain his way of thinking, feeling, and being.

Are you experiencing the abundant life? If you are not, it is because you have never entered through the door of death. The life Jesus promised is on the other side of our personal cross. It is beyond the present life we now live, and it is beyond the reality of death to the self-life. The truth is you will never experience Jesus' fullness until you relinquish your old life on your personal cross.

Let the words of Jesus penetrate your heart, "For whosoever will save his life shall lose it: and whosoever will lose his life for my sake shall find it. For what is a man profited, if he shall gain the whole world, and lose his own soul? or what shall a man give in exchange for his soul" (Matthew 16:25-26)?

---

[7] John 12:32; 1 Corinthians 1:30

13

TO WHOM SHALL WE GO?

Jesus had one simple, consistent call that went out to His disciples throughout His ministry: "Follow me." When you consider this simple solicitation, you wonder why it is hard for many who call themselves Christians to adhere to it. Why is it that people have a problem accepting the challenge to follow Jesus into the life that is full and complete?

The reason many Christians miss this call is because they romanticize about it or they surround it with sentimentality. The reality is that there is nothing pleasant about following Jesus.[1] Granted, it is rewarding, but it is hard on the pride and the flesh. Feelings that surround sentimentality quickly fall to the wayside when the harsh reality of the Christian life begins to challenge present fantasies about the Christian walk.

Jesus' call to follow Him was consistently emphasized throughout His ministry. It went out in three ways. First, there was His *initial call* that went out to all those who would follow Him. He said to Peter and Andrew, "Follow me, and I will make you fishers of men" (Matthew 4:19).

This was reinforced in Luke 9:59-60. Jesus called a particular person to follow Him. The man asked Him to let him first go back and bury His father. Jesus' reply was, "Let the dead bury their dead: but go thou and preach the kingdom of God." Jesus' call is in light of eternity, and it will reveal where your real priorities and treasures lie.[2]

Secondly, there was a *general call* that went out to those who desired to be His disciples. "If any man will come after me, let him deny himself, and take up his cross daily, and follow me" (Luke 9:23). Obviously, the call to follow Him had conditions. Whenever there are conditions, hearts will be tested and proved as to the sincerity of the desire or claim of the person. After all, such a call comes down to testing the person's level of faith as far as following Jesus into the unknown.

Where would a person follow Jesus? The person would follow Jesus into a life of obedience to the will of the Father. Where would such a life lead a person? Psalm 23 gives us the route of the Shepherd, while John 10:14 refers to Jesus as the Good Shepherd. Following Jesus will lead people to a place of complete satisfaction. After all, goodness and mercy will follow those who follow Him all the days of their life. They will also be

[1] John 15:18-20
[2] Matthew 6:19-21

assured of dwelling in the house of the LORD forever.[3] Although many Christians are dissatisfied in their Christian life, the blame does not rest with God. Rather, it comes down to the failure to follow Jesus. People who fail in this area grumble in their dissatisfaction, but they will not do what they need to do to obtain this life.

The first place the Great Shepherd will lead His sheep is to a place of nourishment and rest where their soul will be restored in His presence. Jesus' invitation is to come. Come to Him and you will discover the Bread from heaven that gives eternal life. Come to Him and He will give you Living Water. Come to the Jesus of the Bible and you will find rest for your heavy-laden soul. [4]

The Good Shepherd will lead His sheep in the paths of righteousness for His name's sake. Name implies character. Jesus is righteous; therefore, His leadership will take people in the ways of righteousness.[5] By following Jesus, a person will be following after righteousness.

In 1 Timothy 6:11, Christians are told to follow after righteousness, godliness, faith, love, patience, and meekness. In 2 Timothy 2:22, the Apostle Paul gave this instruction, "Flee also youthful lusts: but follow righteousness, faith, charity, peace, with them that call on the Lord out of a pure heart." Obviously, a person must follow hard after Jesus to walk in righteousness, godliness, faith, charity, and peace.[6]

Psalm 23:5 assures us that as God's sheep, we will walk through the valley of the shadow of death. Most people take this as meaning physical death. However, death marks the Christian life in different ways. When believers talk about death that is experienced in the valleys of humiliation and uncertainty, they are making reference to the death to self, the old man or the old life. Without this death, there is no identification to Jesus nor is there resurrection life.

There is no need to fear as long as Jesus is in the lead. He has the rod, His Word, which is able to direct our steps. Sometimes, the Word serves as a harsh rod of discipline for the sheep that refuse the leadership of the Shepherd. The Word of God, therefore, can bring both bitterness and sweetness to our souls, depending on how we adhere to its instructions. Adherence to His Word means coming into agreement with God about His evaluations on a matter. This will establish our reality according to the leadership of our Shepherd.

The Shepherd's staff is the Holy Spirit. He will nudge at us to change course or stay on the present course. If we become too insistent on our

---

[3] Psalm 23:6
[4] Psalm 23:2-3; Matthew 11:28-29; John 6:35; 7:37
[5] 1 Corinthians 1:30; 1 John 2:2
[6] Psalm 63:8

personal reality or the right to maintain our life, the staff can become quite harsh, as it is used to steer us away from the snares of the enemy.[7]

Jesus' third call to follow Him was on a *personal level*. This call is about following Jesus in a proper way and finishing the course. In Jesus' personal call to Peter in John 21, He defined Peter's mission. He was to feed His sheep, lambs and the flock. As Jesus defined Peter's mission to feed His followers, He stipulated the condition that needed to be present for Peter to adhere to His instructions. The condition was to follow Him.[8]

Each of these different calls brings about discipline in different areas. For example, those who respond to the *initial call* are prepared to do so. Following Jesus is a natural response. However, these very same people can be harboring personal agendas that will be exposed as they follow Him. Therefore, following Jesus will expose wrong agendas and establish proper emphasis and priorities according to God's will.

The *general call* that goes out to those who desire to follow Jesus will discipline the will of a person. After all, they must make a choice to follow Jesus according to His terms. Following Jesus in this manner requires a determination that must be maintained throughout the person's lifetime.

The *personal call* of discipleship will discipline the walk of the person. When Jesus personally called Peter forth, He geared His instructions towards Peter's own personal call to feed the sheep. From this point on, Peter needed to adjust his walk and commitment to Jesus' instructions. It is at the place of personal discipleship that one must count the cost to personally follow Jesus.

The call into the Christian life is not a call into service or ministry, but a call to follow Jesus into the abundant life. It will become a *personal call* to every devoted believer. The *initial call* to follow is to discover our potential in Christ, while the *general call* is to come to terms with our purpose in His kingdom. The final call points to personal responsibility, endurance and service. Following Jesus is not just a mission or ministry, but the essence of discovering true life in light of God's character, kingdom and eternal purpose.

The simple call to follow Jesus is meant to challenge and revolutionize the way individuals think. Hence, enters the aversion to following Jesus. Although this call seems so simple, its very words can become an affront to people. There are reasons for these words serving as a sharp sword that divides the loyal from the sentimental. One of the reasons for this aversion is because there is more to following Jesus than what many perceive.

The perception is that as long as I can follow Jesus on my terms, all will be well with my world. However, following Jesus can only occur on

---

[7] Galatians 6:16-18
[8] John 21:14-23

His terms, according to His conditions. It is a personal call, and as Jesus pointed out to Peter, who tried to concern himself with another disciple's walk, "If I will that he tarry till I come, what is that to thee? follow thou me" (John 21:22).

As you study the Christian life, you begin to realize that following Jesus is a personal discipline. It begins with denying self and picking up the cross. Denying self changes agendas, while the cross fine tunes the walk to keep the person in step with Jesus. Once these two procedures are accomplished, a person will be able to follow Jesus. As he or she follows Jesus, the cross eventually becomes the yoke by which the person becomes a co-laborer with Jesus in the harvest field.[9]

The yoke continues to discipline the walk of believers. They must stay in step with Jesus who is carrying the heaviest portion of the yoke. This requires sensitivity and concentration because it is easy to walk out from underneath this yoke. It is at this point that following Jesus becomes one of the toughest forms of godly discipline. The reason is that it involves focus.

Following Jesus means that you must keep your eyes on Him. Keeping your eyes focused requires a lot of concentration. It involves your other senses as well. In other words, just because a person is looking in a certain direction does not mean they are actually seeing. Focus means your complete attention is directed at the source you are following.

People's attention spans are very self-serving. A person's attention often hinges on whether or not it can hold his or her emotional zeal. As soon as the zeal is gone, the attention will go to another source that will begin to lay claims to the person's concentration. This is especially true in America, because Americans are used to being entertained. Sadly, this is the way many Christians function. They take the same worldly mentality to church. In order to maintain numbers, many churches have become places of entertainment. As a result, Christians lack character, causing them to act as if they are corks on the ocean, going from one entertaining fad to the next.[10]

Concentration means that the mind must be clear of diversion. It also means that you are tuned to the call or desires of the leader. Above all else, your heart must be in it. In other words, your affections must also be directed at your source.[11] Therefore, to focus means not only putting your very being on alert, but also your inclination is directed towards the One you are following. The concentration is so great, that all possible distractions are blurred or become non-essential in the scheme of what is important and necessary in light of your leader.

---

[9] Matthew 11:29; 1 Corinthians 3:9
[10] Ephesians 4:14
[11] Matthew 6:21; Colossians 3:2

Jesus always challenged His disciples' focus and understanding. Keep in mind, focus will determine your reality. Reality is based on influences. In other words, what you expose yourself to on a consistent basis is what you will express in your life. These influences will determine your conscience or moral conduct.

Many people establish their own moral code. This is not only self-centered, but also unrealistic. In such a scenario, people exalt themselves to be god of their own world. When challenged by reality, such people are devoid of character and harbor fragile egos. Reality always proves more than they can handle; therefore, they become angry, disillusioned and fall into despair.

When people establish their own moral code, it is because they do not recognize any real authority. This results in chaos, as people do what they perceive to be right. There is no real standard by which to test their reality, as they claim the right to express themselves in any way they desire. Such an attitude ultimately abuses the freedom of others.

Americans are proud of their freedom. They see it as a means to express their individuality and independence. They speak of being tolerant and susceptible to others' cultures and beliefs. However, what is the real purpose of freedom? Is it to be independent from what is right? Does it allow for the liberty to do what seems right in a person's own eyes? Such personal judgments will change according to individuals, causing abuse of freedom. Abuse of this nature erodes homes and societies from within, and results in grave offenses against humanity, as in the case of Israel in Judges 20-21.

This incident involved the tribe of Benjamin. The men of Benjamin in a particular city decided they had the right to feed their fleshly desires when they desired to abuse a Levite who came seeking rest in their city. The man's concubine was offered up instead. They abused her to the point that she died. The Levite cut up the body of his concubine and sent it to all parts of Israel. The stir for justice became great, as judgment was demanded for this grave offense. The other men of Benjamin actually decided they needed to protect these men, regardless of their abominable acts against God and humanity. In the end, only 600 men from the tribe of Benjamin survived. How could such a grave sin take place? Judges 21:25 gives us insight into the mentality of Israel, "In those days there was no king in Israel: every man did that which was right in his own eyes."

King Solomon addressed the destruction of man doing that which is right in his own eyes in *Proverbs.* He actually called such a person a fool. He backed his conclusion with such statements as Proverbs 14:12, "There is a way which seemeth right unto a man, but the end thereof are the ways of death."

Proverbs 16:2 states, "All the ways of a man are clean in his own eyes; but the LORD weigheth the spirits." In Proverbs 21:8, he summarizes man's ways by calling them froward and strange to God.

Isaiah 55:8-9 confirms this conclusion, by declaring that God's ways and thoughts are higher than mankind's.

The opposite of liberty is tyranny. Tyranny means that you must come into subjection to the harsh taskmaster that is in rule. One prevalent taskmaster among humanity is sin.[12] Such a taskmaster has no regard for its servants. Tyrants of this nature see people in terms of how they can serve them, and not on a personal plane. These taskmasters are not only self-serving, they are wicked, as they use and sacrifice people along the way.

As you study the purpose of liberty, you begin to realize that its main goal is to give people the freedom to choose what or who will serve as their personal conscience. Man cannot serve as his own conscience. He will basically do that which serves his purpose without regards to others. He will readjust and disregard any moral obligations according to present preference. Therefore, conscience must be established by an outside source. This outside source will not only serve as a final authority, but it will also serve as a point of discipline. Discipline in this text implies a place of accountability and responsibility, where an individual will owe up and face consequences for moral deviation.

Consequences become a type of reality check. Sadly, this reality check is missing in many people's lives, including Christians. As one individual stated, people want you to make them feel good about themselves. They do not want to be called to accountability or made responsible for deviant conduct that reveals evil attitudes and wicked actions. Such people want you to play their games, so they can avoid the inevitable reality of facing their depravity.

For Christians, the Bible must serve as their conscience. It must be considered their final authority, always establishing present reality. Sadly, few Christians see the Word as reality. To them, it is metaphoric or adjustable; therefore, they pick and choose what they adhere to. They will justify wrong attitudes and actions that will make them both an exception to and judge of the Word. Their attitude towards the Word declares that they do not believe every aspect of it in regards to their lives. Ultimately, it will make these individuals liars, as they walk away from following Jesus in delusion and hypocrisy.

As disciples obey God's Word, they will follow Jesus into this life. The Word serves as a point of discipline. It guides saints down this unseen, challenging path of righteousness. I must point out that without self-denial, the inclination to obey the Word will be missing, and without the application of the cross, the intent of obedience will be absent. If this combination is missing, the Word will have no power (right spirit) or authority (truth) behind it. Without the discipline of self-denial and the cross, the Word will become hard and offensive.

---

[12] Romans 6:12, 18-23

We see this happening in John 6:52-71. There were many people following Jesus. However, in one incident, their reality surrounding Jesus was greatly challenged. Jesus was talking about being the Living Bread from heaven. He told of how people needed to partake of Him. This brought confusion to many of His followers. How could they literally partake of His body and blood? Jesus was not talking in literal terms, but in spiritual terms. To partake means to believe upon Him and to believe Him. Such belief points to active faith that is expressed in obedience.

Since understanding eluded Jesus' followers, His sayings became hard to them. This hardness caused offense. The offense resulted in many turning away from Him. And, as John 6:66 stated, "...and walked no more with him." Jesus turned to the 12 remaining disciples, and asked them a heartbreaking question, "...Will ye also go away" (John 6:67)?

Truth will become hard for those whose inclination towards following Jesus is self-serving, and their intention is self-glorification. Eventually, every follower's motive and intention will be exposed by the sharpness of the unchangeable truth that initially produces more darkness to our perception than light and understanding. In these times, our very foundations are being shaken, as we are forced to make a decision about Jesus.[13]

It is at such times that we can put our focus on the darkness created by our limited perception, or keep it on the Light of the world.[14] Although nothing makes sense at this point, the focus must not change from what we know is true, Jesus, to what we are unable to intellectually fit into our present understanding or beliefs. Changing focus at such times will cause us to take a detour or walk away from Jesus.

When Jesus asked Peter the question about his intentions, Peter answered him, "Lord, to whom shall we go? thou hast the words of eternal life. And we believe and are sure that thou art that Christ, the Son of the living God." (John 6:68-69). The ultimate goal of each believer should be to follow Jesus. We can zealously claim our intent to follow Him, but we will never know the extent of our devotion, until it is tested by the harshness of truth. Is our devotion to Jesus conditional or is it sincere and complete? Are we impressed with the Person of Jesus or are we impressed with who we think we are in His kingdom? Is our life before Jesus based on emotional zeal or is it founded on the immovable Rock?

Peter gave us insight into his focus. Although he may have been shaken by what Jesus said, he could not be moved because of what he knew. He knew that Jesus possessed the words of eternal life. He chose to hold onto the character of Christ, and not be sidetracked by mysteries that were beyond his human understanding. Peter also knew that since

[13] Hebrews 4:12; 12:26-27
[14] John 1:3-6

Jesus possessed eternal life, He was the Christ, the Son of the living God.

Sometimes, I wonder how deep and sincere my devotion is towards Jesus. I can con myself about it or focus in on what many could consider noteworthy in regards to my life in Christ. The truth is, I am nothing without Jesus. I have come so far in my life with Him that it is too late and too far to turn back. In fact, there is absolutely nothing to go back to. Jesus has become my life, heart and breath. However, I cannot forget how susceptible I am in taking detours. It is so easy to fall out of step with Jesus' yoke when I take my focus off of Him and put it elsewhere.

Personally, I know that focus is everything in my walk with Jesus. It is the ultimate discipline. It involves all of my senses and affections. I cannot follow Jesus in a life of loving devotion, service, and worship until He becomes my heart's desire, my all in all, my complete focus.

What about you? Have you started out following Jesus in emotional zeal, only to be shipwrecked by hard sayings? Perhaps your religious foundation is being shaken. This has caused you to follow Jesus from afar with an attitude of "wait and see" as to how the situation will turn out, before you draw close to Him again.[15] My hope is that your total focus is on Him, and that you are as close as you can be to Him, regardless of situations and circumstances. In fact, you are walking under His glorious yoke, learning the liberty of enjoying His life, love, mercy, grace, and devotion.

In conclusion, note the diagram on the following page. Consider where the natural preference will lead you, versus the Christian who adheres to Jesus' call to follow Him. The results are obvious.

---

[15] Matthew 26:58

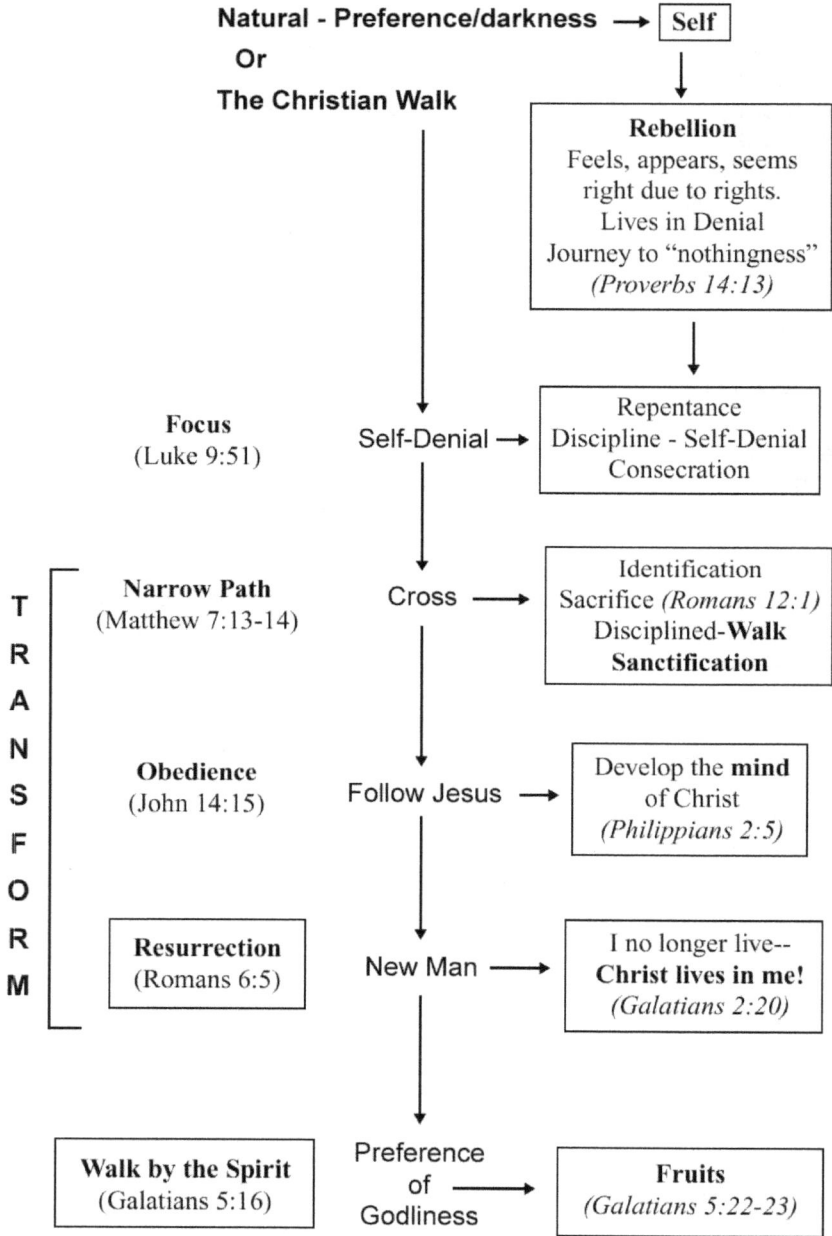

Natural - Preference/darkness → | Self |

Or

The Christian Walk

Rebellion
Feels, appears, seems
right due to rights.
Lives in Denial
Journey to "nothingness"
(Proverbs 14:13)

↓

Focus
(Luke 9:51)

Self-Denial →

Repentance
Discipline - Self-Denial
Consecration

Narrow Path
(Matthew 7:13-14)

Cross →

Identification
Sacrifice *(Romans 12:1)*
Disciplined-**Walk**
Sanctification

Obedience
(John 14:15)

Follow Jesus →

Develop the **mind**
of Christ
(Philippians 2:5)

Resurrection
(Romans 6:5)

New Man →

I no longer live--
Christ lives in me!
(Galatians 2:20)

T
R
A
N
S
F
O
R
M

Walk by the Spirit
(Galatians 5:16)

Preference
of
Godliness →

Fruits
(Galatians 5:22-23)

14

FAITHFULNESS

Faithfulness is the next form of godly discipline that needs to be examined. Faithfulness is a matter of doing right before God. The real discipline in faithfulness is not found at the point of action, but rather at the place of motive.

People can do many things without thinking about motive. They can perform without considering their intention. However, in the kingdom of God, the motive must be right before it is acceptable to God, otherwise it is treacherous. Without the proper motive, the action will have no eternal meaning. If there is no eternal meaning, the action is vanity. In other words, it will be rendered useless in the scheme of things. Granted, an individual may get some recognition, but the exaltation lasts for only a moment; afterwards it is lost. As Jesus said, exaltation sought and secured in this earthly life will be the only reward a person receives.[1]

Motive serves as a real point of discipline. We can con ourselves about our spiritual condition. We can do religious deeds to give the impression that we are going in the right direction. We can talk the talk, so that we can impress ourselves with religious knowledge or insight. In such personal flattery, we can convince ourselves that we are scripturally sound, but all of these attempts may be hiding a wrong motive.

You cannot fake motive. Eventually, your fruits will expose and express your very motives.[2] This is why motives serve as a point of great discipline. To determine our motive requires discipline. Without the right motive, we are untrustworthy. Although we may appear to be upright in action, a wrong motive harbors rights that will cause us to give way to thought patterns that will betray the level and purity of our commitment in any specific situation. In the end, our character will be compromised, making us unfaithful.

This can be observed with married couples. A great deal of what spouses do for their mates has conditions attached to them. They have expectations as to what their deeds will produce. When they fail to get the desired response, they feel they have a right to give way to thought patterns or actions that appease the flesh. These thoughts are not only treacherous, but they are vain, lustful, and in many cases, adulterous. It is our thoughts that define our character and reveal our true intentions. As Proverbs 23:7 states, "For as he thinketh in his heart, so is he..."

---

[1] Matthew 6:2-7
[2] Matthew 7:20

This brings us to our faithfulness with God. How many of us are betraying our relationship with Him by playing the harlot with the world, coming into agreement with the flesh, and doing Satan's bidding? How many of us are treacherous towards God, because the quality of our commitment towards Him depends on how well He performs in regard to the terms we have established?

If such character or integrity is absent, you will be untrustworthy at every level of your life. Everything will be about you and not what is honorable. Faithfulness is not self-centered, but is the product of self-denial. It is committed to doing what is right in regards to others. Regardless of the circumstances, it maintains integrity and purity in its motives and actions.

How do we bring our motives into discipline to ensure integrity? We first must stop to examine our priorities and agendas. These two points of motivation will determine our inclinations towards something and intentions towards the type of outcome we desire. To examine priorities and agendas can be difficult to do, especially if we have been busy avoiding such an examination. The next step of discipline is to make a decision to operate from the point of integrity when it comes to personal motives. This is hard as well because motives often prove to be deceptive, self-centered, and self-serving.

Integrity entails discipline. When it comes to motive, you must be willing to bring all vain imaginations into captivity.[3] The reason vain imaginations must be silenced when examining motives is because they harbor the rights and excuses that will let you off the hook from doing that which is honorable. In fact, you begin to debate or try reasoning with the situation based on these vain imaginations to come up with a conclusion. Ultimately, conclusions inspired by these premises will justify personal rights and will excuse away wicked thoughts and practices.

Once the vain imaginations are brought into obedience to Christ, truth can be exalted. Truth must be exalted in order to bring a comparison. Often, the reason we let ourselves off the hook is because we compare ourselves with our own notions of personal goodness or with others whom we consider inferior. In order to discover our true motives, we must compare ourselves with Jesus.

It is at this point that we begin to consider our attitudes towards God and others. In a way, it is like taking your temperature based on how you feel or react to particular situations or people. For example, the way I discover my true priorities is to be honest about what I value. The means by which I determine my agenda is by examining personal desires or accomplishments. Sometimes, we delude ourselves about what we value or desire; therefore, we need to put our finger on the things we think are important to our well-being and worth. One of the ways I discern my attitude towards what I consider valuable is by asking myself, if God

---

[3] 2 Corinthians 10:5

asked me to give that particular thing up or let go of a pursuit, what would be my attitude towards Him? If I found myself fearful or resentful, I would immediately know that I was walking in idolatry in that area. Idolatry always produces unbelief that expresses itself in fear, ignorance, and resentment.

When I am considering people, I examine my attitudes towards them by considering how I truly feel about them. This means wading through emotions to see if I am regarding them in an idolatrous way, or if I am hateful, bitter, or angry towards them. Recently, I found myself being sarcastic about a particular individual. The Holy Ghost put a check in my spirit that my attitude was wrong and I needed to change it.

It is important to realize that we are responsible for changing our own personal attitudes. The way I change my attitude is by stopping myself when I recognize an unacceptable attitude, reproving my state of mind, and calling myself to accountability in that area. I then come into agreement with God as to what is right. Immediately, my attitude comes into line with God; thereby, changing it.

The reason motive is important is because it will determine your sensitivity and endurance level towards a matter. For example, if you are doing something for recognition, you expect exaltation in return. When exaltation eludes you, you become insulted and obstinate. At this point, there is no momentum left. This reveals that pride was the true motive behind your pursuit.

The other manifestation of a wrong motive is that you will fail to do that which does not bring recognition. Much of life is drudgery. It feels as if nothing will change. It takes integrity to be faithful to what you know is right in times when there is no recognition or indication of change. People who lack faithfulness will become indifferent in such times to the real needs of others, and will fail to work behind the scenes in obscurity to bring about a constructive point of discipline or change concerning their personal attitude.

The greatest work done in God's kingdom is done in obscurity. Obscurity serves as a point of discipline because it will also test your motives. If your motives are not right, obscurity will cause you to become disillusioned. I cannot tell you how many Christians have been close to being brought forth in power and glory, but bolted because of the drudgery of obscurity. They expected great things for themselves, and resented being in the grave of preparation and testing.

This brings us to the discipline that serves as the point of integrity when it comes to developing and maintaining the right motive: that of faithfulness. Faithfulness is the manifestation of true faith in God. It is comprised of an attitude of availability. It has many characteristics. One of the characteristics is that it knows how to occupy, regardless of the circumstances. In other words, it keeps doing when everything seems useless and ridiculous. Jesus mentioned this quality in Luke 19:13. He went on to say that the reason people do not occupy is hatred.[4] Hatred is a product of an indifferent attitude and a spirit of rebellion. Indifference refuses to care, while rebellion refuses to come into submission. People who possess this attitude actually hate anyone who has the authority and power to demand honorable actions and obedience from them.

Another quality of faithfulness is sensitivity. It is aware and observant of what needs to be done. The reason that it has this sensitivity is because it comes from the position of servitude. Faithfulness is devoid of self. It is committed to do the bidding of another. Its motive is pure and its devotion is sincere and single in focus and purpose. Jesus will acknowledge and reward this virtue in His followers. He gave this example in Luke 19:17, "And he said unto him, Well, thou good servant: because thou hast been faithful in a very little, have thou authority over ten cities."

Humility is another important characteristic of faithfulness. To be a faithful servant of God, you must be humble in attitude. Since Jesus is Lord, this attitude is comprised of devotion that is prepared and ready to respond in obedience. This willingness is the result of humility. A faithful servant will do that which is insignificant without being told or have his or her ego stroked. If this simple faithfulness is missing, you will never be entrusted with more in the kingdom of God. Jesus confirmed this in Luke 16:10: "He that is faithful in that which is least is faithful also in much: and he that is unjust in the least is unjust also in much.

There are other honorable characteristics and fruits of faithfulness, such as fear of the Lord. Faithfulness is one quality that is greatly lacking in every area of life. As I deal with the world, I encounter the hard reality that very few Christians are faithful to God. Their words mean nothing, their conduct is not honorable, their attitudes are rebellious, and unbelief is rampant. Solomon apparently had the same struggle. He made this statement in Proverbs 20:6, "Most men will proclaim every one his own goodness: but a faithful man who can find?"

Obviously, it is hard to find faithfulness among people. It is important that Christians understand this virtue. To properly understand faithfulness, we need to study the character of God, for He is faithful. His Word constantly expounds on this reality. It is because of His faithfulness towards man that souls are saved, promises fulfilled, and lives made whole. Most of God's work is behind the scenes, where man cannot see it with his physical eyes. The purpose for this obscurity is to allow God to establish faith in His servants, and to receive the glory when His work is fulfilled in and through them. Faithfulness points to God being true to who He is and to His Word. He will never betray either.[5]

---

[4] Luke 19:14

[5] Deuteronomy 7:9; Isaiah 49:7; 1 Corinthians 1:9; 1 Thessalonians 5:24; 2 Thessalonians 3:3; Hebrews 10:23; 1 John 1:9

This is the greatest evidence of faithfulness. Faithfulness is verified in actions. God's faithfulness has been clearly declared and made known to us.[6] This part of His character is not accepted on blind faith; rather it gives us the reason for putting our trust in Him.

As you study God's faithfulness, you realize that it is not a matter of actions, but of being true to what is said. It is not a matter of performing, but of developing and maintaining integrity in who you are and what you do. As long as you remain true to this personal commitment, you will not betray what you know or who you are.

God is looking for faithfulness among His people. It is a serious matter, because He cannot honor those who are not faithful. Psalm 31:23 says, "O love the LORD, all ye his saints: for the LORD preserveth the faithful, and plentifully rewardeth the proud doer."

Let us examine the core of faithfulness. It finds its source in faith. I am sure you have heard the concept of doing something out of good faith. What does it mean to do something based on this motive? It means that you trust someone to do something before you see the results. You are strictly going on your faith in the character, commitment, agreement, or word of that person.

This describes faithfulness in the kingdom of God. You are simply doing something in good faith because you trust in the character and Word of God. You trust Him because He is true to His character. In other words, He will not step outside of His character; therefore, His ways are consistent and sure. In fact, if there is any discrepancy between God and man, the Apostle Paul makes this statement in Romans 3:3-4, "For what if some did not believe? shall their unbelief make the faith of God without effect? God forbid: yea, let God be true, but every man a liar..."

The Apostle Paul stipulates why many never discover the faithful character of God: because of unbelief. When individuals fail to respond to God's righteous ways, they prevent Him from meeting them. Since they fail to choose faith, they walk in unbelief. They are stating that God is untrustworthy. This sets them up for failure and destruction. When these people pay the consequences for their unbelief, they begin to accuse God's character. They declare that He has failed because He had no intention of honoring His Word. If the intention were missing, then it would make God not only treacherous, but a liar.

This brings us to intentions. Without the right intent or spirit, a person will prove to be untrustworthy. The fruit of being untrustworthy is that of lying. In other words, individuals have no real intention of keeping their word. Sadly, most of us are liars because we fail to be honest with ourselves. Since we think highly of ourselves, we perceive that we have good intentions and that it is good enough, whether we carry something out or not. Jesus addressed this in Matthew 5:37, "But let your

---

[6] Psalm 36:5; 40:10; 89:2, 5, 8; 92:2; 119:90; Lamentations 3:23

communication be, Yea, yea; Nay, nay: for whatsoever is more than these cometh of evil."

For Christians, they must consider their words the same as a vow. If their words are minus integrity, the intent of their words will be evil. The reason for this is because words without integrity produce liars, who will bring a reproach to Christ and to the person's testimony. Keep in mind, lying not only associates a person to the father of lies, Satan, but it also condemns him or her to the lake of fire.[7]

God's intention towards us is pure, but our intention towards Him is often tainted by our self-serving ways. We must make sure that our intentions are upright before Him, in order to ensure faithfulness to our commitment to Him, our words, and our conduct.

The Christian's life before God is about his or her faith in His character. Believers cannot have faithfulness towards God unless they have faith in His character, and walk according to His Word. Such faith runs contrary to the suspicious nature of sin. Sin is untrustworthy; thereby, it transposes its moral deviation onto those who fail to adhere to its demands or standards. Needless to say, this suspicion is often transferred to God, as being the One who is untrustworthy and undeserving of trust or respect.

God ultimately ends up with a bad rap because man fails to acquire faithfulness towards Him. In fact, true faithfulness runs contrary to the essence of man. Man in his fallen state is committed to one entity: self. It is not that man is being true to himself, it simply means that he is committed to upholding self in order to gain the life he thinks he so richly deserves. Self has no boundaries in which to operate; therefore, people often betray their heart to obtain this self-life, as they compromise what is right and become treacherous in their conduct.

Once again, we come back to Jesus' instructions: "Deny self, pick up the cross and follow me." You cannot be faithful to self and someone else at the same time.[8] In fact, you can only be faithful to one entity at a time. The reason for this is because faithfulness is the truest form of commitment. It is simply faithful to do that which is honorable in regards to others. Faithfulness is concerned about the small matters that must be confronted in obscurity, as well as the big matters that are obvious.

As long as the person is serving self, there will be no intention of serving others. This is why there are so many problems in Christianity and marriage because people fail to be faithful in their commitment to each other. As long as people serve self, they will be indifferent to the lives of others.

To be faithful to others, you must become faithful to God. It is only when God is in the proper place that you can be faithful to others in the right way. To become faithful to God, you must deny self. As I have dealt

---

[7] John 8:44; Revelation 21:8
[8] Mathew 6:24

with people over this issue of denying self, I have struggled to remember how I got past self, so that I could be of some use to God. In my mind, it had to be a traumatic experience. Yet, I could not remember any real impact in my life where I was aware that self was no longer freely reigning.

As I was trying to remember the point where I finally got past self, the Lord broke through my meditation and revealed to me how I managed to get past it. I made a choice to accept His Word by faith. Each time I decided to trust His Word over my reality, and walked it out, the more I denied self. Suddenly, I realized that there was no specific traumatic experience because it was simply giving way to God through obedience to His Word.

Galatians 5 talks about the flesh warring against the Spirit. I realized that the battle in this area raged when I insisted on holding on to my rights to self. Since the flesh is contrary to God's Spirit, it caused conflict in my spirit and soul. Who is going to reign in this matter, the flesh or the Spirit? Man's natural tendency is to go with the flesh. However, if he is born again, his inclination is to do what is right according to the divine nature of his Lord. Therefore, the war rages until the man denies his tendency to give in to the flesh and submit to God, because it is the honorable, trustworthy thing to do.

Each time a person denies self, and adheres to God's Word by faith, the greater the work of the Spirit. Spiritual maturity will result from submitting to God. Submission to the Word of God will determine the reality of every saint. However, it is the Spirit of God who makes God's Word a living reality. In fact, the Word becomes a living reality when Jesus is unveiled in it.

The Word serves as our immovable boundary. As the Word takes root and begins to abide in us, the Spirit has the tools with which to work. The more the Word abides in us, the greater the revelation will be that can come forth from it. Sadly, many Christians do not have the Word abiding in them. This prevents the Spirit from working because He has no base from which to work. As a result, many are chasing after religious experiences or falling prey to doctrines of demons.[9]

Today many people are emphasizing the Spirit rather than getting into the Word. As a result, the Spirit is unable to properly establish the life of God in Christians. This unhealthy emphasis is producing a faithless generation that is seeking after signs and wonders, rather than Jesus Christ.

The question that each believer must ask is, am I faithful to God or am I a spiritual harlot or fornicator? We can con ourselves about this point of discipline, but, in the end, Jesus will reject us because we failed to be His true and faithful servant.

---

[9] 1 Timothy 4:1

15

HOLDING THE LINE

We live in a world of illusion. What you often see or perceive is not reality, but an appearance or image. This is why discernment is vital. Discernment is testing the spirit behind something. Most people judge a matter according to appearance, as well as how something makes them feel about themselves and life. Such judgment is fleshly and unrighteous.[1]

It is easy to give way to the appearance, but in so doing, you become part of the fantasy or game that the person is playing. Anytime you give way to fantasy, you are reinforcing delusion. When you play the game with others, you are not only giving way to a form of witchcraft, but you will become part of a treacherous trap of creating and maintaining a reality that is unrealistic and self-serving.

Sadly, many Christians unintentionally fall into these two traps. They either encourage delusion or they help create a reality that is wicked and destructive for other people. It has taken me years to recognize these two traps of Satan. After all, I have given the appearance and played the games. The false appearance was to receive recognition, while the games were a means of controlling my world. How do these two devices work?

To create an appearance, people perceive what others want from those around them. They simply adjust their appearance or presentation according to the apparent preference. This way, their pride can be acknowledged and fed, so they can feel good about themselves. Such exaltation keeps people from facing themselves. They can happily or ignorantly continue to deceive themselves about the environment of sin that freely reigns in their lives.

Since Christian stability and maturity are based on our attitude about personal sin, the individuals who live in a false reality will lack the integrity to face the real issues challenging their lives. In fact, they will become downright unhappy about it. They will resent reality intruding into their world. Ultimately, they will try to conform in other ways. After all, pride must be fed to feel important and significant in the scheme of things. This keeps individuals from having a sense of the extent of their disposition of sin. The Apostle John made this statement in 1 John 1:8, "If we say that we have no sin, we deceive ourselves, and the truth is not in us."

---

[1] John 7:24; 1 John 4:1

The reason we play games is to control the reality of our world. To control the reality of our world, we must get others to see it our way. There are a couple of ways we do this. Our first means is to reason with someone about how they are affecting our reality. The goal is to get people to see it our way and adjust to our world. If I get people to adjust to my reality, my surroundings will change according to my perception. The result is I do not have to face the character flaws in my life that are causing me discomfort. In essence, I want my world to change around me, so that I do not have to be responsible for confronting personal selfishness and insecurities. In a way, I simply transpose these insecurities by getting others to bow down to them, so I can be happy once again in my fantasy.

The second way that people try to control their own world and reality is to erect façades that give an appearance of adjusting to someone else's reality. The purpose for this outward adjustment is so that my purposes will be served in the end. These appearances are nothing more than sinister performances designed to gain a person's confidence so that he or she will line up to my world or way of thinking. As you can see, it is all about me, and there is no consideration as to how my selfishness and manipulation are affecting others. I simply want it my way.

Control and manipulation at any level will eventually create strife. When the strife comes, people will do one of two things. They will insist that they are right, cop an attitude, and hide behind a haughty look, or they will reform outwardly. Reforming is putting on an image or giving an appearance, but there is resentment and self-pity behind it. Either way the spirit is wrong, but at least reforming outwardly gives the appearance of nobility, or what I call the martyr syndrome.

Christians who fall into these traps are either sacrificed or the life is sucked out of them. They are sacrificed when they fail to live up to the façade, or else they have the life sucked out of them as they struggle to adjust the "reality" to someone else's drumbeat. Sadly, most well-meaning Christians are abused before they learn how to discern spiritual leeches. Their faith is undermined and their energy robbed from them, rendering them useless in ministering to those who are sincere and needy.

How must a Christian respond when they discern such people? They must hold the line of righteousness. Holding the line of righteousness is a powerful discipline. It not only calls for restraint, but it actually puts unseen pressure on those who are failing to uphold righteousness in their lives.

Righteousness is the main theme or product of a godly walk. It is a disposition. In other words, it is not a matter of doing right, but being right before God. If a person is right before God, he or she will do right by others. Righteousness that comes from a right disposition before God will not only result in obedience, but it produces godliness or godly conduct. Godliness means that our conduct is a product of God's influence and Spirit.

Righteousness is also comprised of truth and is maintained in obedience and faithfulness before God. Jesus instructed people to first seek the kingdom of God and His righteousness. It is righteousness that is accounted to those who walk by faith. There are various verses in Proverbs that talk about the glorious benefits of being righteous. The opposite of the state of righteousness is wickedness, and the opposite action of godliness that comes out of righteousness is evilness. Therefore, what is not done in righteousness before God is considered to be evil.

We see godly men holding this line of righteousness in Scripture. In order to hold this line, one must get past the relationship, or personal welfare, to see that it is about the spiritual destination of souls. Without the mirror of righteousness, people will ignorantly remain in their darkness and path of destruction. The problem is that people think in terms of the world, such as relationships and reputation, and never bother to consider it a matter of life and death.

Righteousness in this manner is a line because it is defining what is righteous and acceptable, and demands that a person adhere to its strict boundaries or pay the consequences. Individuals such as Samuel, David, John the Baptist, and Jesus held the line of righteousness. For example, Samuel held this line with King Saul. God had commanded Saul to destroy everything associated with Amalek.[2] Saul failed to kill the king and the animals. When Samuel confronted him, Saul reasoned with Samuel that his disobedience to God was noble and beneficial to Him. Samuel differed with him. He confronted Saul with truth. He brought a contrast between his actions and that which is right in 1 Samuel 15:22, "And Samuel said, Hath the LORD as great delight in burnt offerings and sacrifices, as in obeying the voice of the LORD? Behold, to obey is better than sacrifice, and to hearken than the fat of rams." He called Saul's actions as rebellious and stubborn.

David also held the line with King Saul. Saul had been chasing after David out of jealousy and fear of losing his kingdom. Saul's actions displayed wickedness. On two occasions, David had the opportunity to rid himself of his enemy. Instead of justifying personal rights to kill him, David chose to do right by leaving Saul's life in God's hands.[3]

In both cases, David confronted Saul, bringing a powerful contrast between righteousness and Saul's wicked actions. In 1 Samuel 24:17, Saul acknowledged that David was more righteous than he was. In 1 Samuel 26:21, he admitted that he was sinning against David. Ultimately, David's righteousness heaped judgment upon Saul.

---

[2] 1 Samuel 15
[3] 1 Samuel 24 & 26

John the Baptist held the line of righteousness with Herod over committing fornication with his brother's wife. Knowing the possible consequences, he maintained that line. In the end, John was imprisoned and beheaded.[4] Righteousness in John's case not only brought guilt and fear to Herod because he knew John was a righteous man, but it continued to haunt him even after John's death.

Jesus held the line with those who abused the things of God. He overturned the tables of the moneychangers twice, at the beginning of His ministry, and three years later before He was offered up as the Passover Lamb. In John 2:16, He said, "...Take these things hence; make not my Father's house an house of merchandise." He also exposed the self-righteous and self-serving motives of the Pharisees.[5]

Each of these men held the line of righteousness. They spoke truth to illuminate wicked intentions and evil actions. They refused to play the game by maintaining righteousness. For Samuel, he walked away from Saul. As Saul tried to prevent him from leaving, judgment was passed on him. Samuel stayed, but it was to kill the king of Amalek, as the means to maintain righteousness.[6]

Jesus spoke the truth to the rich young ruler. This young man declared that he was in search of eternal life. When Jesus brought the rich young ruler down to the last obstacle in his life, he still was not willing to lose that which bound him to the world to gain the One who would loose him from its entanglements. In this case, Jesus exposed the man's real sin: that of idolatry. His worldly possessions were more important than embracing God for eternity. The young man walked away in sorrow. Jesus did not chase after him, nor reason with him. It was obvious that the rich young ruler did not want to go the way of righteousness. There was nothing more that could be said to the ruler. The young man walked away from life, facing the harsh consequences of choosing the insignificant and temporal over the eternal.[7]

By upholding righteousness, these different men cut through appearances and brought people to a place of decision. Their unwillingness to play these people's games served as a sorrowful mirror to those who would not choose the ways of righteousness.

When people are first confronted with righteousness, their initial reaction is to conform. Saul asked for forgiveness before Samuel, and admitted his sin to David. However, it was all words. When actions are simply words or an outward show of repentance, it is nothing more than conformity. There is no real heart change, and God is aware that it is all show. Hebrews 12:17 makes this statement about Esau who was considered a fornicator or profane person, "For ye know how afterward,

---

[4] Mark 6:16-28
[5] Matthew 15:1-20; 23:13-36
[6] 1 Samuel 15:24-33
[7] Matthew 19:16-26

when he would have inherited the blessing, he was rejected: for he found no place of repentance, though he sought it carefully with tears."

To hold the line of righteousness, one must begin on a personal level. We see this with Moses. Hebrews 11:24-26 says this about Moses,

> By faith Moses, when he was come to years, refused to be called the son of Pharaoh's daughter; Choosing rather to suffer affliction with the people of God than to enjoy the pleasures of sin for a season; Esteeming the reproach of Christ greater riches than the treasures in Egypt: for he had respect unto the recompense of the reward.

Moses took action in three ways. He refused to be identified with the world. He chose to suffer affliction and become identified with his people. Finally, he changed his focus from the earthly to the eternal. Moses could have had the riches of earth, but he chose the hope of heaven. His choice caused him to reject the riches and prestige of Egypt and share in the suffering of the bitter bondage of his people.

I have discovered that people fail to hold the line of righteousness in regards to others, because they are not holding it for themselves in the same areas. For example, the priest Eli warned his sons of pending judgment, but partook of certain aspects of their sin because it served his purpose. In the end, he was also judged with his sons.[8]

King David had not maintained the personal line of righteousness when it came to Bathsheba. Later, when his oldest son raped his half-sister, David did not have the authority to hold the line with his son. The results were tragic. He experienced great sorrow, as the ordeal violently cost him two of his sons and divided his family.[9]

The character flaws or wickedness of others serve as incredible mirrors to us as they reveal the imbalances of our own character. Most of the time, we excuse these flaws as we ignore the mirrors. This is dangerous, because we need a reality check. We do think too highly of ourselves, which blinds us to personal flaws that will eventually cause us to become entangled in sins.[10]

It is only as you hold the personal line of righteousness with yourself that you will be able to hold it with others. It is hard to hold this line with others, because you must be both discerning and enduring. The line of righteousness is meant to put pressure on people. In order to get the person's attention, you must first jerk the line of righteousness. You do this by bringing the truth to the forefront about a matter. However, once you jerk the line, you must maintain it. This is where the real pressure begins.

---

[8] 1 Samuel 2:12-17, 22-36; 4:10-18
[9] 1 Samuel 11; 13; 15:7-23; 18:19-30
[10] Romans 12:3; Galatians 6:3

Hence, enters your level of endurance. Righteousness must be maintained. People must understand that there are consequences to wickedness. When their rope is jerked by truth, people's tendency is to conform, perform, or reform in order to relieve the pressure. These attempts are their way of getting you off their backs, so they can continue to play their games and maintain their reality.

Discernment is vital at this point. You must wade through their words and façades, to see if they are lining up to righteousness. The tendency for most people who are holding this line is to believe the words or outward performance. The main reason for believing these outward attempts is because many of us are lazy.

Outward conformity lets those holding the line off the hook. People who do this can appear noble because they are willing to let bygones be bygones, allowing the culprit to come back into fellowship. This relieves these individuals of the responsibility and pressure of maintaining a consistent pressure on the line. Once again, personal unwillingness or excuses for letting go of the line become a mirror to each of our personal characters and levels of commitment.

Doing right in regards to other souls is not a sacrifice, but our reasonable service. The Christian life is not about what is comfortable or convenient for me, but what is right before God, and what is right in regards to others. If someone is playing a game, giving way to it so I can relieve the pressure the line is putting on both parties as a means to create a semblance of peace, it is not only self-serving, but it is partaking of the other person's sin.

When I am holding the line of righteousness with someone, I take their words lightly and consider their outward conformity in light of attitudes and fruits. This is my way of proving someone. The Apostle Paul said, "Prove all things; hold fast to that which is good" (1 Thessalonians 5:21). People must be proven before you let go of the line. Granted, I would like to believe people's words and accept outward conformity, but such individuals are still on the path of destruction. Therefore, I will not partake of their sin nor make them feel good about themselves while they are on their way to hell. I must do right by them, in order to be right before God.

I will also not make people feel good about themselves, or play the game, so I can be friends with them. I will not take the pressure off of them for one minute. If I do, they will feel justified, and what will ultimately be revealed will be my personal level of commitment to God.

What about you? Do you need to hold the line with someone or are you holding it right now? If you are failing to hold the line of righteousness with someone, take a good look in the mirror, and see what that person is saying about your commitment to God and your character in His kingdom.

16

OTHER DISCIPLINES

The Christian life is full of disciplines. Some disciplines are more obvious than others, such as studying the Word of God.[1] We all know this is a necessary discipline, but how many people have substituted Christian TV, radio, and religious exercises, such as going to church, for this discipline. The Word of God is both milk and meat to our spirits and souls, but how many really know the Word of God? How many Christians are establishing the right environment with the Word of God that allows the Holy Spirit to bring forth the life of Jesus in them, establishing them unto all good works?

As we study the different responsibilities of the Christian life, we can see how every aspect of it points to some form of discipline. Whether it is our attitude, responses, or how we conduct our lives before God and others, it involves a point of personal discipline.

In this chapter, I want to cover other disciplines of the Christian life. Most of these disciplines have to do with giving way to God, and trusting Him to be God. After all, the greatest source of Christian disciplines are motivated by love, inspired by faith, and maintained in hope.

The first two disciplines that we must consider have to do with the Holy Spirit. We are told that we must walk after the Spirit to avoid condemnation, and we must be led by the Spirit to possess our inheritance. There are clear differences in walking after the Spirit and being led by the Spirit. To walk after the Spirit means you are pursuing after the Spirit. Such pursuits involve obedience that finds its source in righteousness, godliness, faith, love, meekness, peace, and purity of heart.[2] Being led by the Spirit implies that you are giving way or coming into submission. It is the Spirit who leads you into a complete life in Christ. Another difference between walking after the Spirit and being led by the Spirit is that walking points to being aggressive, while being led by the Spirit implies a call for restraint.

The Apostle Paul talked about these two types of discipline of the Spirit. All battles in regard to leadership in our lives come down to the battle between the flesh and the Spirit. As Christians, we give way either to the tyranny of the flesh or the liberty of the Spirit.[3] The flesh is our

---

[1] Matthew 4:4; 2 Timothy 2:15; 3:16-17; Hebrews 5:11-14

[2] Romans 8:1, 14; Ephesians 1:11-14

[3] 2 Corinthians 3:17-18; Galatians 5:16-18

natural preference, while the Spirit is a choice of the will. Giving way to the flesh ends in death.

Giving way to the Spirit always ends in righteousness and life.[4] Giving way to something is submission. Submission is a discipline of the will. This act involves humility and subordination to that which is greater. Humility addresses pride, while in the case of subordination to God's will, the works of the flesh will be mortified. These virtues and actions will prove to be contrary to our natural preferences.

As you can see, it is through the Spirit that the deeds of the body will be mortified. As you give way to the Spirit, you will not fulfill the lusts of the flesh. The Spirit will lead you away from the condemnation of the Law, as well as confirm the relationship you have with the Father. This will bring both liberty and freedom to possess your life in Christ. Your mind will be transformed, as you develop the mind of Jesus. The mind of Christ means you will begin to seek and grasp the heart of God. Once you put down the flesh, you will be able to discern between the flesh and the Spirit, and walk according to the ways of God instead of in condemnation.[5]

The Holy Spirit also will have the freedom to pray through you.[6] Prayer is another discipline. The discipline in prayer is not based on putting a certain time aside for this activity, but on stepping over self to truly find the mind and heart of God. Prayer involves seeking God's perspective about a matter. It takes discipline of mind and focus to seek after God in prayer. If you are interceding, it also takes endurance until the burden lifts. You actually must pray through until you know that God will honor it on earth.

Prayer is also discipline because people must pray according to the name of Jesus. This means they must pray according to Jesus' character. To pray according to His character requires a person to know Jesus. Prayer; therefore, ceases to be about personal desires, but becomes about realizing the mind and heart of God. It is as His heart is realized that people can pray according to His will. By praying in line with Christ's character, and in the light of His will, righteousness will be present in the prayer, giving authority and power. In the end, Jesus will be lifted up. It is at the point of Jesus that the Father can meet us. And, when Jesus is lifted up, He will draw those who are heirs of salvation to Himself.[7]

Prayer is also a point of preparation. Preparation is another type of discipline. It takes time to prepare for spiritual challenge and growth. To be spiritually prepared, I first must cleanse myself. Most people think that

---

[4] Romans 8:1-4
[5] John 12:32; Romans 8:1, 4-17; 12:1-2; 1 Corinthians 2:14-16; Galatians 5:13-25; 1 Timothy 6:11; 2 Timothy 2:22
[6] Romans 8:23-27
[7] John 14:13-14; James 5:16; 1 John 5:14-15

God is the one who cleanses the person. In the spiritual sense, He does cleanse us with the sacrifice of Jesus, but in the physical realm, we must cleanse ourselves. We see this even in the case of the priests in the Old Testament. They had to offer sacrifice as well as physically cleanse themselves at the laver.[8]

"Cleansing" in this text points to separation and consecration. Cleansing involves separating ourselves from the environments that would defile our lives before God, and abandoning all unholy practices and influences. James 4:8-9 states, "Draw nigh to God, and he will draw nigh to you. Cleanse your hands, ye sinners; and purify your hearts, ye double minded. Be afflicted, and mourn, and weep: let your laughter be turned to mourning, and your joy to heaviness."

Preparation involves waiting before God. In fact, you must learn to listen as you wait. Waiting is a product of patience or long-suffering. Patience is worked in us through testing, trials, and tribulation. It involves a process that will end in experience. Experience is a product of a perfect work of God and will produce perfection in our life and service to God. Perfection establishes hope that results in satisfaction or the state of wanting nothing. The process of patience is a way of possessing our very souls in such a way that we will not be moved in times of grave challenges.[9]

As Christians, we are constantly being tested. We have the tendency to think that the other guy is responsible for our personal attitudes and actions that come out of these testings. This is not true. The other guy often serves as a mirror that is testing the extent of our Christian character.

Others will always test my character. Will I have the mind of Christ towards these individuals, regardless of how they treat me?[10] Do I want truth or do I want my own opinion to be recognized or exalted above truth because of my fragile ego? Sadly, most people do not want truth to win out, but their opinions. They must be right because the alternative is that they might discover they are human. If they are human, they are subject to the same failures that the rest of humanity struggles with. Due to religious arrogance, these people perceive that they have become an exception to humanity, rather than the rule. Somehow, they have to reach heights of excellence in their own power and understanding.

Jesus said that His servants were to turn the other cheek and go the extra distance for those they encounter, whether they are enemy or friend.[11] The truth is, those who will not agree with my personal reality will always test my character. This testing is an enlargement of

---

[8] Exodus 29:1-4

[9] Psalm 27:14; 33:20; 37:34; Proverbs 20:22; Luke 21:19; Romans 5:3-4; 2 Corinthians 2:3-8; James 1:2-4

[10] Philippians 2:1-5

[11] Matthew 5:39-48

character. It calls for restraint or action. In challenging situations, I must restrain certain responses, in order to do right by others. In some cases, I must take action when it requires me to stand for truth and withstand the enemy. Perhaps I want to verbally strike out at someone who has offended me, or ignore attacks against truth. As a Christian, I must rein in fleshly reactions, and display godly attitudes and actions. And, when standing for the truth, I must display authority and power.

People are not the only ones testing my character. The Word tells me that I must test or examine myself! The Apostle Paul tells me that I must examine myself to see if I am in the faith.[12] This is another type of discipline. It requires me to step outside of my perception of self and truthfully examine personal attitudes and fruits. I have to exhibit integrity in such times, because the natural tendency is to justify away wrong attitudes and fruits. My main goal is to see how much of the life of Jesus is evident in attitude and conduct. Such a test is not based on how good I am, but how much of Christ is being manifested through me. This is determined by how much I allow Him to reign in my life as Lord.

Our instant society does not produce patience in us. If anything, it produces rudeness, and in many cases, frustration and rage. People, who do not have character, do not know how to humble themselves and simply be wrong. They are easily offended, lonely, and isolated. They become insulted because most others dare to disagree with their reality. They are lonely because they must come out on top, and people get tired of feeding their egos. They eventually become isolated because they can't afford to let anyone into their fragile world to see their lack of character.

Patience produces character because it also entails experience. Experience implies facing the harsh reality of life and allowing it to bring maturity. Sadly, most people avoid or resent experiences that would enlarge their perception. They want to hold on to their ridiculous comfort zones so that they never have to face the reality of their own character and inability. They prefer their ignorance. Ignorance is not the lack of intelligence about something, but the lack of experience. Without experience, people can remain in blissful ignorance about what is going on around them. They can maintain their own opinions, and arrogantly discard anyone's opinions that do not agree with or pay homage to their reality. This not only produces superstition in the Christian life, but fantasy and self-delusion.

This brings us back to waiting. God's Word talks about waiting before the Lord. Waiting is necessary in such places as weariness and drudgery. Isaiah 40:31 states, "But they that wait upon the LORD shall renew their strength; they shall mount up with wings as eagles; they shall run, and not be weary; and they shall walk, and not faint." It is hard to wait on God. It calls for restraint when we want action. Sadly, instead of people waiting on the Lord, they either close down or give up.

---

[12] 1 Corinthians 11:28-32; 2 Corinthians 13:5

Waiting on the Lord involves maintaining a state of expectancy. This expectancy has to do with deliverance or salvation. It actually keeps an individual ready for action when the proper doors open. Luke 19:13 refers to it as occupying. The problem is that people either get ahead of God's timing, and find themselves in a precarious position, or, they are not prepared or available to respond to God's deliverance because they are not looking for it. Isaiah 64:4 says, "For since the beginning of the world men have not heard, nor perceived by the ear, neither hath the eye seen, O God, beside thee, what he hath prepared for him that waiteth for him."

To wait for God means that your soul is quietly and in confidence waiting for God to move. This attitude of quietness and confidence is based on faith in God.[13] This faith cannot be moved from what it knows to be true of the character of God. The soul finds rest in this confidence in spite of the state or the environment that surrounds it. Isaiah 30:15 confirms this, "For thus saith the Lord GOD, the Holy One of Israel; In returning and rest shall ye be saved; in quietness and in confidence shall be your strength: and ye would not."

Lamentations 3:25-26 states, "The LORD is good unto them that wait for him, to the soul that seeketh him. It is good that a man should both hope and quietly wait for the salvation of the LORD." The first part of this verse tells us that it is good to wait for God. Waiting does not involve sitting around or being complacent. As already stated, it involves a state of expectancy. You are actually doing something. For Christians, they are seeking God in service and maintaining spiritual sharpness.

Hope always points to expectancy. It is the hope that not only produces confidence in the waiting, but it quiets a person's soul during the time of waiting.[14] Romans 8:25 says, "But if we hope for that we see not, then do we with patience wait for it?" And, what is the Christian waiting for?

Many Christians are waiting for God to open the door, so they can serve Him. This may seem noble, but there is no Scripture that tells believers to wait for God to open the doors of ministry. The reason for this is because ministry is all around us. Every arena we enter becomes a mission field. Every soul we encounter is a potential child of God. In fact, if you are waiting for some great door of ministry to open up, you are probably not being faithful with what is in front of you. God told Jeremiah's companion, Baruch, not to seek great things for himself because God was going to bring evil upon all flesh. However, He would give Baruch his life.[15]

Therefore, what are Christians waiting for? Each believer is waiting for one event, and that is to realize the fullness of salvation. The Apostle

---

[13] Isaiah 8:17
[14] Hebrews 11:1
[15] Luke 16:10-12; Jeremiah 45:5

Paul said this in 2 Thessalonians 3:5, "And the Lord direct your hearts into the love of God, and into the patient waiting for Christ." The fullness of our salvation means one main event, seeing Jesus face to face. Whether it involves the flesh giving way to physical death, so that we may be ushered into His presence, or, whether we will be caught up with His Body when He comes back for His Church in the future, our ultimate hope is seeing Him.[16] It will be a glorious time of celebration, for we will be home to enjoy our Lord, King, and Savior forever and ever. Are you possessing your soul in patience? Are you waiting for the fullness of your salvation to come in quietness and confidence?

Another discipline is meditating on the Word. We have already mentioned the need to study it. Studying the Word is different than meditating on the Word. Most people try to read the Word, but few study and meditate on it. Solomon reminds us that too much studying creates weariness. Therefore, how does one meditate on the Word? The way to effectively benefit from the Word is to meditate on what you are studying. The Word will actually cleanse a person's way. Some people simply like knowledge, but if knowledge does not become revelation, it has no impact in a person's life. It never becomes a sharp sword that penetrates through self-delusion or spiritual oppression, to expose the motives and intents of the heart.[17]

Motives point to spirit, while intents represent inclination and tendencies. People may have good hearts or intentions toward God, but if their motivation is about self, it will defile their intentions. In fact, they could walk in self-delusion about their motivations as they seek vainglory for their deeds. This will cause them to pursue the things of God, rather than God. Such people are prone to be caught up with ministry, rather than knowing God. They will consider the significance of their life in light of what they do for God, rather than what God has been allowed to do in and through them.

Another important discipline can be found in God's promises. They are known as conditions. God cannot honor His promises, unless the person is in a proper state to receive His promises. The reason for this is that people who are not prepared to receive God's promises will defile or improperly handle them, thereby, bringing judgment upon themselves. Since God is merciful, He has set various disciplines in His promises as a means to prepare people to properly receive them with a correct spiritual condition.

For example, take the famous promises found in Psalm 37:3-7. Psalm 37:3-5 says, "Trust in the LORD, and do good; so shalt thou dwell in the land, and verily thou shalt be fed. Delight thyself also in the LORD; and he shall give thee the desires of thine heart. Commit thy way unto the LORD; trust also in him; and he shall bring it to pass." How many

[16] 1 Corinthians 13:10: 15:51-52; 2 Corinthians 5:6-10; 1 Thessalonians 4:13-18
[17] Psalm 19:14; 104:34; 119:15, 48, 78, 97, 99, 148; 119:9; Ecclesiastes 12:12; 2 Timothy 2:15; Hebrews 4:12

disciplines can you see in these promises? I see at least six different disciplines that must be put into practice before God can bring forth a few promises. Sadly, most people quote the promise, but never walk out the disciplines. The promise is not fulfilled, and they blame God, instead of recognizing that they failed to adhere to the conditions or disciplines involved.

This brings us to another discipline: That of abiding in Christ. The meaning of abiding speaks of discipline. It means to be given a place, state, relation, or expectancy. It includes such words as continue, dwell, endure, be present, remain, stand, and tarry.[18]

The Apostle John talked about this state in his Gospel and epistle. In John 15, we have a beautiful picture of what it means to abide in Jesus. He is the Vine, and we are the branches, while the Father is the husbandman. Great care goes into maintaining our life in Jesus. He is our source, and without Him, there is no life. Without this abiding, we will become worthless in the scheme of things, and will be separated from the Vine to face judgment.

The Christian life is meant to make a difference. We have been given every means to produce fruit worthy of bringing glory to the Father and attraction to our Lord. But, what does it mean to endure? John answers that question in 1 John 2:6.

To abide in Jesus, you must conduct your life as He conducted His life. In order to do this, you must be born again of the Spirit. It is the Spirit who anoints believers and helps them to embrace life, keep the commandments, avoid sin, and walk as Jesus walked. He is the one who sheds the love of God in people's hearts, so they can love both God and their brother.[19]

"To abide" in Jesus means that the Word is abiding in you. If the Word is abiding in you, it will keep you on the right track, as it keeps you from sin. It will help you overcome the wicked One, and walk in confidence before God. By abiding in the doctrine of Christ, you are assured of having both the Father and the Son.[20]

If you are abiding in Jesus, you will be walking in the light. The light ensures forgiveness, cleansing, and fellowship, as you enjoy the reality of God and agreement with other likeminded believers. The light will expose your steps and keep you from stumbling. It will uphold truth and keep you in the ways of God. It will keep you in line with God's will, ensuring that you will abide forever.[21]

These are other disciplines that must be quietly working in our lives, as they effectively change our limited perception. People may not see these disciplines, but they will taste the fruits of them. They may not be

---

[18] Strong's Exhaustive Concordance: #3306
[19] Romans 5:5; 1 John 2:6, 24-27; 3:6, 14
[20] Psalm 119:11; 1 John 2:13-14; 2 John 9
[21] John 1:4; 1 John 1:2-7; 2:10, 17

aware of these disciplines, but they will see the character that is being established in their lives because of them.

Are these disciplines working in your life? If so, they will be evident in your fruit, attitude, and conduct. Examine your fruit and see if you can detect godliness in your life.

17

JUST DO IT!

Discipline is active, whether you refrain from responding or you act upon what you have committed to do. It is always active in some way. Any attitudes or actions that are not active within these boundaries do not constitute discipline. For example, some people's inaction is nothing more than complacency. The actions of giving way to what is natural are anything but discipline. Discipline implies that some pressure or control is being applied in the situation that is running contrary to what is natural or pleasant.

The characteristics of discipline can be clearly seen in God. When God is refraining from acting in holiness, it becomes an act of mercy. If He responds in graciousness and faithfulness, it becomes an act of grace. If He does move upon evil, it is an act of righteous judgment. Therefore, the whole essence of God's character shows tremendous discipline. He does what He says He will do, but He also shows tremendous discretion and restraint in whatever He does.[1]

Man is a creature of action as well. He is always doing. However, much of what man does is self-serving.[2] This is the opposite of discipline because it simply means man is giving way to what is comfortable, convenient, and self-exalting. When challenged to discipline themselves, many people do not have the initiative or endurance to see it through. When it comes to spiritual discipline, many well-meaning people start out in religious zeal, but quickly lose momentum. At this point, many give in to complacency, apathy, and anger.

Spiritual discipline is often a passing fancy for most people. Few are willing to discipline every aspect of their lives. As a result, many Christians do not experience the spiritual maturity they dream about. Although the milk of the Word eventually leaves them hungry for more, they will not stir themselves up to seek the meat. If they do, the initial discomfort of trying to "chew" on it causes some to give up in despair.[3]

Spiritual maturity will not come unless there is spiritual discipline. For Christians to begin the preparation for running this incredible race, they

---

[1] Genesis 6:17; 9:13; 18:19, 25, 30
[2] Genesis 11:6
[3] Hebrews 5:11-14

must lay aside every weight of the world and the sin that easily besets them, and begin to run the race with patience.[4]

Jesus understood the power of personal discipline. His discipline as man came out of preparation, servitude, and suffering. For thirty years, He was prepared in obscurity. As man, he came into subjection to the Father's will. He never moved outside of it. Therefore, He was always in step with the situation. He never got ahead of the plan nor was he ever late. He was not indifferent to what needed to be done, and He never missed any opportunities to touch people in a miraculous way. Jesus' obedience not only defined the attitude, strength, and power of His servitude, it perfected Him as man in His sufferings. Hebrews 5:8-9 states, "Though he were a Son, yet learned he obedience by the things which he suffered; And being made perfect, he became the author of eternal salvation unto all them that obey him."

The Apostle Paul talked about how he maintained the endurance to run this race. First, he talked about how he died daily. Death to self is the main way to lay aside every weight that would hinder a person in his or her Christian walk. Next, he talked about how he had to keep the members of his body in subjection to avoid becoming a castaway.[5]

Paul also spoke about running with the intent of receiving a prize. In order to receive this prize, he talked about counting all things as dung, and pressing forward towards the mark in order to gain this incredible prize.[6] At the end of his life, he summarized the extent of this discipline in 2 Timothy 4:6-8. He acknowledged that he was about ready to be offered up. He declared that he had fought a good fight, finished his course, and kept the faith. He ended by saying he would receive the crown of righteousness that was laid up for him.

Can you see the discipline in Paul's life? He made the choice to die and keep his body under control. He kept his focus single, pressed through the obstacles, and managed to keep his purpose unclouded as he reached forward with everything in him. As a result, he finished the course and received the prize.

Spiritual discipline adheres to what is right. Since you cannot please God without genuine faith, you must choose to believe all spiritual truths and matters by faith. I realized a long time ago that I had nothing to lose by believing God, but I had everything to lose if I did not respond to Him in faith.[7]

Sincere faith always produces discipline that translates into righteousness. We see this in the life of Jacob. He had been shrewd when he caught his brother at a vulnerable time, and purchased the birthright from him for a bowl of lentils. He showed shrewdness when he

[4] Hebrews 12:1
[5] 1 Corinthians 9:27; 15:30
[6] 1 Corinthians 9:24; Philippians 3:14
[7] Hebrews 11:6

plotted with his mother to deceive Isaac about his identity, in order to receive the blessing. Later, he would come to a place where he encountered God. This encounter would permanently change him.[8]

Jacob sought out his uncle Laban, as he sought for a wife. His uncle was also a shrewd businessman. He took advantage of Jacob, and set him up to fall into a clever trap. In the end, God blessed his uncle due to Jacob's presence. The uncle made a deal with Jacob to watch his flocks. In spite of how much Jacob's uncle took advantage of him, Jacob did right by him. As a result, God was able to bless Jacob.[9]

The reality of godly discipline is that it simply does what is right. It does not have to debate about such matters. In fact, the key to discipline can be summarized in two words: Do it. You see the concept of "doing it" throughout Scriptures. When the children of Israel were ready to possess the land, Joshua reminded the Reubenites, the Gadites, and the half-tribe of Manasseh that even though they had their land on the other side of Jordan, they promised to help the children of Israel possess the Promised Land. Their response was an example of discipline, "...All that thou commandest us we will do, and whithersoever thou sendest us, we will go" (Joshua 1:16).

I appreciate King David's attitude and approach in regards to the building of the temple. He had provided the means and plans to ensure that his heart's desire would be carried out. This great task had been passed down to his son, Solomon. David told his son that all that was left for the temple was to build it. His instruction to Solomon was to be strong and do it.[10]

In Ezra's day, he was in despair to find that the children of Israel had intermarried with women of pagan backgrounds. He rebuked the people for their grave trespass against God. He then instructed them to make a covenant with God to put away all their foreign wives and the children born to them. After the instruction, he challenged them with these words, "Arise; for this matter belongeth unto thee: be of good courage, and do it" (Ezra 10:4).

When the lawyer asked Jesus what it meant to love his neighbor, Jesus gave the example of the Good Samaritan in light of indifferent and uncaring religious leaders who knew what was right. He asked the man which one showed himself to be a neighbor in the situation. The lawyer had to admit that it was the one who showed mercy. Jesus made this statement in Luke 10:37, "...Go, and do thou likewise."

Every successful saint has understood the dynamics of spiritual discipline. They knew that it entailed laboring in different types of situations. Some of the laboring was of a physical nature, but most laboring in the Christian's life has to do with the spiritual. Spiritual

---

[8] Genesis 25:34; 28:6-22
[9] Genesis 29:23-30; 30:25-33
[10] 1 Chronicles 28:1-10

laboring can be compared to the travail that takes place in birth. This travailing has to do with laboring to see the kingdom of God realized in people. As John 6:27 says, "Labour not for the meat which perisheth, but for that meat which endureth unto everlasting life, which the Son of man shall give unto you: for him hath God the Father sealed."

This labor had to be in the confines of God's will and purpose, or it would all be in vain.[11] Such labor involves endurance and confidence, in spite of the challenges and circumstances. The Apostle Paul made this statement, "To the weak became I as weak, that I might gain the weak, I am made all things to all men, that I might by all means save some" (1 Corinthians 9:22).

Laboring in the harvest field of humanity requires servants of God to deny self in order to become identified with those around them. This allows them to become sensitive to souls. Sensitivity of this nature positions God's servants in the place of being His co-laborers.[12]

As you study God's people, you see both restraint and aggression that was contrary to what they perceived or felt. They were simply being obedient or doing what they were told. As a result, these people accomplished great feats in the kingdom of God.

Let us consider a few of these people. Joshua helped the children of Israel possess the Promised Land. He had to go against the grain of what appeared to be the impossible. God made this statement to him, "Have not I commanded thee? Be strong and of a good courage; be not afraid, neither be thou dismayed for the LORD thy God is with thee withersoever thou goest" (Joshua 1:9).

The first part and the last part of this instruction called for Joshua to put his faith in God. He had to believe Him if he was to accomplish the task before him. Joshua had to be strong, in spite of his human limitations. He had to take courage in the promises of God, rather than consider the obstacles. Joshua could not give in to fear or dismay. Once again, we see that discipline is a choice.

This choice is a matter of the heart. Nehemiah brought this out. He was a man who had to overcome various obstacles to rebuild the wall around Jerusalem. His endurance level was tested in many ways. However, he confessed that this discipline was a matter of the heart, "And I arose in the night, I and some few men with me; neither told I any man what my God had put in my heart to do at Jerusalem: neither was there any beast with me, save the beast that I rode upon" (Nehemiah 2:12).

The children of Israel had to display discipline. Much of their discipline came in the form of submitting to leadership. Submission to godly leadership meant obedience to God. The one consistent discipline that can be seen in all godly people is this form of obedience to God.

---

[11] Psalm 127:1
[12] 1 Corinthians 3:9

Without it, there is nothing that will be accomplished in God's kingdom. Without this submission, the children of Israel never would have possessed the Promised Land. They had to rise up, out of their comfort zones, and be willing to lose their very life to gain all that God had for them. In contrast, God was not happy with the people of Israel when they failed to rise up and possess the land.[13]

As Christians, we must rise up to inherit the kingdom of God. The rich young ruler came to Jesus to inquire about eternal life. When he was challenged about what was dear to his heart, he walked away in sorrow. The man came to Jesus, but he failed to rise up to meet the challenge. As a result, he never inherited or possessed eternal life.

Ruth showed tremendous discipline when she chose to leave all behind, to follow her mother-in-law, Naomi, to Bethlehem. In fact, when Naomi tried to send her back to her own people, Ruth clung to her. She declared that she wanted Naomi's God and people to be hers. Although Ruth faced an uncertain journey and future, she risked it all to gain both Jehovah God and a new life that in the end would place her in the lineage of King David and the Promised Messiah.[14]

Ruth proved to be an incredible woman of faith. No matter what obstacle she encountered, she believed. This reminds Christians how the walk of faith disciplines them to endure the unpredictable and the unknown in order to embrace the unseen, the impossible and the eternal. Without the walk being disciplined by faith, many walk after things that do not profit their spiritual well-being. [15]

There is no victory without discipline. Gideon proved this when he faced the Midianites with 300 men. God had instructed Gideon every step of the way. As you follow Gideon, you must observe how God prepared him for this challenge. God called him to defeat this pagan army. We see where Gideon offered an acceptable sacrifice to God. He brought down the idol in his midst, allowing the Spirit of God to come down upon him. He blew the trumpet for battle. God reduced his army to 300 men. His obedience led to victory that was wrought in the miraculous with trumpets, empty pitchers, and lamps.

For the Christian, the trumpet points to their call to go forth in their life in God, the empty pitchers point to their lives before God, and the lamps point to Jesus. The pitcher was broken, signifying brokenness before God, so that the light of Christ can shine forth. This was all accomplished by faith. After all, each step of obedience required discipline on the part of Gideon. Each step was a step of faith in regards to the great God of heaven who would ensure a miraculous victory.[16]

---

[13] Joshua 13; 18:1-8

[14] Ruth 1; Matthew 1:5

[15] Jeremiah 2:8; 2 Corinthians 5:7; Hebrews 11

[16] Judges 6-7

120

The victory always belongs to God. He is the One who fights for us, but we must rise up and obey His instructions. In other words, we must give Him something to work with. He cannot show Himself mighty, unless finite man believes. Christians must understand this principle. Many are sitting around waiting for God to do something, so they can possess this incredible life. They refuse to step into the Jordan River, so God can part the waters for them to walk through on dry land, and possess the life He has for them.[17]

Jonathan, the son of Saul, also showed discipline in the form of commitment. Godly commitments always require some type of discipline. He made this statement to David, "...Whatsoever thy soul desireth, I will even do it for thee" (1 Samuel 20:4). For Jonathan, he had to oppose his father to maintain his friendship with David. In the end, he became a sacrifice so David could take his rightful place as king. Jonathan's commitment was sincere, sacrificial, and complete.

Christians must also possess a sincere commitment towards God. This commitment can only come out of devoted love. Many Christians are in love with their idea of God, but not in love with the Person of God who is found in the Bible. This type of fleshly, self-serving love is nothing more than sentimentality that falls short of enduring commitment that produces sacrifice.

King Saul made this statement about David, "...Blessed be thou, my son David: thou shalt both do great things, and also shalt still prevail" (1 Samuel 26:25). David was a man of integrity. He had faith, was obedient, and could be humbled. He knew his God, and was led by God through many ordeals. David revealed the greatness of God through many of his feats, but also mirrored the devastating ripple effects of sin and its consequences.

In 1 Kings 9:4, we read about the character of David, "And if thou wilt walk before me, as David thy father walked, in integrity of heart, and in uprightness, to do according to all that I have commanded thee, and wilt keep my statutes and my judgments." The main discipline of David's life was his obedience to God. This is constantly being brought out in Scripture.[18]

Obedience is the key to a victorious life in Christ. Part of obedience is not forgetting God's Law.[19] The Law keeps the ways of God ever before us. By walking according to His Law, we avoid giving way to iniquity. Psalm 119:3 states, "They also do no iniquity: they walk in his ways."

Psalm 119:153 says, "Consider mine affliction, and deliver me: for I do not forget thy law"

---

[17] Joshua 3:13-17
[18] Deuteronomy 6:1-3; 8:1-3; Psalm 119:8
[19] Deuteronomy 8:11

121

As Christians, we must walk out the Christian life. To ensure righteousness, we must fulfill the Law through love, obey Jesus' instructions, and line up to His examples.[22] These all serve as points of discipline that will produce the disposition and attitude of Jesus.

Obviously, every aspect of the Christian life involves discipline. Without the proper discipline, Christians will fail to stand, withstand, overcome, finish the course, and receive the prize. Granted, we can downplay discipline in our life, as we hide behind one excuse after another. However, in the end, the life of Jesus will be missing. His glory will not be evident, and His attitude will be absent.

Do you have spiritual discipline or are you giving way to the preference of the flesh and the exaltation of your pride? If so, you are not developing godly discipline. You will be rendered ineffective and powerless as you confront life, the world, and Satan.

Discipline in God's kingdom is never a matter of debate. It always comes down to doing what is necessary. As Christians, we will do it because it is right before the One we love with all of our being. We will do it because it identifies us to that which is eternal and magnificent. We will do it because it will bring glory and honor to the One who so loved us that He gave His only begotten Son. We will just do it because there is nothing else that will bring meaning and substance to our lives.

---

[22] Romans 10:8-10

Book Two

PRAYER
AND
WORSHIP

INTRODUCTION

When one thinks of the Christian life, prayer and worship come into the picture. No one would debate that these two subjects are of the utmost importance to promote and ensure the fulfillment and completion of our spiritual journey on earth. Prayer marks the entrance into the Most Holy Place of communion, while worship represents the place of communion.

There are many books on prayer and worship. I am sure that I will not add any new revelations to these two topics, but I feel that my approach may add a balance and a simple perspective. For those who are new in Christ, the complication and religious notions will be removed, so that they will be able to see the simplicity in these two vital subjects. To those who are mature, I hope that it will cause them to pause, consider, or rediscover the Most Holy Place of intimacy with God.

The challenge for each reader is to discover the beauty and power in effectual prayer and the sacrifice of true worship. Once the beauty and power are discovered, it will allow the individual to touch the throne of God. This will allow God to move in power and majesty on his or her behalf.

Section I

Prayer

1

HARSH REALITY

And it came to pass, that, as he was praying
in a certain place, when he ceased, one of his
disciples said unto him, Lord, teach us to pray,
as John taught his disciples.
(Luke 11:1)

How many of God's people know how to pray? There are many religious notions about prayer, but few ever hit the mark of what constitutes acceptable prayer before God. This is made obvious by the despair and disillusionment that many Christians have in regards to prayer. They never see answered prayers; therefore, unbelief is prevalent in their life before God. Few realize that unanswered prayers have nothing to do with God, but with their inability to touch the throne of God. Therefore, God is often perceived as being an unfeeling, unfair, indifferent, and cruel God to those who fail to come to terms with this subject.

This is why one of the harshest realities that most believers must initially face about prayer is that they do not know how to pray. Regardless of religious experiences, most Christians have been left to figure out prayer on their own. This has caused misconceptions, ignorance, or superstition on their part.

The Apostle Paul emphasized the fact that Christians do not know how to really pray in Romans 8:26, "Likewise the Spirit also helpeth our infirmities: for we know not what we should pray for as we ought: but the Spirit itself maketh intercession for us with groanings which cannot be uttered."

Amazingly, the disciples recognized their ignorance in the area of prayer. However, this reality check probably was a result of witnessing Jesus in His prayer life. Surely, His example brought a visible contrast to their lives in the areas of attitude and answered prayer.

This harsh reality made them teachable resulting in their request, "Teach us to pray." I wonder how many Christians have made such a request to the throne of God? It was only after years of silence and struggle that I came to terms with prayer. Surprisingly, I found that the greatest denominator in effectual prayer was child-like faith. I only learned this after understanding the heart of God about this subject.

Once a person initially faces the reality that he or she does not know how to pray, knowledge can be imparted. As proper knowledge is imparted, religious notions or superstitions about prayer will be brought down and replaced by truths that will change a person's attitude and approach to the throne of God. These truths will create a confidence that will give believers authority and boldness to enter the throne room of God.[1]

This brings us to the significance of this first chapter. Before we can understand what constitutes prayer, we must come to terms with the religious activities that become sick substitutes for effectual prayer in the kingdom of God. Jesus addressed some of these substitutes in Matthew 6:5-8.

The first sick substitute for prayer comes by way of religious show.[2] I have witnessed people who could say flowery prayers to impress or entertain others with their religious piousness. I could tell by their mannerisms that they were most impressed with their ability to pray, but in the end, it was an exercise in futility.

Prayer is for the purpose of getting a hold of God, not impressing others around you with your so-called "piousness." To use prayer as a means of impressing others or as a form or religious entertainment is the worst affront against the privilege of prayer. Jesus said of these people that man's recognition would be their only reward.

If you want prayer to count, you must recognize that it is between you and God. There is a story about a young girl praying at the dinner table. Her voice was so low that others could not hear her. Someone commented to her that no one could hear her. She quickly reminded the individual that she was not talking to anyone at the table. Prayer should be a personal, intimate time between you and God. Effective prayer will often take place outside of religious activities. Jesus often left the noisy activities of the world and sought a solitary place to be with the Father.[3] The reality of prayer is that it can be a time of rest, a point of great personal struggle, or a place of intense conflict. After all, spiritual battles are first won in the prayer closet.

As a result, Jesus instructed people to find a secret closet and close the door behind them. Granted, it is hard to pray when there is no audience. Silence is the loudest noise in the world today. It is frightening because you will sense various aspects about yourself that can be hard to confront.

In such times it will become obvious that prayer is one of the most challenging disciplines of the Christian life to anyone who embarks on this journey to discover its power. In the prayer closet, one must discipline his or her thoughts, open up his or her heart to God, and learn

---

[1] Hebrews 4:16
[2] Matthew 6:5
[3] Matthew 14:22-23; 15:29; Mark 6:46; Luke 22:41

when to be quiet before Him. People must be persevering in their requests and confident in their spirit.[4] Psalm 46:10 says it best, "Be still, and know that I am God: I will be exalted among the heathen, I will be exalted in the earth."

This brings us to another important issue: to whom are you praying? The priests of Baal made a tremendous amount of noise to get their idol's attention in 1 Kings 18. They leaped upon the altar, cried aloud, cut themselves, and prophesied. Elijah mocked them because their god remained silent, "...Cry aloud: for he is a god; either he is talking, or he is pursuing, or he is in a journey, or peradventure he sleepeth, and must be awaked" (I Kings 18:27).

To whom are you talking? How are you approaching God? Most people are always speaking in prayer. Those who always talk, usually fail to be good communicators because they do not know how to listen.

It is hard to remember that whenever two parties are involved in some form of conversation, both parties must be involved in the conversation to effectively communicate. What some Christians fail to realize is that God actually wants to talk with us. He sometimes intrudes or steps into the midst of our lives when we are not even looking for Him. He occasionally initiates the conversation. When the boy Samuel, first encountered God, he did not know who was calling him. He kept running to the priest, Eli. Eventually, Eli realized God was trying to get Samuel's attention. Eli instructed Samuel to reply with this statement, "Speak, LORD; for thy servant heareth."[5]

How many of us would resent any kind of intrusion? I wonder how many times I have failed to hear the voice of God because it represented an intrusion. For God to even speak to us would serve as a test to see if we were ready to hear Him speak. The response should be so simple from us, "Speak Lord."

Samuel was a servant at heart; therefore, he was always ready to hear the master's call. We must always be ready to hear and respond as a servant when we hear God's voice.

The first thing we must acknowledge about Jehovah God is that He is not an idol. You cannot accuse Him of being deaf, blind, dumb, or asleep. You do not need to yell at Him, for He can hear the silent cries of the heart. He is not impressed with religious antics because He weighs your spirit.[6] He does not care if you leap up on the altar or wave a flag to get His attention. He is aware of you. However, He is God and you must learn to be still before Him. You must learn to carefully listen.

This was brought out to Elijah in 1 Kings 19:11-12 after he fled for his life. Elijah had just experienced a powerful victory over the priests of Baal at Mount Carmel. God had shown Himself in a mighty way. Such

[4] 2 Corinthians 10:5
[5] 1 Samuel 3:4-10
[6] Psalm 121:4; Proverbs 16:2

victories are preludes to valleys of humiliation. Elijah was probably operating off of adrenaline when Jezebel threatened to kill him. This caused him to run the other way and go into deep depression. After all, he had been jealous for God; therefore, why was the victory short-lived? How could people like Jezebel refuse to see the truth? Eventually, God stepped on the scene to bring matters into perspective. He gave Elijah these instructions,

> Go forth, and stand upon the mount before the LORD. And, behold, the LORD passed by, and a great and strong wind rent the mountains, and brake in pieces the rocks before the LORD; but the LORD was not in the wind: and after the wind an earthquake; but the LORD was not in the earthquake: And after the earthquake a fire; but the LORD was not in the fire: and after the fire a still small voice (1 Kings 19:11-12).

Many Christians perceive that they will encounter God in His majesty, only to find out that His ways are found in simplicity. Others expect to meet Him in His power, only to find out that He moves through that which seems insignificant. There are still some who expect to see Him in mighty judgment, only to realize that He wants to express Himself in practical ways. Elijah encountered God when he heard His still small voice.

Christians need to consider Elijah's encounter with God. It was so sweet, simple, and practical. There was no fanfare or entertainment. He actually intruded through the majesty, power, and judgment with a still small voice.

Jesus said when you pray do not use vain repetition.[7] Consider the usual prayers that we often hear in churches. They all have the same flavor. Some sound more sincere than others. These prayers are safe, but in some cases they are repetitious. They are comfortable, but prove to be redundant at times.

How about the prayer books? Such books have a prayer for every occasion. This seems acceptable since many people don't know how to pray. Therefore, people use these prayers to try to get God's attention regardless of how repetitious or dead they sound. Such prayers are at least fulfilling religious obligations.

Jesus said of such prayers that even the heathen operate in this manner. Obviously, prayers must have more meaning and purpose behind them than some generic, religious exercise. Prayer must be a matter of the heart. Our Lord confirmed this in Matthew 15:8: "This people draweth nigh unto me with their mouth, and honoureth me with their lips; but their heart is far from me."

Christians are commanded to not be like the heathen. They are religious and sincere, but they do not know to Whom they need to be

---

[7] Matthew 6:7

praying. Their prayers are all outward show, rather than a heartfelt means of approaching the true God of heaven. They are self-serving, rather than seeking the heart of God to know how to serve Him.

This brings us to self-serving prayers. These prayers are all about what we want from God. Needless to say, these requests don't even get close to the throne room of God. James 4:3 makes this statement, "Ye ask, and receive not, because ye ask amiss, that ye may consume it upon your lusts."

Most people pray to God to get things from Him. They see Him as a Santa Claus or a big Sugar Daddy. Their prayers are for those things that will bring personal happiness. Many of these individuals equate happiness with things. Prayers that are focused on obtaining personal benefits are exiting from the mouths of many fleshly Christians. They simply want to heap more upon their already worldly, extravagant lifestyles. They believe that since God loves them, it is His desire and good pleasure to give them such things. In fact, a whole new "faith movement" has been created to enhance the pursuit of the things of the world in the name of Jesus.

James is very clear concerning when we ask for things that will feed our idols of lust and greed that we are asking amiss. He explained why in James 4:4, "Ye adulterers and adulteresses, know ye not that the friendship of the world is enmity with God? whosoever therefore will be a friend of the world is the enemy of God." Self-serving prayers reveal the spiritual harlotry of our hearts. They prove that we do not desire the things of God. Rather, we use God in hopes of heaping the things of the world to feed our personal, selfish desires.

Jesus said this in Matthew 6:8, "Be not ye therefore like unto them: for your Father knoweth what things ye have need of, before ye ask him." If God knows what we need, then why pray? Remember, prayer is a Christian discipline, but it also becomes a means by which God can teach us valuable lessons and form character. However, do you know what you have need of? One of the greatest lessons we must learn in prayer is the difference between our needs and our wants.

We have this promise in Philippians 4:19, "But my God shall supply all your need according to his riches in glory by Christ Jesus." God will supply our needs. The riches in Christ Jesus have more to do with experiencing the spiritual life, rather than possessing the things of the world. Much of the riches that surround Jesus are eternal in nature.[8]

Most of the requests ascending to the throne of God have to do with wants. These prayers never hit the target. As a result, many misinformed Christians end up discouraged about the Christian life, disillusioned about prayer, and skeptical about God.

It is Jesus' heart to teach us how to pray. He gave both instructions and examples to help us discover the extraordinary place of prayer. Are

---

[8] Colossians 2:3

you taking advantage of it? A good way to test yourself in this area is by considering how many of your prayers are hitting the target.

2

A MATTER OF COMMUNICATION

...Speak LORD; for thy servant heareth...
(1 Samuel 3:9)

Prayer is one area I have struggled the most with in my spiritual life. Jesus said that His sheep will hear His voice. I have always desired to have a close relationship with my Shepherd. However, my idea of this powerful prayer life was influenced by comparisons. After reading about the prayer lives of great people of faith, I felt inadequate in mine. In some cases, contemporary Christian acquaintances have bragged about their great moments of inspiration during their prayer times. Comparing myself with others was scripturally wrong, but regardless of such unproductive implications, I have often perceived my prayer life as lacking.[1]

When I did manage to sit down to quiet my soul before God in prayer, my mind became incredibly active with daily demands. Every time I tried to schedule a time of prayer, it became a powerless duty. In fact, all personal attempts to discipline my prayer life in the past have ended in failure. It is as though I missed the mark no matter how much I struggled. This left me feeling like a failure.

I have found that the struggle I have just described is not uncommon among Christians. When asked what seems to be lacking the most in their spiritual lives, many Christians confess it is their prayer life.

How can one come to terms with prayer without going into extremes? For example, some become so spiritually minded in prayer, they cease to deal with the practical world around them. Other people create formulas about praying, only to rob its real purpose or potential. Some people become so confused or condemned in their prayer life that they become discouraged and walk in hopelessness.

It is only by God's help that I have come to terms with this subject. It is not unusual for people to complicate something that is quite simple. I know I have complicated prayer by making it a religious duty, a means of disciplining my Christian life. I still don't have all the answers about prayer, and the struggle remains. However, in spite of all of the confusing issues that surround prayer, I know how to come into peace about this subject in my spiritual life.

---

[1] John 10:1-18; 2 Corinthians 10:12-13

The first lesson I learned about prayer is that it is simple communication with God. This is why Jesus condemned repetitious or flamboyant prayers. It is meant to be an exchange between God and man. God is not interested in platitudes or flowery prayers. A Christian's time with God should be natural interaction and fellowship.

This is where we get into the art of communication. There are two important aspects to effective communication. The first one is to listen. Few Christians enter their prayer closet to listen to God. They come in to fulfill their duty or tell God what they want or desire, but not to listen.

The second aspect to effective communication is motivation. My motivation behind communication is to establish some kind of common ground with the person I am trying to develop a relationship with. In order to develop a relationship, my communication must be directed toward discovering who that person is. This means three things: 1) The conversation must be about the person and not about me; 2) I must truly listen to what the person is saying to understand what is important; and 3) I must seek to know that person for who he or she is.

Most communication with people begins at the point of self. Self-glorification in conversation is a sure way of proving to the rest of the world that you couldn't care less about their persons. You are simply out to be heard.

It is not unusual to encounter Christians of this caliber. There was one woman who spent all of her time talking as a means to receive what she considered the proper recognition. When she was not talking, she was judging others according to her perverted perception. Needless to say, no one lived up to this woman's expectations. She became critical towards everyone. Later, she wrote a letter to the church group to criticize and condemn them. Her evaluations were not only perverted, but also insane. Obviously, her conclusions were based on her vain imaginations and perverted expectations. As the people of the group struggled with her unwarranted and demonic accusations and abuse, they all had to come to one conclusion: she had no real concept of who they were as individuals. She had constantly talked, but she had never listened. Her only way of evaluating them was by sitting back and judging them for not bowing down to her expectations and paying idolatrous homage to her.

Communication involves true interaction that is directed at getting to know the individual. The idea of evaluating a person based on personal expectations is not a way of discovering that person's identity or character. Rather, it is a way to determine the worth of a person according to how he or she affects you. Obviously, this approach is not about knowing the other person, but a sinister means to make everything revolve around oneself.

This is how many Christians approach God in prayer. It is not about developing a relationship with God, but a means getting one's own way about a matter. Many individuals act as if God does not know them or really understands what they have need of. God knows every hair on our heads.[2] Many times He answers prayers before they are even spoken. The problem in man's relationship with God never rests with God's ignorance of man, but with man's ignorance of God. Many individuals know about God, but few know Him in a personal way. The focus of prayer should be to know God. We need to discover the depth of His glory, the beauty of His grace, the abiding power of His faithfulness, and the commitment of His heart.

This brings us to the real heart of prayer: identification. Relationship with God points to intimate fellowship or communion. Communion with God is for the purpose of identifying with Him. Effectual prayer simply means that a saint is identifying with the heart, mind, and will of God. The Apostle Paul made this statement in Romans 11:34, "For who hath known the mind of the Lord? or who hath been his counselor?" How can one know the real heart of God unless there is a viable communion taking place? Therefore, prayer is not a means to communicate our agendas to God, but to find out His agendas.

As I began to understand that prayer was simply communicating with God, I realized that it was not a matter of personal discipline on my part, but a matter or habit of making communication with God a natural course throughout my day.[3] As I submitted to this concept, I began to see how prayer disciplined me as far as my focus, goals, and direction. As communion with God became as natural as communicating with a close friend, I began to enjoy my life in God.

In most encounters with a new person, you have to listen to know how to open the person up. This is necessary to determine the extent of your relationship and ministry with that person. Most people like to talk about themselves, but there are others you must listen to, to know the right questions to ask because they will not volunteer much information.

The Word of God tells us how to get God's attention or draw Him out into the open so that we can learn of Him. We can find this important information in two of the Gospels—Matthew 7:7-11 and Luke 11:9-13. We are going to consider Luke 11:9-13. Luke 11:9 states, "And I say unto you, Ask, and it shall be given you; seek, and ye shall find; knock, and it shall be opened unto you."

These three responses are in correlation with the summary of Jesus' ministry among man. He said He was the way, the truth and the life.[4] As the way, Jesus will affect our focus and direction. As the truth, He will establish our perspective of God. Our perspective of God will determine our walk of faith. The type of faith we possess will establish not only our level of righteousness before God, but our life in Him.

---

[2] Matthew 10:30
[3] 1 Thessalonians 5:17
[4] John 14:6

As the Truth, Jesus will also set man free to pursue his life in God. This liberty will allow people to reach their potential in God.[5] As they reach their potential, they will discover the essence of real life that comes by way of greater revelation of Jesus. When Jesus becomes the life, people will discover what it means to possess resurrection power. Out of this type of life flows authority and power.

As you compare your responses with Jesus' ministry, you will begin to see the simple correlation. Jesus taught that if a person asks, it should be given to him or her. This is where the right request or question comes into play. Obviously, the concept of asking could not embrace just any area because many people ask God for various things and never receive the things for which they ask. Therefore, what should we ask God for to ensure that our request evokes a response from Him? It is simple. We need to ask Him to have His way in our lives.

The Israelites walked in unbelief because they did not know the ways of God. His ways are perfect and eternal, and they lead to righteousness and salvation.[6] Psalm 86:11 makes this request, "Teach me thy way, O LORD; I will walk in thy truth: unite my heart to fear thy name."

Asking God to have His way will test your faith. It implies that you are trusting God with all the details of your life. In our moments of zealousness, we declare that we trust Him with our salvation, but we refuse to put confidence in Him when it comes to the preferences of our personal lives. This lack of confidence reveals that such faith is a concept that makes safe declarations about unseen matters, but is clearly missing in present situations. After all, faith is reliance on God to have His way in all matters, and to trust Him in all circumstances. In fact, such reliance allows God to move incredible obstacles out of the way.[7]

Once you ask God to have His way, you must now seek it out. Only 60% may ask God to have His way, but only 35% bother to seek out this way in spirit and truth. Christians can prove to be complacent about possessing God. They are slothful in their pursuit to know Him. They may declare they want God, but it is on their terms. These terms are always self-serving and will avoid paying the necessary price to know God. Without paying the price, such people will end up abusing the things of God.

Every search will bring the person to the door of communion. This door will present obstacles as it represents judgment or separation. For example, you cannot enter this door carrying excess baggage of the old-life. Therefore, this spiritual door has a tendency to stop those who are slothful or self-serving. This is why it represents a test.

Ultimately, the door serves as a mirror. Is your motivation and desire to know God greater than the comfort zones and excuses of self? Will

---

[5] John 8:32-36
[6] 2 Samuel 22:31; Psalm 1:6; 18:3; 139:24; Hebrews 3:9-12
[7] Matthew 17:20; 1 Peter 1:6-8

you knock regardless of the circumstances? Will you be persistent until the door is open or will you give up before you finish the course?

People fail to enter this door for various reasons. They fear the other side of the door because of unbelief towards God. Some are too weary to be persevering in knocking. Such weariness is a result of people trying to live the Christian life in their own strength.[8] Then, there are those who are carnal people. They get bored with knocking because they lack commitment.

Knocking on the door is about exercising your faith in the character and commitment of God. Can you truly trust God that in His timing, the door will open? Will you stand assured that when the door opens, you will find eternal blessings on the other side? Jesus put it in this perspective in Luke 11:11-12, "If a son shall ask bread of any of you that is a father, will he give him a stone? Or if he asks a fish, will he for a fish give him a serpent? Or if he shall ask an egg, will he offer him a scorpion?" Do you trust God with your life and being? Is He who He says He is or is He a fraud who does not deserve your confidence? If you answer yes, do you trust Him with the presence of the different doors in your life?

If you choose to trust Him, He will open the door. What will you find on the other side of the door? You will find a greater revelation of Jesus Christ. This revelation will unveil greater depths of God. It will bring you higher in Him to discover greater truths. Each door, regardless of size and difficulty, represents possessing greater eternal treasures.

Finally, we come down to the main thrust or intent behind effectual prayer. Luke 11:13 reveals it to us, "If ye then, being evil, know how to give good gifts unto your children: how much more shall your heavenly Father give the Holy Spirit to them that ask Him?"

Matthew's Gospel leaves out the part about the Holy Spirit. However, Luke is clear that we need to ask God to give us His Spirit. The Holy Spirit is referred to as a gift and a promise.[9] This shows God's desire to give us the fullness of His life and blessings by giving us more of Himself in the presence and power of His Spirit. If a person is full of self, he or she will limit the reality of God. If he or she fails to seek God's way, he or she will prevent the Holy Spirit from penetrating every area of his or her life.

A person needs to persistently knock on the door of communion until it opens. Once it is open, the Holy Spirit will be able to enlarge his or her boundaries to discover God in greater measure.

Prayer is not a complicated matter. It is about God, not about you or me. To discover God, we must get past self and become identified with His heart, mind and will. Our motivation has to be pure as we seek after Him as an inquisitive child. We must have one main focus, ask for His

---

[8] Hebrew 12:2
[9] Luke 24:49; Acts 2:38;

way, seek for His truth, and knock until the door is opened to commune with Him and to possess His life in greater measure.[10]

How is your prayer life? Is it about you or discovering the reality of God? Are you talking or listening? Do you desire to commune with Him or is your association with Him based on self-serving purposes? There is a way to test your prayer life. How much of the unseen treasure of heaven do you possess? This will reveal whether you have an effectual prayer life.

---

[10] John 14:6

3

THE GOAL

...Our Father which art in heaven....
(Matthew 6:9)

Religious people struggle with the concept of addressing God when it comes to prayer. Are there certain criteria, terms, opening statements, or proper acknowledgement that would catch God's attention? After all, who would not like to immediately acquire God's attention in times of prayer?

When the disciples asked Jesus to teach them to pray, He provided a model prayer. He confirmed this when He instructed them to pray in this manner or in this fashion. We refer to this model prayer as the "Lord's Prayer." This is incorrect because it had nothing to do with Jesus' prayer life. He was providing a model for His disciples that would bring understanding of the attitude, purpose, and goal behind effective prayer.

Today, many people use this model prayer found in Matthew 6:9-13 as a catchall prayer. It serves as a safe prayer that covers all bases, but sadly, it has become a repetitious prayer that has no meaning or purpose. This type of approach to any prayer leaves it lifeless. The model prayer established by Jesus is simply a form or pattern that allows a person to see the heart, purpose, and goal of prayer. It is a means to reveal the attitude or disposition behind effectual prayer.

One of the struggles I have had in my prayer life is to Whom I should direct my prayer. Christians have voiced concerns about the confusion they feel when appealing to God. For example, which Person of the Godhead am I addressing or invoking?

Prayer is never meant to get God's attention, for He is not asleep or indifferent to our lives. It is simply a means to discipline the person's focus and attention, so that God can speak. It is never a means to invoke God, for He is always ready to do His will and good pleasure through His people. However, it is a way of provoking a person to consider Who he or she is addressing.[1] If a person has a right attitude towards God, prayer will provoke him or her to lift up God in praise, adoration, and worship.

Prayer is about getting a hold of God. Scripture reveals that all three Persons of the Godhead are involved in effectual prayer. My struggle

---

[1] Psalm 121:3-4; Ephesians 1:5, 9; Philippians 2:13

over this issue has shown me that there are two Persons of the Godhead who can be personally addressed in prayer. I have also recognized that the approach or attitude of prayer is often based on Who is being addressed and for what purpose. For example, I open some prayers with an appeal to the "Lord GOD Almighty." When I approach God in this matter, I am appealing to all three Persons of the Godhead to appropriate their intervention and power in an effective way.

Another term I use to address God is "LORD." Notice the word "lord" is in all caps. When I use this term, I do so in light of Isaiah 45:3 and 5, that I, the LORD, which call thee by name, am the God of Israel...I am the LORD, and there is none else, there is no God beside me." When I say LORD, I am acknowledging in my mind and believing in my heart that He is the one true God and Savior. He is in fact, the covenant keeping God. I am calling to Him, seeking His will and way for my life. My concept of powerful prayer is that it must be properly targeted to give God the room to respond. He is Lord over all. Understanding Who He is invokes a certain attitude in me as well. The way I address God is often determined by my understanding of the work of the three Persons of the Godhead. By understanding both the nature of God and the distinct work of the three Persons of the Godhead, prayer can become an effective means of witnessing the intervention of God in light of His nature and covenants.

You see this same type of approach to God with the men and women of the Bible. In fact, it is interesting to see how these people addressed God. Sometimes, the word "Lord" is in all caps, while at other times, the word "God" is in all caps. I realize that the different emphasis of these words has to do with God's different names, but there is clearly a personal side behind the usage of them as well. The way that the different names of God are used recognizes various aspects of Him as Creator and owner. For example, a particular name or usage of that name can connect you at the point of His covenant, to His will, power, inheritance, blessings, and grace. I am not an expert on such matters, but people of prayer personally know God, and will have a sense of how to connect with Him. The way they address Him is a very personal matter.

I use these different names to express my own personal knowledge of God when I approach Him. My approach to Him is not based on any formula, but on a personal knowledge about Who He is and His work in my life. After all, the three Persons of the Godhead are involved in every aspect of a person's Christianity. By understanding their distinct work, there can be more clarity in approaching Him.

Let's consider how some of the following people approached God. As you will see, there is a personal awareness of Who He is to these individuals. This is not only found in their approach, but in their attitude. For example, Hannah addressed God as LORD in her prayer of rejoicing for an answered prayer. In her prayer, she honored His work of salvation and His faithfulness and compassion.[2]

After God established a promise of an everlasting kingdom with King David, he addressed Him as "O Lord GOD." Obviously, David was recognizing His sovereign ability to carry out His will and promises even for generations to come.[3]

In the dedication of the temple, King Solomon called upon the "LORD God of Israel." Israel was the only nation that knew the true God of heaven. They knew Him to be "Jehovah," Lord over all. This term has to do with identification. The God of Israel was being addressed in light of the people who had been redeemed by His intervention.[4]

In Ezra's prayer of adoration, he addressed God in two ways, bringing the past and present together. This prayer has to do with identification. The first type of identification has to do with history: "LORD God of our fathers." History, in light of God, points to His faithfulness to uphold His Word and His power to bring forth His promises. The second type of identification was "LORD my God." Ezra was acknowledging that his present Lord was the same One who could be traced back to the God of his father.[5]

When Daniel addressed his Lord in intercession on behalf of Israel, he referred to Him as, "O Lord, the great and dreadful God" (Daniel 9:4). He was recognizing His holiness in order to appeal to His mercy and grace.

In her prayer of adoration and submission, the handmaiden Mary addressed God as both "Lord" and "God my Saviour." The term "Lord" stipulated her Master or authority, and God her Saviour revealed her personal status and need before the One Who was entrusting her with the Promised Messiah.[6]

In His prayer, Jesus addressed the Father. This shows relationship. Obviously, Jesus was recognizing His place and showing His submission to the Father's will and heart.[7]

One of the terms I have a problem with is when the Father is referred to as "Daddy." I realize the term comes from "Abba, Father" in Romans 8:15. This term points to a relationship of a child to the father. "Daddy" is a sweet, sincere term, but the usage of it today often speaks of blatant abuse. There is no respect or awe in it. Many of the people I hear using it sound like spoiled children who are demanding something from their father. This concerns me. If Jesus, who was the only begotten Son, approached God, the Father, in a reverent, respectful way, and

---

[2] 1 Samuel 2:1-10
[3] 2 Samuel 7:19-22
[4] 2 Chronicles 6:5
[5] Ezra 7:27-28
[6] Luke 2:46-54
[7] John 17:1

addressed Him accordingly, who are we to do differently? I also recognize that it depends on attitude, but I feel that "Abba, Father" encourages and maintains the proper attitude more than "Daddy." I may be a child of God, but I must never forget Who I am approaching. He is God, and He deserves my awe, respect, and worship.

It is vital that a person strive to personally know God. Scripture commands us to seek to know God.[8] Daniel 11:32 confirms the importance of personally knowing God, "...but the people that do know their God shall be strong, and do exploits." Knowing God allows a person to stand strong in prayer because he or she believes God about a matter. Standing strong in God is what ensures exploits. Therefore, personal knowledge of God will establish a prayer life that will be powerful, individual, and distinct from others.

Sometimes, I use the name of Jesus when I approach the throne. In the right spirit, this name can make hell tremble and demons flee. Anytime I use Jesus' name, I am trying to encourage one of two atmospheres: that of worship or deliverance. The name of Jesus in true worship can bring the presence of God down in a powerful way. This will open up the way into the Most Holy Place.

Jesus stated that He was the only way to the Father.[9] He serves as a door into a relationship with the Father. He became this door when He died on the cross. The veil of the temple was ripped from the top to the bottom, opening up the Most Holy Place to the common man.[10] The writer of Hebrews made this connection in Hebrews 10:19-20: "Having therefore, brethren, boldness to enter into the holiest by the blood of Jesus, By a new and living way, which he hath consecrated for us, through the veil, that is to say, his flesh."

In intense spiritual battles, Jesus' very name establishes an authority that is able to push back the powers of hell.[11] Jesus talked about this authority in Matthew 16:18, "And I say also unto thee, That thou art Peter, and upon this rock I will build my church; and the gates of hell shall not prevail against it."

In His closing remarks in Matthew 28:18, He stated, "All power is given unto me in heaven and in earth."

In the model prayer, the Father is being addressed. The first point we must recognize is that we are talking to someone who is real. Even though He cannot be seen because He is spirit, He is a person who can be approached.[12] Therefore, the Father is not a concept or a romantic notion. He resides in heaven. This means our prayers must be directed to someone who is not of this world. His title reminds us of what our

---

[8] Jeremiah 29:13; Amos 5:4-8
[9] John 14:6
[10] Matthew 27:51
[11] Luke 10:17-20
[12] John 4:24: 5:37

position is in light of Him—that of a child. John 1:12-13 confirms this, "But as many as received him, to them gave he power to become the sons of God, even to them that believe on his name: Which were born, not of blood, nor of the will of the flesh, nor of the will of man, but of God."

Based on what Jesus accomplished on the cross, as believers, we can approach Him in child-like faith and appeal to Him as a loving Father with the goal of knowing Him in an intimate way. This personal introduction to Him reveals His heart. He wants to intimately commune with each of us. First, we must get past the temporary to embrace the eternal.

At the heart of the desire to commune with us is the Father's incredible love toward us. 1 John 3:1 states, "Behold, what manner of love the Father hath bestowed upon us, that we should be called the sons of God: therefore the world knoweth us not, because it knew him not." It is the Father Who sent the Son to reach out to the world and die on the cross on our behalf.[13] Jesus made this fact clear.

It was Jesus' love toward the Father that enabled Him to carry out His will to bring each of us back into a relationship with our Creator. However, Jesus' love for us is contingent upon our being loved by the Father. The Father's love hinges on us keeping Jesus' commandments.[14] This shows us that the Father's love is extended to all, but it can only be experienced in the right environment. Therefore, it is not unconditional as many people present it. In other words, God's love may be extended towards a person, but that does not mean the individual will receive it, thereby, benefitting from it.

God is love. It was out of love that He provided salvation. This devoted love is associated with the Father. People must receive this salvation to encounter the incredible love of the Father. Otherwise, they will not encounter a loving God, but His condemnation because they did not believe upon the Son of God.[15]

Whenever the word "God" is used in conjunction with the "Son" or the "Holy Ghost," it is in reference to the Father. 1 Corinthians 8:6 confirms this, "But to us there is but one God, the Father, of whom are all things, and we in him; and one Lord Jesus Christ, by whom are all things, and we by him."

2 Corinthians 13:14 beautifully brings out the distinction of the three Persons of the Godhead, "The grace of the Lord Jesus Christ, and the love of God, and the communion of the Holy Ghost, be with you all. Amen." Grace is associated with Jesus for He is full of grace and truth, and it is by grace that we are saved. Love is linked to the Father, for He so loved the world that He sent His only begotten Son to secure

---

[13] John 14:24; 20:21
[14] Luke 22:42; John 14:21
[15] 1 John 4:8; John 3:16-19

salvation. Communion is associated with the Holy Ghost. Communion points to agreement and fellowship. It is the Holy Ghost's responsibility to bring us into agreement and fellowship with God and with each other in the right spirit according to truth.[16]

The Father sent the Spirit to bring forth communion. Jesus is the door to this communion, but the Holy Ghost leads people through this incredible door into the presence of the Father. Jesus' main goal is to bring reconciliation between God and man. This is why He clarified that He was the way to the Father, the truth about Whom He is, and is the One Who establishes a person in a life or relationship with the Father.[17]

In John 14:13-14, Jesus made this statement, "And whatsoever ye shall ask in my name, that will I do, that the Father may be glorified in the Son. If ye shall ask anything, I will do it." These Scripture verses show us that we must come by way of Jesus. The concept of asking in His name does not mean that His name serves as a magic wand or word in prayer. His name mainly refers to Who He is. If you study Jesus' name throughout Scripture, you will see how it is used to reveal His character. To be effective, everything in a Christian's prayer life must line up to the cornerstone of Jesus Christ.[18]

This gives us another insight into the purpose of effectual prayer: That the Father will be glorified in it. Therefore, our prayers must ultimately glorify God in intent and purpose. If they fail to do so, they cannot be properly honored.

Finally, the only person of the Godhead who is never personally or directly addressed in prayer is the Holy Ghost. Scripture shows us that we must either go to the Father or to the Son in order to encounter greater measures of the Holy Ghost in regard to our spiritual lives. He is the promise and gift of the Father. Jesus confirmed this in John 14:16 and 26. This brings out a very important point, you never directly go to the promise to see it fulfilled. Rather, you go to the One who gave the promise to ensure its fulfillment. You never seek the gift. Rather, you seek the one who gives it. Clearly, we must not personally seek the Holy Spirit; rather we must give way to His leading and work. As a result, we are told that one of the areas He leads us in and must work through is prayer. He is the One who prays through us in line with the heart of God. Obviously, in prayer He would never address Himself. [19]

This brings us to the different work of the Holy Spirit and of Jesus. The Spirit's responsibility is to exalt Jesus as a means to convict the world of sin. He will also lead followers to the knowledge or truth of

---

[16] John 1:14; 3:16; Ephesians 2:8; 4:12-16
[17] John 14:6-7, 26: 16:13; 2 Corinthians 5:18-19
[18] 1 Peter 2:6-8
[19] Luke 11:13; 24:49; John 7:37-39; Acts 1:8; 2:38; Romans 8:26-27

Jesus as He works His very life in us. Jesus, on the other hand, points to the will and the purpose of the Father being realized in our lives.[20]

The Holy Ghost gently works behind the scenes. He dwells within the believer, therefore, serving as the abiding presence of God in this world. He serves as the legal seal or witness of heaven, verifying that a believer has been adopted into the heavenly family, and is heir to an eternal inheritance.[21]

A believer is a vessel, and as he or she gives way to the Holy Ghost, he or she becomes His vessel and means to communicate with the Father. As a result, the Spirit is the One Who inspires and empowers effectual prayer. Such prayer will reach up to the Father in compliance with His will and for His glory.

Obviously, to effectively stand in prayer, believers must seek to know God and understand His work. Continual submission to the Holy Ghost will usher the person through the door of Jesus, right into the presence of the Father. It is in His presence that one can enjoy the Father's heart, joy, and commitment.

As a child of God, have you ever been in the presence of the Father? If your answer is no, you have failed to take advantage of your position and relationship with the Father. As a result, your prayer life probably falls short in making a difference in heaven and on earth.

---

[20] John 16:7-13, John 5:30; 6:38-40
[21] Romans 8:14-17; Ephesians 1:11-14

4

THE ATTITUDE

Hallowed be thy name.
(Matthew 6:9c)

People try to invoke God in various ways. They use His Word, promises, bargaining, and flattery to try and stir Him up to respond to their requests. The Word is adamant about what God responds to: the right attitude. Psalm 34:18 confirms this: "The LORD is nigh unto them that are of a broken heart; and saveth such as be of a contrite spirit." A broken heart points to an open heart desirous of God, and a contrite, repentant, humble spirit before Him.

The last part of 1 Peter 5:5 through verse 6 reinforces this simple truth about attitude, "...and be clothed with humility: for God resisteth the proud, and giveth grace to the humble. Humble yourselves therefore under the mighty hand of God, that he may exalt you in due time." Answered prayer is a matter of grace. In other words, no one person deserves God's attention to any matter. This is why the throne we come before is referred to as the "throne of grace."[1]

Grace is an attribute of God. He does not answer prayer because of who we are, but because of who He is. Therefore, prayer should always begin with the reality of who He is. He does things solely according to His character, will, and ways. It must be about what He wants to accomplish in a person's life or in a situation, and ends with the reality of His abiding presence.

We see this attitude when God's people approached Him in regard to certain matters. For example, Moses approached God according to His reputation when it came to Him destroying the Israelites after they refused to enter the Promised Land. In fact, he came to God in confidence because he knew His character. He was bold in intercession because he knew God's desire. He appealed to His power in light of restraint, not judgment. He basically reasoned with God. He reminded Him of His reputation among the pagans, and His great power to carry out His will in light of His longsuffering and great mercy.[2]

Hannah rejoiced in who God is: LORD. She acknowledged His holiness and declared Him to be her Horn, Rock, and Judge. She exalted

---

[1] Hebrews 4:16
[2] Numbers 14:13-18

Him in His ability to subdue enemies. She brought out His just ways to bring down the proud and mighty men, and how He showed His compassion by exalting the poor in spirit.[3]

King David acknowledged his smallness in the sight of God's greatness. He also recognized His commitment towards an undeserving servant such as himself, and His redemption of Israel. He acknowledged God's greatness and that His words are true. Therefore, he could believe and trust Him to fulfill all promises.[4]

In his dedication of the temple in 1 Kings 8, King Solomon declared there was only one God. He acknowledged His mercy and promise to his father, David. He then said this in 1 Kings 8:27, "But will God indeed dwell on the earth? behold, the heaven and heaven of heavens cannot contain thee; how much less this house that I have builded?" Solomon had a sense of God's greatness. Nothing could contain God, but God still makes His incredible presence known to His people in spite of His vastness and glory.

In his prayer of confession, Daniel first set his face and prepared himself. He then acknowledged the mercy, holiness, and greatness of God before he confessed the iniquity of Israel. The realization of sin in light of God's character created a proper attitude in Daniel to approach God on behalf of Israel. Daniel never asked God to be any less then He was, a righteous God. However, He was asking Him to regard Israel in light of His mercies.[6] Many times our prayers would require God to cease to be who He is. He is perfect, and you can see where Daniel was asking God to regard the plight of Israel for His sake, in light of His character.

Mary, the mother of the Man, Christ Jesus, talked about how her soul magnified the Lord. She was rejoicing because He had regarded her. She recognized His power and praised Him for His mercy. Like Hannah, Mary also made reference to how He brings down the arrogant and exalts those seeking after Him.[7]

Each of these people displayed a proper attitude towards God. Their attitude can be observed in how they approached God. David sat in awe, and Solomon stood with arms lifted up in surrender, praise, and worship. Daniel approached God in sackcloth and fell before Him in a prostrate position. The attitude of these people was a product of personally knowing God. They recognized Who He was, and their own status in light of His awesome attributes. This gave them the authority and confidence to approach Him in light of His grace.

Sadly, most people approach God with an attitude of pride. They perceive that they are worthy of His attention and blessings. They

[3] 1 Samuel 2:1-10
[4] 2 Samuel 7:17-29
[6] Daniel 9:4-19
[7] Luke 1:45-54

become insulted when He remains silent before them. This silence usually means He is resisting their arrogant attitude.[8]

Jesus clearly defines the acceptable attitude by using the word "hallow". "Hallow" in this text means to consecrate something in order to separate it or make it holy.[9] Consecration is our responsibility. It means we are separating something from those things that would defile the work and ways of God in our lives.

Jesus then goes on to clarify what must be consecrated: God's name. "Name" points to both God's character and authority.[10] Therefore, God's name immediately brings forth identification as to whom we are addressing. The reference to His name should remind us of the third commandment, "Thou shalt not take the name of the LORD thy God in vain; for the LORD will not hold him guiltless that taketh his name in vain" (Exodus 20:7).

If someone truly knows Jehovah God, His name will invoke reverence and worship, not indifference or rebellion. When people use God's name outside of a right attitude, it becomes an offense to Him. The reason for this is because He is the only One who has a legitimate right to be called God or recognized as deity. He alone is God, and there are no other gods before Him or beside Him. This is why the third commandment is preceded by the first two commandments that denounce all forms of idolatry.[11]

The name "God" identifies an entity that stands apart from all creation, including man. At the mention of His name, hearts should bow, minds immediately should become focused, and bodies posed in humility. His name should silence wandering thoughts, cause doubts to flee, drown out the world's activities, and prepare trembling lips to proclaim His majesty and glorious ways. God's name should automatically cause worship.

The reason for this response comes down to Who He is. He is a holy God who stands distinct in heaven. In fact, He is recognized for His holiness, for even the seraphim covered their faces in His presence.[12] The writer of Hebrews made this observation about His holiness, "Wherefore we receiving a kingdom which cannot be moved, let us have grace, whereby we may serve God acceptably with reverence and godly fear: For our God is a consuming fire" (Hebrews 12:28-29).

King David made this statement in 2 Samuel 7:23,
> And what one nation in the earth is like thy people, even like Israel, whom God went to redeem for a people to himself, and to make him a name, and to do for you great things and

---

[8] Luke 18:1-4

[9] Strong's Exhaustive Concordance of the Bible; #37

[10] Ibid; #3686

[11] Exodus 20:3-5; Isaiah 45:21-22

[12] Isaiah 6:2

terrible, for thy land, before thy people, which thou redeemedst
to thee from Egypt, from the nations and their gods?

Obviously, God wanted to make Himself a name among His people that
would stand distinct and separate from all other peoples and nations. He
did this by redeeming Israel. In 2 Samuel 7:26, David requested that
God's name be magnified or lifted up.

God chose the temple of Jerusalem on which to put His name as a
constant reminder of His desire to dwell among men. It was King David's
heart to build a house for the name of the LORD God of Israel. As we
know, it was Solomon who built the temple.

God told Solomon that He wanted to put His name on the temple
forever. Solomon in turn asked the Lord to forgive those who had gone
astray if they turned towards the temple, confessed His name and
forsook their sin. He asked Him to answer prayers so, "that all people of
the earth may know thy name and fear thee" (2 Chronicles 6:33).[13]

The handmaiden Mary declared, "...and holy is his name" (Luke
1:49). His very name should instill fear, awe, and humility in us. His
name should be exalted in His people's hearts and minds, as well as on
their lips. This can clearly be seen as His people constantly exalted His
name.

Hebrews shows us that we dare not approach God flippantly. We
must know and acknowledge Who we are approaching. He is holy!
Holiness in the life of the saint is not an option. Peter insists that since
God is holy, His people must be holy. The writer of Hebrews warns that
without holiness, people will not see the Lord.[14]

In heaven, we see ongoing worship. It must be glorious to hear the
worship of heaven as those around His throne declare God's holiness
and recognize His worthiness to be honored, adored, and exalted. It
must be wondrous to witness all crowns being cast before the One who
possesses all power, riches, wisdom, strength, honor, glory, and blessing
of heaven.[15]

Jesus is implying in the model prayer that before we approach God,
we must have this awareness of how distinct and separate He is from all
creation. The glory of man cannot begin to hold a glimmer of light in the
light of His glory. The beauty of the world would immediately fade in the
light of the majesty of heaven. The power of governments would flee at
the revelation of His power. In the end, all the power, glory, and beauty
of man and the world will come into subjection to the Lord's power,
beauty, and glory. And, at that time the fading beauty and glory of the
world will all be turned into darkness and judgment.

His name not only stipulates His identity, but His authority. God has
the authority and power to move heaven and earth to answer people's

---

[13] I Kings 9:2-8; 2 Chronicles 6:6-7, 26
[14] Hebrews 12:14; 1 Peter 1:15-16
[15] Revelation 4:9-11; 5:11-14

prayers. King David recognized this in his prayer, "And now, O LORD God, the word that thou hast spoken concerning thy servant and concerning his house, establish it for ever, and do as thou hast said. And let thy name be magnified for ever" (2 Samuel 7:25-26).

Those who know their God know that all of creation and its elements are at His disposal. He will show Himself mighty and worthy of all praise and worship because He will keep His promises and preserve His covenants. Daniel knew this when he interceded on behalf of Israel. Jeremiah had prophesied that Jerusalem would lie in waste for 70 years. Daniel knew the 70 years were up and it was time for Israel to return home.[16]

When Mary discovered that God had chosen her to be the mother of the Promised Messiah, she did not debate with Him. She chose to believe Him and submit to His work. She simply praised Him for choosing her to bring forth the Anointed One.[17]

God is not limited on any front to bring forth His promises except in one area: man's faith. Faith comes down to a person's perception of God. People limit God because their perception of Him is often self-centered and worldly. They actually bring Him down to their way of thinking and doing. Even though the Word is clear about God being beyond the limited and perverted thoughts and ways of man, people continue to think of God in terms of themselves, not according to His character.[18]

This limited perspective often demotes the idea of God into a puppet that can be impressed, bribed, or controlled. Such faith is directed at what God can do, rather than who He is. God never reacts according to His abilities, but only in line with His character. This is why a person must get His character right before he or she appeals to Him in light of His power.

Distinction of God must take place on a personal level. Each person must personally consecrate or set God apart. The Apostle Peter actually gives us insight in accomplishing this feat. "But sanctify the Lord God in your hearts..." (1 Peter 3:15). God must be your only God. He must take center stage in your focus, affections, and devotion.

Ezekiel also talked about the idols of the heart and mind.[19] Idols of this nature reside in secret corridors of the heart or in high places of imagination that are inconspicuous. This makes these idols hard to detect. They often reign unhindered because few ever check out their agendas, rights, and where their affections are being directed. This is why the Apostle Paul gave us this instruction in Colossians 3:2, "Set your affection on things above, not on things on the earth."

---

[16] Daniel 9:2
[17] Luke 1:28-38
[18] Isaiah 55:8-9
[19] Ezekiel 8:6-12; 14:3-8

Affections directed at any source other than God are idolatrous in nature. It means someone or something holds our heart besides God. God will not share our affections or reign with any other gods. Therefore, to sanctify Him in our hearts requires us to love Him with our whole heart.[20] It is love that will exalt God to a place of authority, adoration, and worship.

The heart where God has been sanctified is singular in love, purpose, and service.[21] Such a heart points to an undivided heart. A divided heart is where a person circumvents his or her heart with excuses that will justify ungodly attitudes and actions. These individuals find themselves struggling as their heart is pulled in various directions. Division keeps a person from focusing and walking in the straight path.

King David had a heart that was focused. This was made obvious by his walk before King Saul. 1 Samuel 18:5a and 14 says, "And David went out whithersoever Saul sent him, and behaved himself wisely... And David behaved himself wisely in all his ways; and the LORD was with him."

David knew his God. He walked according to the character of His God, rather than those around him. 1 Kings 9:4 reveals the virtue behind David's walk, "And if thou wilt walk before me, as David thy father walked, in integrity of heart and in uprightness..." David was both honest and humble before the Lord. His integrity kept him on the narrow path of wisdom and discretion before God and his enemies. One cannot have this type of integrity without possessing a healthy fear of God.

We should come to God in a reverent manner. We have this example in the prayer lives of the David's, Daniel's and Mary's. We should display the wisdom and discretion that come out of possessing a realistic understanding of whom God is. This godly fear will produce godly submission. The Apostle Paul made reference to this submission in Ephesians 5:21, "Submitting yourselves one to another in the fear of God."

There is great authority in godly submission, for it gives way to that which is worthy and excellent for the sake of God and the benefit of others. It is sacrificial in disposition and obedient in action. As a result, it allows the person to walk in the power and authority of God.

The combination of a humble heart, integrity, and godly submission produces a right attitude before God. It will allow God to be God, as it displays wisdom and discretion towards His ways. It will confidently declare God's promises for it will be cognizant of the seasons and times. Most of all, God will draw near to such a person with this attitude. When God draws near, you can be assured that you will have His ear.

---

[20] Mark 12:29-34
[21] Ephesians 6:5-7

5

THE DESIRE

Thy kingdom come...
Matthew 6:10

The next part of the model prayer has to do with God's kingdom. How many of us perceive the importance of coming to terms with the concept of the kingdom of God? Obviously, it is significant because it is placed first in line as far as the requests that are to be made to God. This request in regard to His kingdom points to desire. According to Jesus, the first desire a Christian should have is to see God's kingdom come forth in power and glory on earth.

It is important to define kingdom. According to *Strong's Exhaustive Concordance*, kingdom points to royalty.[1] This clearly implies that royalty or a king governs a kingdom. In the case of God's kingdom, believers already must know where to direct their allegiance and loyalty. The Apostle Paul makes this clear in 1 Timothy 6:14-15, "That thou keep his commandment without spot, unrebukeable, until the appearing of our Lord Jesus Christ: Which in his times he shall shew, who is the blessed and only Potentate, the King of kings, and Lord of lords."

The Apostle John said this about Jesus, "And he hath on his vesture and on his thigh a name written, KING OF KINGS, AND LORD OF LORDS" (Revelation 19:16).

Kingdom also points to a realm or dominion. Today, there is much controversy over what constitutes the kingdom of God. Many people advocate that it is up to believers to usher in the kingdom of God on this earth before Jesus will come back to reign. To many, this means taking dominion over the earth. However, is this concept an incorrect presentation?

In 2 Samuel 7:12-16, King David made reference to who will establish this kingdom. He clearly stated that God would bring forth this kingdom and not man. This kingdom will be forever. The angel confirmed this to Mary in Luke 1:33 when he made this proclamation about Jesus: "And he shall reign over the house of Jacob for ever; and of his kingdom there shall be no end." Once again, man can only establish what is temporary, while all that God ordains and institutes is forever.

In Mark 1:14-15, Jesus is preaching the Gospel of the kingdom of God saying, "The time is fulfilled, and the kingdom of God is at hand:

---

[1] # 932

repent ye, and believe the gospel." Jesus was saying that God's kingdom was drawing near to those who were hearing His message. In order to embrace, partake of, or become part of this kingdom, one had to turn from his or her present way and believe the Gospel or good news.

What is the Gospel or good news? It is that the long-awaited for King and Messiah had come to fulfill God's promises. The essence of becoming part of this kingdom required one to embrace the King.

Jesus made this statement in Matthew 6:33, "But seek ye first the kingdom of God, and his righteousness; and all these things shall be added unto you." Here again, Jesus is reiterating the believer's responsibility to first seek the kingdom of God. We must note that the heavenly kingdom is referred to as the kingdom of God and the kingdom of heaven. Is there a difference? I have concluded from my studies that the kingdom of God is associated to God's will being done in heaven and on earth, while the kingdom of heaven has to do with His work being accomplished on earth or within the lives of men.[2]

However, do God's followers seek some kind of location, physical realm, or dominion as some advocate today? No! The Word clearly tells us to seek God. Jesus said to first seek Him for He is the source of God's kingdom, work of redemption, and the essence of righteousness. If a believer chooses this initial pursuit, he or she can be assured that all needs will be provided for.

Therefore, it is erroneous to seek God's kingdom outside of Jesus. Acts 28:23 makes reference to this fact, "And when they had appointed him a day, there came many to him into his lodging; to whom he expounded and testified the kingdom of God, persuading them concerning Jesus, both out of the law of Moses, and out of the prophets, from morning till evening." The Apostle Paul was contending with others about the kingdom of God in relationship to Jesus.

Luke 21:31 says, "So likewise ye, when ye see these things come to pass, know ye that the kingdom of God is nigh at hand." This instruction is about the end days. What is near?

Luke 21:28 answers the question, "And when these things begin to come to pass, then look up, and lift up your heads; for your redemption draweth nigh." Both Scripture verses are about Jesus Christ's second coming.

If you possess Jesus, you possess the kingdom of God. One must consider what it takes to possess Jesus. John 3:5 says, "...I say unto thee, Except a man be born of water and of the Spirit, he cannot enter into the kingdom of God." According to Matthew 25:34; 1 Corinthians 6:9, and Galatians 5:21, you will actually inherit this kingdom. Obviously, a person must first be born into it before he or she can lay claim to the inheritance associated with this kingdom. The spiritual birth comes from

[2] Jeremiah 29:13; 1Corinthians 1:30; Philippians 4:19

above, and it brings some type of identification. However, what does this have to do with Jesus Christ?

Matthew 18:3 gives us this insight, "Verily I say unto you, Except ye be converted, and become as little children, ye shall not enter into the kingdom of heaven."[3] To be born again, people must regress in self-importance by turning from their self-sufficient ways. Then they must come to Jesus, recognizing personal sin in order to receive in sincerity their need for salvation. This regression points to a change in disposition and perception. Such a change is necessary for receiving the provision of salvation that comes through Jesus. When we come with the open heart and hands of a child, God can impart Jesus to us as Savior and Lord. His presence and reign are represented by the presence of the Spirit of God in our lives.[4] This constitutes the born-again experience

At the point of salvation, a person is placed in Jesus Christ, the Vine.[5] There, he or she depends on the Vine to supply all needs and govern all spiritual growth. Therefore, the key to realizing the kingdom of God is abiding in the King.

This brings us to leadership. The Word is clear that there is only one king or ruler in this kingdom. Amazingly, my secular dictionary associates the word "kingdom" with the eternal kingship of God.[6]

A kingdom does embrace a realm or dominion. However, does the kingdom of God include a physical realm as some are advocating today? Jesus answered this question in John 18:36, "My kingdom is not of this world: if my kingdom were of this world, then would my servants fight, that I should not be delivered to the Jews: but now is my kingdom not from hence." God's kingdom is not of this world. In other words, it does not operate from the basis of the world or according to it.

The Apostle Paul said this about the makeup of the kingdom of God in Romans 14:17, "For the kingdom of God is not meat and drink; but righteousness, and peace, and joy in the Holy Ghost." It is not a fleshly kingdom that depends on the world for its substance or purpose. Most kingdoms are designed to rule with a worldly emphasis from a fleshly nature. God's kingdom is of a spiritual nature. It works in the unseen world. Jesus related it to a costly hidden treasure that must be discovered, and a net that is cast into the sea.[7] It cannot be seen by the naked eye.

---

[3] The kingdom of God is also used in many cases as synonymous with the kingdom of heaven. You can see this by comparing *Matthew 18:4* with *Mark 10:14.* The main point is that God is the sovereign ruler and the kingdom of God which would also embrace the kingdom of heaven.

[4] 1 Corinthians 3:16

[5] John 15:1-7; 1 Corinthians 1:30

[6] Webster's New Collegiate Dictionary © 1976 by G. & C. Merriam Co.

[7] Matthew 13:44-48

Where is this kingdom found? It is found in the hearts of those who believe God. People, not earthly or worldly realms, make up the kingdom of God. Fruits and power can only distinguish or identify this kingdom. The Apostle Paul made reference to this when he said that the kingdom of God was righteousness, peace, and joy. Here we see that fruits confirm the existence of this kingdom in a person's life.[8] These fruits will attract others to His kingdom.

The second form of identification to God's kingdom is power. 1 Corinthians 4:20 says, "For the kingdom of God is not in word, but in power." People will not catch a glimpse of this kingdom by the words that are said, but by the power that backs up the words with authority.

Christians may talk about authority and power, but how many display it in their devotion to God and in their lives? Many appear to live powerless lives. There is no power in the Gospel they claim to believe. There is no power to overcome the world, the flesh, and the devil. There is no power to live the Christian life in victory when circumstances are overwhelming.

Keep in mind that both the fruit and the power point to the Holy Ghost. The Holy Ghost is the seal that identifies us to this kingdom. He makes the King real to each believer. As each saint submits to the sovereign rule of Jesus, the Holy Ghost begins to do the work of sanctification by developing the King's disposition in him or her.[9]

This brings us to our position and responsibility in this kingdom. The first thing we must recognize is that we are citizens of this heavenly kingdom. Our patriotism, allegiance, and loyalty must be solely to Jesus. As citizens of heaven, Christians are entrusted with two responsibilities: 1) Preach the Gospel and 2) make disciples of Christ.

Preaching the Gospel is the means of stirring up and attracting people to this kingdom. It offers hope and salvation. In fact, it is the power of God unto salvation.[10] This power does not rest in the message alone, but in the Spirit behind it. The Apostle Paul confirmed this in 1 Thessalonians 1:5, "For our gospel came not unto you in word only, but also in power, and in the Holy Ghost..." Not only do believers have the power to carry out their responsibility, but they also have the authority.

Saints have been made ambassadors for this kingdom.[11] An ambassador is the highest government official who represents the interest of his or her country in a foreign nation or kingdom. Believers need to remember they are representing the King of kings in a foreign place, and not their own interests. Yet, many Christians live for this present world, while representing personal interests that have nothing to

---

[8] Matthew 7:15-16; Romans 14:17; Galatians 5:22-23
[9] John 16:13-14; Romans 15:16-20; Ephesians 1:13-19
[10] Philippians 3:20; Matthew 28:18-20; Mark 16:15; Romans 1:16
[11] 2 Corinthians 5:18-19

do with the kingdom of God. Therefore, they fail to adhere to their position and responsibility in this unseen, eternal kingdom.

Jesus gave this contrast in regard to discipling people in Matthew 5:19, "Whosoever therefore shall break one of these least commandments, and shall teach men so, he shall be called the least in the kingdom of heaven: but whosoever shall do and teach them, the same shall be called great in the kingdom of heaven." Discipling people comes by two main avenues: example and teaching. Jesus stated that those who obey (His examples) and teach His commandments will be great in God's kingdom, but those who discard them and teach others to do the same will be least.

The Gospel presents the keys to the kingdom of God, but discipleship is about putting the Christian life into daily practice. It points to discipline. One must deny self and apply the cross to ensure godly discipline. This can create inner conflict and turmoil.

Separating from the world, putting down pride, and crucifying self can prove to be a traumatic experience, but it is necessary if one is going to enter into the narrow gate of the kingdom of God.[12] Acts 14:22 makes reference to this difficulty, "Confirming the souls of the disciples, and exhorting them to continue in the faith, and that we must through much tribulation enter into the kingdom of God." Proper godly discipline will make the kingdom of God a reality, rather than a concept.

Jesus defined the desire that needs to be prevalent in effective prayer. This desire may seem insignificant, but it is of the utmost importance. It identifies us to a King, a kingdom, a position, and an inheritance. Therefore, the kingdom of God must be personally realized in each person. Fruits and power serve as the evidence of the presence of this kingdom in a person's life.

Just as the Word is clear that the kingdom of God must be visible in a person's life, it also stipulates those who will fail to inherit this kingdom. Jesus said in Luke 9:62, "No man, having put his hand to the plough, and looking back, is fit for the kingdom of God." Those who are divided in loyalties will not possess the desire or inclination to inherit this kingdom regardless of the cost.

The kingdom of God is righteousness and the Holy Ghost. Therefore, one must be upright to obtain this kingdom. If a person fails to operate or walk according to the Spirit of God, he or she will not inherit the kingdom of God.[13]

Jesus' words in Matthew 7:21 give us another reason why people will not enter into God's kingdom, "Not every one that saith unto me, Lord, Lord, shall enter into the kingdom of heaven; but he that doeth the will of my Father which is in heaven." Jesus must be ruling in a person's heart.

---

[12] Matthew 7:13-14; 16:24; 2 Corinthians 6:14-18; Galatians 2:20
[13] 1 Corinthians 6:9-10; Galatians 5:21; Ephesians 5:5

His heart, goal, and ways will be in line with the Father. The natural response to His rule will be love and obedience.

Do you have the kingdom of God within you? Are you willing to pay the price to realize the power and authority of this kingdom in your life? Do you desire to see this kingdom realized and fulfilled in others? Is your heart's desire and cry the same as the Apostle John's, "Even so, come, Lord Jesus" (Revelation 22:20)!

6

THE PURPOSE

...Thy will be done in earth,
as it is in heaven.
Matthew 6:10b

Why do people pray? We have discussed the various reasons for praying, but the main reason for praying is to see some purpose fulfilled. The *spirit* or *intent* behind prayer determines the quality or spiritual condition of this purpose as to whether it is holy or unacceptable to God. *Pursuit* or *emphasis* determines the intent behind prayer. Emphasis finds its source in the will of man. Therefore, prayer is about seeing someone's will be fulfilled.

As I studied the word "kingdom," my secular dictionary implied that kingdom is a realm in which God's will is fulfilled.[1] Here we see that the order in this model prayer is very important. The goal is to enter into an intimate communion with the Father, but one must approach Him in a right, worshipful attitude. A person's desire for approaching God is to see His kingdom realized in him or her as well as in others. To realize the presence of His kingdom, a person must be doing the will of God. Therefore, the one distinction about God's kingdom here on earth is that His will is being carried out in the lives of His followers.

Many Christians declare a desire to see God's will done. This appears quite noble, but few realize that doing God's will is not an option or a noble, self-righteous act, but a prerequisite to entering into His kingdom. Matthew 7:21 confirms this harsh reality. Jesus declared in this verse that He will not recognize those who fail to do the Father's will. 1 John 2:17 verifies this: "And the world passeth away, and the lust thereof: but he that doeth the will of God abideth for ever.

Sadly, even though most religious people talk about the importance of prayer and doing God's will, they fail to finish the course. Such failure points to good intentions. Good intentions are nothing more than a cover-up for the lack of commitment and determination. As a result, many fail to discover God's will for their lives.

This lack of personal vision and commitment towards God carries over into these people's prayer life. They usually pray according to their personal will. They believe that if they say the right things, earn a certain

---

[1] Webster's New Collegiate Dictionary

amount of credits, and wrestle long enough with God, He will adhere to their will and way regardless of His plan. They perceive this pursuit to be righteous because they conclude that such measures are good and would make the world a better place. Since their requests appear to be good, they believe that God will see their logic and ultimately comply with their will. This is a delusion and a clever way to hide personal selfishness. Selfishness has one goal: personal happiness.

Peter deals with this selfishness in his first epistle, "Forasmuch then as Christ hath suffered for us in the flesh, arm yourselves likewise with the same mind: for he that hath suffered in the flesh hath ceased from sin; That he no longer should live the rest of his time in the flesh to the lusts of men, but to the will of God" (1 Peter 4:1-2). As Christians, we must cease from pursuing the lusts of the flesh, and begin to pursue the will of God. Living for, and according to the flesh, make a person's prayers ineffective. Whenever the flesh is present and reigning, a person's prayer life will focus on selfish desires and pursuits. This simply means that the individual will ask amiss so that he or she may consume it upon personal preferences and desires.[2]

In John 9:31, Jesus confirmed the fact that God will not answer a person who is giving way to wickedness, "Now we know that God heareth not sinners: but if any man be a worshipper of God and doeth his will, him he heareth." You must be a worshipper of God and obedient to His will to ensure answered prayers. This is why Jesus is very clear about the purpose behind acceptable prayer. It is about seeking the will of God to ensure the necessary authority to move heaven and earth in prayers, as well as see promises fulfilled for His glory.

Jesus noted that God's will is fulfilled in heaven, and our main emphasis should be to see His will done on earth. God's Word is also clear that if one wants God to answer his or her prayers, one must pray according to His will.[3] After all, it is His purpose or will that must be realized in our lives and the lives of others.

Many Christians pray to see God's promises fulfilled, but these promises are conditional. Hebrews 10:36 tells us what the condition is to see God honor His promises, "For ye have need of patience, that, after ye have done the will of God, ye might receive the promise." You cannot receive the promises of God unless you are carrying out His will in your life.

Obviously, we need to understand God's will to be effective in prayer and to see His best upheld, carried out, and maintained in our lives and in regard to His kingdom. The concept of will points to purpose, determination, or inclination. Purpose is associated with focus or vision, determination with enduring strength, and inclination with the natural direction one will lead or travel. Interestingly enough, the will of God in

[2] James 4:2-3
[3] Romans 8:27; 1 John 5:14

the New Testament is associated with the Father. Jesus stated that He did not seek His own will but the Father's will. Jesus gave way to, and carried out His Father's will in every area including the cross. This means that His Father's will became His will.[4]

Amazingly, many religious people treat God's will as a mystery or spiritual truth that only the elite can know. The Apostle Paul contradicts this perception, "Having made known unto us the mystery of his will, according to his good pleasure which he hath purposed in himself" (Ephesians 1:9).

Paul declared that God's will has been revealed to us. In fact, Jesus explained His Father's will in John 6:40, "And this is the will of him that sent me, that every one which seeth the Son, and believeth on him, may have everlasting life: and I will raise him up at the last day." There you have the will of God. His main purpose is to see man saved and raised up in everlasting life. This salvation was established by the will of God. To fail to understand the simplicity of His will, will cause individuals to become unwise in their ways.[5]

God's will brings us back to the goal of prayer, and that is to lead a person into an intimate childlike relationship with the Father. In fact, doing the will of God identifies a person with the heavenly family and inheritance that is being established by the Spirit of the Living God. Jesus made this statement in Matthew 12:49-50, "And he stretched forth his hand toward his disciples, and said, Behold my mother and my brethren! For whosoever shall do the will of my Father which is in heaven, the same is my brother, and sister, and mother."

This family relationship with God and other believers is not only His will, but also it is His good pleasure. The Apostle Paul confirmed this, "Having predestinated us unto the adoption of children by Jesus Christ to himself, according to the good pleasure of his will" (Ephesians 1:5). It is interesting how accomplishing the will of someone is associated with happiness or pleasure. For example, people believe that if their will is done they will be happy. This is true to some extent, but such happiness will often prove to be temporary. However, Scripture clearly states that doing God's will, will bring Him pleasure. Such pleasure will translate into the servant's life as salvation, peace, and contentment.

Salvation is a gift, but the reality of it must be worked out in our lives. Ephesians 1:11 states, "In whom also we have obtained an inheritance, being predestinated according to the purpose of him who worketh all things after the counsel of his own will." This gift from God is worked out in our lives as we give way to His work. Our part in His work is submission and obedience.

Jesus stated that the will of the Father is for those who see the Son to believe upon Him. The word "believe" is associated with active faith

---

[4] John 5:30; Philippians 2:7-11
[5] John 1:12-13; Ephesians 5:17

that always results in submission to a greater authority, and obedience to what is right. Jesus tells us to do the Father's will, but the Father's will is that we obey the Son. Obedience to the Son will bring glory to the Father.[6]

It is through obedience to the Son that God's will becomes personal. Disobedience makes a person indifferent to God. Indifference to God makes our loving Creator seem impersonal and unrealistic. Because of this perception, many people look at God's will as being unobtainable. Hebrews 13:21 tells us that God is the One who works His will out in our lives, "Make you perfect in every good work to do his will, working in you that which is well-pleasing in his sight, through Jesus Christ; to whom be glory for ever and ever. Amen." He does this through the means of transformation.

Romans 12:1-2 tells us what our part is in this work of transformation,

> I beseech you therefore, brethren, by the mercies of God, that ye present your bodies a living sacrifice, holy, acceptable unto God, which is your reasonable service. And be not conformed to this world: but be ye transformed by the renewing of your mind, that ye may prove what is that good, and acceptable, and perfect, will of God.

People must first present their bodies as a living sacrifice, so that God can have His way with them. This allows Him to transform their minds. A transformed mind implies having the mind of Christ. The mind of Christ is to do the will of the Father. As one develops the mind of Christ, he or she will be able to ultimately prove what is the good, acceptable, and perfect will of God.

The Scripture verse in Romans 12:2 instructs us to actually prove what is that good, acceptable, and perfect will of God. "Prove" in this text means to test, to approve, allow, discern, and examine.[7] Obviously, it is our responsibility to make sure that we know and do the will of God. Keep in mind that to know God's will we must know the character and work of God.

The Apostle Paul revealed this prayer request towards the Colossians,

> For this cause we also, since the day we heard it, do not cease to pray for you, and to desire that ye might be filled with the knowledge of his will in all wisdom and spiritual understanding; That ye might walk worthy of the Lord unto all pleasing, being fruitful in every good work, and increasing in the knowledge of God."

In Colossians 1:9 we see where Paul wanted the Colossians to be filled with the knowledge of God's will. This knowledge would enable them to

---

[6] Philippians 2:12; John 14:6-24; 15:4-17
[7] Strong's Exhaustive Concordance, #1381

walk worthy of the Lord, as well as be fruitful in good works, and continue to increase in the knowledge of God.

Ephesians 6:6 instructs Christians to do the will of God from the heart. The heart points to the source of inclinations. Godly inclinations are developed as one disciplines his or her thoughts and actions. In other words, a person must choose to do right regardless of how he or she feels or his or her circumstances. Such discipline will change the inclinations of the heart. Once the inclinations are properly aligned to God's will, it will be natural for a person to do His will without debate or doubt.

This brings us to the different ways in which God's will operates. There are three aspects in which God's will may manifest itself towards man. If God allows man to act according to his own will, this is considered God's *permissive will*. If He somehow directs man in order to accomplish His way in a situation, it is determined to be His *providential will*. And, if His order in a matter is adhered to, carried out, and honored, it is considered His *perfect will*. Let us now examine these three aspects of His will.

God's *permissive* will manifests itself when a person insists on having his or her way. Man's way falls short of God's way, but He will not stand in the way of a person pursuing his or her own desires. The problem with God's permissive will is that He removes the restraints of His grace. Without His grace, the protection is missing and the flesh will reign unchallenged. In fact, His grace cannot abound as long as a person is heading away from His protection. The lack of God's grace will subject a person to consequences or judgment. Sadly, this is how many of His followers learn hard lessons that are not easily forgotten. They are actually allowed to taste the bitter fruits of their own will and way of doing things.

The *providential* will of God is manifested for three reasons: 1) To keep someone from being destroyed, 2) to teach someone important lessons or 3) to bring forth His plan in a person or situation. Since God will not step over people's wills, He uses circumstances or events in order to have His way in a situation in spite of the person walking in the flesh or in confusion. Even though God will allow His children to taste consequences, He will warn, guide, instruct, or create situations to bring forth maturity or keep them from walking into destructive traps.

God's providential will also comes into the picture when He wants to accomplish something in a person or in a situation. It is in this arena He will open and close doors for those who are uncertain in the way they must walk. I have also witnessed Him using some unusual people or circumstances to put certain things into place, in order to save people, show Himself mighty, and fulfill His plan.

There was an incident with one of our former co-laborers. We all lived in the same house. The Lord has graciously given Jeannette a little dog. The other co-laborer decided she wanted to have a dog of her own.

She had this idea of how a dog would make her happy and serve her purpose in other ways.

Both Jeannette and I felt this was not God's perfect will for her life. Even though she sought Him about this issue, she already had her mind made up. She saw no reason why God would deny her something that seemed insignificant. After all, it was just a dog and she was simply asking God to bless her desire.

Although this individual perceived that she wanted God's will, she had her own agendas, desires, or fantasies as to how God would fulfill His will in her life. She was still holding on to some personal rights that seemed insignificant to her, but had the potential to hinder God's perfect will in her life. Fleshly agendas often blind people to the real work of God and prevent them from recognizing or accepting God's perfect will. Since they are working on the limited plane of fleshly desires, they are unable to see the eternal picture of what God wants to accomplish in their life.

Since it was in our companion's will to have a dog, God, Jeannette and I permitted it. At this point, this individual was about to experience God's permissive will by tasting the consequences of what seemed to be a harmless desire. However, on the other hand, we also changed the rules by asking God to have His way in this incident. This put the situation in the arena of God's providential will. He chose the dog with the intent of tearing up this woman's fantasy and bringing some much-needed sobriety about the various issues of life. The concept of God's perfect will is not a matter of His will being done around us, but in us.

Amazingly, many people fail to perceive that the real goal of God is to have His perfect will done in their lives for the purpose of bringing them to spiritual perfection. He will not do a trade off where He will do His will according to self-serving flesh or arrogant terms just to get something accomplished. God's will is His will. His thoughts and ways are much higher than ours are; therefore, it is up to each of us to line our wills up to His will.[8] This means that our will must cease to exist and God's will must become our primary focus or desire. To accomplish this means seeking His perspective about everything in our lives regardless of how small or large.

God chose the dog, and what was meant to fulfill this woman's good pleasure became a nightmare. The dog exposed and tore down every concept she had about her abilities to control and bring about her fantasy. What she saw as a good pleasure became a responsibility that produced a harsh reality about her fantasy.

The harsh reality this individual had to face was the difference between fantasy and reality. Fantasy feeds our imagination as to how something will make us feel, while reality causes us to land with the harshness of responsibility. God eventually delivered her from her cursed fantasy, but not until she learned some important lessons.

---

[8] Isaiah 55:8-9

I learned this same lesson the hard way. Sadly, it was not over a dog, but a marriage partner. There came a time in my life that I felt that I was supposed to be married. I never thought about asking God if He wanted me to be married. I just assumed that it would be in His heart for me to experience this relationship.

I fervently prayed for the right partner. Needless to say, a man came into my life. I did seek God's will about him, and felt it was within God's will for us to marry. At the time, I did not understand about God's permissive or providential will versus His perfect will. I failed to realize that my failure to seek God as to whether it was even His will to marry automatically put me in His permissive will, but my desire to honor Him, put me in His providential will.

To this day, I believe God had His hand in the type of man that I married, but it was to teach me some hard lessons and to bring forth maturity to ensure that His perfect will would be accomplished in my life. Our marriage ended in divorce, but I look back at my experience and can see how God used it to do a deeper work in me. I do not consider those years as a waste, but I do see my shame and failure to seek God about every aspect of my life. I learned never to assume that because something is acceptable or logical, that this must be what God wants for my life.

Personal expectations are the main reason many people fail to realize and accept God's will for their lives. They keep His will separate from their personal desires and dreams. They speculate how God's will would fit into their personal ideas or concepts.

This brings us to God's *perfect* will. God's perfect will has to do with His order being carried out and fulfilled in a person's life. Order not only establishes a right environment, but becomes a breeding ground to right attitudes. Whether God's perfect will is carried out depends on the vessel. The vessel or person must be in total surrender or abandonment to the work of God within him or her, through him and her, and in situations where the person is personally affected. This abandonment is a form of consecration. It is only when everything is lined up to God's will in a person's life that His perfect will is accomplished. His perfect will is verified by the order it will bring to a person's life or environment. When a person truly abides in God's perfect will, he or she will know personal contentment and peace.

Total surrender involves three stages: trust, submission, and obedience. A person must first decide to trust God with every detail of his or her life. To trust God with every detail of our personal lives is difficult because it involves self-denial. This is hard because God will go against the grain of personal agendas, expectations, and ideas. In other words, God's will, will not look attractive to our flesh. Instead of making us feel good about self, it will challenge us, especially since He often uses iron to sharpen iron.[9] Instead of making us look good, it will sometimes make us feel or look insignificant in the scheme of things.

Once a person trusts God with every detail of his or her life, then the cross can be properly applied through submission. The cross is a point of discipline where character is established. Submission is where a person makes the decision to line up to God's will regardless of the claims of the flesh and the challenges of the circumstances. It is at the point of submission that a person becomes a co-laborer with God.[10] This is an important part about God's will. He wants to make each of His followers, co-laborers in carrying out His work and plan to fulfill His perfect will in their lives and in the lives of others. The problem is that few ever become a co-laborer in ensuring God's will. Many may talk about it, but few deny self and apply the cross to become identified as co-laborers with God.

As a person submits to God's work, He is able to bring forth spiritual maturity. Spiritual maturity involves integrity, character, and uprightness before God. These virtues are necessary to make the right decisions or stand when all of hell comes against an individual.

People who are happy in being nominal Christians pose no threat to Satan. However, those who desire to do the will of God represent great opposition to his kingdom. Such people will have authority and power to overcome this enemy of God. They will know their position in Christ, and will possess peace, as well as display contentment regardless of the circumstances.

Submission also means that one will gain an eternal perspective. People have such a high opinion of what they think they know. Yet, they only know in part.[11] If people could gain God's perspective, they would realize how insignificant, or even acceptable things, could hinder God's work in and through them. This eternal perspective can only be revealed to a person when he or she is walking God's will out in his or her life.

Obedience will enable us to realize God's will in our lives. In order to obey, one must be walking in the Spirit. Needless to say, this is unlike God's permissive will and providential will where a person is walking according to some aspect of the flesh. By walking in the Spirit, the person will walk out God's will. This ensures that God's perfect will is accomplished in the person just as it is in heaven. The results of this are peace of mind, contentment in whatever state one is in, and His perfect order.[12]

Order is missing from Christians' lives because they are not walking out God's will. This causes chaos and contention as the soul wrestles with doubts, accusations, lies of Satan, and irritating problems and questions that flood their world with a mocking vengeance. All of this

---

[9] Proverbs 27:17
[10] 1 Corinthians 3:9
[11] Roman 12:3; 1 Corinthians 13:9; Galatians 6:3
[12] Isaiah 26:3; Philippians 4:5-7, 11; 1 Timothy 6:6, 8

leaves them empty. The reason for emptiness is because God's perfect will is the only thing that makes sense in the confusing and unpredictable world we live in. Once God's will is accomplished in His followers' lives, they begin to see that God does know best.

To do God's perfect will means that His will, will replace our will. This requires total surrender or abandonment. Let us consider what needs to be done to ensure God's perfect will.

Coming Into God's Perfect Will	Trust	Submission	Obedience
Response	Self-denial	Application of the cross	Walk by the Spirit
Goal	Change Inclination	Become Co-Laborer with God	Walk out the Christian life
Result	Change Focus	Develop Eternal Perspective	God's perfect will, will be done.
Evidence	Confidence In God	Contentment/ Peace with God	Order in a person's world

As you can see, His perfect will has to do with the person more than with the situation. God can always move around a situation to fulfill His plan, but His desire is to move in, through, and with the person to accomplish His perfect will in his or her life. This is why it is up to each believer to prove what is the good, acceptable, and perfect will of God in his or her life. When it comes to good, this points to upright conduct that produces good works. Acceptable has to do with sacrifice. And, perfect has to do with the complete or fulfilled work of God in that particular area of a person's life.

God's perfect will must be sought. To know His will, one must know His heart, mind, and plan. This cannot occur unless a person is developing a relationship with the Father through Jesus Christ. As one grows in the knowledge of Jesus, he or she will know what pleases God. Obedience to God's will, will give Him the opportunity to entrust the person with more of His life, authority, and power.

Are you operating in His permissive will, His providential will, or within His perfect will? His perfect will is the safest place to be. And, if you are abiding in this place, not only can you be assured that His grace is abounding, but also that you will have the authority to move heaven and earth in your prayer closet.

7

SIMPLICITY

Give us this day our daily bread.
Matthew 6:11

The first part of the model prayer has to do with establishing ourselves before God in relationship, attitude, desire, and emphasis. Once God is in His rightful place in our lives, our attitudes will be properly adjusted and agendas redefined. It is at this time that we can bring prayer down to a personal level.

How many people make prayer about personal crusades instead of seeking out God? How many people make prayer all about themselves and their pursuits, rather than God's kingdom? How many people make prayer like a Christmas list where personal desires are lifted up instead of God's will being sought out? Is it any wonder people's prayers are ineffective? So many people have it all wrong when it comes to their prayer life. They take detours and find themselves in the oven of afflictions before they finally realize what prayer is all about.

Jesus exalts the emphasis of God's will in order to reveal the simplicity of prayer. After we establish a relationship, then we can begin to ask God for our needs. Jesus actually shows us what to ask for. It is incredibly simple: Ask God for our daily bread.

I don't know about you, but I used to have a whole list of things to ask God for. After all, "Ask, and it shall be given."[1] However, Jesus clearly puts the things we personally ask for down to the simplest form: Ask for what you have need of. Don't complicate or confuse your life with those things that represent vanity. Be wise and discreet about what you ask for.

The walk of faith has taught me the difference between needs and wants. Ninety-nine percent of what I personally ask for is nothing but wants. Granted, my flesh declares I have need of such things, but when I get down to the basics of life, I realize they are nothing more than insatiable wants that feed my flesh.

Why is it important that we understand the difference between needs and wants? Scripturally, I am guaranteed that God will supply all my needs, "But my God shall supply all your need according to his riches in glory by Christ Jesus" (Philippians 4:19). "Need" means occasion,

---

[1] Matthew 7:7

demand, requirement, distribution, lack, and necessary.[2] God will supply our needs according to His riches in glory. This puts His provision in light of the eternal realm. Ultimately, His provision will bring Him glory.

This brings us down to what constitutes a need. A need comes down to the bare necessities to keep something functioning. For example, a car needs gas to function, animals need food and water to exist, and man needs food and water to live. Therefore, things that have nothing to do with one's ability to exist or live are wants or blessings. This narrows the field down to what is important.

The problem with wants or blessings is that they often become points of spiritual testing. Testing reveals the extent of a person's carnality. In many cases, these tests end in some type of judgment. Like the quail that God gave the Israelites to feed their fleshly wants in the wilderness, it brought both physical death and leanness to their souls. [3]

Humans have two types of needs: spiritual and physical. Spiritual needs ensure well-being, while physical needs maintain physical life. However, as you consider the physical needs in Scripture, they are for the purpose of maintaining the spiritual aspect of our lives with God and before God.

The Apostle Paul tells us that God provides such needs according to His riches in glory by Jesus Christ. Riches in this context can mean wealth or possessions, but they also point to fullness, abundance, or valuable bestowal. Many people consider riches in light of worldly wealth or possessions, but this Scripture emphasizes spiritual treasure in light of Jesus Christ. Such treasure is eternal and results in satisfaction to the soul. Although all wealth is at God's disposal, His greatest desire is for us to possess the fullness of His kingdom.

We must now determine what we have need of. Jesus once again defines our needs in Matthew 6:31-32, "Therefore take no thought, saying, What shall we eat? or, What shall we drink? or, Wherewithal shall we be clothed? (For after all these things do the Gentiles seek:) for your heavenly Father knoweth that ye have need of all these things." Jesus tells us that we only have three basic needs to function properly: food, water, and clothing. Anything outside of these basic needs can be considered wants and blessings. These basic needs are not only true on a physical level, but on a spiritual one as well. Obviously, the Father provides both types of needs. In the spiritual realm, the Holy Spirit serves as the water, Jesus is the bread from heaven, the Word of God is the milk, God's will the meat, and the life and disposition of Christ serve as our spiritual clothing of humility and righteousness.[4]

Jesus also told us in what light to consider these needs on a daily basis. People are always looking forward to secure their future. Such a

---

[2] Strong's Exhaustive Concordance #5532
[3] Numbers 11:31-34; Psalm 106:14-15
[4] Luke 13:11; John 4:34; 6:35; 1 Corinthians 1:30; Hebrews 5:12-14

169

pursuit causes much anxiety or worry, which is a form of unbelief. In fact, most people worry about the future, while overlooking present problems. Present reality shows us that we are never prepared for tomorrow. In fact, present reality proves that we do not control our lives. This is why many live in the past or in the future. People can change the past in their minds or consider everything in light of how they can secure the future, while the present slips past them. Such practices point to fantasy, which produce vain imaginations. The Apostle Paul dealt with this tendency in Ephesians 5:16, "Redeeming the time, because the days are evil."

James also condemned such practices.

"Go to now, ye that say, To day or to morrow we will go into such a city, and continue there a year, and buy and sell, and get gain: Whereas ye know not what shall be on the morrow. For what is your life? It is a vapour, that appeareth for a little time, and then vanisheth away" (James 4:13-14).

He went on to call such planning evil boasting.[5] Yet, this practice of planning for tomorrow is encouraged by the world. It declares that a person must prepare for his or her future or who will take care of the person's personal well-being? Who will ensure that the person will have the lifestyle he or she is accustomed to?

When you consider these scenarios, you can see that this need to secure tomorrow is self-centered and a means to control one's life. The focus is on this life, as we know it and not on heaven. Jesus warned about the futility of such a focus, "For whosoever will save his life shall lose it.... For what is a man advantaged, if he gain the whole world, and lose himself, or be cast away" (Luke 9:24-25)?

Jesus gave a good example of this self-centered attitude in Luke 12:16-21. A rich man's investments brought forth many fruits. He realized he did not have room for all of his abundance. He decided to pull down his old barns and build bigger ones to contain all of his goods. Then, he decided that he was going to live a life of ease by eating, drinking, and being merry. However, God called him a fool and that night, life as he knew it and had planned, ceased by the hand of God. Jesus ended the parable by saying, "So is he that layeth up treasure for himself, and is not rich toward God."

The unwillingness to deal in the present is a matter of unbelief. We are to walk by faith. This walk involves walking Christianity out daily by confidence in God. This faith produces obedience. Faith never operates according to the future; therefore, faith is not given for future events, but for present challenges. If people are always dealing in the future, they will fail to be faithful in the present.[6]

---

[5] James 4:16
[6] Luke 16:10-13; 21:34-36; 2 Corinthians 5:7

Unfaithfulness is a fruit of faithlessness. Faith deals in the present, but unfaithfulness is a product of not believing God for the present and walking according to unbelief. In the kingdom of God, the greatest preparation for tomorrow is being faithful today. After all, we will be judged according to our days on earth and not in light of an uncertain and uncontrollable future.[7]

As you study James' exhortation about the foolishness of planning for tomorrow, you see that it is in light of doing that which is right on a daily basis. James confirmed this, "Therefore to him that knoweth to do good, and doeth it not, to him it is sin" (James 4:17).

The Apostle Paul made this statement in Romans 14:23, "...for whatsoever is not of faith is sin." So much of Christianity is pure drudgery. Christians start out thinking that the Christian life is marked by greatness. This is a wrong perception. Christianity is marked by drudgery that expresses itself in faithfulness, availability, and practicality. The test is to occupy in whatever capacity comes your way. After all, character is refined by drudgery as individuals are tested and tempted to give up and forego the ways of righteousness in order to find purpose and excitement in life.

Jesus is trying to keep people in the present reality by exhorting them to ask for what they have need for that day. The physical life is a fragile reality. It is like a vapor that quickly disappears or a flower that fades away.[8] As one lives in the present, he or she will be able to clearly discern present needs.

Our test is to be wise with what we have been entrusted by the great I AM THAT I AM.[9] God has been greatly involved in history as well as upholding the future in His hands, but He actively deals in the present needs and details of His people. Imagine what it would be like if He were not involved with your daily life? None of us would be here. Clearly, God deals in the present, but many of us refuse to face it.

Do you understand what you have need of? It is a discipline to come to terms with our needs. It is also a discipline to trust God to meet those needs. People wonder why they need to ask God for their daily needs when He already promised to provide them. There are three reasons: 1) Asking God for our daily needs keeps us aware that He is the Great Provider, 2) it is a point of faith or putting our confidence in God, and 3) it allows Him to show us how faithful He is in providing people's needs when He answers prayer.

Do you know what you have need of? Maybe you are pursuing your wants as you look to the world's possessions as a means of security and happiness. Both security and happiness are a false illusion outside of God. And, as Jesus pointed out in Luke 12:15 about the essence of real

---

[7] 2 Corinthians 5:10-11
[8] 1 Peter 1:22-24
[9] Exodus 3:14

life, "Take heed, and beware of covetousness: for a man's life consisteth not in the abundance of the things which he possesseth."

The Apostle Paul counted worldly possessions and prestige as dung in light of gaining Christ. The people of faith gave up the comforts and the glories of the present world to obtain a greater resurrection.[10]

Do you know what you have need of? Jesus Christ gave up the glories of heaven and became poor so that we could be made rich in Him. Are you willing to become poor or a cringing beggar in this world to discover the riches of heaven?[11]

Do you know what you have need of? God promised that He would supply all our needs according to the riches in Christ Jesus. His storehouse is endless, but the real purpose for providing for our needs is so that we can bring glory to Him. Sadly, we want to honor ourselves by heaping things upon ourselves, instead of using our lives as a means to bring glory and honor to the only One who deserves it.

Do you know what you have need of? If you do, you can use prayer as a means to make a difference in God's kingdom, instead of an avenue to pursue worldly things that have no value. You will be able to hit the target in prayer, as you remain faithful by trusting God for the present, so that you will be prepared to face the future in confidence. As the Apostle Paul stated in 2 Corinthians 5:9-10, "Wherefore we labour, that, whether present or absent, we may be accepted of him. For we must all appear before the judgment seat of Christ; that everyone may receive the things done in his body, according to what he hath done, whether it be good or bad."

Do you know what others have need of around you? Are you recognizing the needs of your family or Christians? Do you even care? It takes time and energy to get past self to discover what others have need of, so that you can be an avenue of prayer and blessing.

Do you understand what you have need of? Jesus instructed us to ask God to meet our daily needs. In essence, people have only one basic need. Within this basic need, all other needs are realized. A person needs the fullness of God in Christ Jesus. Out of this fullness will come satisfaction as His kingdom is realized in a person's heart, and His reality penetrates every area of that person's life. Pleasures evermore are obtained as God's will is completed. And, all needs, spiritual and physical, are provided for. As you can see, the life that is surely founded in Christ lacks nothing for it is full and complete.

Do you really understand what you have need of? Ask, and you will receive.

---

[10] Philippians 3:7-8; Hebrews 11:34-40
[11] Matthew 5:3; 2 Corinthians 8:9

8

THE CONDITION

And forgive us our debts,
as we forgive our debtors.
Matthew 6:12

Jesus taught His disciples how to pray by giving them a model prayer. This model prayer is not to serve as a catchall prayer, but to clarify the attitude, the desire, the emphasis, and the simplicity behind effective prayer. As a result, Jesus brought a valuable contrast that exposes the hypocrisy of man's heart, the cloak of self-righteousness, the self-serving attitude of the flesh, the foolishness of misconceived notions, and the vanity of complicated prayers.

I am often awed by the model prayer laid out in the Sermon on the Mount. In its purity, you see God's heart, and in its simplicity, you can see His purpose and will. Such an example of prayer reveals that it is man who complicates prayer with his religious, romantic notions about God, His kingdom, and the privilege and uniqueness of being able to communicate with the Creator of the Universe, the ever-present, unchangeable, and all powerful I AM.

This brings us to an important condition that must be met when making sure God will hear our prayers. Such a key guarantees that God will hear by ensuring uprightness, authority, and power before Him. The condition is forgiveness.

Sadly, forgiveness is often overlooked as a vital condition in our Christian life. Granted, Christians talk about forgiveness, but few understand the significance it plays in the Christian walk. The truth is that one cannot experience salvation or walk out the Christian life unless forgiveness is in operation.

Forgiveness lies at the heart of salvation. We must be forgiven in order to be open and receptive to the salvation of God. This means we must recognize that we have offended God by trespassing His Law. We have betrayed Him by treading into areas of idolatry and moral deviation. We have used the bodies He has given us to carry out unacceptable activities. We have wasted the gift of life He has given us by coming into unholy alliances with the world. We have filled our minds with the useless philosophies of the world and Satan.

Offenses have broken both the heart of God and our fellowship with Him. However, the harsh reality of sin does not stop with a separation from God. These offenses also require restitution. In other words, we have created a debt that must be satisfied.

Scripture clearly states that we cannot properly pay this debt without it costing us our very souls. If we received our just judgment, we would spend eternity in hell, forever separated from God who is the essence of love, mercy, grace, and life. Thus, enters forgiveness.

Forgiveness ensures that we can be delivered from our hopeless plight. After all, the debt is too great to pay. Since we cannot make the proper restitution to satisfy God's holy Law, mercy and grace must be allotted to us. This is where forgiveness comes into the picture. Forgiveness represents the mercy and grace that must be extended to each of us to satisfy the debt. Ultimately, it is able to bring about reconciliation and complete restoration or healing.

Jesus is clarifying in the model prayer that forgiveness is not an option, but a necessity. He confirms this in Matthew 6:14-15, "For if ye forgive men their trespasses, your heavenly Father will also forgive you: But if ye forgive not men their trespasses, neither will your Father forgive your trespasses." If forgiveness is missing, then our prayers will have no power. We must come to God in prayer, forgiven, reconciled, and restored. This will mean that we have been cleansed from our sins, our consciences no longer condemn us, our hands are clean, our hearts pure, and our minds correctly focused on God.[1]

God's forgiveness is conditional. Even though He desires to bestow forgiveness on us by not giving us our deserved lot, as well as providing us with the means of deliverance, it still hinges on our walking in forgiveness towards others. This is a bitter pill for many people to swallow. In fact, people justify their lack of forgiveness by convincing themselves that only God is capable of forgiving because of His nature and His love. This is a misconception.

God is holy. However, forgiveness is often considered in light of God's love. This is incorrect. Forgiveness must be considered in light of God's holiness before people can understand its significance. God showed His love to the world through His Son on the cross, but He required His Son to become a sacrifice because of His holiness. Holiness demands that our sin be dealt with in a proper fashion; therefore, sin cannot be downplayed or ignored. People must realize that God could not accept sin-laden individuals until the price was paid for their sins.

Sadly, many people miss the necessity of forgiveness because they figure God will overlook their discrepancies because of His love. In fact, many hide behind a syrupy idea of love to justify unwillingness to sell out to God and to do what is right. As long as God's love is considered in this ridiculous light, people will never see the need to truly repent and seek God's forgiveness for the way they are.

---

[1] Hebrews 10:22; James 4:8; 1 John 1:7-9

God's holy character actually demands restitution just as the makeup of man requires restitution once offended. Forgiveness is a choice. God chooses to forgive us because His emphasis is saving our souls. It is this choice of forgiveness that constantly activates His mercy and grace. This is true for man. He must choose to forgive in order to give way to mercy that restrains from judgment, and grace that freely gives.

This brings us to the different aspects of forgiveness. Like many, I have struggled with the issue of forgiveness. There is no way that you can avoid being offended. There are many reasons why we become offended. One of the greatest offenses will be caused by our encounter with Jesus. God often insults us when He challenges us with the truth of Jesus Christ. Jesus offended many people during His short ministry.[2]

There are three conditions that will guarantee that each of us will be offended in this life. We live in Satan's world, we encounter fallen man on a daily basis, and we are self-centered. Such offenses are personally considered unfair, illegal, or unacceptable; therefore, it requires that restitution must be paid. However, as a Christian, Scripture tells me that I must forgive in order to receive God's forgiveness.

What does it really mean to forgive? The concept of forgiveness seems quite noble, but I can assure you that it is not a point of personal nobility. It actually serves as an important element of spiritual survival or well-being. Without forgiveness, a person will become unhealthy in his or her body, soul and spirit. Such an individual will display a hard heart, a critical, skeptical attitude, and perversion.

There are two aspects of forgiveness that we must come to terms with to understand how it works. These aspects are: release and pardon. Scripture outlines these two aspects. For example, in the model prayer, Jesus is referring to forgiveness in light of releasing someone, while in 1 John 1:9, the Apostle John is making reference to pardon.

What does it mean to forgive or to release someone? It is important to point out that God, as the just Judge of the universe, is the only One who can give a pardon to those who have broken His Law and cause treacherous offenses toward Him.[3] However, in the model prayer, Jesus is saying that a person must let go of his or her right to demand justice. This implies that one must cease from seeking restitution from those who have offended him or her. Amazingly, this release is not for the benefit of the one who committed the offense, but for the one who has been offended. When a person personally releases someone from paying restitution, he or she is releasing self from the traumatic experience of trying to satisfy personal judgment. The reason that this experience is so traumatic is because such judgment will never be sufficient.

God is offended because He is holy. However, God provided the means by which His judgment upon such offences could be satisfied.

---

[2] Matthew 13:57: 18:7: Mark 6:3: John 6:61; Romans 9:32-33
[3] Hosea 6:7; Luke 5:20-26

This provision came by way of Jesus' cross. The part or makeup of man that is often offended is his pride. Pride can never be satisfied. It will always want more recompense as its insatiable appetites grow and demand to be avenged. As you can see, there is no limitation or provision to suffice judgment when it comes to the harsh judge of personal pride. Due to its nature, pride is unable to display any type of mercy and grace. It does not have such characteristics nor can it conjure them up.

The characteristics of pride are anger, resentment, bitterness, and hatred. These fruits are why offences cause one to escalate in his or her emotional cycles. Unrequited hurts, wounds, and offences become unresolved issues. The unresolved issues intensify anger. Anger turns into resentment. This ill will becomes bitterness to the soul. As bitterness takes root in the soul, it begins to defile a person's reasoning or perception.[4] He or she becomes restless as he or she is tormented by the need for restitution. Such torment turns into hatred.

The Apostle John describes this condition in 1 John 2:11, "But he that hateth his brother is in darkness, and walketh in darkness, and knoweth not whither he goeth, because that darkness hath blinded his eyes." People who are at this stage are not only in darkness, but they cannot see the destruction ahead of them. Their heart has become harder, thereby, becoming more unreasonable. Their arrogance escalates as their right to demand restitution is mentally justified. Their hatred becomes acceptable as they become judge, jury, and hangman. In fact, this hatred becomes so intense that even if they receive the payment of the offender's very life, they would desire to resurrect that person just so they could make that individual pay over and over again.

Through the years, I have had to examine my heart towards those who have offended me. I guard my heart by touching those places that have been wounded by betrayal, cast down by false accusations, unfairly treated by selfishness, and mocked by arrogance. The reason for touching these areas is for the purpose of exposing my true heart attitude towards those who offended me. My emotional response reveals whether God is healing that area or whether I am holding onto it because I am declaring my right to do so. If I am holding onto it, I realize that bitterness will take root and become an open door to Satan. If my reaction is too strong, I release it by giving it to God and declaring that I choose to forgive or release this person from tasting my personal judgment.

Recently, I had to face my attitude towards someone who was close to me. This person had offended me at different times and I simply ignored it. Finally, this person showed disrespect that became unacceptable. As I waded through my emotions and responsibilities towards this person, I was surprised to discover anger towards the individual that bordered on total resentment. This was not only unhealthy

---

[4] Hebrews 12:15

for me, but also unacceptable to God. I realized that He used the situation to unveil the unforgiveness that was subtly taking root in my life.

Forgiveness or release can only be found at the point of self-denial. Jesus proved this on the cross. His first statement was, "Father, forgive them; for they know not what they do" (Luke 23:34). Jesus had denied Himself in the Garden of Gethsemane when He gave way to the Father's will. On the cross, He chose to release people from their actions or participation in His suffering and death by interceding for them. He recognized that most of them had no concept of what they were doing. Many were carrying out a responsibility or caught up by religious ignorance or emotional zeal that was raging during His ordeal.

When it comes to most offences, this is usually the case. The offender never sets out to offend, and in many cases, has no idea that he or she has trespassed personal boundaries. Like most individuals, offenders are just trying to get through life, but they find themselves in the wrong place and position, rubbing someone's touchy disposition in the wrong way. Jesus gave humanity a much-needed break, and so must we when it comes to personal offences.

The forgiveness Jesus humbly displayed in His time of great suffering released Him to endure the cross. After all, He was not on the cross to bring judgment, but to become judgment so that all who would believe upon Him could have life.[5]

All forgiveness begins with a choice that produces self-denial. On the other hand, unforgiveness is self-centered, while forgiveness is caught up with a greater purpose. It actually takes the focus off of self and allows one to look beyond unresolved issues to the One who resolved all issues on the cross. When issues are resolved, it results in restoration or healing and new life.

The cross of Jesus is also a place of pardon. While release is for the benefit of the one offended, pardon is directed at the offender. However, it is important to understand the dynamics of pardon. This is where there is a lot of confusion. Pardon involves holding the line of righteousness with the intent of reconciliation.

In order to receive a pardon, one must acknowledge the offence and ask for forgiveness. Jesus confirmed this in His parable about forgiveness in Matthew 18:21-35. He pointed out that forgiveness came because it was desired.[6]

The Apostle John also brings this fact out about forgiveness in 1 John 1:9, "If we confess our sins, he is faithful and just to forgive us our sins, and to cleanse us from all unrighteousness." A person must confess or acknowledge his or her offence. Until the acknowledgment is made, a person cannot be released from the pending judgment. This is

---

[5] Acts 16:31; 2 Corinthians 5:21
[6] Matthew 18:32

why forgiveness lies at the heart of salvation. As the servant in Jesus' parable, a person seeks mercy by seeking forgiveness.

If people are in denial about sin, they will see no need to seek pardon or forgiveness. They will blindly and happily walk in their delusion while judgment awaits them. Salvation, on the other hand, is a matter of seeing how one has offended God, and taking responsibility for the offence by confessing it and seeking God's forgiveness at the foot of the cross. Such forgiveness results in reconciliation as God releases the person from pending judgment and restores him or her in a relationship with Him.

The Apostle Paul said this,

> And all things are of God, who hath reconciled us to himself by Jesus Christ,...not imputing their trespasses unto them; and hath committed unto us the word of reconciliation. Now then we are ambassadors for Christ, as though God did beseech you by us: we pray you in Christ's stead, be ye reconciled to God (2 Corinthians 5:18-20).

This Scripture tells us that Jesus came to reconcile man back to God, and that we as His servants must be in the same business. As Christians, our main goal should always be reconciliation, not judgment.

In order to ensure reconciliation, a person cannot be released from personal accountability until he or she has repented. This was clearly brought out in the situation involving the fornicator in the Corinthian church.[7] Paul instructed the church to bring disciplinary actions against this man. These actions had one goal: to bring the man to repentance in order to restore him. The man refused to repent, forcing those of the Corinthian Church to separate themselves from him.

The Corinthians held the line of righteousness with this man in the hope of seeing him confess and repent of his sin. Repentance would allow him to once again be reconciled to God and restored into fellowship. Apparently, the man did repent because the Apostle Paul gave these instructions, "So that contrariwise ye ought rather to forgive him, and comfort him, lest perhaps such a one should be swallowed up with overmuch sorrow. Wherefore I beseech you that ye would confirm your love toward him." (2 Corinthians 2:7-8).

Christians who are compelled by the love of God will strive to walk in forgiveness. They will handle offences in meekness. Their desire is to show mercy as they release the offender from personal restitution, and seek grace on his or her behalf for the purpose of reconciliation and restoration.

Jesus gave this instruction about forgiveness, "So likewise shall my heavenly Father do also unto you, if ye from the heart forgive not everyone his brother their trespasses" (Matthew 18:35). God is able to not only forgive our sins but also to forget them. He will cast them from

---

[7] 1 Corinthians 5

His sight. This is not the case for man. He has a problem forgetting. Therefore, he must forgive from the heart. Pride, rights, and judgment operate from the heart.[8] To "forgive from the heart" means that a person has totally released the offender from restitution. A forgiving heart implies a peaceful heart that finds its origins in an active relationship with God.

One of the problems that plague people on the issue of forgiveness is that offences cause a broken heart. When the heart is broken, a person is unable to forgive from the heart. Although they may wrestle mentally with letting go, their broken heart remains an unresolved issue. Jesus addressed this in Luke 4:18, "...he hath sent me to heal the brokenhearted,..." Jesus can heal a broken heart, allowing a person to forgive from the heart to experience wholeness.

Forgiveness must always be available. Jesus brought this point out in Matthew 18:22. Peter came to Him and asked how often he should forgive his brother who sinned against him. Jesus said, "I say not unto thee, Until seven times: but, Until seventy times seven." God confirms this practice by showing long-suffering towards us when we are in our sins.[9] He patiently waits for us to seek His forgiveness and is quick to render it when once sought. Since God shows each of us long-suffering, we must show the same virtue to those who constantly offend us.

Christians who harbor or seek judgment because of offences are mocking God and what He accomplished on the cross. God, who chose to satisfy His judgment by sending the sacrifice, and Jesus, who chose to deny self and offer up His life, serve as visible examples of how offences need to be addressed. There are no exceptions to the rule. Each offence must be humbly brought to the foot of the cross where rights are denied, pride neglected, and the flesh crucified in order to know spiritual wholeness in God.

Jesus tells us that forgiveness is a key to ensuring that God hears our prayers. His heart is to see others reconciled to Him, and to each other. Such reconciliation cannot take place unless there is forgiveness.

Are you walking in forgiveness or are you maintaining your rights to judge? If you are maintaining your rights to judge, you will be judged in the same manner.[10] Probably, the most important question you can consider is whether your right to walk in unforgiveness is worth going to hell for. Think about it. Repent and seek God's forgiveness, leaving your rights to maintain any unforgiveness at the foot of the cross.

---

[8] Psalm 103:12; Micah 7:18-19; Matthew 15:18-20
[9] 2 Peter 3:9
[10] Matthew 7:1-5

9

THE FOUNDATION

And lead us not into
temptation but deliver us from evil.
Matthew 6:13

Jesus carefully guided His disciples through valuable steps that would ensure effective prayer. He started with relationship, defined the acceptable attitude, and stipulated what needed to be one's initial desire in prayer. He revealed the purpose behind communicating with God and brought it down to the simplicity of learning to ask for one's needs. He unveiled the condition that had to be present before God could meet a person. At this point He revealed the foundation of effective prayer. Without this foundation, prayer will not stand.

Jesus used two very important words in Matthew 6:13, lead and deliver. When you consider Jesus' words, you must keep in mind that His teachings and examples must be considered in light of what is the acceptable way of doing something in order to bring proper contrast. Jesus told people to ask God to lead them from temptation and deliver them from evil. It is never enough to examine a Scripture in light of what we must not do, unless we are willing to consider the proper motivation.

Before we can consider the importance of these two requests, the first thing we must recognize in this part of the request is that it is in relationship to our walk. For Him to lead, we *must* follow by faith. For Him to deliver, we *must be* willing to follow in obedience. Jesus clearly stipulated what it will take for one to maintain an effective prayer life.

To find the contrast to Jesus' instructions, one must find the common factor between the concept of leading and delivering and effective prayer. For example, where does God want to lead one, in what way does God want to deliver a person, and what establishes authority in prayer? The answer to this question about the common factor is righteousness.

Psalm 23:3 states that the Lord leads us in the paths of righteousness. Psalm 5:8 puts forth this request, "Lead me, O LORD, in thy righteousness because of mine enemies; make thy way straight before my face." The writer is asking God to lead him in righteousness because of His enemies.

Psalms 71:2 says, "Deliver me in thy righteousness, and cause me to escape: incline thine ear unto me, and save me." It is righteousness that clearly causes one to escape. Also, notice how out of righteousness, He will incline His ear. This brings us to prayer.

Righteousness serves as a point of confidence that personal prayers are heard. Psalms 34:15 confirms this, "The eyes of the LORD are upon the righteous, and his ears are open unto their cry."

James 5:16b states, "...The effectual fervent prayer of a righteous man availeth much." Righteousness is the foundation upon which we can stand. It gives us authority before God. In fact, it is the connecting thread that can be seen in this model prayer. It is associated with God's character. It must be sought for in the same way, as well as preferred with the same intensity as we should His kingdom. Such preference ensures that our needs are met.[1]

God's will is for all to be saved; and the visible evidence that assuredly marks the born again experience is righteousness. 1 John 3:9-10 confirms this, "Whosoever is born of God doth not commit sin; for his seed remaineth in him: and he cannot sin, because he is born of God. In this the children of God are manifest, and the children of the devil: whosoever doeth not righteousness is not of God, neither he that loveth not his brother." These Scriptures also show us that righteousness is associated with forgiveness.

Righteousness is likewise associated with the Christian walk. One is to hunger and thirst after it. This means a person is pursuing or following after it. It serves as a breastplate over the believer's heart since it is by the heart that he or she believes unto righteousness.[2] Such belief serves as truth. Truth will manifest itself in righteous acts.

Righteousness establishes a correct disposition. Disposition will determine a person's attitude towards God and life. As a result, righteousness will express itself in godliness, while the disposition of wickedness will manifest itself in evil before God. Therefore, God's people must be clearly established in righteousness. Isaiah 54:13-14 says, "And all thy children shall be taught of the LORD; and great shall be the peace of thy children. In righteousness shalt thou be established: thou shalt be far from oppression; for thou shalt not fear: and from terror; for it shall not come near thee." Righteousness ends in peace, and keeps one from oppression.

God is close to the righteous. He will hear their prayers because their sincere faith is actually being counted for righteousness. It is faith that moves mountains of obstacles in prayer. This virtue perseveres because it believes God and stands sure of His character and intentions.[3] Jeremiah 29:11 gives us this promise, "For I know the thoughts that I

---

[1] Psalm 7:17; Isaiah 51:8; Matthew 6:33

[2] Isaiah 51:1; 59:16; Romans 10:9-10; Ephesians 6:14; 1 Timothy 6:11; 2 Timothy 2:22

[3] Matthew 17:20; Romans 4:5; Hebrews 11:1-6

think toward you, saith the LORD, thoughts of peace, and not of evil, to give you an expected end."

Godly obedience is faith in action. Such faith serves as an access into God's grace and promises, resulting in peace or reconciliation.[4] Reconciliation establishes confidence to enter the very throne of God. Hebrews 4:16 reiterates this, "Let us therefore come boldly unto the throne of grace, that we may obtain mercy, and find grace to help in time of need."

What does it mean to maintain righteousness or this authority before God? Jesus gives us insight into ensuring uprightness in this model prayer, "And lead us not into temptation, but deliver us from evil" (Matthew 6:13). Does this request actually mean that God leads a person into temptation? This seems almost a contradiction to other well-known Scriptures. Scripture states that God never tempts man with evil, and that He will never let a person be tempted above what he or she is able to endure.[5]

To understand this request, one must understand what constitutes temptation. There are three popular meanings to this word. They are chastisement, test, or prove. Temptation can become a form of discipline, serve as a test to our character, or prove our heart condition. Therefore, this particular request points to one being led or carried away from temptation that would ensnare a person into moral deviation due to character flaws or inconsistencies.

The key to avoid such temptation is to be upright before God, and to walk in the ways of righteousness. The battle is not with temptation in and of itself, but with the old man within us. For example, the greatest door that opens us up to temptation is our pride. The Apostle Paul brings this out in 1 Corinthians 10:12, "Wherefore let him that thinketh he standeth take heed lest, he fall." Pride is an idol that gives us a false sense of self, which sets us up for defeat. When it reigns, it makes us unreasonable, cruel, and unteachable. We always have to come out on top of every issue or somehow come out with our dignity intact. It also sets us up to give in to the enticements of the flesh or to blindly fall into Satan's traps.

It is important to understand how these different forms of temptation work. For example, why must God chastise or discipline us? Hebrews 12:6 states that He only chastises those whom He loves. The reason He disciplines His children is found in Hebrews 12:10-11,

> For they verily for a few days chastened us after their own pleasure (earthly fathers); but he for our profit, that we might be partakers of his holiness. Now no chastening for the present seemeth to be joyous, but grievous: nevertheless afterward it yielded the peaceable fruit of righteousness

---

[4] Romans 4:13; 5:1-2; James 2:21-26
[5] 1 Corinthians 10:13; James 1:13

unto them which are exercised thereby. (Parenthesis added.)

Discipline is associated with humbling self, fleeing fleshly lusts, and pursuing righteousness. Such discipline must occur when the flesh is reigning. The flesh always defiles the things of God and causes a person to become entangled in the things of the world. Therefore, discipline in this sense is for the purpose of causing one to partake of God's holiness. Holiness will cause one to walk in the ways of righteousness. The holiness of God is also associated with the fear of the Lord.

The fear of God is the beginning of wisdom. The Apostle Paul made this statement about Jesus Christ in 1 Corinthians 1:30, "But of him are ye in Christ Jesus, who of God is made unto us wisdom, and righteousness, and sanctification, and redemption." Righteousness always walks in wisdom.

Proverbs 8:20 says this about wisdom, "I lead in the way of righteousness, in the midst of the paths of judgment." Wisdom will lead God's people in the ways of righteousness as it guides them in the midst of judgment. It will keep His people's steps from slipping as well as keep them from walking in foolishness.[6]

The Apostle Paul tells us that God will give us a way out of temptation.[7] Once again, the key is following Him, but people must choose to do so. Such a choice requires them to neglect their pride. Once pride is put down, they can make the necessary moves to follow Him through the temptation. The initial move is repentance where a person humbles self, turns around, and gives way to the leadership of God.

To test something in the spiritual realm means to reveal its character. To test character, a person's spirit or motivation will be exposed. When pride is reigning, it means we are operating according to our natural spirit or the spirit of the world, Satan. Once again, pride is setting us up to fall into Satan's traps. Therefore, when our character is tested, it will reveal the ways of wickedness rather than righteousness. This is why the Apostle John instructs people to test the spirits, while Proverbs 16:2 says, "All the ways of a man are clean in his own eyes; but the LORD weigheth the spirits."[8]

Everything man concludes seems right and logical to his way of thinking.[9] Clearly, this is not what God considers. He considers the spirit that is motivating or prompting the person. A wrong spirit defiles that which is right, while the right spirit maintains righteousness in disposition as well as in conduct.

---

[6] Proverbs 9:6-11
[7] 1 Corinthians 10:13
[8] 1 John 4:1
[9] Proverbs 14:12; 16:25

Testing the spirit reveals the disposition of a person. The level or extent of pride will not only determine a person's character, but also his or her level of maturity. Pride lacks wisdom and will always express itself in obstinacy, foolishness, or folly.

Philippians 2:5 tells Christians to have the mind of Christ. In His humanity, His mind consisted of a lowly disposition and a meek attitude. This type of disposition not only made Him manageable, but sensitive. When people are obstinate, they cannot be managed or led. If they are self-centered, they are indifferent to reality. When people are indifferent, they cannot be warned of impending destruction or judgment.

God allows testing that comes through trials or tribulation. Such testing not only works character in us, but also tries our faith.[10] Romans 5:3-5 says, "And not only so, but we glory in tribulations also: knowing that tribulation worketh patience; And patience, experience, and experience, hope."

James 1:2-4 gives us this encouragement, "My brethren, count it all joy when ye fall into divers temptations; Knowing this, that the trying of your faith worketh patience. But let patience have her perfect work, that ye may be perfect and entire, wanting nothing."

Christians will be tempted, but hopefully it will not be for the goal of exposing rebellion, but to establish and refine both faith and character. Those who are righteous will not only endure such temptation in confidence, but will come forth with greater spiritual depth and maturity.

To ensure temptation that will enlarge our character, we must be walking according to righteousness. Otherwise, the testing will be to expose a person's wrong disposition. This type of testing will involve pressure that is designed to break a person at his or her pride in order to bring him or her to repentance.

Temptation also involves proving something. God used the wilderness to prove Israel. Deuteronomy 8:2 confirms this, "And thou shalt remember all the way which the LORD thy God led thee these forty years in the wilderness, to humble thee, and to prove thee, to know what was in thine heart, whether thou wouldest keep his commandments, or no."

It is interesting to observe the different types of temptation. God uses diverse means to expose the different aspects of a person's spiritual condition. For example, God personally disciplines his children. He uses fiery ovens to test or refine godly character, but He uses the wilderness to prove His people.

The purpose of proving is to expose the heart. The heart is either close to God or far from Him. The condition of the heart will depend on the focus or direction or our affections. For the children of Israel, much of their affections were with the attractions of Egypt. Their hearts secretly

---

[10] 1 Peter 1:6-9

remained divided, and when they were proved in the wilderness, they erected a golden calf and eventually rebelled against God.

The problem is that most people think more highly of themselves than they should.[11] They do not realize how deceitful their heart is. It is usually divided which points to idolatry. It claims loving devotion to God, while maintaining rights contrary to His character and ways. In fact, a heart that has not been completely changed or regenerated has no inclination towards God. It may be attracted to the concepts or religious notions surrounding Jesus, but it is not in love with the Person of Jesus.

God allows His people to be proved so they can see their hearts. The problem with a revelation about the heart is that if a person fails to keep it in proper perspective, he or she falls into despair and condemnation. Much of religious life is outward conformity, but temptation proves that the real test to a person's spiritual life comes down to his or her inward disposition. This means it comes down to the heart. For the heart to be changed, the mind must be transformed and the inward man must be sanctified by the life of Jesus.[12] This life will manifest itself in godly wisdom and righteousness.

Temptation can serve as a narrow path between spiritual growth and destruction. It can lead to the ovens of affliction where character is established, or to the fires of hell where judgment is experienced. It can be a form of pruning to produce greater fruits, or a means to burn up that which avoids the leadership of God. It can lead to the establishment of righteousness or to the destruction of the clutches of evil.

Jesus is basically instructing His followers to ask God to lead them not into temptation that will result in despair, destruction, or judgment, but deliver them from evil practices. This last statement in regard to evil practices, points to temptation that would cause one to fall into the evil snares of Satan.[13]

Evil in this Scripture points to a person's essential character.[14] This means a person has to be delivered from him or herself. The Apostle Paul confirmed this in Romans 7:21, "I find then a law, that, when I would do good, evil is present with me."

Man is hopeless unless God delivers him. He does not have the ability to do that which is right. Instead of temptation bringing him to heights in God, he would not only taste the depths of his own bitterness and hopelessness, but the destruction of his soul.

Deliverance points to God's mercy, grace, and redemption. This brings us back to Paul's words in 1 Corinthians 1:30. Jesus serves as our wisdom from heaven, our righteousness within, our sanctification throughout, and the complete work of redemption. We need to line up to

---

[11] Romans 12:3

[12] Romans 12:2

[13] 1 Timothy 3:7; 2 Timothy 2:26

[14] Strong's Exhaustive Concordance; #4190

His wisdom, give way to His righteousness, yield to His sanctification, and believe His complete work of redemption to ensure uprightness in our life.

Righteousness will bring us under the control and leading of the Holy Spirit and will result in heavenly benefits. Proverbs 12:21 tells us that no evil shall happen to the just, while Proverbs 14:19 declares that evil will bow before the good and the wicked at the gates of the righteous. Obviously, the righteous will ultimately be delivered and exalted.

Are you maintaining your Christian walk in the wisdom, righteousness, sanctification, and redemption of Christ? Are you indifferent to God's Spirit or are you sensitive to His leading? Would temptation refine you or serve as a form of chastisement or judgment? Would it reveal maturity or a wicked disposition and evil practices? The answers to these questions will determine how effective you are in your prayer closet.

10

THE REALITY

For thine is the kingdom, and the power,
and the glory, forever, Amen.
(Matthew 6:13b)

We have been considering the model prayer that Jesus presented to His disciples. They had admitted they did not know how to pray. This confusion was probably caused by religious influences.

Man's religion has a tendency to make prayer a matter of ritual and duty, rather than a simple, sincere form of communication from the heart with God. This practice has often been reduced to methods and procedures, rather than serving as a means to realize God's kingdom, discover His will, and present daily needs and concerns to Him in confidence and faith.[1] For the religious, prayer has been mistaken for the expression of outward piousness, rather than a means to uncover and rectify inward problems such as unforgiveness. It has been used as a form of self-exaltation, rather than a way to keep vigilant in order to discern Satan's traps, endure temptation, and avoid the destruction of evil.

Jesus introduced the model prayer by introducing the Father. This introduction unveiled the heart of the Father by showing His desire to have a relationship with each of us as a loving Father. He so wants us to sit on His lap in loving adoration, to sit at His feet in wonder and expectation, and sit beside Him in relaxation and rest as we enjoy His presence.[2]

God wants us to know the benefit of enjoying the reality of who He is. In this enjoyment, we will realize thankfulness that comes out of praise, contentment that originates with gratefulness, joy that find its basis in comfort, and peace because of His presence. He wants us to understand the satisfying, abundant life that comes from being in His presence.[3]

Prayer must start with a relationship with God, but it will end with a revelation of His character. This is made obvious in the final part of the prayer, "For thine is the kingdom, and the power, and the glory, for ever. Amen." Even though this part of the Scripture cannot be found in older

---

[1] Matthew 15:7-9; 1 Peter 5:7
[2] Psalm 16:11; John 14:6; Luke 10:38-42; Romans 8:14-15; Colossians 1:20
[3] John 10:10

translations, it maintains the intent and consistency of the model prayer. After all, the main goal of prayer is to discover God, and all we can say to all of this is amen, so be it on earth, for it is so in heaven. Therefore, all successful prayer will conclude with a greater sense, revelation, or reality of God. This benediction sums up the heart of prayer. It is always in regards to His kingdom, while answers are brought forth by His power. His power gives us a glimpse of His glory. His glory reminds us that He is eternal, and His ways everlasting.

The recognition of the incredible reality that surrounds our God is a worthy benediction. Moses ended his intercessory prayer to God in light of the greatness of His mercy. Hannah concluded prayer by advocating God as judge who will give strength to the future King, and exalt the horn of His Anointed One.[4] King David finished his prayer with these words in 2 Samuel 7:28-29,

And now, O Lord GOD, thou art that God, and thy words be true and thou hast promised this goodness unto thy servant: Therefore, now, let it please thee to bless the house of thy servant, that it may continue forever before thee: for thou, O Lord GOD, hast spoken it: and with thy blessing let the house of thy servant be blessed forever. David extolled God as One who keeps His word.

Both Solomon's and Daniel's prayers were prayers of intercession. They reminded God of His promises to His people, and how He separated them as an inheritance for Himself. They asked Him to forgive His people and out of mercy honor their supplications.[5] Daniel's prayer was interrupted by the angel, Gabriel, after he had made this request, "O Lord, hear; O Lord, forgive; O Lord, hearken and do; defer not, for thine own sake, O my God: for thy city and thy people are called by thy name" (Daniel 9:19).

The prayer of Mary, the mother of Jesus, exalted God in adoration. However, she ended with the reality that whatever He spoke remained true forever.[6]

Prayer is about God, discovering His character, and remembering who He is. His unchangeable attributes are what stir up confidence in the hearts of those who seek Him, as they begin to cling to His promises and abide in His faithfulness.

The benediction of this model prayer signifies both the end and the beginning. A person may have come to the end of his or her time with God, but prayer in itself signals the endless character and reality of God. After all, there is no beginning or end with Him.[7]

---

[4] Numbers 14:19; 1 Samuel 2:10
[5] 1 Kings 8:50-54; Daniel 9:2-21
[6] Luke 1:46-56
[7] Revelation 1:8

One of my favorite benedictions in the Bible is Aaron's benediction in Numbers 6:24-27, "The LORD bless thee, and keep thee: The LORD make his face to shine upon thee, and be gracious unto thee: The LORD lift up his countenance upon thee, and give thee peace." Ruth Specter Lascelle related this benediction as an appeal to the Godhead.

For example, "The LORD bless thee and keep thee," points to the Father's abiding love and care. The Apostle John made this statement, "Behold, what manner of love the Father hath bestowed upon us, that we should be called the sons of God: therefore the world knoweth us not, because it knew him not" (1 John 3:1).

The next statement of Aaron's benediction is, "The LORD make his face to shine upon thee." This reference points to the Son. Jesus is the visible image of the Father. He is the light of the world. Revelation 22:16 makes this statement, "I, Jesus, have sent mine angel to testify unto you these things in the churches. I am the root and the offspring of David, and the bright and morning star." Wherever Jesus' life is shining, He will be reflecting the reality of God. His face is shining brightly with power and glory, pointing to revelation of the heavenly. [8]

The final part of Aaron's benediction points to the Holy Spirit, "The LORD lift up his countenance upon thee, and give thee peace." The Holy Ghost resides in us, allowing God to view us as His inheritance. He is our Comforter and gives us an abiding peace in God, in spite of circumstances and overwhelming circumstances. He leads us into communion with the Father.[9]

As you consider the model prayer, you realize that it ends with the reality of God in His fullness. The kingdom points to God the Father, power to God the Holy Spirit, and glory to God the Son. This benediction reminds us of the commitment of the Father, the work of the Holy Ghost, and the revelation of the Son. It shows us that it begins with the Father and ends with a greater revelation of the glory of Jesus. In between the love of the Father and the revelation of the Son is the glorious work of the Spirit to bring forth communion. This communion or fellowship can only be realized at the point of grace. This grace came forth on the cross through Jesus' death. Let us consider the significance of this benediction of the Disciple's Prayer Matthew 6:13b, "For thine is the kingdom, and the power, and the glory for ever. Amen."

The word "thine" points to something that is personal or a possession. It implies to seat oneself in the company of something or someone.[10] This statement tells us that the heavenly kingdom belongs to God and is open to all who will accept His invitation to come.[11] It is His power to do as He will: That is to save, change, and bring forth a desired

---

[8] John 1:4-5; 14:9; Revelation 1:16
[9] John 14:15-18; 1 Corinthians 3:16; Galatians 5:22; Ephesians 1:10-14
[10] Strong's Exhaustive Concordance, #4675
[11] Matthew 22:1-14

result. It is His glory that He desires to express through His kingdom in His power and through the Body of Jesus. As the Apostle Paul stated in Ephesians 2:6, "And hath raised us up together and made us sit together in heavenly places in Christ Jesus." Positionally, we are seated together in Christ, but God's desire is that His kingdom or reign be realized in us. After all, it is His kingdom.

The key to advancing His kingdom is power.[12] This power is in reference to the miraculous to do the impossible, the ability to carry it out, and the abundance that will be the obvious product.[13] The main purpose for this power is to be a witness for God's kingdom in this world. A great example of this in found in Acts 2 when the people in the upper room were endued with power from on high. The reason is revealed in Acts 1:8, "But ye shall receive power, after that the Holy Ghost is come upon you: and ye shall be witnesses unto me both in Jerusalem, and in all Judea, and in Samaria, and unto the uttermost part of the earth." The power from above enables believers to be effective witnesses in attitude and conduct. They not only have the ability to be silent witnesses in example and deed, but verbal witnesses with authority and confidence.[14]

Adhering to God's kingdom and walking in the power of His Spirit brings a person to His glory. Glory means dignity, honor, praise, and worship.[15] God in His glory deserves adoration and worship. Prayer is to lead a person to not only discover His will but a greater revelation of Him. Each revelation will enhance his or her worship as it enlarges him or her to embrace a greater reality of God's eternal character.

God's heart is to reveal His glory to each of us. This glory lifts us above this world to realize the beauty of His incredible majesty. The Apostle John talks about God's glory, "And the Word was made flesh, and dwelt among us, (and we beheld his glory, the glory as of the only begotten of the Father,) full of grace and truth" (John 1:14). God's glory is found in His Son. He wants to unveil the One who is king over His heavenly kingdom. It is the Son who gives the power of the Spirit to those who believe to become children of God.[16] Once again, we are reminded of an intimate relationship with the Father. It is in this relationship that the glory of the Son is not only unveiled to those who partake at the communion table, but also, He Himself will be unveiled to those who commune with the Father.

The Apostle Paul made this statement in 2 Corinthians 3:18, "But we all, with open face beholding as in a glass the glory of the Lord, are changed into the same image from glory to glory, even as by the Spirit of the Lord."

---

[12] 1 Thessalonians 1:5
[13] Strong's Exhaustive Concordance, *#1411*
[14] 2 Corinthians 3:2-3
[15] Strong's Exhaustive Concordance, #1391
[16] John 1:12

The benediction found in Matthew 6:13 reminds us of how we need to seek God and His kingdom early in our day to maintain the integrity of our life before Him. We must be persevering in prayer until His power is displayed.[17] Communion with God inspires us to live in an expectant state in relationship to seeing the fullness of His glory. The Apostle Paul made this statement, "When Christ, who is our life, shall appear, then shall ye also appear with him in glory" (Colossians 3:4).

God's kingdom, power, and glory are eternal. There is no end to His kingdom, no limit to His power, and no boundaries to His glory. We can bank on His kingdom, experience His power, and reflect His glory. This combination is meant to establish, enlarge, and exalt us to realize our life in heavenly places with Jesus. This place in Christ allows us to enjoy an inheritance, partake of the eternal, and walk by faith in a God who never changes.

The reality of God is forever. Man can see His intervention in the past, His abiding presence in the present, and His power to shape the future. God's work can be seen in creation, is revealed to and in the humble heart, and will be expressed in a sanctified saint.

It is this sure reality of God that allows us to declare amen. Amen means, "so be it", "surely" and "trustworthy".[18] Seeing His kingdom realized through His will and provision is "amen." Witnessing His power in our lives, as well as others is "so be it." God being exalted in His glory is a sure reality pointing to a matter as "being so." Knowing Him as God is the most trusted assurance we have in this present world.

This model prayer is about God. It points to a relationship that speaks of privilege. Having a relationship with the Living God has to be the greatest privilege a person can have. But, how many of us take this privilege for granted? We allow the glitter of the world, the appetites of the flesh, and the demands of self and pride to blind us to this awesome privilege. Jesus brings this privilege out in this model prayer. He reveals that it is about a relationship with God. In this relationship, His kingdom can be realized, His will discovered, His provision enjoyed, His forgiveness embraced, and His leadership trusted.

Your prayer life before God will not only say much about your relationship with Him, but your worship as well. What does your present relationship say about your life before God?

---

[17] Psalm 63:1; Matthew 6:33; Luke 18:1-8
[18] Strong's Exhaustive Concordance, #281

Section II

WORSHIP

11

LET US COME AND WORSHIP

O come, let us worship and bow down:
let us kneel before the LORD our maker.
(Psalm 95:6)

Worship started out to be a vague concept to me in my initial years as a Christian. It was nothing more than a time of singing a few hymns in church. After all, that is what the church bulletin called the experience. Therefore, I never thought much about worship. At best, it was an insignificant time set apart for singing some songs on Sunday. Otherwise, it held no real meaning to me.

As I grew in my relationship with God, I began to realize that my concept of worship was far from the Biblical presentation of it. Worship was not a time of singing once a week, but a daily reality. It was not just an activity, but a state or attitude of the mind and heart. It was more than an invitation to worship, but a product of an active, acceptable life before God. In fact, true, acceptable worship is a natural act of a saint who truly understands the character of God.

The challenge to come to terms with the subject of worship caused me to rethink my understanding of worship, and to study what God's Word had to say about it. My study started with the meaning of the word, "worship."[1] Worship encompasses body language, as it points to bowing or prostrating oneself to pay homage. It involves the attitude as a person humbles him or herself to show reverence, adoration, veneration, and devotion. It also serves as point of piousness for those who love God. The meaning seemed simple enough, but I began to realize that worship could not be understood on an intellectual basis. It had to be experienced.

The request in Psalm 95:6 is an invitation for all to come and worship God. However, this invitation to come and worship is not a simple call, but implies that there is a compelling desire. This compelling desire reveals that the call may go out to everyone, but worship is a personal encounter that must take place with God.

The greatest insight about worship came from two main sources: The study of the tabernacle in the Old Testament and Jesus' encounter

---

[1] Strong's Exhaustive Concordance; #5457, 6087, 7812 (OT); 2318-2323, 3511, 4352, 4573-4576 (NT)

with the Samaritan woman in John 4.[2] The tabernacle revealed what it would take to come into a place of real worship, while Jesus explained the attitude behind acceptable worship to the woman. The tabernacle study brought awe to my heart as I realized the simplicity and beauty of worship, while Jesus' teachings concerning it in John brought both sobriety and excitement in my spirit.

As I pondered Jesus' words to the Samaritan woman, I recognized that Jesus had stepped outside of heaven, time, and His present course to answer the Samaritan woman's question about worship. This made me realize that Jesus greatly valued this subject; therefore, it was an important issue to God. I could no longer accept a vague concept of it or any weak presentation about it. I had to know for myself the purpose of worship in my spiritual life.

The more I studied worship, the more I realized that worship rests at the heart of everything a godly man and woman does in regards to God. Isolated knowledge about worship will make people indifferent to God. Making worship a matter of fleshly activity makes it pagan in nature. Stamping the word "worship" on some religious ceremony demotes it to a simple religious exercise that has no life or meaning to it. It dawned on me that until true worship is practiced and experienced, it remains shrouded by doctrine or man's theology.

My first real experience of worship occurred when God brought me to my knees. I had been in sin, and felt I had stepped over the line of no return. I knew I had left Jesus behind as I covered my idolatry with outward devotion to Him, and tried to make atonement for my transgression with religious deeds. All my attempts brought me to spiritual bankruptcy. As I faced my spiritual poverty, I became broken over my sins. I didn't realize it then, but I had just entered one of the doors that lead to true worship.

Later, I learned that there are two main doors to worship. One is brokenness, while the other one is praise. Brokenness brings you to the end of self, so you can embrace God in His pardon and restoration, while praise brings you to the foot of His throne, where you can experience Him in His greatness.

As I began to repent in tears and confess in brokenness my blatant affront against God's character, and my failure to obey the first commandment to love Him, I found myself at the feet of Jesus. My brokenness had produced humility in my disposition, causing my heart to bow, my knees to shake, my lips to tremble, and my hands to reach out for mercy.

In His love, the Lord met me in His mercy and grace. He was quick to pick me up, wipe away my tears, and give me assurance that I was forgiven. The weight of my sin lifted, and I stood before Him in adoration, awe, and excitement.

---

[2] Exodus 25:8-9

This was my first experience of worship. It made an impact on my life that changed the way I perceived God. However, I knew I was still in much ignorance about this subject. I had taken so much for granted in my Christian life, due to my intellectual arrogance. Intellectual arrogance can only produce spiritual ignorance. Spiritual ignorance is nothing more than superstition. I realized that I harbored superstition when it came to worship, and I wondered how many other people possessed such ignorance.

In my brokenness before God, I had gotten my feet wet, but I had greater depths to plumb about worship before I would gain God's perspective. One of the obstacles I had to overcome was making sure that worship was not a duty, but a compelling desire. Underneath, I knew this was the secret to true worship, but how does one develop this desire? The first thing I had to do was answer the question, "Why does one worship God?"

There are two answers to this question: Man was created to worship, and God is worthy of worship. Man must worship something. If you don't believe me, study human nature. People are forever looking for something to worship outside of the essence of self. This search has led people down into dark, pagan, idolatrous worlds where their gods are harsh and destructive. The Apostle Paul dealt with this issue in his travels and in his epistle to the Romans.

In *Acts 17:16-27*, Paul takes on the people of Athens with their many altars erected to their various gods. In Romans 1:18-30, he condemns those who worship the creation rather than the Creator. At one point, he was even considered the mythical god, Mercurius, which is something he clearly rejected and refuted. He was also persecuted because he put a dent in the financial gain of idol makers.[3]

Man desires to worship in order to fill the empty spiritual vacuum of his spirit and soul. Sadly, he erects his own gods and surrounds these gods with superstition and religious activity. Ultimately, his god or gods will feed his fleshly appetites and appease his pride, but they will also leave him miserably lost.

The God of heaven deserves worship because of who He is. In Revelations 4:10-11, we see the elders worshipping the Lord, saying, "Thou are worthy, O Lord, to receive glory and honour and power..." Due to God's own nature, He formed man with the ability to respond and interact with Him at the point of worship. Worship implies communion and fellowship with God.

How important is it to understand what constitutes acceptable worship? The truth is many Christians are unsuspectingly worshipping idols, while giving lip service to God. This idolatry is caused by ignorance. Worship in many cases is not being properly taught.

---

[3] Acts 15:12-19

Ignorance of this nature allows people to interpret or define a spiritual matter according to worldly or lifeless religious perceptions.

Do you know how to worship God? Perhaps you are ignorantly bowing down to other gods, while the God of heaven is shrouded in superstition. You go through an exercise at church called "worship," but it is vague to you and has no meaning. If you fit into either category, quit assuming that you understand this subject. You need to take up the challenge to come to terms with real worship that is acceptable to the living God of heaven and earth.

12

WORTHY OF WORSHIP

Ye worship ye know not what...
John 4:22a

In Jesus' discourse with the Samaritan woman in John 4:22, He stated that she did not know whom she worshipped. Obviously, the woman worshipped something, but her concepts of God and the real God of heaven were far apart. She assumed that she knew God because of her religious affiliation, but Jesus explicitly stated that she had no idea whom she worshipped.

This statement should cause each person to pause and consider whom or what he or she is worshipping. Just because one worships some idea or entity does not mean he or she knows whom or what he or she is bowing down before. It is vital that each person come to terms with the focus of his or her adoration. Assumption or religious affiliation is not enough. Worship is determined by a person's understanding of the focus of his or her adoration. Obviously, people's attitude is going to be greatly affected by their perception of whom or what they worship.

To properly worship God, we must know whom we are worshipping. By knowing the true God, we can do nothing but worship Him in the right spirit and according to the truth as to His identity. We see this in Scripture. When people encountered God's presence and power, they immediately responded by worshipping Him.

For example, each time the visible presence of God came down on the tabernacle, the Israelites would worship Him. When Joshua encountered the captain of the hosts of the LORD, he bowed down and worshipped the pre-incarnate Son of God. When the people of Israel witnessed God accepting the sacrifice of Elijah in a miraculous way, they worshipped Him. [1]

Jesus received the same reaction in His humanity from those He encountered. After he healed the leper, he came back and worshipped Him. Jairus, a leader, came to Jesus and worshipped Him by showing a certain respect for Him before he asked Him to heal his daughter. Jesus' disciples worshipped Him after He calmed the raging sea. A woman from Canaan worshipped Him as she was seeking Him to deliver her daughter

---

[1] Exodus 33:9-10; Joshua 5:13-15; 1 Kings 18:38-39; 2 Chronicles 7:2-3;

from a devil. Even a demon-possessed man worshipped Jesus in spite of his grave oppression.[2]

People desire to worship something. They are forever erecting altars and idols. They are looking for something outside of their limited self to make sense of their lives. They are looking for something beyond themselves that can change the course of their lives. They are looking for something that can give them hope in spite of the world and events that plague them.

Man's desperate search for God reveals his ignorance about God. This ignorance is nothing more than superstition. To make God a matter of superstition means that God will appear to be indifferent, and that things happen according to chance, punishment, or personal merits, rather than in light of God's unchanging character or eternal plan. Such a person's concept of God's power hinges more on the idea of magic or the supernatural, rather than on His character. This ignorance means that much of the person's response towards God will be out of a fear of the unknown, rather than a fear or respect for the true, living God of heaven.

The Apostle Paul confronted this superstition in *Acts 17*. He was in Athens where there were many altars erected to different gods. Paul passed by an altar with the inscription: *"TO THE UNKNOWN GOD."* He addressed the people by telling them that they ignorantly worshipped this God. Then he proceeded to explain who this God was.

Who is this God? Since His presence results in worship and His power in awe, each of us must be sure that we know Him. Obviously, knowing Him confirms that He is worthy of worship. The angels worship Him before His throne. In Isaiah 6:2-3, the seraphim covered their faces as they cried, "Holy, holy, holy, is the LORD of hosts." The elders around the throne worship Him as they cast their crowns before the throne, declaring His worthiness to receive glory, honor, and power. In fact, there are thousands upon thousands who worship Him before His throne, always declaring that He deserves to be exalted, adored, and honored.[3] This worship is inspired by a heart revelation of Him. Such a revelation will ensure a right attitude that will humble the heart in worship.

Why does God deserve worship? The Apostle Paul gives us insight into this answer in Acts 17:24-25, "God that made the world and all things therein, seeing that he is Lord of heaven and earth, dwelleth not in temples made with hands; Neither is worshipped with men's hands, as though he needed any thing, seeing he giveth to all life, and breath, and all things."

The first reason we should worship God is because He made all things. He is our creator or maker. Psalm 95:6 instructs us to kneel before our Maker. Hebrews 1:1-10 speaks of how God made the world

[2] Matthew 9:18; 14:25-33; 15:22-28; Mark 5:1-6; Luke 17:12-19
[3] Revelation 4:10-11; 5:11-12; 7:9-15

and upholds all things by His word. He laid the foundation of the earth, and the heavens are the work of His hands. Revelation 14:7 invites people to come and worship Him that made the heaven, earth, sea, and the fountains of water. Since God made us, we owe Him our service, adoration, and worship.

Secondly, He is the Lord of heaven and earth. In other words, He is the overseer of all of creation. As part of creation, Jesus has the right to be Lord in our lives. As Lord, He deserves our servitude, obedience, and commitment.

The final reason we must worship Him is that if we fail to do so, we have no part in Who He is. He stands alone in His position and in His creation. He has need of nothing, while we have need of everything. In fact, He holds our very life and breath in His hands. Knowledge such as this should create not only awe, but also fear. We will answer to Him alone. He alone has say over the length and essence of our lives. In light of Him, our life is like a vapor; our flesh is as grass that withers, and our glory as a flower that falls to the wayside.[4]

In Acts 17:30, the Apostle Paul also warned that God would not continue to wink at ignorance towards Him. This is a serious warning. God has provided the means by which people can know Him. His creation declares His existence. His Son came to earth to quench the ignorance of man. His Spirit was sent to draw man to Himself. Now, we have His written Word to unveil Him to all who seek to know Him. Therefore, there is no excuse for not knowing the true God. However, many people have no desire to seek out the real God. They prefer their ignorance, so that they can merrily go on their way to judgment and spiritual ruin.

In light of who God is, man can do nothing more than fall at His feet in worship. His holiness produces fear and humility. His incredible love inspires sacrificial love. His longsuffering encourages repentance, while His mercy gives way to forgiveness, and His grace offers salvation. He freely promises Living Water to the parched soul and Living Bread or Manna to the spiritually hungry. There is not one aspect of His character that does not reach out to man with the intent of providing him with a complete life, and restore him to a place of fellowship in Him.

Throughout the Bible, we see man personally worshipping God. The responses are similar. There is always sobriety or fear and not sensual fleshly foolishness. Moses and Joshua reverently took their shoes off when they were in His presence. The Israelites stood and worshipped God from afar because they witnessed His power and holiness. Isaiah felt undone or exposed before God. The Apostle John fell down as if he were dead when He encountered Jesus as the Alpha and Omega, the King, and righteous Judge.[5]

---

[4] James 4:14; 1 Peter 1:24
[5] Exodus 3:5; 20:18-21; 24:1-2; Joshua 5:13-15; Isaiah 6:5; Revelation 1:17-18

Worship does not come from emotional zeal. Rather, it comes from a deep abiding sense of who God is. This sense is not silly, but sober. It is not fleshly, but based on a healthy fear of God. It is not casual, but cautious and aware. It is not a matter of duty to win God's favor, but one of diligence to seek and find God in order to please Him.[6]

Man must worship someone or something, but it is clear that there is only one true God who deserves such worship. Sadly, everything and everybody seems to be vying for this position in people's lives. Idolatry is rampant. People look to every possible source outside of God to find purpose and happiness. These pursuits lead to dead ends, but people continue to avoid God. Ultimately, each pursuit and attitude reveal his or her gods, as well as their identity.

For example, some peoples' god is money. This idol leaves people discontent and miserable. Other people worship man, causing them to become disillusioned and closed down. Self is another god that many bow down to. This god leaves people hard and indifferent to others. Another popular god is education. It leaves people arrogant, unteachable, and foolish. The world is also another highly preferred idol to some individuals, but it leaves them empty and depressed. Religion is another god that is clamored after by many. Religion can break off into various idols. But, whether the god is exalted doctrine, arrogant knowledge, or heretical leaders, these gods leave people self-righteous, legalistic, hypocritical, and isolated.

Satan offered all of these gods to Jesus when He was in the wilderness. Jesus said of the god that involved the aspects of the flesh that His existence did not rest in the things that maintained His physical life. He declared that the Word of God maintained the type of life that should be desired and is significant and lasting.[7]

When Satan offered the god that honored self, Jesus revealed that adhering to this god would put the true God to a foolish test. In a way, the god that surrounds the pride of man subtly demands that God bow down to it, and adheres to it according to its games and whims.[8]

The final god was the world, with all of its glory and attractions. This test revealed that Satan's real goal was to get Jesus to bow down and worship him. Satan is the god of this world. The world offers the flesh the fulfillment of all of its needs and desires, even though they represent temporary pleasures and satisfaction. It appeases the pride with illusive promises of success and happiness. And, hidden behind the world's glory is a façade, but most people are attracted to its false majesty. Needless to say, this false glory hides the ignorance, darkness, delusion, and destruction that plague those entangled in its deceptive web.[9]

---

[6] Hebrews 11:6
[7] Matthew 4:1-4
[8] Matthew 4:5-7
[9] Matthew 4:8-10; 2 Corinthians 4:3-6; 1 John 2:15-17

People are either worshipping God or Satan. God's Word is clear that there is only One true God. There is no god that stands beside Him or deserves to be worshipped. As a result, the first two commandments instruct His people that they must not have any other God, but Jehovah God. God warns them of the devastating consequences if they bow down to idols erected in their minds and hearts or made with their hands. It is man who gives such idols their identity as he declares them to be his god. However, God is a jealous God, and He will not compete for people's hearts and minds.[10]

Obviously, people must know God before they can properly worship Him. By knowing God, people will have a right attitude in which to approach Him. They will have an abiding confidence about His ways. These individuals will have a tried and tested faith that will take God at His Word. Ultimately, they will be able to declare His faithfulness to others

Do you know God? If you don't, you do not know whom you worship. You will exhibit a carnal attitude, while your approach will be fleshly. In the end, you will be worshipping an idol rather than the God of heaven.

Finally, what does your attitude and way of worship say about the identity of the God you honor?

---

[10] Exodus 20:3-5; Joshua 24:14-24; Psalm 115:4-9; Isaiah 45:19, 21-22

13

A MATTER OF SALVATION

...we know what we worship:
for salvation is of the Jews.
John 4:22b

Jesus explained to the Samaritan woman that she did not know whom or what she worshipped. Ignorance of this nature is nothing more than spiritual superstition. He then went on to explain that the reason for her ignorance was because salvation is of the Jews.

The Jews knew God because they were entrusted with the lineage that would bring forth the Messiah. To establish and maintain this lineage, God had to keep the Jewish people separate in their beliefs and conduct. As a result, the people of Israel have paid a high price for this distinction.

To establish this distinction, God instructed Abraham to circumcise his household. Circumcision would serve as an outside mark, to not only set his descendants apart from the rest of the world, but to remind them of the covenant that He made with Abraham.[1]

The children of Israel have found themselves in unbearable bondage due to their association with Jehovah God. They spent time in the wilderness where they were entrusted with the Law of Moses that pointed to man's need for a savior. They were given the Promised Land as a lasting heritage to ensure a lineage and future kingdom. They battled in and for this land, as well as experienced tyranny, struggled with idolatry, fell into paganism, experienced judgment, were scattered and tasted the bitter cup of persecution. They have been made the tail in most other countries. However, through it all, Israel's survival is one of the greatest testimonies that Jehovah God exists, and that He is very much involved in man's affairs.

The salvation that came through the Jews would serve as the means by which those of spiritual ignorance could discover the true God of heaven and earth. This discovery would not only lead to salvation, but worship.

Hebrews 6:9 states, "But, beloved, we are persuaded better things of you, and things that accompany salvation, though we thus speak." The virtues that accompany salvation are the natural byproducts of those who

---

[1] Genesis 17:9-14

are truly born of Spirit and water. Jesus was the firstfruits to come forth because of what was accomplished on the cross.[2] This salvation speaks of God's character and commitment. As the Holy Ghost works the very means of salvation in a person, it will create a right attitude and response towards God: That of worship. This worship will be in accordance with the nature and accomplishments of God, and will be expressed in various ways.

For example, salvation implies deliverance. Every time God intervened on behalf of His people, He would deliver them. We see this in the case of the children of Israel. He delivered the people of Israel from the tyranny of Egypt. He brought distinction to them when His wrath was abiding on Egypt, and showed great miracles on His people's behalf such as the parting of the Red Sea. After His people's deliverance through the Red Sea, they worshipped God by singing a song to Him. They made this declaration in the song, "The LORD is my strength and song, and he is become my salvation: he is my God, and I will prepare him an habitation; my father's God, and I will exalt him" (Exodus 15:2). The children of Israel acknowledged Jehovah God as their strength and song. As a result of His deliverance, He became their salvation, and they exalted Him as God.[3]

Christians have this same reality about God through Jesus. His death on the cross was the way to deliver those from the tyranny of sin.[4] As the chains of sin fall to the wayside, worship comes forth from the heart. Ephesians 5:19 instructs us as believers in this way: "Speaking to yourselves in psalms and hymns and spiritual songs, singing and making melody in your heart to the Lord."

Psalm 144:9 summarizes the abiding reality of God's deliverance, "I will sing a new song unto thee, O God..."

Deliverance represents a glorious time indeed. It produces a song in the heart that is directed upwards to the Great Deliverer of all. Hebrews 5:9 gives us this insight into Jesus, "And being made perfect, he became the author of eternal salvation unto all them that obey him."

Since salvation is deliverance, it points to rescue. The psalmist made this request in Psalm 35:17, "Lord, how long wilt thou look on? Rescue my soul from their destructions..." There are so many traps in this world. Pride blinds people in such a way that they are set up to fall into traps, while the flesh is used to entice people into the traps. The traps represent death or separation from God.

Jesus came to rescue our souls from these traps of death. He did this with His own death on the cross. His victory over death destroyed the power of the one who had the power of death, Satan. As a result, Jesus rescues those who come to Him from the bondage caused by the

---

[2] John 3:3 & 5; 1 Corinthians 15:20 & 23
[3] Exodus 12:23; 14:30; 15:1-22
[4] Romans 6:14, 17-18

fear, the hopelessness, and the defeat caused by death.[5] As the Apostle Paul declared in the last part of 1 Corinthians 15:54 and the first part of 1 Corinthians 15:55, "Death is swallowed up in victory. O death, where is thy sting?"

Salvation implies safety. It is God who places man in safe places. He put Noah and Moses in an ark. He hid Elijah away from the tyranny of Ahab and Jezebel. He provided refuge cities for the stranger, sojourner, and manslayer. He hid His Son away in obscurity for thirty years.[6] These are examples of literal places, but the truth is, there is only one perfect hiding place for all saints, and that is being in the perfect will of God.

God's will is that all be saved. However, this salvation is a place in Jesus Christ. The Bible talks about believers being in Christ Jesus. For example, He is the Vine, and saints are the branches. It is abiding in the Vine that ensures Christians the life that endures, withstands, and overcomes. He is the eternal place that is being prepared in John 14:1-3. By being in Jesus, believers have been raised up to sit together in heavenly places in Him.[7]

Jesus is truly the place of safety for all who abide in Him. As the Apostle Paul said in Colossians 3:3, "For ye are dead, and your life is hid with Christ in God." A person's life can be hid in Christ, but he or she must first be dead to self, the flesh, and the world. A person who is dead in Christ is alive with His life and reality. Since Jesus is eternal, nothing can touch or destroy this incredible place. As Psalm 3:8 declares: "Salvation belongeth unto the LORD."

Salvation points to liberty. The concept of spiritual liberty is not the right to do as one pleases, but the ability to do what is right. Physical bondage may cause certain limitations that will keep a person from doing certain activities, while worldly bondage often causes emotional and mental oppression that limits a person's ability to properly function. However, when it comes to spiritual bondage, it keeps a person from moving forward in his or her relationship with God. This limitation means a person cannot embrace what God has for him or her.

Bondage causes distress. Psalms 118:5 says, "I called upon the LORD in distress: the LORD answered me, and set me in a large place." One must spiritually be in a large place to come into rest in God. This large place represents liberty, allowing the person to explore God and discover His treasures. It especially encourages communion with God.

The Apostle Paul made this statement in 2 Corinthians 3:17, "Now the Lord is that Spirit: and where the Spirit of the Lord is, there is liberty." The presence of God's Spirit represents liberty and power to move forward. Paul also talked about the communion of the Holy Ghost.[8] God

---

[5] Hebrews 2:14-15

[6] Genesis 6:14: Exodus 2:3; I Kings 17:3, 9

[7] John 15:1-8; 1 Corinthians 1:30; Ephesians 2:6; Colossians 3:3

[8] 2 Corinthians 13:14

wants to bring us to a place where we can have liberty to enter into communion with Him.

Much of the worldly bondage that exists occurs because of guilty consciences. It is not unusual to see worldly people whose consciences have become seared.[9] Sadly, what has replaced the vacuum that has been left by an unresponsive conscience is anger and hatred.

As long as God's people harbor unclean consciences, they are unable to enter into the place of worship and communion. They lack the authority, thereby, lacking the boldness. Their hands are dirty, preventing them from reaching up to God in need. They feel shame; therefore, they are unable to look upward into His glorious face. As a result, they must cleanse themselves from filth though confession, humility, mourning, submission, and obedience.[10]

Spiritual liberty results in spiritual victory. There is victory over all that would hold a believer from finding his or her life in Christ. Jesus proved this when He rose from the grave. The grave represents the hopelessness and darkness of bondage, but it could not hold Jesus. He had victory over it because His life and power were greater than the grave. Genuine salvation ends in victory. As Paul stated, we are more than conquerors in Christ Jesus. The key to victory is being hid in the Victor. This victory is wrought by faith that will endure all testing until the appearing of Jesus Christ.[11] His appearing represents the real essence of victory for every saint. The concept of being enfolded in the everlasting, reality of Jesus should humble us, and cause us to worship in spirit and truth.

Genuine worship will accompany salvation. There is no way people can experience salvation, and not be compelled to worship God. When people understand the different ingredients of true adoration, they begin to understand the implications of worship. Worship is an automatic response to the reality and work of God. If worship is missing, individuals must examine themselves to see if they are truly in the faith, or if Jesus has become simply a lifeless concept.

Consider why worship would accompany salvation. It is established by an immovable foundation. Psalm 95:1 says, "O come, let us sing unto the LORD: let us make a joyful noise to the rock of our salvation." The Rock is Jesus.[12] He can never be shaken.

The response to this salvation is joy or celebration. One can only rejoice because it lifts a person above the temporary to experience the eternal. It reveals God's great glory, allowing one to be bathed in His majesty. Out of this reality comes a hope that will never fade in light of temporary circumstances or defeat. This reality caused the Psalmist to

---

[9] 1 Timothy 4:1-2
[10] Hebrews 10:22; James 4:6-10
[11] Romans 8:37; 1 Corinthians 15:55; 1 Peter 1:6-9
[12] 1 Corinthians 10:4

declare, "We will rejoice in thy salvation, and in the name of our God we will set up our banners: the LORD fulfill all thy petitions" (Psalm 20:5).

The reality of God in His salvation will establish a disposition or attitude of worship. It will be stirred by an abiding joy and confidence, founded in peace, clothed in humility, and beautified in meekness. Psalm 149:4 says, "For the LORD taketh pleasure in his people: he will beautify the meek with salvation."

This type of disposition will produce a desire to possess and obtain God's salvation. Psalm 119:81 gives this perspective, "My soul fainteth for thy salvation: but I hope in thy word." If only I could taste the fullness of salvation... If only I could touch the face of salvation... It can only be realized by faith in what God says. Paul was compelled to apprehend the knowledge of Jesus. He was willing to enter into His sufferings and press forward regardless of the obstacles.[13] Does your soul desire God's salvation above all riches and promises?

How does one obtain this salvation? It involves a walk. Isaiah 12:2-3 gives us insight into the walk, "Behold, God is my salvation; I will trust, and not be afraid: for the LORD JEHOVAH is my strength and my song; he also is become my salvation. Therefore with joy shall ye draw water out of the wells of salvation." People must walk by faith.[14] Faith is the opposite of fear, which is a form of unbelief. Faith will push past the fear in order to come to the wells of salvation where those who desire all that God has for them can freely drink of Living Water.

We know the Living Water is the Holy Ghost.[15] We also know the well is Jesus Himself. His invitation is clear in John 7:37, "If any man thirst, let him come unto me, and drink."

Genuine salvation brings an eternal perspective. Isaiah 51:6 says,
Lift up your eyes to the heavens, and look upon the earth beneath: for the heavens shall vanish away like smoke, and the earth shall wax old like a garment, and they that dwell therein shall die in like manner: but my salvation shall be for ever, and my righteousness shall not be abolished.

Salvation is forever. This is the reality of the saint who gets beyond self and this world. As Hebrews 2:3 warns, "How shall we escape, if we neglect so great salvation; which at the first began to be spoken by the Lord, and was confirmed unto us by them that heard him."

Are you saved? This means you have encountered God and His work. You have received it by faith, and now you have an eternal inheritance that will be realized in the unhindered presence and glory of God. If you are an heir of salvation, worship will accompany this eternal hope and reality. And, as Jesus said in Luke 21:28b, "...look up, and lift up your heads; for your redemption draweth nigh."

---

[13] Philippians 3:7-14

[14] 2 Corinthians 5:7

[15] John 7:38-39

14

THE PLACE

Our fathers worshipped in this
mountain; and ye say, that in
Jerusalem is the place where men
ought to worship.
John 4:20

Worship is at the core of effective Christianity. There has been much debate concerning where worship must take place. This debate raged among the Jews and Samaritans in Jesus' day. The Jews maintained that the only acceptable place for worship was Jerusalem. The Samaritans maintained that it was Mount Gerizim.

This debate was understandable. The Jews had distinct instruction as to where the center of all of their religious activities was to be. We are given insight into this in the Old Testament. Deuteronomy 12:5 tells us, "But unto the place which the LORD your God shall choose out of all your tribes to put his name there."

First, we see that He will place His name upon this place. Remember, name points to character. He will choose a place where His character and ways will be made known. This place would remind His followers of Who He is. The Lord goes on to say that this place is where the Israelites will bring all of their offerings.

Deuteronomy 12:11 gives us this next insight to this place, "...Then there shall be a place which the LORD your God shall choose to cause his name to dwell there." The Scripture verse tells us that God's representation will dwell there. This reveals that what sets this place apart will be some type of physical representation. This representation would come in the form of His presence. His presence would be a fulfillment of prophecy where He said that He would dwell among His people.[1]

In Deuteronomy 12:21, the Lord instructs people that the location He chooses will be the main place where sacrifices will be offered to Him. This was God's way of deterring idolatry and unholy sacrifices. By designating one place, it would take the flippancy out of sacrifice, and hopefully cause people to consider the God they were paying homage to. After all, His name would be on this place.

---

[1] Exodus 25:8; 29:43-46

In the case of the priest eating that which was holy, He gives this command in Deuteronomy 14:23, "And thou shalt eat before the LORD thy God, in the place which he shall choose to place His name there." This Scripture implied that all that was associated with this chosen place must be holy. Holiness must be maintained at every level. The Lord revealed the reason for this in the last part of the Scripture: "...that thou mayest learn to fear the LORD thy God always."

The Passover was also to take place at this designated place.[2] Passover reminded the Israelites that they were strangers in a foreign country. God miraculously stepped on the scene and delivered them from the judgment of death and the tyranny of Egypt, which was wrought by the blood of the lamb on the doorposts. Such deliverance also pointed to the great deliverance that took place at the Red Sea, allowing them the liberty to pursue their inheritance.

God chose Jerusalem to be this designated place. Its name means the "habitation of peace." Its very name was to remind the children of Israel of the peace that comes when God's abiding presence and leadership was in their midst. As most know, Jerusalem has been anything but a habitation of peace. War and oppression have plagued its history. There are two reasons for this: 1) The children of Israel forsook Jehovah God, and 2) it is designated as Israel's inheritance. When these two entities, God and Israel, are missing in the land, this land becomes worthless real estate. For example, when Israel is present, but God is missing, there is grave conflict and oppression. When Israel is dwelling in the land in light of their God, He greatly blesses them.

The Samaritans believed that the designated place was Mount Gerizim. Mount Gerizim faced Mount Ebal. It was between the bases of these two mounts that the blessings and curses were read in regard to the children of Israel entering Canaan.[3]

According to their tradition, the Samaritans believed it was on Mount Gerizim that Abraham offered Isaac up as a sacrifice. They also believed that Melchizedek, the priest, blessed Abraham on this mount. We know that Jacob dug a well in the vicinity where the Samaritan woman and Jesus stood discussing Living Water.[4]

The Samaritans built a temple on Mount Gerizim after conflict arose over the temple at Jerusalem. Due to their questionable lineage, they were not allowed to participate in the building of the temple in Jerusalem after the Jews had returned from 70 years of captivity in Babylon. This caused tremendous animosity between the two parties. About B.C. 409, a certain man named Manasseh, who was of priestly lineage, built the temple after being expelled from Jerusalem for an unlawful marriage.[5]

---

[2] Deuteronomy 16:2, 6
[3] Joshua 8:30-35
[4] Smith Bible Dictionary, pages 583-584
[5] Ibid

The Samaritan woman wanted to understand what place was correct to worship God. Jesus made this statement, "Woman believe me, the hour cometh, when ye shall neither in this mountain, nor yet at Jerusalem worship the Father" (John 4:21). Scripturally, the Jews were correct, but many did not have a real attitude of worship. To many of the religious Jews, worship became a ritual that was carried out with a verbal exercise, but not offered from the heart.[6] Jesus stipulated in this Scripture that those who are the true worshippers of God would be able to grasp the reality of His statement.

God deserves worship, but it must be in line with who He is. Jesus confirmed this in John 4:24, "God is a Spirit: and they that worship him must worship him in spirit and in truth." Even though Jesus was the bodily representation of God on this earth, John declared that no man has seen God.[7] In order to see God, one would have to see all three persons of the Godhead. In John 5:37, Jesus declared that no one has heard the voice nor seen the Father's shape. The Father is an unseen spiritual entity. Therefore, a person must worship Him in a right spirit.

The right spirit brings us to the Holy Ghost. He must be present in your life before you can properly worship God. Keep in mind, God declared that His presence (Holy Spirit) would distinguish the place upon which He chose to put His name. His presence would signify that He dwells in the midst of His people.

Is there a present-day place of worship that is able to fit the qualifications of the Old Testament? The answer is yes. It is the person who is truly born of Spirit and water (the Word). This person's heart serves as a permanent place for the Spirit to reside within. Individuals born of the Spirit and water serve as the temple of the Holy Ghost. They will carry the name of God as Jesus is embedded in their hearts, and His name will be always on their lips.[8]

Like the temple of old, each believer has been chosen. It is the presence of the Spirit of God that brings about distinction in the Christian's life. Eventually, the believer who abandons all to know God will become a stranger in a foreign country.[9]

Is there a location? The answer is yes. There are two boundaries people must worship within: spirit and truth. The Holy Ghost inspires true worship from the heart. He can only do this within the framework of truth. Truth points to the character and work of God. This virtue is summarized in two words: Jesus Christ. Jesus declared that He is the truth.[10]

As truth, Jesus is the only way to communion with the Father. He serves as the entrance into an intimate life with the Father. Jesus said

---

[6] Matthew 15:8-9

[7] Matthew 3:16; John 1:18; 5:37; Colossians 2:9

[8] John 3:3, 5

[9] John 15:16 1 Corinthians 3:16-17; 1 Peter 2:11

[10] John 8:32-36; 14:6

that He was the door to the sheep.[11] In John 14:13, He states, "And whatsoever ye shall ask in my name, that will I do, that the Father may be glorified in the Son."

Everything Jesus does for His followers and through His followers is for the glory of the Father. In a way, Jesus serves as the location in which the New Testament temple must be firmly placed. He is the location where man meets with God. This communion takes place at the point of who He is and His redemption.

Since Jesus serves as the location or place for meeting God, it is the Holy Ghost's responsibility to guide a person into all truth.[12] Jesus adds this insight in John 16:14, "He shall glorify me: for he shall receive of mine, and shall shew it unto you."

The ultimate goal of the Holy Ghost is to lead a person into Christ at the point of communion. 2 Corinthians 13:14 makes reference to the communion of the Holy Ghost. He is the right Spirit, and if He is present, He is the one who inspires worship, as well as ultimately leading to greater revelations of God. Revelations simply point to truth taking on life and greater dimension.

The final point of Jesus' discourse with the Samaritan woman was that the Father seeks people who will worship Him in the right way. God deserves genuine worship; therefore, He is actually seeking those who will truly worship Him in Spirit and truth.

The Word instructs us to seek God with all of our hearts, but few realize that God is also on a search. Jesus talked about searching for the lost sheep.[13] We are also told that God is in search of certain specific traits. His search presents us with a picture of what is important to His heart. We know that the souls of men are His top priority, but consider one of the traits He is searching for within man.

2 Chronicles 16:19 states, "For the eyes of the LORD run to and fro throughout the whole earth, to shew himself strong in the behalf of them whose heart is perfect towards him." God is looking for those who have a perfect heart before Him. This implies a complete or whole heart in its devotion to Him. Such a heart is just and righteous in its ways. It is made ready to serve, and is quiet before God. It is whole because it is at peace with God. This is the type of heart that God can show Himself mighty in and through.

Ezekiel 22:30 says, "And I sought for a man among them, that should make up the hedge, and stand in the gap before me for the land, that I should not destroy it: but I found none." Who is God looking for? He is seeking a person who has the authority to stand in the gap for his or her home, church, and nation.

---

[11] John 10:7

[12] John 16:13

[13] Jeremiah 29:13; Luke 15:3-7

Finally, He seeks those who truly worship Him. People, who have embraced His salvation by faith, possess an undivided heart towards Him. Because of the influence of the world, many struggle with this issue of worship and fall short of knowing what it means to worship God. Without worshipping God, they will never discover how to bring glory and honor to Him. These individuals will also fail to understand the presence of the Spirit in their midst. On the other hand, those who know how to worship, will know their place in Jesus, and will have experienced both the communion of the Spirit and peace with the Father.

Christianity is about having an intimate relationship with God. It is about possessing the authority of the Spirit that subdues, and His power that overcomes. This life is about the boldness to enter in at the place of Jesus and His work of redemption. It is a life that finds its base at worship where one experiences the reality of God as He alone is lifted up in honor and glory.

God is testing your heart. Will He find a perfect heart? He is searching for one who has authority to stand in the gap. Will He find such a person in you? He is seeking those who truly worship Him. Will He be able to identify you as a true worshipper, or would He declare that your heart is far away from Him?[14]

---

[14] 1 Samuel 16:7; Jeremiah 11:20; Matthew 15:8-9

15

SACRIFICE

I beseech you therefore, brethren,
by the mercies of God, that ye
present your bodies a living
sacrifice, holy, acceptable
unto God.
(Romans 12:1)

Worship encompasses every aspect of the Christian life. Sadly, Christians can make the mistake of keeping worship as an activity that happens during a religious meeting. As previously discussed, worship is much more than a religious activity. It is an attitude that must be present in everything we do for God. It must be present in service to God, towards those we minister to, and in our lives.

There are three ways we minister in regards to God. We minister *before* God. This involves our earthly ministry to others. It must be motivated by benevolence that is sacrificial. Its main intent is to glorify God before others.

The second type of ministry is ministering *because of* God. Such a ministry involves praise where God is exalted for who He is. Our focus is changed to embrace greater depths of His incredible nature and the possibilities of His unlimited power. An upward focus inspired by His nature can translate into a heavenly perspective, allowing God to be glorified in our lives.

Finally, we minister *to* God through worship. Praise allows God to lift us up into heavenly places with Him, bringing us into the inner, personal sanctuary of sweet communion where we simply enjoy who He is. It is in the "most holy place" of our hearts where an intimate relationship is established with God. Our spiritual senses are heightened and brought into line with the Holy Ghost, bringing us into oneness with the heart of God. It is in oneness with our Lord that our disposition is changed to reflect His glory. Therefore, it is vital that we understand the importance of each of these levels of ministry. Without an attitude of worship, God's glory will never be realized in our lives.

Attitudes towards God are a manifestation of our disposition. Disposition is determined by the spirit motivating us. As you consider attitudes, you realize they are influenced by how we look at life in light of God, and not according to circumstances. The way we look at life will affect our relationships with both God and people. If the attitude of worship is missing in our lives in regards to God, our relationship with Him will be minimal or non-existent. As a result, we will miss greater revelations of Jesus.

There are three reasons that an attitude of worship must be present at all times: 1) A Christian's life must be totally dedicated to do what is right and acceptable to God in and out of season; 2) God is always in the midst of His people, and is worthy of worship whenever He makes His presence known; and 3) a person will never know when God might suddenly intrude into his or her life.[1] When He does, one must be ready to worship Him in Spirit and truth.

An attitude of worship keeps people in a mode of preparation and readiness. It keeps a person sensitive to the moving and leading of the Holy Ghost. It also keeps an individual prepared and ready to offer up the necessary sacrifices for the glory of God.

In the last chapter, the place of worship was addressed. In the Old Testament, the place of worship was also a place of sacrifice. The patriarchs brought this out. Their worship was often associated with two things: altars and sacrifice. The altars were used as a memorial where the character, promise, and work of God were upheld; or, it was a place where sacrifice was offered up for God's pleasure.[2]

2 Chronicles 7:12 states, "And the LORD appeared to Solomon by night, and said unto him, I have heard thy prayer, I have chosen this place to myself for an house of sacrifice." Since Christians serve as the temple, they not only are to serve as a place of worship, but a place of sacrifice. Worship and sacrifice walk hand in hand. Worship reminds Christians of their responsibility before God, but sacrifice reminds the saint that there is a preparation and cost to have such a privilege. For example, it cost God His Son, and the Son of God, His life, for believers to have the privilege to boldly enter the throne of grace.[3]

Sacrifice is not only an act of worship, but it prepares one to approach God. When you study the Old Testament tabernacle, you can see how God worked from the Most Holy Place outward. God's approach points to the work of sanctification. Sanctification transforms the disposition of a person.

The Christian begins at the outer court and works inward. This approach points to the work of consecration. Consecration is total abandonment and involves physical and emotional separation. It must be noted that God begins with the Ark of the Covenant in the Most Holy Place. The ark represented Jesus and His complete work of redemption and reconciliation. The Christian starts with the Altar of Burnt Offering in the outer court. It was at this altar that the atonement for sins was made.

---

[1] 2 Timothy 4:2
[2] Genesis 8:20-21; Exodus 17:13-16
[3] Hebrews 4:16

God must start with Jesus and His ministry towards man, while man must begin with Jesus' sacrifice.[4] Therefore, the location where man meets God will be at the point of Jesus' redemption.

For the Christian, the Altar of Burnt Offering points to the cross of Jesus. A Christian's life and journey into this intimate place with God begins with the revelation of Jesus' cross. Without this revelation, the right attitude and spirit will be missing.

The cross of Jesus serves as the narrow gate or entrance way into this new life.[5] Christians must enter in by way of Jesus' death in order to embrace the life they have available in Him. However, the person can only enter this place at the point of sacrifice.

There are four sacrifices a Christian must be willing to offer up at all times to ensure an attitude of worship. Each sacrifice represents the four main aspects of the Christian life. The first sacrifice is found in Romans 12:1. In this Scripture, the Apostle Paul instructs believers to present their bodies as a living sacrifice. This means to make one's body ready to be yielded up at all times for God's work.[6] This concept of total abandonment or consecration gives three valuable insights: 1) The body is strictly for God's use; 2) a person's life is being set apart unto God for His purpose because it belongs to Him; and 3) it must be prepared at all times to be offered up in death.[7]

The Apostle Paul understood what it was like to be such a sacrifice. He said this at the end of his life, "For I am now ready to be offered, and the time of my departure is at hand. I have fought a good fight, I have finished my course, I have kept the faith" (2 Timothy 4:6-7).

Our bodies are much like the vessel that Mary brought the night that she anointed Jesus for His burial in John 12. The costly contents were poured out on Jesus to anoint Him for His burial. The fragrance that came forth filled the room. According to 2 Corinthians 2:15-16, "fragrance" is to symbolize Jesus' life. As His life fills up the empty lives of His saints, it reaches God, edifies the Church, and challenges the unsaved.

To be a living sacrifice, a person must be dead to self and alive unto God. Everything that is brought by way of the sacrifice of Jesus must be offered up for God's will and glory. We see this principle in the life of King David.

King David was in the midst of a fierce battle. He was thirsty and mentioned to his men how he longed for a drink of the water from the well of Bethlehem. Three of his valiant soldiers broke through the enemies' line to bring him water. When they brought it back to him, he refrained from satisfying his physical thirst and poured it out to the Lord

---

[4] 2 Corinthians 5:18-20; Hebrews 13:10-13
[5] Matthew 7:13-14; John 10:9
[6] Strong's Exhaustive Concordance; #3936
[7] Luke 9:23-25; 1 Corinthians 6:19-20; 7:23; 15:31; 2 Timothy 4:6

as a sacrifice. When questioned about his action, he admitted there was no way that he could enjoy the water from the well knowing the possible cost of it. Three men had risked their lives to secure the water for him. Since their acts were sacrificial, all David could do was to offer a drink offering to the One who is worthy of such offerings.[8]

The purpose for believers to present their bodies as living sacrifices is to allow God to do His work in them. This is how He touches and prepares lives to do His will. Philippians 1:6 says: "Being confident of this very thing, that he which hath begun a good work in you will perform it until the day of Jesus Christ."

The Apostle Paul said this in 2 Corinthians 9:8, "And God is able to make all grace abound toward you; that ye, always having all sufficiency in all things, may abound to every good work." Christians must present their bodies to God, so that He can do a good work in and through them. He alone will sanctify them to be a vessel fit for His use, and prepared unto every good work.[9]

A living sacrifice will always be prepared to be offered up for the purpose and glory of God. Such sacrifices face the reality of death. This brings us to the next acceptable sacrifice. It is found in Psalms 51:17, "The sacrifices of God are a broken spirit: a broken and a contrite heart, O God, thou wilt not despise."

This was part of King David's prayer after the prophet, Nathan, reproved him for his sin concerning Bathsheba and her righteous husband, Uriah. David had fallen into the sin of adultery with Bathsheba, but he planned Uriah's death to cover up the sin. Both transgressions required his death according to the Law of Moses. There was no sacrifice he could offer to make atonement for his offenses against God. If there were, he would have made the necessary offerings.[10]

The only sacrifices he could offer were a broken spirit and a broken, contrite heart. "Broken," in this Scripture verse, means to be crushed, destroyed, and afflicted.[11] David was truly "crushed" and "afflicted" by his sins. He was in emotional ruin and spiritually devastated over his actions.

King David's spirit was not only crushed, but so was his heart. His heart was also contrite or repentant. It was collapsed by the reality of his conduct.[12] This breaking of his spirit and the collapsing of his heart also made him a candidate for God to draw near in mercy, show His grace in forgiveness, and bring forth reconciliation and restoration because of His love. Since David's spirit was in a humble condition, he could ask his merciful God to create a clean heart and renew a right spirit within him.[13]

---

[8] 1 Chronicles 11:16-19
[9] 2 Timothy 2:21
[10] Deuteronomy 22:22; 19:11-13; Psalm 51:16
[11] Strong's Exhaustive Concordance, #7665
[12] Ibid #1794
[13] Psalm 51:10

In a sense, David was broken and spilled out before God. He was an empty man because of his brokenness over sin. He needed his heart to be healed and cleansed. He realized his spirit needed to be revived by God's Spirit.

As a result, God could forgive David, accept his sacrifice, and take away his sin and its devastating consequences of death.[14] He could restore the joy of David's salvation and uphold him with a fresh, new liberty.

The next acceptable sacrifices are found in Hebrews 13:15-16, "By him therefore let us offer the sacrifice of praise to God continually, that is, the fruit of our lips giving thanks to his name. But to do good and to communicate forget not: for with such sacrifices God is well pleased." We have considered how worship begins with presenting our bodies as a living sacrifice so that God can have His way. This brings us to the two main doors that lead into God's presence. They both are sacrifices.

The first door is brokenness. If a person is truly broken in spirit and heart, God can meet him or her. This humble state allows God to have His way to forgive, heal, reconcile, and restore.

The second door that leads to the presence of God is praise. Psalm 22:3 states, "But thou art holy, O thou that inhabitest the praises of Israel." We have already highlighted the significance of praise, but it is vital that we come to terms with this important sacrifice that can be offered at any time and in any place. As previously stated, praise is where God is lifted up with the intent to worship Him. Real praise originates when a humble man is out of the way. Genuine humility will always abase a person, allowing God to be lifted up in one's heart in His goodness, majesty, and power.

A grateful heart that recognizes God's goodness motivates praise. Psalm 107:8 declares, "O that men would praise the LORD for his goodness." Goodness includes such acts as salvation, provision, and intervention.

Praises exalt God, so that He can lift man up above his limited world to consider the One who created the heavens and the earth. When saints consider His majesty, there is no way they can keep their lips from joyously lifting Him up in honor, awe, and adoration. The world becomes insignificant, problems fade, and the reality of God lifts the person from the earth to meditate on the eternal and the impossible.

As one considers God's majesty, he or she begins to grasp a sense of His incredible power. God created all things. His power is expressed in every aspect of His character. His mercy holds back the power of His judgment. His grace channels His power to show His commitment to man. His longsuffering shows the strength of His power as He refrains from showing His wrath. His holiness reveals how His power upholds that which is righteous and acceptable. The wisdom of His power is

---

[14] 2 Samuel 12:13

revealed in His faithfulness, as He silently works on behalf of man to bring desired results.

Praise and worship are about God. They are about who He is, which is expressing the majesty of His character. A heart that stands in awe as well as in thankfulness, and is overwhelmed because of His faithfulness is inspired. The awesome reality of His character humbles us as we begin to realize that His ways and works are too wondrous to describe.[15]

Praise is man's way of lifting God up above all those things that demand his attention. It helps him change his focus. As man lifts God up in praise, God can in turn lift man up into heavenly places. This is when a person's attitude is adjusted to consider God's wonders, his or her perspective is enlarged to see Him in His glory, and hope is inspired to come alive with the reality of His greatness.

In the midst of trying and adverse times, true praise becomes the purest of sacrifices. It takes a lot to offer praise when the feelings are missing, the circumstances are ready to destroy you, and life appears to be a cruel joke. This is when the sacrifice of praise becomes pure. It is at the point of this purity that God can step on the scene to bring comfort and perspective.

The next sacrifice is good works. Praise is sacrifice of the lips, but works are sacrifices of the heart and hands. The Bible is clear that personal, righteous works do not save us. Rather, we are saved unto good works.[16] Ephesians 2:8-10 says,

> For by grace are ye saved through faith; and that not of yourselves: it is the gift of God: Not of works, lest any man should boast. For we are his workmanship, created in Christ Jesus unto good works, which God hath before ordained that we should walk in them.

Paul is clear that man is not saved by his works, but by God's grace. This is to ensure that man does not take credit for salvation that cost God His Son. He goes on to say that we are created in Jesus unto good works that God ordained before we ever came into existence, and that we need to walk in them.

Walking in works is a form of consecration, as well as the product of faith. We walk by faith in what Christ did for us. This faith results in good works.[17] Faith in Christ directs our steps in the right direction so that God can work the desired works in us and through us. Philippians 2:13 states, "For it is God which worketh in you both to will and to do of his good pleasure."

These works will cause our lives to shine. This will bring glory to God and please Him.[18] In Philippians 2:14-15, the Apostle Paul goes on to

---

[15] Psalm 50:23; 106:1-2; 138:1-2

[16] Ephesians 6:5-7; Titus 3:5

[17] 1 Corinthians 5:7; Galatians 2:20; James 2:17-18

[18] Matthew 5:16; Colossians 1:10

say this in regard to works: "Do all things without murmurings and disputings: That ye may be blameless and harmless, the sons of God, without rebuke, in the midst of a crooked and perverse nation, among whom ye shine as lights in the world."

The Apostle Paul also talked about Jesus purifying a people who are zealous unto good works. In Titus 2:7-8, he gives this instruction: "In all things shewing thyself a pattern of good works: in doctrine shewing uncorruptness, gravity, sincerity, Sound speech, that cannot be condemned; that he that is of the contrary part may be ashamed, having no evil thing to say of you." Obviously, a pattern of good works comes down to behavior or conduct. In fact, believers should abound in good works and stand distinct in this world as a testimony of their God. This is not popular and will be resented by the world as the believer's light exposes its foolishness. When good works bring the reproach of the world upon saints, this makes them truly a pleasing sacrifice to God. Therefore, the author of Hebrews instructed believers to provoke each other unto love and doing good works.[19]

Good works bring us back to becoming a living sacrifice. God must have His way in a person's life before he or she can know what is acceptable to God. Each person must first be made fit for the master's use, which will prepare him or her unto every good work.[20]

As we can see, worship is to be in every aspect of our lives. It must be evident in our lives as we present our bodies for God's work and service. It will be realized in our praise as we lift God above our lives, circumstances, and world, allowing Him to lift us up into the heavenly. It should be seen in our works by bringing Him glory and honor. These works are an extension of our love for God, and our desire to serve and please Him as bondservants.

What about you? Are you offering any of these sacrifices? Are they pure or defiled? Do they glorify God or yourself? Do your sacrifices make you distinct from the world, or do they make you hypocritical in the world's eyes? Are you truly offering the sacrifices that serve as worship to our wondrous God?

---

[19] 2 Corinthians 9:8; Titus 2:14; Hebrews 10:24
[20] 2 Timothy 2:21

16

CLEANSING

How much more shall the blood
of Christ, who through the eternal
Spirit offered himself without
spot to God, purge your conscience
from dead works to serve the
living God?
(Hebrews 9:14)

If you could summarize worship, you would say it is coming into a secret place with God. This secret place is the key to a victorious Christian life. It is a place of communion and rest. It is where God is lifted up as God in one's heart and mind. In fact, in worship, there is no other abiding reality but God. It is a place where man is lifted above self and the world to consider the possibilities of the wonder and greatness of His Creator and Maker. It is where man's heart is in tune with God, and his mind is at rest and peace because God is his focus. It is a place of pleasure and satisfaction because it is there that man is able to enjoy the reality and fellowship of his God.[1]

Sadly, few people get into this place with God. They run on the outside edges of this secret place, but never enter in. This reminds us of the priests of the Old Testament. They were required to enter through three different entrances: the gate in the outer court, the door into the Holy Place, and the veil in the Most Holy Place. Communion was to take place in the Most Holy Place between the cherubim.[2]

In the Most Holy Place was the Ark of the Covenant. On top of the ark was the mercy seat. Two cherubim were facing each other, but peering down upon the mercy seat with their wings extended towards each other. Many people talk about the grace of God, but before individuals can obtain grace, they first must seek His mercy. Mercy cannot be realized until people understand their need for forgiveness. It is at the place of mercy that God is able to meet each person to impart His grace.

The Ark of the Covenant pointed to Jesus' ministry, but the mercy seat pointed to His redemption. It was here that judgment of the Law and

---

[1] Psalm 16:11; Isaiah 26:3; Philippians 4:6-9
[2] Exodus 25:10-22

the bountiful mercies of God came together to produce grace. It is at this place that God is able to meet with those who make this journey into the secret place.

The High Priest only entered the Most Holy Place once a year on Atonement Day to make a sacrifice for sin. Before he entered the Most Holy Place, he took two goats and a bullock. One goat was offered up as a sin offering. The bullock was also offered up as a sin offering on his behalf. The blood of both sin offerings was taken into the Most Holy Place where it was sprinkled upon the mercy seat on behalf of all of the people of Israel. After atonement was made in this manner, the live goat had all the sins of Israel placed upon it by the laying on of hands. It was then taken to the wilderness where it was turned loose to wander. This goat was considered the scapegoat, a popular term most of us are aware of.[3] Jesus became our scapegoat. He was not only offered up for our sins on the cross, but He took our sins to the grave so they could not plague us once we accept His provision of salvation.

As you study this journey into the Most Holy Place where the abiding presence of God resided, before the High Priest entered this place, he had to offer up a sacrifice for himself to prevent his demise. There were two types of sacrifices offered—a sin offering and a burnt offering. We see the same similarities for Christians. Two types of sacrifices have to be prevalent before the modern-day priests can enter this secret place. The first sacrifice points to Jesus. He became the sin offering, so that the Christian can come before God. The second sacrifice points to the Christian. The burnt offering represents complete surrender. The only sacrifice Christians can offer up in complete surrender is their bodies.[4]

These sacrifices mark the beginning of this journey to the secret place. It involves a process. A person must be separated from the influences of the world and self in order to get into this secret place. Sadly, most people avoid the process because it involves sacrifice. This will keep them on the outside of the secret place. These people may have a sense of this life, but they will never experience it.

Some of these people may make it to the gate, but not through the door. Others may manage to get through the door, but fail to enter in through the veil. Jesus said the Father seeks those who are true worshippers.[5] These are the people who in repentance, humbly walk through the gate, and in submission enter the door of the Holy place, as they make their way in adoration, love, and praise to enter through the veil into the Most Holy Place.

These three entrances show us there are three ways Christians practice worship. The first type of worshipper is the one who keeps worship a matter of ritual. This person may go through the motions, but

---

[3] Leviticus 16

[4] Leviticus 16; Romans 12:1

[5] John 4:23

has no sense of its purpose in his or her spiritual growth and life. These people simply have an intellectual perspective, but it never becomes an experience where God is real and lifted up to allow His glory to fill the human temple of man's spirit and soul.[6] These individuals remain indifferent to the Holy Ghost and their spiritual condition.

Those who enter the door represent the second type of worshipper. These are the people who keep worship a soulish or fleshly exercise. They get caught up with fleshly hype. As a result, they feel on top of the world when doing this exercise, but it has nothing to do with the reality of God. They are simply caught up with the experience. When questioned, this is clearly brought out for they zealously speak about how they felt in their time of worship. They may refer to it as the moving of the Spirit or revival, but there is no greater sense of God in their declarations. Their testimony is about the experience, which is nothing more than sensual entertainment. After all, one can get the same hype at a sports game and similar feelings by listening to good music or watching an inspirational movie.

The one element that distinguishes true worship from the intellectual ritual or the fleshly experience is a greater sense of God. If God is missing in the exercise, then it was not true worship.

True worshippers prepare themselves to meet with and worship God. They initially prepare their mind by remembering what had to occur for them to enter into this secret place with God. This is why they first come to the altar or cross. There they remember what Jesus did on the cross. The Apostle Peter talked about how people became barren and unfruitful in the knowledge of Jesus. He stated they were blind and could not see afar off because they had forgotten that they were purged from old sins. Peter claimed that by remembering their humble beginnings at Jesus' cross, they would be established in their life in Christ. He also admitted they had to be stirred up. Therefore, he endeavored to keep the truth ever before them in his epistle.[7]

Remembering the cost of redemption stirs up gratitude and prepares the mind to enter through the gate in humility. By entering into the gate, one is leaving the world behind. The world vies for people's attention and worship. It encourages idolatry and wants to possess a person's mind and heart. The Bible classifies Christians who belong to the world as adulterers and adulteresses. To be in agreement with the world is to commit a form of spiritual harlotry.[8]

In order to worship, God's people must come out from the clamor of the world. They must separate themselves from the world's demands in order to embrace the reality of God. Entering the gate represents leaving the world behind, while the cross points to crucifixion to the world. This

---

[6] Isaiah 6:1-3
[7] 2 Peter 1:8-9, 12-15
[8] James 4:4

crucifixion deals with the affections of the world. These affections can pull people back into the influence of the world.[9]

After a person encounters the altar, he or she will have to be cleansed from the entanglements of the world. The Apostle Paul put it in this perspective in 2 Timothy 2:3-4, "Thou therefore endure hardness, as a good soldier of Jesus Christ. No man that warreth entangleth himself with the affairs of this life; that he may please him who hath chosen him to be a soldier." These entanglements once again point to affections that can cause a person to forget who he or she belongs to, and their purpose for being in this world.

The altar of burnt offering is what all the people viewed in the tabernacle. It reminded them of sacrifice, death, and atonement, for it pointed to the work of the cross of Jesus. The laver was the next object. It stood between the altar of burnt offering and the Holy Place. It was designated to cleanse the priests of any unholy influences or residues before they did their priestly duties in the Holy Place. This object was made of brass that came from the looking glasses of the women who assembled at the door of the tabernacle or in the outer court.[10]

Brass was symbolic of the judgment on man's sin. Obviously, man had to see his sin before he could be cleansed and begin his spiritual journey into the secret chamber with God. The problem is man deludes himself about his spiritual condition. He becomes indifferent to it through various means such as justification, declaring rights to enjoy aspects of the self-life and the world, and self-pity. He lets himself off the hook; therefore, he never has to be responsible to do what is right.

What serves as the mirror for Christians? James 1:23-24 reveals the mirror, "For if any be a hearer of the word, and not a doer, he is like unto a man beholding his natural face in a glass: For he beholdeth himself, and goeth his way, and straightway forgetteth what manner of man he was." James is talking about the Word of God. It reveals man's spiritual condition and reminds him that he has been cleansed.

This brings us to the unpopular work of the Word. It does contain the revelation of God, but it also reveals the wretchedness of man. It was meant to deal with sin. Since the laver was brass, it shows us that the Word serves as a point of judgment on sin.[11] It brings people to a point of separation. Either a person will choose to separate him or herself unto God, or he or she will go the way of sin and death.

The laver not only gave the priest a reality check about his need for separation and cleansing from the unholy, but it served as a point of cleansing. He was to wash his hands and feet. Hands that have handled or partaken of the world cannot properly minister before God or to God in worship. After all, His people are to raise holy hands to Him in service,

---

[9] 2 Corinthians 6:14-18; Galatians 6:14; Colossians 3:2
[10] Exodus 30:17-21; 38:8-9
[11] Jeremiah 23:29

prayer, adoration, and honor.[12] James reaffirms the need for such cleansing in his epistle, "Draw nigh to God, and he will draw nigh to you. Cleanse your hands, ye sinners; and purify your hearts, ye doubleminded" (James 4:8).

The Word of God cleanses. The Apostle made this statement in Ephesians 5:26-27, "That he might sanctify and cleanse it with the washing of water by the word. That he might present it to himself a glorious church, not having spot, or wrinkle or any such thing; but that it should be holy and without blemish."

The priest had to wash his feet. The feet are the means by which people touch the world. Although individuals may remain separate from the world, they cannot help but be affected when walking through it. In fact, people must walk through the world and still remain separate from it in their hearts, minds, and actions. The walk is what actually distinguishes a person. John instructed believers to walk through this world as Christ walked through it. His walk was that of self-denial and the cross. It was also a walk that identified Him to His Father's will and work, for He did nothing outside of the heart, mind, and will of the Father.[13]

The walk is what poses the greatest challenge for Christians. The attractions are great and many. If one attraction cannot trip a person up, another one will. These attractions take Christians on detours, entangle them into the world's deadly tentacles, and rob them of their testimony.

God instructed Moses and Joshua to take off their shoes for they were standing on holy ground. Obviously, God wants us separated from the world so that we can truly stand in His presence.[14] Jesus washed the feet of His disciples. When Peter became zealous and asked Him to wash his hands and his head, Jesus said, "He that is washed needeth not save to wash his feet, but is clean every whit: and ye are clean, but not all" (John 13:10).

In the Christian's armor, our feet are to be shod with the Gospel of peace. This procedure is necessary to prevent soreness or lameness in our Christian walk. If crippled, we would not only be hindered, but inconsistent. The Christian walk points to conduct as well as marching orders. The Word guides our steps. We can avoid unnecessary detours by applying the principles of God's Word to our lives. We can be assured of staying on the right path as we allow God's Word to discipline us in our conduct through obedience. By preparing our feet with the Gospel, we will keep our focus in the right place. The right focus will cause us to walk in the right path.[15]

The Word also serves as a sword. It cuts through personal delusion to expose true motives and intentions. It is the hammer that knocks out

---

[12] Exodus 30:19-21; 1 Timothy 2:8

[13] John 5:19; 1 John 2:6

[14] Exodus 3:5; Joshua 5:15

[15] Psalm 119:11, 105; Ephesians 6:15

the silliness caused by pride, so one can walk in sobriety and fear before the Lord. It is the fire that burns up the dross of the old man, and purifies that which belongs to God.[16]

Just as the laver prepared the priests of the Old Testament to enter into the place of worship, God's Word prepares the New Testament priest to come into this life-changing place.[17] Many Christians are either indifferent or act silly about God and His ways. They lack the right spirit. Therefore, they have no consensus about the truth of God. They may dance around the outer court and wave their flags, but they still have failed to enter through the door. Obviously, they are still in the outer court, pretending they are in the inner chamber with God. This is all show, for men are still seeing them. When considering their fruits, there is no sense of the reality of God in their lives.

Have you visited the laver lately? In other words, have you allowed the Word to be your mirror? Has it cleansed you from the residue of sin? Has it set you free from the entanglements of the world? Has it exposed your wicked motives, your self-serving intentions, and the depth of your pride? Has it knocked some silliness out of you, and replaced it with fear before God and His Word? If you have not allowed the laver to sanctify you, you are not yet ready to enter into the secret chambers. Bear in mind, the priests had to wash their hands and feet, and offer a sacrifice so that they would not die. After all, no one can see the Lord without holiness.[18]

---

[16] Jeremiah 23:29; Hebrews 4:12

[17] 1 Peter 2:5, 9

[18] Exodus 30:20-21; Hebrews 12:14

17

THE HOLY PLACE

Follow peace with all men, and
holiness, without which no man
shall see the Lord.
(Hebrews 12:14)

The purpose of the outer court was to separate God's priests from the associations of the world and the consequences of sin. The Altar of Burnt Offering dealt with sin, while the laver addressed the influences of the world. Both objects were made of brass. Brass represented judgment on sin. The sacrifice of Christ and the unchanging truth of the Bible are able to deal daily blows to the reign of sin. The judgment of sin entails cleansing. Cleansing is a means of preparation. These preparations were necessary to enter the Holy Place.

The Holy Place represents holiness being established in the life of the saint. The objects in this room were made of gold. Gold represented deity. This pointed to Jesus; therefore, the Holy Place was a place where self regressed and Jesus became the consuming reality. In the presence of His wisdom and righteousness, sanctification would become evident. Sanctification is the work of holiness. Without this characteristic, one will not see the Lord.[1]

Holiness or separation is not an option. This is why a person must be separated from the world and self. Both defile the work of God and lead to spiritual ineffectiveness and death. This ineffectiveness becomes obvious, especially when entering the secret chambers of communion. People who have sin and are uncertain about their life in God will not enter into this secret place. They may run about on the outside fringes of the Christian life, but it is all show. The fact that they fail to enter in proves there is an inconsistency in their lives that has not been resolved before God. Perhaps they still have known attachments to the world and maybe pride is reigning. Nevertheless, their hands, feet, or conscience are not clean before God. Underneath, they do not have the confidence or authority to enter the throne of grace.[2]

It is important that cleansing take place in the outer and inner courts of our lives. We first must consecrate our lives from all worldly influences

---

[1] Romans 6:19-22; 1 Corinthians 1:30; Hebrews 12:14; 1 Peter 2:5, 9
[2] Hebrews 4:16: 10:22; James 4:8-10; 1 Peter 1:15-16

to set our bodies free to serve as living sacrifices. We must be sanctified in the inner courts of our soul area to be used of God and bring Him glory.

Sanctification points to the inward work of the Holy Ghost. He is the one who separates man from his way of thinking and way of being. The Apostle Paul made this statement about sanctification in 2 Thessalonians 2:13b, "God hath from the beginning chosen you to salvation through sanctification of the Spirit and belief of the truth." Notice how salvation comes by the work of sanctification. Salvation must be worked in, through, and out of a person's life by the work of sanctification. After all, salvation points to deliverance. Very few people ponder how far this deliverance must go. Man has been enslaved totally to the mentality and ways of sin. Therefore, deliverance is an ongoing process that can only take place as a person gives way to the work of the Holy Ghost.

Each area that is given to the Holy Ghost is purified. Sometimes this purification means the total loss of something that would hinder the complete work of sanctification. In some cases, it might mean a refining to set something apart for God's purpose and glory.

In this process, the mind is transformed.[3] Priorities are changed, personal agendas are exposed, and self-serving rights lose their power. The mind ceases to be conformed to the world's way of thinking. As the mind is transformed, the inward disposition changes.

As stated, wrong attitudes are a product of how one views life. This view determines the value that people place on something. Such value establishes attitude. For example, when people are greedy and self-serving, they value the world. When individuals are controlling, selfish, and jealous, they value the idea of self.

Man's religion always clouds the issue of attitudes. People can put on a good mask, scurry around in their religious activities, and say all the right things to delude themselves about their spiritual condition, but the fruits will tell on them. Fruits are one of the manifestations of the disposition. Disposition is influenced by the spirit in operation. This is why we are instructed to test the spirits, and why Jesus said that you would know people by their fruits.[4]

The Holy Place gives us insight into how preparation must take place in the soul area to enter into the secret chamber of worship and communion. There were three articles in the Holy Place that enlightened one as to what kind of preparation needed to take place. There were the Table of Shewbread, the candlestick, and the Altar of Incense.[5] When the priest entered the Holy Place, the Table of Shewbread was to his right, while the candlestick was to his left. The Altar of Incense was located straight ahead of him.

---

[3] Romans 12:1
[4] Matthew 7:15-16; 1 John 4:1
[5] Exodus 25:23-40, 26:35; 30:1-8

To understand our journey into this place, we will begin on our right. The Table of Shewbread reminds people of what they need to partake of to sustain life: the bread. The table also reminded Israel that God is Jehovah-Jireh, the Great Provider. This object also pointed to the Bread that God provided for all mankind. The bread came from heaven. The Gospel of John identifies Jesus as the Bread from heaven who gives eternal life. The table pointed to a type of communion where we actually partake of the bread provided by God to ensure our spiritual well-being. [6]

The bread on the table had to be ever before God as a memorial. Frankincense had to be poured on this bread, and only the priest could eat of the hallowed bread. To the saints, this represents the fact that Jesus' life must be evident in believers. It is His life that serves as a fragrance to God. But, for Jesus' life to be evident, one must partake of Him.[7]

Jesus talked about eating of His body and drinking of His blood.[8] The Apostle Paul elaborated on His statement in 1 Corinthians 10:16-17, "The cup of blessing which we bless, is it not the communion of the blood of Christ? The bread which we break, is it not the communion of the body of Christ? For we being many are one bread, and one body, for we are all partakers of that one bread." To partake of the life of Jesus refers to believing or assimilating the example and life of Jesus that will serve as a form of communion.

If a person fails to partake of Jesus in communion, he or she cannot be guaranteed eternal life. Jesus confirmed this when He said in John 6:58, "This is that bread which came down from heaven: not as your fathers did eat manna, and are dead: he that eateth of this bread shall live for ever."

Keep in mind the outer court is a separation from the world. The Apostle Peter made this statement in 2 Peter 1:4, "Whereby are given unto us exceeding great and precious promises: that by these ye might be partakers of the divine nature, having escaped the corruption that is in the world through lust." We are called to partake of Jesus' divine nature in order to realize the precious promises that are available to us. These promises point to a banquet table that possesses everything a person needs that pertains unto life and godliness.[8] In order to benefit from this spiritual feast, a person must have escaped the corruption that is in the present world that comes through the lust of the flesh. Then, they must partake of the Bread.

Partaking not only points to communion, fellowship, companionship, and sharing, but of actual participation or being part of something.[9]

---

[6] John 6:32-35: 2 Peter 1:4

[7] Leviticus 24:5-9; 2 Corinthians 2:15-16

[8] John 6:53-58

[8] 2 Peter 1:3

[9] Strong's Exhaustive Concordance; #2841-2844; 4791; 4829-4830

Therefore, a person must partake of the Bread on God's table for communion to be a reality.

What must people partake of to possess the fragrance of Christ? They must partake of Jesus' sufferings.[10] His sufferings point to identification. It is in identification with Jesus that a person's hope becomes steadfast or sure. As Hebrews 3:14 states, "For we are made partakers of Christ, if we hold the beginning of our confidence stedfast unto the end." By holding confidently to our life in Christ, we will be made partakers of His abounding promises.

Promises remind saints of their inheritance. This eternal inheritance is made a reality through the Gospel. By believing the Gospel in our hearts, we will be made partakers of an eternal inheritance that carries untold spiritual riches.[11]

Identification in this text of eternal inheritance means that people will also partake of the Holy Ghost. The Spirit of God assures a person of authority and power.[12] Without the authority, Christians will not subdue the forces that oppose their spiritual well-being, and without the power, they will not overcome. Therefore, authority and power point to victory. A victorious life in Christ declares that a person is a partaker of His holiness.

To partake of something means one is also active in properly applying it for spiritual growth. The more a person partakes, the more the mind will be transformed. The key here is exposure. Believers must expose themselves to the character and work of God. They must avoid taking the things of God and defiling them. Rather, they must let such things make them holy in their way of thinking and doing. As individuals partake of the Bread from heaven, they will be more desirous to enter into the secret chambers to worship. Partaking of the Bread is the means of developing a taste for this Bread that cannot be satisfied with one taste. In fact, the taste motivates the person to eat of this incredible Bread on a daily basis.

Now that the mind has been transformed, one can begin to walk out this separated, consecrated life. To walk this life out takes the light of Christ. The candlestick points to both Christ as the light and to the Christian walk. This walk entails applying and walking out the life of Christ. The Apostle John made this statement about Jesus, "In him was life; and the life was the light of man" (John 1:4). It is Jesus' life that serves as the light. His life points to both His disposition of meekness and His righteousness. His meekness and righteousness resulted in a walk of obedience and sacrifice.[13]

---

[10] 2 Corinthians 1:7
[11] Ephesians 1:13-14; 3:6; Colossians 1:2-3, 12;
[12] Hebrews 6:4-5
[13] Matthew 11:28-30; Hebrews 5:8-9; 1 Peter 2:21

The Apostle John made this statement in 1 John 2:6, "He that saith he abideth in him ought himself also so to walk, even as he walked." Self-denial produces meekness and righteousness, while the cross produces the disciplined walk of obedience and sanctification. Sanctification comes out of regression or sacrifice.[14]

Jesus told His followers that they had to deny self and pick up their cross daily. The candlestick had to be maintained daily by the priests to keep the flame going. After all, it was the only light in the Holy Place. Since Christ is the only light in the midst of the believer's life, denying self and giving way to the life of Christ is a daily exercise. It is through self-denial that the right disposition is established, and through the daily application of the cross that godly conduct is produced. This daily working out of Jesus' life establishes a living testimony of His life and work in the life of the saint. [15]

Jesus' life, instructions and examples bring the necessary contrast to a person's life. People have a tendency to compare themselves with others. The Word is clear that only Jesus can bring the right contrast to reveal a person's true spiritual condition. When people compare themselves to others, it is almost like comparing darkness with darkness. No matter how many lights one perceives is shining in the midst of their darkness, it is still spiritual darkness.

Jesus' light exposes three elements. First, it reveals mans' condition. This light comes through the Gospel. It actually shines into the darkened mind with the reality of what Jesus accomplished on man's behalf. Next, His light reveals the glory of God. John tells us that Jesus serves as the glory of the only begotten of the Father. The Father's glory will not only be unveiled to saints as they walk in the light, but it will be unveiled in and through them.[16]

The light of Jesus also maintains our spiritual lives through cleansing and fellowship. "But if we walk in the light, as he is in the light, we have fellowship one with another, and the blood of Jesus Christ his Son cleanseth us from all sin" (1 John 1:7). To maintain the Christian life, believers must have fellowship with and in the light. They also must recognize, acknowledge and bring their sins to the cross. The light of Christ is vital to keep saints from detours, snares and destruction. They must be able to see in order to come into the place of worship.

A final note on the candlestick, it is useless unless the light is shining. There is no light without the oil. Each Christian serves as a candlestick in this dark world. If the light of Christ's life is missing, then the candlestick is also in great darkness. If the light of Christ is missing, it is because there is no oil.

---

[14] See 1 Corinthians 1:30
[15] Exodus 27:20-21; Luke 9:23; 2 Corinthians 3:1-3; Revelation 12:11
[16] John 1:14; 2 Corinthians 3:18; 4:3-6

Oil brings us to the necessity of the Holy Ghost's work in the soul area. What has not been sanctified belongs to darkness and not God. Wherever darkness reigns, there is ignorance towards God and delusion in regards to self. This darkness also represents a hard heart that will be indifferent to truth and the work of the Spirit. The Holy Ghost cannot sanctify what has not been consecrated or totally abandoned to God. Without the presence of the oil daily penetrating every area of a person's life, there will be inconsistencies in the person's walk, and the quality of fruits will reveal his or her hypocrisies.[17]

Preparation for communion with God will always lead us to the candlestick. The candlestick produces the necessary light to come to the next object: the Altar of Incense. This altar stood before the veil that separated the Holy Place from the Most Holy Place. The priests were to burn incense every morning after they dressed the candlestick. The incense was to be perpetual or ongoing before the Lord.[18]

The Altar of Incense points to prayer. Prayer needs to be ongoing before the Lord. It stands before the veil that leads into the Most Holy Place. The veil points to Jesus. Nothing can be accomplished in prayer unless it is done in the name or character of God Incarnate.[19] Prayer stands in light of real brokenness when coming to God for forgiveness and restoration, and it stands in light of praise that exalts God in heart and mind. It stands in the ongoing shadow of Jesus and His redemption. After all, God can only meet us at the point of Jesus and what He accomplished on the cross.

As we can see, each object points to the reality of God. The Table of Shewbread shows us our need and dependency on God, while the candlestick gives us a reality check about our spiritual walk and the work of the Holy Ghost. The table prepares our disposition, while the candlestick becomes the place where the mind of Christ is worked in us. It is the mind of Christ that displays meekness in His disposition and obedience through His conduct.

A meek disposition and obedient conduct equals righteousness. Once righteousness is established, one may now boldly approach the throne of grace, and be confident that his or her prayers will avail much. It is important to realize that in the Holy Place, regression takes place. Self must lose its place of honor before the life of Christ can come forth in a powerful light.

In the Holy Place, it becomes less about man and more about God. Focuses are enlarged by the light and forever changed by the perpetual incense of Jesus' life. His life forever permeates the lives of His saints, while its fragrance reaches heaven and becomes a sweet fragrance to

[17] Matthew 25:1-13; Ephesians 5:18
[18] Exodus 30:1-9
[19] John 14:12-14; 1 Thessalonians 5:17; Hebrews 10:19-20

God.[20] This must happen because both prayer and worship are about God. It is about exalting Him in His character, praising Him for His ways, honoring Him for His will, and glorifying Him for His work.

What makes a person holy is the reality of Christ. It is His wisdom that brings spiritual insight into the character of God. It is Jesus' righteousness that makes one upright and acceptable before God, while it is Jesus' sanctification that makes a person worthy to approach God, and His redemption identifies that person to the complete work of sanctification.[21]

Like the priest, it is up to each saint to keep the life of Christ flowing through every facet of his or her life. This can only be accomplished through prayer. Prayer keeps the veil or the ever-abiding presence of Christ accessible to all who will come to Him in sincerity. It opens the way into the inner chamber through dependency and need. It alleviates any fear through humility and brokenness. Prayer is a place where saints can take stock of their lives before they enter into that place in Jesus. It also produces confidence through repentance, and prepares the way through love and faith.

The altar of prayer is not the door into worship or communion. It stands before the veil; rather, it simply marks the entrance. This is how prayer works. It is not the entrance into this place. It is simply a point to make sure all of self is out of the way before entering through the veil. This is why many people fail to enter into this secret chamber. Prayer often serves as a religious exercise, not a point that marks the Most Holy Place of communion. The reason prayer stays on a lower level is because the spiritual life has never become a spiritual journey to seek after, to discover, and to enjoy God.

Many Christians are missing it. It seems they have never separated themselves from the world or regressed past themselves to discover God in sweet communion. To them, Christianity remains about how they will benefit from some type of religious life. It never becomes about God.

I have witnessed people walking up to the Altar of Incense. Often, they become blessed in their religious experience, but as soon as prayer begins to give way to the veil, they begin to back up in fear and uncertainty. There is something about the veil that can seem almost foreboding. Even though all the preparations have taken place so that the person could live in the presence of God, they fail to enter in. Keep in mind that until now, a person can somewhat play the religious game of personal piousness. They can give the impression they have the goods, but once a person is in the secret place, he or she will find out if he or she is prepared to meet God in His glory, and in His holiness. After all, once a person is beyond the veil, there is no turning back.

---

[20] 2 Corinthians 2:15-16
[21] 1 Corinthians 1:30

Where are you in this journey? Perhaps you are on the outside looking in. You are saying to yourself, "I am too unworthy to enter in." This is a lie. The truth is you don't want to pay the price of the world. Maybe you are standing on the outside of the door. Your excuse for not entering in is that you have not prepared enough. Once again, this is a lie. It is not that you are not prepared to enter in. It is that you are not willing to give up your rights to self to embrace the life God has for you.

Perhaps you are standing on the outside of the veil. You have been convincing yourself that you already have enough of God. This is another lie. You are still operating in the soul area. There is more, and when self is out of the way, an overwhelming desire will remain. This desire is to possess it all. In fact, your claim will be the same as Moses was after being in the presence of God, "I beseech thee, shew me thy glory" (Exodus 33:18).

18

THE MOST HOLY PLACE

Then saith Jesus unto him, Get
thee hence, Satan: for it is written,
thou shalt worship the Lord thy God,
and him only shalt thou serve.
(Matthew 4:10)

True worship is a hard subject to deal with. Anyone can worship because it is within man to worship. However, the battle rages as Satan does everything to hinder man from worshipping God. The truth is, whatever a person serves is also the very object or being that will receive his or her worship. This is why Satan's whole purpose is to rob God of His rightful place in man's heart and mind; so ultimately, he receives the worship that only God deserves.[1]

Through the years, I have struggled with why God was not moving on His people and in His Church in America. I have been aware that He is moving in other places. Recently, He revealed why He is absent from much of the religious activities: it has ceased to be about Him and His will and works. People rely on secular methods and fleshly experiences; therefore, they do not expect Him to move on behalf of their lives and they fail to tarry until He does move. Through the years the American churches have adjusted to the soulish preference of the world. They have put God in a timeframe, exalted religious activities and experiences over His simple truths, and developed methods to bring people into their sanctuary to have some type of religious experience that is acceptable to their worldly ways. Sadly, these experiences are equated with the move of God. However, God is clearly missing.

As I struggled over the issue as to why people are not being saved, healed, and delivered, the failure or urgency to wait on God is due to a lack faith that will patiently wait before God. As a result, the tendency for many is that they will settle for having enough religious experience as a means to soothe their religious conscience. Once they have soothed their conscience, they feel justified to count the rest of the day as belonging to them. It is as though they have "given at the office;" therefore, they have paid their required dues.

---

[1] Matthew 4:8-10

Since many in the American Church appear as if they have slid into the habit of not expecting anything to happen, they have become spiritually dull. This simply means they do not care if anything really happens. Numbers of people have become a sick substitute for the salvation of souls. Soulish worship has become a counterfeit to the presence of the Holy Spirit. Religious activities have taken the place of sincere devotion, and "so-called" religious TV has drowned out the fact that most people are spiritually dying on the vine due to a smorgasbord of fluff, candy-coated truths, and a feel-good religion that hides the desperate state of the Church. This condition is evident in both the prayer life and the type of worship that is taking place.

In this book, we started out with prayer. Prayer is the means of seeking God to discover His heart and will, while worship indicates that you have finally found Him. Godly worship is personal and involves a personal encounter with God. It is an experience that impacts a person in the depths of his or her soul. It can be so consuming that no words can describe the experiences that take place in the inner court. These experiences become nuggets too precious to share with others. All one can do is encourage a person to risk it all to come into this place of communion.

The late A. W. Tozer spoke a lot about worship in his writings. He talked about how the Church is trying to make workers out of new converts without first teaching them how to worship.[2] Man was not redeemed so that he could work for God; he was redeemed so that he could worship Him in Spirit and truth. It is only out of godly worship that acceptable service to God will manifest itself.

Because of ignorance about real worship, Christians are not striving to come into the place of worship. Much of the worship going on is fleshly and popular because it creates a feeling, an idea, or an image, instead of giving the person a desire to seek and find the One who deserves worship. If true worship is done in the right spirit, it will lead to a greater revelation of Jesus. It is at this point that Jesus ceases to be a concept, and becomes nourishment and life to a person's soul and spirit.

The Most Holy Place represented this place of communion. Here, God resided in the midst of man. Shadows of His abiding presence were seen in the wilderness during the day in the form of a cloud, and could be seen through the night in the form of fire.[3] The Jewish people witnessed these manifestations of God's abiding presence in their midst, but there was so much more to this life. There was the inner court, and in this place, His glory shone forth in unhindered majesty.

The cloud and fire represented God's presence in the midst of His people, but the glory of God in the inner court symbolized what it would mean for His people to be in the midst of His presence. God's presence

---

[2] *Born After Midnight*; pg. 125
[3] Exodus 13:21-22

in the midst of people may touch them, but when a saint is in His glory, it changes him or her from glory to glory.[4] As A. W. Tozer pointed out, all worship originates with God and ends up being reflected in the lives of God's people. According to Mr. Tozer, this is the only kind of worship that is acceptable to God.[5] It is the presence and reflection of His glory in our lives that honors Him.

This is why believers must never be content with merely encountering God's presence. Only the priests could enter the inner chamber of the tabernacle. It was their responsibility to minister before God and stand in the gap for Israel. As priests and kings in God's kingdom, Christians are not only privileged to enter this place, but it is their responsibility to do so.[6] They have been set apart for God's use. They have the responsibility of entering into the tabernacle of their souls to minister before God and to stand in the gap for others. In the end, they will reign with Him. Understanding this position is vital.

The intensity and effectiveness of Christianity hinges on whether a saint makes it from just witnessing God's presence to fellowshipping with Him in His presence. Without this fellowship, Christianity remains a matter of religion and activities, and it never becomes a life that is rich, full, satisfying, and powerful.

We have been making our way into the tabernacle. This journey has been for the sole purpose of preparing to meet with God and worshipping Him. Ultimately, it points to having an intimate relationship with God where He is truly lifted up in glory. In one of the many books I read, I was surprised to learn that some of the early Christians in America ended their services with what we would call worship. These people must have perceived that the preaching of the Word was to prepare their congregations for worship, and not worship for the preaching of the Word. After all, isn't the purpose of the Word to prepare us to be receptive towards God? If you consider our journey through the tabernacle thus far, worship following inward preparation is in compliance with coming into this secret court. Worship comes after the preparation of sacrifice, the cleansing of the Word, and the work of sanctification. This implies that all Christian exercise should end with worship.

As we consider the present order of most churches, it is as though Christianity is about the preaching of the Word, rather than worship of God. This is a subtle way of exalting man, redefining the Christian life, and demoting God. Keep in mind, the impartation of the Word is strictly for the saint's benefit. It builds up a person in his or her faith. It cleanses and prepares him or her to approach God in a right attitude. It becomes a point of conviction and preparation to meet with God and know what it

---

[4] 2 Corinthians 3:18
[5] Whatever Happened to Worship? pg. 45
[6] 1 Peter 2:5, 9; Revelation 1:6

means to please Him. When a person fails to end with God, the Word will be rendered dead letter or lifeless.[7]

Real Christianity is always about God being glorified. Therefore, is the wrong emphasis on worship to blame for the Church's ignorance towards God? As a whole, are we missing the secret to victorious Christianity because all is geared towards man's mind rather than unadulterated heart worship of God?[8]

Indeed, the Holy Ghost takes the seed of the Word to enlarge our perception of God, but true worship changes a person's perception about God. Without a doubt, worship is taking a back seat as far as importance. It has been demoted to an affect or activity rather than the whole sum of the saint's life. Therefore, the preference to pursue after or know God has never been developed. Without this development, worship will never be natural. Instead, it will become a boring duty or a terrible exercise in vanity. This will be a tragedy. An individual who does not have the proper perspective about worship will not be ready for heaven because the foremost emphasis in heaven is the worship of God.[9]

Let us once again consider the preparation to the inner chamber of worship to bring proper balance to this issue. After all, preparation is everything when it comes to acceptable worship. As Mr. Tozer commented, no worship is wholly pleasing to God until there is nothing displeasing in a person's life.[10] The purpose of this preparation is that the person must regress in unholy attachments, self-importance, and vainglory. A person who fails to confront the influence of the world, the flesh and the self-life in his or her journey to the Most Holy Place, will end up operating in the flesh instead of worshipping in the Spirit. This will prove to be an exercise in vanity.[11]

For the priest, this preparation started with the outer court. For those of us who call ourselves believers, it involves separating ourselves from the outer court of the world in order to face our sin at the altar of sacrifice, Jesus' cross. There, we must be reminded of the sacrifice of Jesus, lest we forget that the privilege to come into this intimate place with God was wrought by a high price, and is maintained by God's mercy and grace.[12]

Next, we come to the Word of God, which was represented by the laver. There, we cleanse ourselves from the entanglements of the world and any remaining residues of sin. Clearly, the outer court pointed to the work of consecration from the world. This consecration is necessary in every saint's so that each of us can now enter the Holy Place.

---

[7] Romans 7:6; 10:17; 2 Corinthians 3:6; Ephesians 5:26
[8] Revelation 4; 5:8-14: 7:9-12
[9] Isaiah 6:1-3; Revelation 4, 5
[10] Tozer on Worship and Entertainment; pg. 7
[11] 1 Corinthians 2:14; Galatians 3:3; 6:8
[12] Romans 5:20; 1 Corinthians 6:19-20; 2 Peter 1:8-9

The Holy Place pointed to the work of sanctification. This place was for the purpose of dealing with self in light of God. The Table of Shewbread addressed self-sufficiency, by reminding God's people that as God, He alone is the One who provides all of their needs. To Christians, this table points to partaking of the Bread from heaven and sweet communion or fellowship as each follower partakes of the reality of Jesus.[13]

The next article in the Holy place was the candlestick. The candlestick was a reminder that saints cannot walk out this holy life in their personal strength. They must realize that it takes both the oil and the light to walk in the way of salvation. The oil points to the Holy Ghost, and the light to the life of the Son of God.

Zechariah 4:6b says, "Not by might, nor by power, but by my spirit, saith the LORD of hosts." As holy people, we must become dependent on the Holy Ghost to guide us to the light of truth in all matters. This light of truth is Jesus Christ.[14] His life is the light that guards us against ignorance about God, delusion about ourselves, and spiritual darkness that hides Satan's destructive devices.

Finally, man is brought to the third article in the Holy Place, the Altar of Incense. This altar represented prayer. It revealed how man's attempts are useless unless God is first sought out in prayer. Effective prayer begins in a heart that is always inclined toward God, open to hear His voice, and ready to respond to His instructions. This type of prayer is honored because it upholds righteousness, expresses itself in godly conduct, and has the authority and boldness to approach the throne of grace.[15]

The articles in the outer court were made of brass. Brass pointed to judgment on sin. However, the articles in the Holy Place were made of gold. "Gold" represented deity or God. The reality of the Holy Place was that self must cease to reign in its vainglory, and God must be exalted. This is true for the Christian. Jesus must be exalted in all matters. Without the reality of Christ, a person cannot enter into the Most Holy Place.

The outer court was to encourage fear of God as people came face-to-face with the inevitability of their hopeless condition of sin and death. From this premise wisdom would cause those who were receptive to seek out God and His ways. The Holy Place was the place where righteousness was established as sanctification was worked in, through, and out of God's representatives. This work reminds us as Christians that at each point of wisdom, righteousness, and sanctification, Jesus is to be lifted up and made more real to us.[16]

---

[13] John 6:35; 2 Corinthians 3:5; Philippians 4:19
[14] John 1:4; 14:6; 16:13-14; Galatians 5:16-17
[15] Hebrews 4:16
[16] 1 Corinthians 1:30

Exaltation of this nature is vital. Mr. Tozer maintains that people do not have a high enough opinion of God.[17] This means that they do not know God. Psalm 99 deals with the reality of God by establishing three places of worship. These places point to the character of God that will produce the necessary attitude in us to ensure worship. As you will see, these three places point to a place of humility, submission, and subjection. Humility is a product of the fear of God, submission comes out of respect, and subjection is a response of obedience that comes out of love.

To set this scene up in Psalm 99, the psalmist establishes the Lord's position. HE REIGNS! He sits among the cherubim. This reminds us that we are to meet Him at the mercy seat.

> And thou shalt put the mercy seat above upon the ark; and in the ark thou shalt put the testimony that I shall give thee. And there I will meet with thee, and I will commune with thee from above the mercy seat, from between the two cherubim which are upon the ark of the testimony…(Exodus 25:21-22).

That Ark of the Covenant was the only object in the Most Holy Place. The mercy seat was made of pure gold, while the ark was overlaid with gold. Cherubim covered the mercy seat with their wings as they looked down upon the seat. Within the ark were three objects that served as a testimony of God's intervention on behalf of man. There were the tablets of the Law, manna from heaven, and Aaron's rod that had budded. Arks in the Old Testament always pointed to Jesus Christ. For Christians, Jesus serves as that place of mercy, for God can only meet each of us at the point of His redemption. As believers, we are hid in Him. Jesus is summarized as the way, the truth, and the life. He is the fulfillment of the Law, as He leads us beyond the Law in the ways of godliness. He is the truth about God's ultimate provision for mankind, and He is the only one who can bring resurrected life out of that which is lifeless and dead.[18]

Once again, we are reminded that everything begins with God. The psalmist reveals the necessary attitude to effectively approach Him: That of trembling. Because of Who He is, praise is the automatic response. Psalms 99:5 states, "Exalt ye the LORD our God, and worship at his footstool; for he is holy." All is under His domain. We must worship Him at the point of His holy character. All of us must not only bow, but also become subdued and humble before Him.

Psalm 99:9 says, "Exalt the LORD our God, and worship at his holy hill; for the LORD our God is holy." We worship according to our knowledge of God. Much of worship reveals that few know the God of the Bible. It is vital that as His people, we must learn to worship God on His terms. This is necessary if we are going to come into this place of

---

[17] Tozer on Worship and Entertainment; pg. 23

[18] Exodus 25:10-22; John 14:6; Romans 6:3-5; 10:4; Colossians 3:3; Hebrews 9:4

communion, but many fear giving up such control. As a result, God seems far away from these people, even though He is in the next room, separated by a veil that is over their hearts and minds.[19]

God seems far away because Jesus is not being properly lifted up. Many people have become familiar with their own concepts about Jesus, but few know Him. This familiarity has caused many to accept their perception of Him as final or complete. The demotion of Christ in people's way of thinking has taken the fascination out of discovering the depths and heights of God. It has taken away the awe, fear, and wisdom to pursue Him in humility. It has made people casual, redefining righteousness as they adjust their perception to what is tolerable and comfortable. This compromise has defiled the place of worship, opening people up to embrace the substitutes of dead or fleshly worship.

Jesus is the visible expression of God in word, deed, and purpose. He is the way to worship, the truth about worship, and the life that will come out of worship. He is the way to the Father's heart; the truth about what pleases Him, as well as the abundant life that is realized in His presence.[20]

This brings us to the veil. The Altar of Incense stood before the veil that marked the entrance into the Most Holy Place. This is why prayer and worship go together. Prayer marks the place of worship that will produce communion, while the actual veil served as the entrance into this Most Holy Place. The veil pointed to Jesus Christ. This is brought out in Hebrews 10:19-20, "Having therefore, brethren, boldness to enter into the holiest by the blood of Jesus, By a new and living way, which he hath consecrated for us, through the veil, that is to say, his flesh." As Christians, we can boldly enter through this veil because of what Jesus did on the cross. He represents a new and living way to this place of worship and communion with God.

The outer court reminded us that we must come to terms with sin in order to accept the price God paid on the cross to redeem us. The Holy Place revealed that man must come to terms with the person or character of his Creator, Jesus Christ. After all, He stands between man and worship. He is the mediator and the High Priest who stands in the gap for us. In His humanity, He offered up the ultimate sacrifice so that we could enter into this place with God.[21] Hebrews 9:12 states: "Neither by the blood of goats and calves, but by his own blood he entered in once into the holy place, having obtained eternal redemption for us."

Jesus also stands between prayer and the glory of God: "And whatsoever ye shall ask in my name, that will I do, that the Father may be glorified in the Son. As Jesus declared in John 14:13-14, if a person

[19] 2 Corinthians 3:14-16
[20] John 10:10; 14:6-9; Colossians 2:9
[21] Hebrews 9:22-26

asks any thing in His name, He would do it. It is in light of His character that we have authority to see things accomplished in prayer.

The Son of God prepared the way for man to enter into this Most Holy Place. In the New Testament tabernacle, there is no foreboding veil to hide the glory of God. Today, believers can get a glimpse into the Most Holy Place by considering the glory of the Son of God. His glory will cause humility, stir up fascination, put awe in the heart, and inspire one to bow down and reach up in complete surrender. However, a person must come by way of Jesus. Sadly, many people choose other means than Jesus to try to enter in.

The veil served as a harsh reality that only the high priest could enter such a place once a year. Even this priest had to prepare himself to ensure he would not die in the holy presence of God.[23] The other priests had to stop at the place of incense or prayer. The veil makes us realize that it was a place of division. Only one person could go into this place at a time.

This brings us to the three entrances. In order to enter the gate, the world had to be left behind. The door required one to leave all worldly attachments outside. As you can see, each entrance becomes more restrictive. When one comes to the veil, he or she must leave the essence of self as well as others behind. This entrance through the veil brought everything down to this one moment, one sacrifice, and one encounter with God. Entering through the veil shows that the Christian life would be brought down to the individual. He or she alone will enter through the veil and stand before God in preparation to worship Him in spirit and truth. In the end, each individual will give an account of his or her life.

Once again, we are reminded of the distinct works the three entrances represent. The gate in the outer court pointed to Jesus' redemption on the cross. For the Christian this represents the place of salvation. The door into the Holy Place represented the abundant life as the High Priest leads a person to the place of rest in God where self has ceased to struggle against His Spirit. The veil represented the place of worship and communion. This place was to house God's unhindered glory. Due to Jesus' redemption and the indwelling presence of the Holy Spirit, a person now has the means to enjoy the majesty of God, making life complete.

The Tabernacle reminds us that the Christian life will always bring us down to one reality: the Person of Jesus Christ. This Tabernacle represented Jesus in His deity, glory, and humanity. As stated, gold represented His deity, while the Ark of the Covenant pointed to His abiding presence. It was in the midst of His presence that one could encounter His glory.

---

[23] Leviticus 16

The Tabernacle also pointed to Jesus' humanity: The Altar of Burnt Offering, the Table of Shewbread, the Altar of Incense, and the Ark of the Covenant's inward structure were made of shittim or acacia wood. This wood was found in the wilderness and pointed to Jesus' humanity. As man, Jesus came out of the barren wilderness of the world into the midst of fallen humanity. Each of these articles represented the necessary work that Jesus accomplished as Man. For example, the Altar of Burnt Offering represented Jesus as the Lamb of God bringing judgment on sin by taking it away. The Table of Shewbread represented His broken body, so that man could partake of Him in communion. The Altar of Incense pointed to Jesus as the High Priest or Mediator that now stands between man and God. The Ark of the Covenant reminded us that our life is hid in Him. He is the One who instructs us in His ways, becomes the example of truth, and reveals to us how real life can only come out of death to that which represents the old rebellious, fallen ways.[24]

The candlestick was pure gold, beaten into shape. Its oil was pure, and it had to be attended to daily to keep it ever burning. It represented the light of Jesus' life leading us by the power of the Holy Spirit (oil) into a life of service and communion.

For a complete picture, consider the following diagram on the following page.

---

[24] Mark 14:22-25; John 1:29; Colossians 3:2; 1 Timothy 2:5; Hebrews 7:22-28

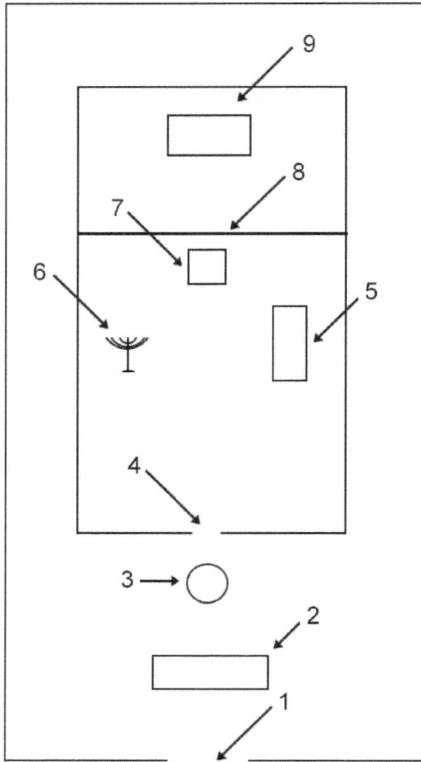

1. Gate: Jesus' redemption / Eternal life

2. Altar of Burnt Offering: Cross/Jesus as the Lamb of God that takes away the sin of the world.

3. Laver: The Word of God

4. Door: Jesus, the abundant life

5. Table of Shewbread: Communion, God's provision, Jesus as broken bread.

6. Candlestick: Jesus as the light—Christian walk

7. Altar of Incense: Prayer / Jesus as the High Priest and Mediator

8. The Veil: Jesus as the entrance into the place of worship and communion.

9. The Ark of the Covenant: Jesus the place of mercy, *& the way, truth, life.*

Because of what Jesus did outside of the gate and the present leadership He now offers each of us, the veil is now gone. All that remains is the Person of Jesus, arms open wide and His invitation clear, "Come." The fact that He is a lone figure reminds people it is a narrow way into this place. He is the only way into the place of rest and communion. To enter it requires preparation that will separate a person from the life in the world that stands condemned.

Such a reality can be frightening to those who have been playing the game. They must get rid of their cloak of pretense. They must embrace the light of truth, and be cleansed and sanctified. They must be ready to enter in to the secret places of communion. It is for this reason that many people never enter in. They know underneath that they are not prepared. Some are also afraid that God's holiness will expose their lukewarm life, thereby resulting in judgment.[25]

---

[25] Revelation 3:15-20

This brings us to the final aspect of worship. It enables a person to stand not only before God in loving adoration, but in the midst of trials and tribulations. Everything can be taken from us except the intimate place of worship where God remains an abiding reality. No one can destroy this place. It stands immovable, and will serve as a testimony of the reality of God in a person's life. We can see this in the life of Paul and Silas in Acts 16. These men were sold out for the glory of God. They were dead to their own agendas and crucified to the world.

Satan had been harassing these two men through a young girl who was in witchcraft. Paul ignored the harassment until he could no longer tolerate it. He then rebuked the spirit of divination. The spirit had to bow to Paul's authority in Christ. The girl's newfound liberty meant loss of financial gain for her master. Her master had both Paul and Silas beaten and thrown into prison.

In the midst of their persecution, Paul and Silas began to worship God in the darkest time of the night. Their sacrifice of praise and worship reached the throne of God. God met them. He shook the prison with a great earthquake. As the foundations shook, the prison doors were opened and everyone's bands were loosed.

The Roman guard perceived that all prisoners had escaped. Just as he was about to take his own life, Paul called out to him. Paul and Silas' confidence in God was expressed in unhindered worship, allowing God to meet them. In the end, the prison doors were opened and the shackles fell away. This is what occurs in worship: liberty in the Spirit. We actually have the liberty to move or walk in our life in God regardless of the physical prisons that surround us. Ultimately, this is when worship serves as a testimony to the reality and greatness of Jehovah God. Like the guard, such confidence and worship will result in salvation coming to hopeless souls.

Godly worship is the glue that brings the Christian life together. It serves as the means by which God will make Himself known. In the end, it will produce an unwavering testimony where one's flame will grow brighter in the midst of trials, testing, and tribulations.

Have you come to the Most Holy Place to develop your life in God? The tribulations of your life will reveal if this place exists or not. If it exists, tribulations will result in worship. If it does not, they will end in self-pity.

What significance does worship hold for God's people? After studying worship, I believe it will be a natural extension of salvation, and that salvation will be worked out and realized in worship. If this is true, worship serves as a pivotal point in salvation. Salvation will bring us to the point of worship, but worship will cause us to walk this salvation out as we come to a greater awareness of the beauty, power, and majesty of our God.

In conclusion to this whole matter, we also can see worship as a pivotal point in the model prayer. Matthew 6:13 not only serves as a benediction in prayer, but it also summarizes the one glorious reality about God that leads to all godly worship, "For thine is the kingdom, and the power, and the glory, for ever. Amen."

Book Three

DON'T TOUCH THAT DIAL!

(Hearing God's Voice)

INTRODUCTION

One of my greatest desires is to hear and know the voice of God. This incredible search has been challenging and glorious as I have learned the secret of hearing His voice. My search often reminded me of the story of the great preacher, Jonathan Edwards; and the missionary, David Brainerd, in the video "*Wings of the Morning*." David wanted to understand the secret of God's strength, so he asked Edwards about this mystery. Edwards compared the secret of strength with the power of God. He told David that the reason God's power appears to be a secret is not because God hides it, but because it is so simple man fails to see it.

I have found that God's voice is not hidden or far away from man, but man fails to hear it because it is so simple to perceive. It is hard for intellectual, prideful minds to accept its simplicity. It is often lost by personal confusion and doubt as various voices penetrate the airways, finding their way into our ears and drowning out His voice. Then there is human wisdom that is often mistaken for His voice. Some even dare to use God's voice for their own purpose or glory, while others abuse it in the name of fanaticism. Still others simply ignore His voice.

God wants to talk to His people. He uses many different means to communicate, but believers need to get past all of their personal concepts and ideas to hear Him. They have to get beyond self to fine-tune their spiritual ears. They must press through the obstacles of the world to tune into what the Spirit is saying.

My hope in writing this small book is to explain the different ways God speaks to us. The Word of God tells us how we can know our Creator's voice, and learn how to be led by it. It lines out basic criteria for testing and discerning the voices we hear.

I believe it is vital that Christians know how to distinguish the voice of God and follow its leading and direction. I believe it will be the voice of God that will not only establish us to stand in these end days, but its leading will also keep each of us on the straight and narrow path.

Do you recognize the voice of God?

1

HE THAT HAS EARS

As humans, we use our senses to perceive what we call reality or truth. Each of our five senses is used to confirm our conclusions. It amazes me that throughout Scripture, Jesus appears to deal with only one of the senses—that of hearing. *Strong's Concordance* reveals that the term "hearing" actually implies the other senses as well.[1]

Throughout the scriptures, Jesus' teachings, and parables, and, at times, rebukes had this famous statement attached to them, "He that hath ears to hear, let him hear." Jesus was appealing not to the physical ears, but rather a spiritual sense of hearing. He was forever challenging people to get beyond the physical world, and begin to understand His spiritual kingdom and the life-changing implications of His words.

In Mark 4:24, Jesus instructed the people around Him to take heed as to what they heard. In Luke 8:18, He instructs them to take heed in how they perceived. Obviously, we humans have a hard time correctly perceiving the things of God. After all, the things of God can only be understood by the spirit, and not by the carnal or natural abilities of man.[2] Due to the influence of our natural abilities and responses, there is much to wade through. We have our selfish disposition that perverts what is holy, our flesh that subdues the things of God and entices us towards the lust of the world, and pride that competes with, judges, and discredits spiritual truths.

When I consider the odds of hearing God's voice accurately, I know it is an impossible task unless God steps on the scene. We are told all things are possible with God, and over 20 centuries ago He did step on the scene in a personal way. Jesus, the Son of God, clothed Himself in humanity, and came to revolutionize man's limited and destructive understanding.

We see from Scripture that Jesus wanted men to learn to hear the distinct voice of God. He wanted them to taste of the real Bread of Life, and be immersed into the rivers of Living Water. He wanted them to touch the throne of God, as well as smell the sweet fragrance of His life. He wanted them to experience this new life in every way.[3]

---

[1] #191

[2] 1 Corinthians 2:13-14

[3] John 6:35; 7:37-39; 2 Corinthians 2:15-16; Hebrews 4:16; 1 John 1:1

Jesus, who was the very reflection of God, physically spoke to the physical ears of people.[4] He led them by outward example, leaving the physical eye to ponder and evaluate what it witnessed. He physically touched the lives of men to bring healing, comfort, and hope. He allowed people to taste His greatness as He fed the crowds with fish and bread. He embraced humanity at every level as He inspired the hearts, minds, and emotions of men to rise up and consider the impossible, the spiritual, and the unseen.

The truth is, God spoke to man in the past, continues to speak today, and ultimately will have the final say in the future. His voice will never be silent. If man does not hear His voice, it is not because God is still or silent, but because man is spiritually dull.

According to *Strong's Concordance*, "dull" means heavy, grievous, weightier, and burdensome.[5] Man is weighed down by the things of the world and overwhelmed by the many demands that burden him down. He is often weak because of his inability to change the status of those things that lay heavily upon his mind, and continues to be grieved by endless struggles.

This dull hearing is associated with a wrong heart condition. In fact, Jesus said in Matthew 13:15, "For this people's heart is waxed gross." Obviously, spiritual hearing is a matter of the heart.

The gross heart that Jesus is referring to is a rebellious heart. A rebellious heart has become callous and is devoid of humility and purity. Therefore, people may hear with the physical ear and see with the physical eye, but they will not be able to understand or perceive the real spiritual meaning. Their spiritual ears have become dull, and their eyes blinded so they cannot understand with their hearts.

Matthew 13:14-15 tells us this is the fulfillment of Isaiah's prophecy. These scriptures indicate this type of heart is under judgment. Salvation and spiritual healing will elude such a person.

What a great tragedy for the souls of men to confront! Jesus came to heal, give sight, and set the captive free; but a hard heart is unable to receive such a blessing. It rejects Jesus, scoffs at His truth, and resists the conviction of the Holy Spirit.

No wonder Jesus gave a comparison of the different heart conditions of man by using the parable of the sower and the seed in Matthew 13. He described four heart conditions; three of these conditions will ultimately lead to rejection of Him and His truths. Each of these unreceptive hearts met with failure because they were either overcome or challenged by Satan, self, or the world. Satan managed to rob the seed of the Gospel from the hard, unsubmitted heart as given to us in the first example. In the case of the second heart, the Gospel found no room

---

[4] Colossians 2:9
[5] #917

for growth because it was full of the follies of self. Due to divided loyalties, the world choked out the life from the third heart.

Obviously, an unregenerate heart may be receptive to the Gospel, but if not changed, it will eventually reject Jesus and His truth. It will give way to the dictates of the flesh and the world, thereby, producing weeds and thorns. Jesus made this statement in Matthew 12:35, "A good man out of the good treasure of the heart bringeth forth good things: and an evil man out of the evil treasure bringeth forth evil things." We can play religious games and look righteous, but eventually our hearts will tell on us.

Jeremiah 17:9 tells us the heart is wicked and deceitful. Our hearts must be changed. God promised to give His people new hearts. The fruits of this new heart will be brought forth through the work of regeneration.[6]

This is why the Apostle Paul in Romans 10:9-10 tells us salvation is a matter of the heart receiving the message of the Gospel by faith. He states, "That if thou shalt confess with thy mouth the Lord Jesus, and shalt believe in thine heart that God raised him from the dead, thou shalt be saved. For with the heart man believeth unto righteousness; and with the mouth confession is made unto salvation." The heart that receives the Lord Jesus Christ by faith results in both salvation and righteousness.

It is obvious why many miss the narrow path to heaven! Man easily complicates the things of God and misses the simplicity of His truth. We also know that many are not receptive because they are blinded by Satan, the god of this world, to the glorious light of the Gospel.[7]

What kind of heart is able to perceive and receive the things of God? The answer is found in Luke 18:17, "Verily I say unto you, Whosoever shall not receive the kingdom of God as a little child shall in no wise enter therein." A child-like heart is an open and receptive heart. It is pure and does not have to wade through the entanglements of the world. It has no set concepts or ideas; therefore, it can simply receive and accept truth. Its confidence does not rest in self, but in the One who oversees their well-being. A child-like heart does not have to make sense out of all the problems that rise up to challenge its world because it finds rest in the Person of God.

I know in my own case when I allow Satan, self, or the world to rock my boat, my heart becomes subject to fear instead of to the Prince of Peace. When I take matters into my own hands to try to figure out a situation, I hit confusion and doubt. As I try to look into the future with my physical eyesight instead of looking into the face of my Lord, I fall into despair and hopelessness.

---

[6] Ezekiel 36:26; Titus 3:5
[7] Matthew 7:13-14; 2 Corinthians 4:3-4

Each detour of Satan, self, and the world has bought me back to square "A" in my spiritual walk. I must regress and become a dependent child on the One who loved me enough to die for me. My heart-felt prayer is always the same: "Oh Lord, make my heart child-like so that I can hear and see in order to understand and perceive your pure, simple truths. Help me, Lord, to have the faith of a child so I can trust you without reservation. Help me become pure, for the pure in heart shall see you."[8] I know that if I would continue to look into the face of my precious Lord, the things of the world would grow strangely dim. My perspective would change, and my focus would become single and clear.

How can we receive a new, child-like heart? The answer is simple: give way to the work of the Gospel of Jesus Christ in our life. There are many gospels being preached today. Each of us must make sure the gospel we choose to believe is the one presented in the Bible. There are four parts to the Gospel found in the Word of God. The Apostle Paul defines it this way in 1 Corinthians 15:1-4,

> Moreover, brethren, I declare unto you the gospel which I preached unto you, which also ye have received, and wherein ye stand; By which also ye are saved, if ye keep in memory what I preached unto you, unless ye have believed in vain. For I delivered unto you first of all that which I also received, how that Christ died for our sins according to the Scriptures; And that he was buried, and that he rose again the third day according to the Scriptures.

Paul verifies that the Gospel he received was confirmed by Old Testament prophecies. He reminded the Corinthians that not only does this message save, but it also gave them strength and confidence.

The first point of the Gospel declares that we are sinners. As sinners we are separated from God. This knowledge is capable of making us dependent children upon God. We cannot save ourselves, so we must look to the One who saves. Our reliance on God's provision becomes an act of child-like faith.

The Word of God constantly confirms our hopeless spiritual condition. 1 John 1:8 and 10 tell us if we say we have no sin, or that we have not sinned, the truth (Jesus Christ) is not in us, and we are making God a liar, proving that His Word is not in us. Romans 3:23 declares we have all sinned and fallen short of the glory of God. Romans 6:23 states that the wages of sin is death or separation from God, who is the essence of real life.

The second point of the Gospel is that Jesus died for us. Romans 5:8 gives us this insight, "But God commendeth his love toward us, in that, while we were yet sinners, Christ died for us." Jesus did an exchange with us. He took our place on the cross and faced the judgment of death that hung over our heads.

---

[8] See Matthew 5:8

The Apostle Paul explained it in this manner in 2 Corinthians 5:21, "For he (God) hath made him, (Jesus) to be sin for us, who knew no sin; that we might be made the righteousness of God in him." (Parenthesis added.) Jesus was without sin. He was God Incarnate. He came into this world as fully man, ready to become a sacrifice to suffice the judgment of sin. As deity, He was perfect and able to save to the uttermost.[9] John 3:16 confirms this by telling us that His death was to ensure everlasting life to those who would believe this simple truth.

The third part of the Gospel is that Jesus was buried. Romans 6:4 explains the importance of the grave experience, "Therefore we are buried with him by baptism into death: that like as Christ was raised up from the dead by the glory of the Father, even so we also should walk in newness of life". There must be a grave experience, which is death to the "old self" or "way of life," that can never bring accusation against us to ensure the next and final point of the Gospel: the resurrection.

For there to be a resurrection, there must first be a death. Resurrection represents the new life coming forth out of the grave, leaving behind the old. As the Apostle Paul stated in 1 Corinthians 15:17, "And if Christ be not raised, your faith is vain; ye are yet in your sins." The whole Gospel is confirmed and our salvation secured by the fact that Jesus rose from the grave three days after He was brutally crucified.

We must believe by faith all four points of the Gospel in order for salvation to occur.[10] This Gospel is simple in meaning, but profound and powerful in its ability to save and change lives forever. This is why Paul declared this message to be the power of God unto salvation.[11]

One would wonder why people have such a hard time receiving the genuine Gospel by faith. The Apostle Paul admitted that this simple, powerful message would be a stumbling block to the Jews and foolishness to the Gentiles. The main problem with the Gospel is that it goes against the human need to be glorified.

Arrogant man finds it difficult to accept the fact that he is saved by grace, through a child-like faith, and not by any of his good deeds or works. Since man cannot take any glory for his salvation, he will look to religious fervor or deeds. Like the Pharisees of Jesus' time, man will often substitute his relationship with God for religious vanity.[12]

The Gospel also has the power to change hearts and produce new life. However, the problem with many Christians is that they will not adhere to their new heart. They continue to give way to the old selfish disposition. This old man or self will drown out the regenerated heart that is capable of hearing the voice of God.

---

[9] Hebrews 7:25

[10] If you would like to know about the Gospel, see the author's book,
Presentation of the Gospel, in the 5th volume of the foundational series.

[11] Romans 1:16

[12] 1 Corinthians 1:23; Ephesians 2:8-9

I encourage Christians who display a pure heart towards God to listen to their heart when it comes to understanding the heart of God. God will never steer anyone away from that which is pure and true.

How about you? What does your heart say about your relationship with God? After all, if your heart is not child-like, you will not be able to hear the voice of God. You may have a form of godliness, but there is neither power nor life that is refreshing to the soul.[13]

If your heart is weighed down, turn to the Lord in humility and repentance. Draw near to Him and He will draw near to you. Cry out for mercy and ask Him to revive your heart and give you clarity of mind. He will be quick to answer you.[14]

Once your heart is restored to a child-like state: *Don't touch that dial!* Rather, adhere to the leading and quickening of the Holy Spirit speaking to your heart. In doing so, you will grow in the grace and knowledge of your Lord. It is that simple.

Perhaps you have not yet believed in your heart all four points of the Gospel. Maybe you have said some sinner's prayer, but you simply mouthed it without perceiving the real spiritual implication of Christ and the cross. Perhaps you have been in church all of your life, but never came to the cross of Christ on bended knees and with a humbled heart.

Coming into agreement with the Word of God is vitally important for fine-tuning spiritual hearing. A pure heart is receptive to the pure Word of God. It will come into agreement with God's evaluation of man's spiritual condition, and the provision of His Son to redeem each of us from eternal doom. It is never too late to ask God to give you a new heart. A new heart will allow you to agree with Him, and come to Him in humility, sincerity, and repentance. He will meet you and save you from the daily claims, delusion, and tentacles Satan, self, and the world.

---

[13] 2 Timothy 3:5
[14] James 4:6-10

2

GETTING RID OF THE STATIC

According to *Webster's New Collegiate Dictionary*, "static" is a disturbance produced in a television or radio receiver by atmospheric or various natural or manmade electrical disturbances. These disturbances create an opposition. As Christians, we contend with much static when it comes to hearing the voice of God.

Countless voices in the world and the church as well, cause confusion and disheartening challenges for people struggling to know God's voice. We must be able to discern different voices in order to recognize the voices of our enemies. The enemies of the soul can cause an array of static in our spiritual lives. We have to contend with the voices of others who claim they are representing God. And finally, we must wade through the predominate voice of self that can be greatly influenced by Satan and the world.

These different voices can sound logical, but will cause us to miss the will of God for our life. The will of God is the main reason we must be able to hear His voice. It is God's voice that leads us into the pastures of His will. Without His leading and direction, we can take detours to the edge of the abyss and be led straight into destruction.

Getting rid of the static in our spiritual lives is essential to hearing the voice of God. Knowing His voice is crucial to fighting a good fight, finishing the course, and keeping the faith. After all, Jesus is the Commander of the army. He is the Trainer and Instructor concerning the course we must run. He is also the Author and Finisher of our faith.[1]

Let us now consider these different voices that are in opposition to God. Keep in mind these voices can sound logical and religious. They can be partially right, but still deny the real truth. The problem with each of these voices is that they are opposed to the will of God in our lives. God's will represents the best for us. The consequences of listening to other voices can be devastating, and could cost us our very soul.

Voices of Self

The greatest challenge to hearing the voice of God is getting past the insipid voice of self. It comes in many forms and can be subtle. It can sound logical, but it lacks godly wisdom. It can come across as religious, but lacks the right spirit. It can be partially right, but lacks complete truth.

---

[1] 2 Timothy 4:7; Hebrews 12:2

The voice of self is often influenced by others, motivated by Satan, and encouraged by the world's notions. Discerning this voice is like trying to find your way through a maze. It takes integrity and humility to separate this voice from the voice of God. It requires self-denial and great determination. You have to be willing to put down reliable standards, reject religious platitudes, and refuse to settle for anything but God's will, heart, and mind in your life.

The battle to get beyond self requires a process. God actually must take us through various stages in our spiritual lives. He will actually show us the depth of our depravity.

The first voice of self that God exposed to me was my *religious* voice. This voice was a substitute for my relationship with God through Jesus Christ. Doctrine, good works, religious talk, and platitudes became my sick way of interpreting and manifesting the Christian life. The Lord showed me I had a form of godliness that was hiding a wrong heart attitude, a carnal mind, and a self-righteous motivation.[2] He revealed to me that the façade I had adopted was my way of covering up the fact that I actually lacked real spiritual goods to be effective in His kingdom.

In the process, He exposed my many sacred cows. Sacred cows are those things that are exalted above the reality, truths, and Word of God. They serve as a person's final authority. Man's religion is often idolatrous at heart and is full of these sacred cows. This is why religion crucified Christ. It could not afford to be challenged because it would easily be toppled by the truth. Today, this type of substitution continues to be the greatest enemy of God's kingdom. It crucified Jesus centuries ago, and continues to repeat its blatant rejection of His truth.

My sacred cows stood strong. My perception of doctrine was down to a fine art. I could argue any point of theology with the best of them. My, how smart I felt over my spiritual knowledge, while ignoring the clear warning of the Apostle Paul that knowledge alone simply puffs up our overrated prideful opinion of self.[3]

I was involved with righteous causes and did various good works. But, behind closed doors I compromised some of the very things I advocated. Hypocrisy surrounded me. However, my religious works gave me a false sense of my spiritual worth in the kingdom of God, while my prevailing hypocrisy revealed my delusion about my real spiritual state.

Lastly, I could talk the talk, but not walk the walk. I justified my discrepancies by convincing myself that my good intentions proved my heart was in the right place. Good intentions fall very short of obedience and holiness. After all, we are instructed in 1 John 2:6, "He that saith he abideth in him ought himself also so to walk, even as he (Jesus) walked." (Parenthesis added.)

---

[2] 2 Timothy 3:5
[3] 1 Corinthians 8:1

I had put confidence in my religious activities rather than God. This misdirected reliance was nothing more than idolatry. I was relying on something other than God to justify my sins and secure my place in His kingdom. Unknowingly, my deceptive way of thinking had broadened for me the narrow path to heaven with a bunch of religious nonsense.

The exposure of my religious idolatry humbled me. What a fool I had been. I had accepted fool's gold to the true Pearl of Great Price, Jesus Christ.

I began to see my prideful disposition was prone to accept imitations and fall into religious traps set by Satan. After all, idolatry is a comfortable practice for the flesh to embrace and pride to accept. However, to worship an unseen, holy God is to expose and challenge the very vanity of the flesh and the loftiness of pride. Neither of these ungodly qualities could comfortably stand in the presence of this powerful God.

The second voice of self that God revealed to me was the voice of *logic*. This voice is very seductive and is often considered wisdom. Like the Apostle Paul stated in 1 Corinthians 1:27, "But God hath chosen the foolish things of the world to confound the wise." At best, the voice of logic is nothing more than man's best attempt to be the wisest fool around. The voice of logic is often based on vain imaginations and philosophies of man.[4] It inspires our standards and establishes our form of truth. This is why this voice is dangerous.

I had relied much on this voice, and considered myself to be quite wise. Some people felt I was one of those individuals who displayed common sense and made good judgments.

When I became a Christian and fell into a religious pattern that led me down the path of great idolatry, my so-called wisdom was called into serious question. As I looked back over my first years as a Christian, I could see my form of wisdom was sensual and devilish, just as James 3:13-14 advocated. It only produced envy, strife, confusion, and every evil work.

It was hard coming face to face with the true identity of my wisdom. It was nothing more than conceit. The Word of God instructs us to not be wise in our own conceits.[5] I realized how my conceit always succeeded in making me look like a fool.

As God began to impart His pure wisdom to me, I was confronted with another challenge.[6] My logic wanted to take credit for His wisdom. I learned that God's wisdom revolutionized my way of thinking. It proved to be so simple and yet profound. It was evident in its ability to change hearts and lives, while making me appear wise for teaching it or using it to instruct others.

---

[4] 2 Corinthians 10:3-5: Colossians 2:8
[5] Romans 12:16
[6] James 3:17

I have watched God graciously impart His wisdom to others who actually thought they came up with the information. They were devoid of discernment to know the difference between their logic and God's wisdom.

I have learned that any truth or deed that possesses the character of God comes from Him, and not human intellect. Christians need to know the difference to avoid touching God's glory. Paul warned in 1 Corinthians 1:29 and 30 to avoid such foolishness. In spite of the seriousness of such actions, many people miss it as they take credit for the things of God. This defiles what is of God and robs Him of His rightful glory.

Another harsh reality about my logic is that it was the greatest enemy of real faith. My logic brought everything of God into question and under my scrutiny. I was shocked to find God's instructions were often classified as illogical, and were cleverly rejected by me. The Apostle Paul put my dilemma in this perspective, "But the natural man receiveth not the things of the Spirit of God: for they are foolishness unto him: neither can he know them, because they are spiritually discerned" (1 Corinthians 2:14).

As I studied the Word of God over the years, I could see where God's instructions to His various prophets like Isaiah, Jeremiah, and Ezekiel would not make a bit of sense to the logical mind. His commands would be considered by the best of men as foolishness. Sadly, many believers still resort to their personal logic, even in light of the Word. The Word states that God's thoughts are higher than ours and asks, "Who can know the mind of God?"[7]

Even though we are reminded that God chooses the foolish things of the world to confound the wise, we still insist that the gentle voice or the startling, passing thought which goes against our logic cannot be God's voice. We conclude it has to be the product of our own imagination in spite of the fact that our imagination would never challenge the comfort zones of our logic.

The logic of man will always reason away the voice of God. It can only operate in the area of what it sees and knows. This is why man's logic is the greatest enemy of faith, and can only produce unbelief, frustration, and a hard heart.

I have encountered many Christians who have the false concept that if only they could hear the voice of God, things would be different. The truth is that Christians are no different than the Israelites. The Israelites heard the voice of God, and ended up requesting that He speak to them through Moses.[8]

The problem with hearing God's voice is that it can be frightening as it challenges our concepts of Him, or becomes a hard saying when He

---

[7] Isaiah 55:8-9; Romans 11:34
[8] Exodus 19-20:21

asks us to relinquish something of value or importance. It can also insult our logic, causing us to write it off as imagination or nonsense. He may ask us to take a step of faith that appears to be leading us over a financial or emotional cliff. In such cases, logic will quickly come to our aid and convince us that God would never ask us to do such a thing.

My walk of faith has put my logic in its proper place. Today, it is rarely given any consideration in my decision making. I take big and small matters to the Lord. I have found safety and protection in seeking God's will no matter how illogical it appears. In the end, God's wisdom always turns out to be an effective and victorious way of doing things.

I have watched Christians, including those in leadership; struggle with the conflict the voice of God causes with their logic. Those who give in to their logic never get very far in their relationship with God. They become stagnant and oppressed. They find the battle they are in includes anger, complacency, and unbelief.

If you are giving way to the voice of logic, you need to repent of conceit and unbelief. The next step is to overcome the fear of looking like a fool in the eyes of the world. It does not matter what the world thinks of you. Rather, your main concern should be how God views you. God can always pick up a floundering Christian who falls when walking by faith more easily than He can pick up a stagnant Christian who refuses to get out of his or her comfort zone. Think about it.

The next voice of self that God challenged in my life was the voice of the *flesh*. This voice is the loudest and hardest to silence. It is not subtle like the voice of logic, but it is blatantly defiant. It is quick to justify because it represents that which is considered normal, natural, and in many cases, acceptable. It gives us great pleasure. It pampers and spoils us. It ultimately gives us free reign to pursue every lust and craving, whether mental, emotional, or physical. In the end, this voice will silence the conviction of the Holy Spirit, make us weak in the area of godly obedience, and entice us into a world of darkness, slavery, and death.

It seems as if I have struggled with this voice on a daily basis. Initially in my faith walk, my victories over its tormenting ways were few. I found this voice nudging me to declare my rights to worldly happiness when I was denying myself of lust. I found it tempting me to curse God when the challenges were great. I discovered it would demand its way and throw tantrums when God withheld my desires.

Amazingly, God put up with me during this process. I would eventually discern when I gave way to the flesh, and would chide myself for allowing it to get a hold of me with its seductive tentacles. Each time I saw the depth of its roots and claims on me, I would humble myself and cry out like the Apostle Paul, "O wretched man that I am! who shall deliver me from the body of this death" (Romans 7:24)? I always knew Jesus would heed such a cry.

The struggles with the voice of the flesh revealed the depth of my depravity and the hopelessness of my plight more than any other part of my humanity. It is hard to imagine how wicked and sinister the flesh is until God reveals it in its ugliness.

My walk of faith exposed it in a greater way. Child-like trust will actually challenge the control of the flesh, while godly repentance will rebuke it in its foolishness, and humility will silence it in its demands. For this reason, we must deny this voice and nail all of its rights and demands to a cross to keep it from being an open door to Satan.

Satan loves it when Christians give in to the voice of flesh. It gives him the opportunity to reinforce his lies, bondage, and oppression. This is why James 4:7 tells us to submit ourselves to God and to resist the devil. Satan will flee from us.

The voice of the flesh is very dangerous because it can deceptively win over the voice of God. In fact, God will quickly turn us over to the underlying dictates of the flesh. I learned this the hard way.

I came to a very important decision in my life regarding marriage. I wanted God's will for my life, and felt I was searching for it diligently. At the time, I was in great prayer, struggling over persistent doubts about the man who appeared to be my future mate. I knew the history of this person and questioned his salvation. I had shared with him my desire to serve the Lord. He seemed to be in agreement with my goal, assuring me that he had rededicated his life to the Lord.

As I struggled over the situation, I found more confirmation towards the marriage than opposition against it. I wrestled with it as I tried to confront each doubt, only to have the doubt vanish with what appeared to be spiritual insight.

I finally came to a place of peace about the issue of marriage. I felt it was God's will. Later, I discover it was far from His perfect order for my life. To my heartbreak, not only had I failed to determine God's perfect will for my life, but also our marriage fell short of meeting the criteria for a godly marriage. It eventually ended in a disgraceful divorce. Lives were torn up, reputations ruined, and people tested.

Incidents such as these are not only humbling, but they force you to go back to the drawing board to find out where you went wrong. What I discovered during my time of examination shocked me. I found out that even though I wanted God's will for my life, my desire to be married proved to be greater than my desire for God's will to be done. Although I had sought God's will, I was still open to be led astray by my own fleshly agendas and logical evaluations. This allowed Satan the perfect avenue to confirm my wrong decision through various avenues.

God had allowed my disastrous decision because I desired it over Him. This is where the voice of God will give way to the voice of the flesh. We must always be on guard when it comes to our desires or personal agendas. We must make sure our heart's ultimate goal is God's perfect will, regardless of how good or logical something may appear.

God did eventually turn my bad decision around for good. I learned a valuable lesson about the significant role fleshly desires and agendas can play in one's spiritual life. Today, I try to recognize those overpowering fleshly desires, influences, or dictates. I do my best to crucify them. And, with God's help I have been successful in overcoming them at important times in my life.

The final voice of self that God dealt with in my life was that of *pride*. This voice can be found intertwined with logic and the source of inspiration when it comes to the flesh. It actually infiltrates every little corner of our humanity. For example, pride can be found in personal standards, religious attitudes, and good deeds. It lurks behind disguises such as vanity, selfishness, personal rights, identity, self-sufficiency, and false humility. It is subtle at times and boastful at others. It can be arrogant, or it can hide behind the insipid masks of fear, self-pity, and self-inflicted martyrdom. It is unteachable, cruel, and relentless in its pursuits. Ultimately, it competes with God and strives to exalt itself at every opportunity. In the end, pride will sacrifice anything or anyone who may get in its way.

The voice of the flesh is obvious, but the voice of pride is hard to detect. For every disguise of pride that is revealed, other masks can replace it. For every layer of pride that God exposes, one becomes aware that there are many more to follow.

As God began to uncover my pride, I became aware of how untrustworthy and treacherous I was. Don't get me wrong. I strive to be very trustworthy, and I hate treachery, but because of my pride the potential of treachery lurked at every corner. I reached a point where I began to question every motive, and found myself overwhelmed by the immensity of the problem my pride was presenting. I could see now how this insidious culprit caused conflict in my spiritual life and my relationships with others.

One day I felt hopeless in the battle against this sinister foe. I kept getting glimpses of how prevalent it was in my life. Everywhere I turned, it was there to defile the holy, pervert the truth, and touch God's glory. The Lord managed to break through my despair. He told me to quit looking at my pride and begin to look at Him. He assured me He would deal with it at the appropriate times. He has never let me down.

The Lord's dealing with my pride varied. At times He has gone after the roots of it with an axe, or taken a sword to expose its sinister ways. In some cases, He has taken a hammer to its ugly head, always displaying the graciousness and capable abilities of a master craftsman.

Pride is bigger than man. This is why it can so easily possess a person's flesh, emotions, and logic. The harsh reality of pride is that it brings people into complete opposition against God, causing Him to resist them. Only God can effectively reveal your pride. Once it is exposed, you must neglect its demands, resist its forms of exaltation, and choose to humble yourself before the Lord. This is the secret in the battle of overcoming this destructive enemy. However, the natural tendency is to make friends with pride or ignore it in our personal lives while condemning it in others.

What about you? Are you listening to the different voices of self? They can do nothing more than lead you astray and bring destruction to your life. Repent of your submission to them. Ask God to deliver you from their power and entanglements in your life. Then, begin to seek God with your whole heart. According to God's sure Word, you will find Him.[9]

Voices of Others

I have depended too much on the voices of others through the years. Some of these voices have represented God, while others have caused me to go on destructive detours.

One such destructive detour that resulted from listening to others' voices was my marriage. A Christian leader and a very good friend advised me that this man was the man for me. I trusted their judgments, but I must emphasize at this point, people will only do what they want to do. I take ultimate responsibility for my wrong decision, and so must others who have incorrectly taken a wrong path based on the advice of those they have trusted.

As a scriptural counselor, I am quite aware that in the end godly advice will lose to the predominate desires of an individual. I cannot begin to tell you the amount of words that have fallen on deaf ears, and the devastating consequences that have followed certain individuals who refused to listen to heavenly wisdom.

Through the years, I have been careful as to the people I choose as my spiritual advisers. Even with the best advisers, I still have a responsibility to test out their counsel. The reason is simple. No person can determine the will of God for another person's life.

Many times, people counsel from their personal frame of reference. I know this is true because I am guilty of it myself. It is easy to judge an incident based on what you think you know or have seen. Getting caught up with some righteous cause or with the plight of someone or even the romance of a situation is a common mistake. Such counsel comes out of human understanding and not godly wisdom. It can cause many problems and prove to be a disaster for the recipient.

Many Christians leave their spiritual well-being in the hands of others. Again, this is an individual's choice to leave such a delicate and important matter in the hands of mere man. If leaders are truly righteous, they will continue to point people to the Lordship of Jesus. If they are not righteous, they will most likely glory in the undeserved recognition and attention. They will end up taking advantage of the person's misguided loyalty.

---

[9] Jeremiah 29:13

Our God is a personal God. His plans for individual lives are designed according to each person's calling and potential. It is His desire to talk to each of us in a personal way, and lead us into His perfect will.

The problem with trusting our spiritual well-being to others is that we could be following a cult leader into destruction. This is why the Apostle Paul's instruction was clear to the Corinthians to follow him as he followed Christ.[10]

The main concern of every Christian leader should be that believers are truly following after Jesus. Like Paul, their main desire should be to ensure that Jesus' sheep do not stray away from truth.

Leaders who refuse to be tested in the different areas of their spiritual life are not of God. They are not building up the kingdom of Christ, but their own kingdoms. They do not care about truth, but about their own personal agendas. That they do not care for or guard the souls of the people reveals that they do not love them. Beware; this is a description of a wolf masquerading in sheep's clothing.[11]

Consider Israel. In Exodus 20, Israel had an encounter with God Almighty. The Israelites heard His voice and got a glimpse of His power and glory. They became frightened, and asked Moses to serve as their intercessor. In the end, the situation was a disaster.

The children of Israel began to question Moses' authority and commands, rebelling against his instructions, while still relying on him to solve their problems. These people were only one step removed from having personal communion with God. This one step caused them to stumble, rebel, and fall. They failed to take personal responsibility for their actions, and completely missed God's will for their lives.

This principle applies today. God is calling us into personal communion with Him. Jesus provided the way for each of us to come into the very presence of God. To allow any mere man to stand between you and communion with God is to be one dangerous step from the real thing.

The entity who is standing between God and you is nothing more than an idol that will fail you. In fact, this individual could easily lead you away from truth, as well as cause you to stumble into the pit of hell. God wants to speak to you personally. Do not allow anything or anyone to stand between you and Him. Enter into His presence, and begin to enjoy who He is.

Are you listening to the voices of others? It is easy to fall into this trap, but it will leave you feeling empty and unproductive. Ask the Lord to bring down any idol or influence that may stand in the way of your fellowship with Him. Make communion with Him your main emphasis; and as the deer that pants after much needed water, pursue this intimacy with relentless tenacity.

---

[10] 1 Corinthians 11:1

[11] Matthew 7:15

Voices of Satan and the World

Satan's voice often comes in the form of fiery darts being thrown at us. These darts are lies, temptations, and damaging suggestions. They can cause destructive fires to flare up in our lives in the form of perversion, lusts, and evil acts.

This is why God has provided us with armor in Ephesians 6. For Satan to be effective in his attempts to rob, kill, and destroy, we first have to give in to his devices.[12] Each piece of the armor protects us from one of his devices. The belt of truth deals with deception, the breastplate and shield protect against all forms of temptation, and the helmet against vain imaginations. The footwear will lead us away from his snares of the enemy, and the sword will put Satan on the run.

The true secret to Satan's defeat is submission to the Lordship of Jesus. The application of the full armor of God implies a person is coming under the total leadership of the Lord of Hosts. This is why the armor of God is so effective against the powers of darkness. On the other hand, if we submit to our logic, flesh, or pride, we are coming under the lordship of Satan.

We must also beware of the voice of the world. The world can only mimic the voice of its leader, Satan.[13] Many Christians have listened to the voice of the world. As a result, the world has come into the Church. This has sent tremors into the Church in order to shake every facet of the Church life. Churches and leadership have fallen. Families are being ripped apart. The sheep are scattered, running to and fro to find some kind of hope, power, or answer to the spiritual leanness that is invading their souls.

Some Christians have substituted the vain philosophies of men for the Word of God. They have defiled true worship with worldly hype and idolatry. These people have replaced godly wisdom with worldly tolerance. They have compromised truth in the name of worldly unity and ecumenism. They have adopted battle cries in place of true repentance and humility. They have justified their pride in the name of worldly titles, prosperity, and aggression. These individuals have minimized the real servants of God by exalting titles over the call of God.

You might wonder how I know these things. The fruits in the Church reveal that something has gone terribly amiss. It appears that all the general consensus of the Church can do is encourage more movements and programs without bringing any viable solution to the problems. In some cases, believers are being called to become more involved, especially in the political arena. In other congregations, leaders have tried to change the face of the Church by rebuking it over such issues as racial problems. It seems like the Church never runs out of good ideas, possible movements, and great causes. Are all these attempts working?

---

[12] John 10:10
[13] 2 Corinthians 4:3-4

By all appearances the world is still in the Church. Movements and programs for men, women, and children may have a nice ring to them, but the world remains entrenched in the homes of Christians, destroying their very core. Rebuking people over issues such as racial problems may sound noble, but the world is still consuming the hearts of many who sit in the pews every Sunday. Getting involved in the political system may be a way to get our voices heard. However, it is the world's voice in the Church that carries the predominate influence in the lives of many who call themselves Christians. The influence of the world has caused many of God's people to become dull of hearing towards the real voice of God.

Where will it all end? I fear it will end with great judgment. In order for the Church to avoid the judgment of God, it must get the world out of the sanctuary and the hearts and minds of its people.

This appears to be an impossible task, but nothing is impossible with God. God can change the face of the Church by changing hearts and minds. However, this change will not occur until the leaders become broken over their failure to serve as an uncompromising voice of God's truth and holiness in the midst of His sheep.

Meanwhile, it is up to each of us, who refer to ourselves as believers, to repent of all worldliness in our lives, and to separate ourselves from the unholy. Separation of this nature is vital if we are going to subdue the voice of the world in our lives so we can clearly hear the voice of God.[14]

What voice are you listening to right now? Is there static in your life because you have not fine-tuned your spiritual life in righteousness? Are you confused because you hear various conflicting voices? Are you in despair because there is leanness in your soul due to a lack of communion with God? Jesus Christ came to clear all conflicting channels in our lives. He provided an avenue that would not only remain open, but would be made available for anyone who sincerely came to Him as the solution to static problems.

Won't you come to Him? He is the Way, the Truth, and the Life, and He is waiting for you to simply come to Him as a child. He will satisfy your longing heart by leading you into the very presence of the Father in sweet communion.[15]

---

[14] 2 Corinthians 6:14-18
[15] John 14:6

3

LEARNING TO FINE-TUNE

A good question to ask at this point is, "How do I learn to fine-tune my spiritual hearing so I can hear God?" The answer is simple. You need to get to know Him personally.

God is merely an acquaintance to many people. After all, it is easy to know *about* God and to know *of* Him, but this does not constitute a growing, vital relationship with Him. For example, there are many people I know of, but I do not know them well enough to recognize their voices on the phone or know what pleases them. They are merely acquaintances. This is true of many Christians. They do not have an intimate relationship with God; therefore, they would not really recognize His voice if they did hear it.

We see this in the case of Samuel. The Lord spoke to Samuel when he was a young boy, but the child did not recognize His voice because he did not know Him. We are told in 1 Samuel 3:7: "Now Samuel did not yet know the LORD, neither was the word of the LORD yet revealed unto him."

Studying Israel during the time of Moses revealed the Lord's desire for Israel to understand who He was. He wanted His people to understand and know Him as LORD. This meant He was their owner and sole leader. As their owner it was vital that they knew His voice. In rebuke, Isaiah pointed out that the ox knows his owner and the ass his crib, but God's people did not know Him.[1]

The Lord wanted His chosen nation to understand and know that He was God and there was none like Him. He is Creator. He controls creation, and He was the only One capable of delivering them from their bondage. He provided for their every need—from the manna that came from heaven to the water that flowed out of the rock.[2]

He not only wanted them to see Him as the Great Deliverer, but also as the ultimate Judge. The children of Israel were shown this contrast when delivered through the Red Sea, only to watch it being used as a tool of judgment on the Egyptians. They were later told that this event occurred so they might know the hand of God and fear Him.[3]

---

[1] Isaiah 1:3

[2] Exodus 6:7; 7:17; 8:22; 9:29; 10:2; 16:12

[3] Joshua 4:22-24

The fear of God is the beginning of wisdom. God wants us to have His wisdom, but such wisdom can only be developed in light of an intimate knowledge of His character. To know His character intimately means we must first know Him personally. If we know His character, we will know His ways and fear Him in a healthy way.[4]

God talked about how the children of Israel did not know His ways, and He gave them up to their own heart desires to walk in their own counsels.[5] We all know the results were devastating. You can hear the Lord's heart cry as He declares, "O that my people had hearkened unto me, and Israel had walked in my ways! I should soon have subdued their enemies, and turned my hand against their adversaries" (Psalm 81:13-14).

The problem is God's ways are foreign to those who do not know Him. His ways can bring unhealthy fear to those who are spiritually shallow, and produce a hard heart to those who are disappointed by His way of doing things. A hard heart produces unbelief. [6]

King David is a good contrast to study as far as a person who knew God. David experienced deliverance many times in his life. He saw God's constant intervention on His behalf, and he watched God bring him into the perfect place of His will. One of the passages of Scripture that caught my attention was when David told Goliath that he would defeat him and, "...all the earth may know that there is a God in Israel" (1 Samuel 17:46). I realized it was because of David's closeness to God that many would recognize the greatness of the God who chose to dwell in the midst of Israel.

I asked myself if people could see the evidence of that very same God in my midst. I had experienced His deliverance and provision in my life in so many ways. However, could I stand up with the same confidence against a Goliath? No wonder Daniel 11:32 tells us those who know their God will be strong and do exploits.

As I considered knowing God, I remembered how the Apostle Paul tells us that we see through a mirror darkly.[7] I know how clouded my vision can be as I look through the various avenues of my flesh, logic, and pride. I have often longed for God to remove all the obstacles so I could make the same declaration as Job, "I have heard of thee by the hearing of the ear, but now mine eye seeth thee" (Job 42:5).

My spiritual search has continually brought me to this conclusion: Nothing makes sense outside of knowing Jesus Christ. I know I must hear His voice, see His face, and embrace Him if my life is going to make any sense.

---

[4] Psalm 111:10
[5] Hebrews 3:10; Psalm 81:12
[6] Hebrews 3:7-19
[7] 1 Corinthians 13:12

Obviously, every believer must know the reality of God on a personal level. God is the only one who can bring meaning and purpose to each of our lives. To fail in this area means that love, faith, and wisdom will be absent. We will not be able to trust God in the areas of deliverance and daily provision. There will be no evidence that the God of the universe is truly in our midst. This is why the Apostle Paul emphasized the need to come to the knowledge of Jesus Christ. In Philippians 3:8, he makes this declaration, "Yea doubtless, and I count all things but loss for the excellency of the knowledge of Christ Jesus my Lord."

Paul gave up self, rights, and the world in reckless abandonment just to know Jesus. In his last letter to Timothy before his death, he stated, "For the which cause I also suffer these things: nevertheless I am not ashamed; for I know whom I have believed, and am persuaded that he is able to keep that which I have committed unto him against that day" (2 Timothy 1:12).

The Apostle Paul knew his Jesus. He had such an intimacy with Him that in his distressful life he had peace and joy, and in the face of his death he had great expectancy and confidence. He was not ashamed or afraid because he knew the character of his God. He had experienced the faithfulness and power of his Lord many times, and was assured that He would never forsake him in life or death.

To know God in such a way should be the main goal of every Christian. We should display the same reckless abandonment as Paul, the same simple willingness to follow Him as the disciples, and the same unwavering confidence as one of the first Christian martyrs, Stephen.

The people that know their God are strong. This strength is evident in joy, for the joy of the Lord is what must serve as each of our strength.[8] It stands sure in times of silence, crises, and uncertainties as you remember to, "Be still, and know I am God" (Psalm 46:10). To have that joy and confidence in the midst of the impossible is the greatest evidence that we truly know our God.

Not knowing God puts us in a precarious position. Paul talked about people who had zeal for God, but not according to knowledge. These people were excited about God, but they were ignorant about His character. In a sense, they were carrying around a loaded gun without knowing how to use it properly. They were establishing a form of righteousness, but it was not God's righteousness. It is no wonder that Paul later talked about people who had a form of righteousness, but denied the power thereof.[9]

As a Biblical counselor, I have found the biggest obstacle to overcome in hurting Christians has been their concept of God. Due to a presentation of a weak Gospel and a lack of proper discipleship, many

---

[8] Daniel 11:32; Nehemiah 8:10
[9] Romans 10:2; 2 Timothy 3:5

Christians have been left to define God on their own. The results have been disastrous.

In many cases, I have had to first instruct hurting individuals about the character of God so He could simply be God in their life. I have been amazed at how many Christians are truly ignorant about the character of Jesus.

To many people, Jesus is simply the loving Savior; but sadly, He is not the holy God, the everlasting Lord, or the righteous Judge. He is their friend, but He is not King. He is a good guy, but He is not Master. They often declare that He loves them and died for them, but fail to understand He did so because of whom He is, and not because there is any redeemable quality in mankind.

As I contend with this lopsided presentation of Jesus in many Christians' lives, I begin to see Jesus has been defrocked of His rightful position. He is no longer Holy God, intolerable Lord, righteous Judge, and soon and coming righteous King who will be bringing with Him a two-edged sword to judge and destroy those who oppose Him.[10] There is no show of fear or respect for Him. He is treated like a "good buddy" who smiles when people defile holy things in His precious Name, will look the other way when they sin, and tolerates all of people's rebellion, idolatry, and foolishness.

Much of the Church seemingly has compromised Jesus so much He has become unrecognizable. He has been made into everything from a groovy rock and roll star that can jam with the best of them to a successful CEO of some big company. Apparently, all of these attempts were to make Him more attractive to the world and somehow make or keep Him happy, right? WRONG!

Our attempts to make Jesus likable, acceptable, and "one of the guys" has stripped Him of the very characteristics that set Him apart from the rest of mankind. It is because of who Jesus is that He can actually bring comfort to the sick, hope to the oppressed, and salvation to the lost.

Jesus said in John 12:32, "And I, if I be lifted up from the earth, will draw all men unto me." What was Jesus talking about here? Was He telling the Church to dress Him up in acceptable fashions so people would be drawn to Him? Was He asking people to exalt Him with some favorable title like CEO? Was He talking about presenting Him as the "good guy" so He could be accepted as a "good old buddy" or an "understanding friend?" What was He talking about?

My friend, He was talking about being lifted up on a cross. When He was lifted up on that cross, He was not wearing the latest fashions. In fact, He wore nothing but a crown of thorns and His own blood.

Christ was given His rightful title while on the cross. It was not the title of CEO, but King of the Jews. Although the title He was given was

---

[10] Revelation 1:13-17; 19:11-16

correct, it did not create the respect due Him. Instead, His title drew the reproach and mocking of most everyone who looked upon Him.

Christ became identified with humanity. He tasted the bitterness of everything that was unclean and unacceptable. In the end, He became the sin offering for us. How did He react to becoming our substitute on the cross? Was He nonchalant? Did He smile? Was He tolerant about it? Hardly! He never smiled once as He took the beatings for us silently. He was far from nonchalant when He asked the Father to forgive people because they did not know what they were doing. There was no tolerance when He cried out in agony as darkness engulfed Him in utter despair.[11]

What have we done to the precious Son of God? We have downplayed the only avenue where people can come to truly know their God.

What about the attitude many have towards Jesus' cross? The cross is the only place where each of us can get a reality check as to our depravity and God's character. The cross is where God has communicated His greatest heart desire for us. The cross is where His will for mankind was established.

Our reliable theology teaches us Jesus was fully man and fully God. As man, He offered up His human body and paid the price for our sins. But as God, He rose again and is now able to save us to the uttermost. He did not go to His cross as just a Savior, but as Lord, King, and Judge, making Him the ultimate Savior. He went to the cross not because He was a "good guy," but because He is love, grace, and mercy who came to satisfy the judgment hanging over every one of our heads. He became sin, not so we could continue in sin and rebellion, but that we could be reborn in the righteousness of God. He became separated so we could be reconciled. He was defiled so we could become justified.

Every Christian's identity begins with the cross of Jesus. To downplay or minimize the devastation, judgment, cost, and purpose of the cross of Christ is to do a great injustice to our Lord and to the souls of man. As believers, we need to come back to the cross of Christ to get our spiritual bearings. We need to come back to the place of redemption to get a right perspective of our God.

I remember one day I was teaching on the character of Christ. I expounded on how many Christians assume they know Him, but only a remnant has a real sound knowledge of Him. At the end of the class, I opened it up for prayer.

A woman came up in tears. She confessed to me that she was not sure she knew Christ; therefore, she was unsure of her salvation. As I prayed for her, she cried sorrowfully. It was as though she mourned the fact she had never searched Jesus out for herself. She had sat in the comfortable pews of her church thinking she was okay because she was

---

[11] Matthew 27:46: Luke 23:34; 2 Corinthians 5:21

going through all the right religious motions. A couple of weeks later, she came to me and shared how she asked the Lord if she really knew Him. He told her she did know Him, but her understanding was very limited.

I believe that God is calling out in the same way as He did in the Garden of Eden, "Adam (man), where are you" (Genesis 3:9)? (Parenthesis added.) God knows where you are, but do you? Make sure you are not hiding behind fig leaves of assumptions, in church pews, behind religious garbs or good works. Find out where you are in your relationship with God. Make sure you know Him for who He is.

If you are not sure you know God, go to the foot of the cross of Christ. The cross is man's connection to God, and He will meet you there. You will see for yourself God's commitment to you. You will feel His love, mercy, and grace. You will sense His power and greatness. You will know His deliverance and provision for you. In fact, you will know you have finally answered the call He made to Adam in the beginning.

The call to Adam was not made because God wanted to find Adam. Rather, it was a call for Adam to find his God, and to be restored back into communion with Him. The cross of Christ offers that restoration to every wandering heart. What a glorious picture of God's gracious commitment and desire to commune with each of us!

4

THE TENDER VOICE OF GOD

God has two voices in the world that confirm and complement each other. These two voices are the Holy Spirit and the Word of God. The first voice we are going to consider is the tender voice of God. This voice can be convicting, but gentle. It can be compelling because of love, but is not demanding and harsh. It can penetrate the hardest heart, soothe the most tormented soul, and bring hope to the hopeless.

The voice I am speaking of is the Holy Spirit. The Holy Spirit is the third Person of the Godhead, and is probably the most misunderstood. His part in the Body of believers is largely ignored or abused, and for the most part serves as a point of great controversy among the popular Christian denominations.

Who is the Holy Spirit? Most agree He is not a force, but a person. In fact, He is God. He is also known as our rivers of Living Water and the author of the written Word.[1] We know He came upon those in the upper room, and gave them great boldness and power to witness in Acts 2.

He indwells every believer and serves as his or her seal to an eternal inheritance. He leads and sanctifies the Christian, as well as distributes the gifts and talents among the Church for the purpose of edifying the complete Body. He convicts people of sin, righteousness and judgment in order to bring them to deliverance and restoration.[2]

The Spirit of God's main goal is always to lift up Jesus; therefore, He never speaks of Himself nor does He bring attention to His work. He is a sensitive gentleman who is constantly wooing believers to the Lover of their soul and their Bridegroom.

In the past, I have struggled with the Holy Spirit in my Christian life. Some of the activities that went on in His name frightened me. My ignorance of Him put a greater wedge between the two of us as I observed that there was no apparent order in what people did under His so-called "influence." The evidence of fleshly hype in most of these activities made me recoil from coming to terms with the complete work of the Holy Spirit in my own life.

Eventually, Scripture inspired me to come to terms with the third Person of the Godhead. Even though I treated Him as a silent partner in

---

[1] John 7:37-39; 2 Peter 1:19-21
[2] John 16:7-13; Romans 15:16; 1 Corinthians 12:8-11; Ephesians 1:11-14;

the first years of my Christianity, I realize that He had a very active part in my life.

I knew the Spirit of God dwelled within me, making me His temple.[3] I must admit, I never really thought about what His very presence in my life actually meant. Like the children of Israel so many years ago in the wilderness, I had the very presence of God in my midst. He was the One that led me during the day. He was the flame in my soul that sustained my very life in the times of great testing. He was the power and authority of God that enabled me to live a righteous life, and to minister effectively. He was my boldness, as well as my peace and compassion.

I never realized how precious the Holy Spirit was until I witnessed a seasoned evangelist minister who had operated in many of the gifts of the Spirit. She had been used as an open door for the Holy Spirit to come as He willed and do miraculous works in people's lives. In her ministry, I witnessed healing of terminal diseases, deliverance of various sorts, and restoration.

As I watched this woman move in power and authority, I pondered what her secret was. On closer observation, I realized the secret was not a secret after all. She simply knew the Person of the Holy Spirit in an intimate way. He was more real to her than her actual physical surroundings. She knew when He was there and when He had lifted. This evangelist never moved outside of His prompting. In fact, as soon as He departed, she sat down.

As I watched this woman minister, I realized she exemplified what I had always felt would be the sincere trademark of the moving of the Spirit. This woman was not a showoff or an entertainer. She quietly and gently moved among those who came to her for prayer. She was not aggressive and boastful; rather, she was a meek and sensitive minister under His guidance. Her meetings displayed a sweet fragrance and were always done in an orderly fashion. The fruits were obvious; therefore, I knew her meetings were of God, and that God was on the scene because His sovereign power was evident.

This godly lady inspired me more than any other individual to get to know the Holy Spirit in greater ways. I knew if I wanted to be led in a right manner, I had to know the person of the Holy Spirit. I also knew I needed to experience the Holy Spirit if I was to know the fullness of God in my life.

As I began to seek to know the Holy Spirit, I realized the third Person of the Godhead often comes across as a silent partner because He is the still, small, tender voice of God in our midst. His voice is meek and tender because He is so sensitive. His sensitivity causes Him to be easily quenched and greatly grieved when He encounters any unholy ground due to the presence of a wrong spirit.[4]

---

[3] 1 Corinthians 3:16
[4] Ephesians 4:30; 1 Thessalonians 5:19

In my experience with the Spirit, I have found that the loudest He gets is when He is grieved. People who have undergone the grief of the Spirit will tell you it is heart-wrenching. I have suffered this grief many times. The first time I encountered this emotion, I became confused and overwhelmed.

I had been attending a church that had become very important to me. The Lord had given me a real love for the people, and my heart's desire was to see them experience the fullness of God in their midst. I had done my best to work towards this goal, but sin and a change of leadership brought the work to a complete stop.

In the very beginning, the Lord showed me what was going to happen to the church if they hired a particular pastor. I knew the pastor and the church were a bad combination. They hired him, and the Lord challenged me to do right by him. I offered my services and found opportunities to speak into his life, but he was very inexperienced and full of pride. Eventually, our spirits began to collide, and I started to become a threat to him.

One day as I was walking and meditating on church problems, the Lord told me it was time to leave because I was about to cause strife among the congregation. Regardless of who was right or wrong, causing discord among the brethren is an abomination to the Lord.[5]

As I sensed the impending devastating consequences the leadership of this pastor would bring to the church people that I loved, my heart began to break. Great sorrow came upon me like a rushing river. I am not an emotional person, but tears started to flow like a turned on faucet. I remember saying to the Lord, "Why did you give me such a love for these people? Now my heart is broken."

I will never forget what the Lord's response was: "Well, at least you have a heart that can be broken." At that moment I was given a revelation of the broken heart of Jesus on the cross. The insight almost brought me to my knees in the middle of the road.

I realized at that time I was experiencing the sorrow and grief of the Holy Spirit towards the devastation of sin upon the lives of people. His grief showed me the heart of God towards His sheep. This sorrow was a prelude to the devastation that would come upon the pastor and the church. Both barely survived the ordeal.

Since that time, I have been acquainted with the sorrows of God many times. Every time someone I am involved with rejects spiritual healing or restoration, I feel sorrow. I have felt this deep sorrow and mourning over the condition of the family. At times I have felt not only sorrow, but also a sickening feeling over the condition of the visible Church.

There was another incident of personal mourning because a family close to me was on a path of destruction. The Lord told me I could not

[5] Proverbs 6:19

warn them in any way. I knew if I tried that I would be disobedient, and would only put off the inevitable process they had to go through. This process was necessary if there would be any hope of them becoming the people God called them to be. I sensed that the process was going to bring them close to the abyss. I knew it was going to be an intense fire, and everything would be either refined or burned up. The process brought a total separation between this family and me.

Sorrows cause one to become identified with the Man of Sorrows; therefore, I choose not to resent them, but embrace them. I know the grief of the Spirit is simply the voice of God who mourns over the plight of souls. We read about this mourning when Jesus wept over Jerusalem. If only every Christian could feel the mourning of God, I believe our commitment to the lost world would be radically changed from indifference to a burning desire to share the love of God.

This mourning comes out of love that went to a cross to spare people of destruction. Such love cries over souls because salvation will never take root in their unreceptive hearts. It also mourns for people who fail to reach their potential by being conformed to the image of Christ.

The Holy Spirit also is essential to our prayer life. The Word tells us to pray in the Spirit. Only the Holy Spirit knows God's mind and personal will for people, while in prayer the intellectual mind of man can only go so far in grasping spiritually what is important to God. It struggles with limited knowledge, staying focused, and properly discerning self-serving agendas.[6]

If we want our prayers answered, we must pray according to God's will. This is where the Holy Spirit comes into the picture. He knows the will of God. If we allow Him, He will make the necessary intercessions according to the perfect will of God. I have learned it is the Holy Spirit's intercession that makes our prayer life powerful and effective.[7]

The Spirit of God also speaks to the Church through gifts. I know the argument about the cessation of all gifts. I have a problem with this argument for three reasons. One, if the gifts have ceased, why do we continue to see gifts of miracles, faith, and healing going on around the world? The second problem I have with this argument is that I have personally experienced the blessings of these gifts and have been used in them. Finally, the gifts of the Spirit are how the Holy Spirit chooses to manifest Himself to God's people.[8] If they have ceased, then how does He presently move and make Himself apparent to and in the Body?

For instance, in the area of miracles and healing, I am often reminded of the supernatural healing that I received from God. I had injured my knee when I was in the Navy. It actually served as a weather

---

[6] Romans 8:26-27; 9:33-34; 2 Corinthians 10:3-5; Ephesians 6:18
[7] Romans 8: 27; 1 John 5:14-15
[8] 1 Corinthians 12:7

barometer. I could painfully tell when a storm was coming in. This fact concerned me when God began to call us to the Seattle area.

Seattle weather is hard on a knee like mine, and I silently expressed my concern to God about this problem. One night while I was praying with some Christian friends, one of my friends leaned over towards me and laid her hand on my shoulder. Suddenly, I felt the power of God come down from the top of my head, down through my body, and center in the leg with the bad knee. The power was indescribable and lasted only a short time. After it lifted, I began to notice the results. My knee ceased to bother me, and I have never had a bit of trouble with it since. God had heard my one silent prayer and in His sovereign way moved upon me. What an awesome God we love and serve!

God has also shown this power to me in the area of gifts, and has used me in the gifts of wisdom, healing, prophesy, and interpretation of tongues. The noticeable gifts He has used me the most in have been the word of wisdom and interpretation of tongues.

In the case of interpretation, each time I interpreted a tongue, it was like stepping off of a cliff. Up front, He only gave me about four words. I would begin to speak those words by faith, not having any idea where it is going to lead me. Some of the messages that have come forth are tough rebukes. I am often surprised.

One Sunday I was sitting in church and there was a message in tongues. I became quiet just in case He gave me the interpretation. Sure enough four words came into my mind. I allowed for a time of silence just in case God had actually given it to someone else. When no one spoke, I began to speak the four words that ended up being a challenge. The message was a call for people to separate themselves from the unholy.

After the interpretation was over, I relaxed back in my seat while the pastor patiently waited for some kind of response from the congregation. No one stirred, and once again there was a message in tongues from someone else. I thought to myself, surely God will give the interpretation to somebody else. To my surprise, four words ran across my mind. I was close to arguing with God when I realized no one else seemed to have an interpretation. Once again, I gave the interpretation. The message was almost identical to the first one.

After the interpretation was over, the pastor told the congregation that God must be trying to deal with certain people, and those who felt the leading of the Holy Spirit needed to respond. I will never forget what happened next; almost all of the people in the church went forward for prayer. It was as though cisterns were broken in repentance and many tears shed.

After the service was over, the pastor thanked me for being obedient to what God had given me. I think he sensed my struggle and my reluctance to step out and simply respond. I realized if I had not responded, the work of the Holy Spirit would have been quenched. He not only had spoken to reveal that which was hidden, but He was also preparing hearts to respond the second time around.

There has been much abuse in the area of gifts. I appreciate strong leadership that encourages the moving of the Spirit, but will not tolerate any abuse. Considering the pros and cons, I would rather confront the abuse than miss the move and work of the Holy Spirit.

Churches are doing a great disservice to the Body when they quench the Holy Spirit because of fear or ignorance. Through His Spirit, God does want to speak to the hearts of people. He wants to bring down walls, reveal hidden sins and agendas, and do spiritual surgery in lives. He wants to bring deliverance, healing, and restoration to the Church.

These gifts are not to entertain people or make anyone elite. The Spirit's main purpose for the gifts is to edify the Church so Jesus can be lifted up and glorified.[9] Everything the Holy Spirit does in the Church is for the purpose of producing spiritual growth and well-being. He wants to give believers power so they can be effective witnesses. He wants to lead them according to the truth and examples of Jesus. He also wants to guide them up the narrow path of righteousness into the pastures of God's will where they will experience the joy and peace of God.

How about you? Have you experienced the fullness of the Holy Spirit? If you have not, how will you be able to hear the tender voice of God and be led by it? How will you encounter His power and know His authority? How will you ever be able to be part of His powerful move in the Church?

If you have failed to encounter the Holy Spirit in a personal way, I want to encourage you to seek to know Him for yourself. Do not let man's theology or denomination determine your conclusions, but go to the Bible and the One who baptizes you with the Living Water, Jesus Christ. Accept His invitation to drink of this Water. Know also that the Living Water is a promise and a gift from heaven. As a result, ask the Father for more of Him. According to Luke 13:11, He will give you more of the Holy Spirit.

In time, you will be pleasantly surprised to discover how wonderful it is to have a greater connection to God. You will be impressed by the Holy Spirit's sweetness, humbled by His meekness, encouraged by His commitment, and enabled by His power. As you submit to His leading, you will become more sensitive to His still, small voice. In time you will begin to rely on this tender voice of God to keep you from detours and to lead you down the right paths.

---

[9] John 16:13; 1 Corinthians 12-14

5

THE HAMMER AND THE SWORD

The second voice of God that we will address is the Word of God. This is the most reliable voice of God we have available. It is the only tool we can use to test the other voices we hear. For example, we know that the Holy Spirit inspired the written Word; therefore, the Word of God serves as our reality check as to whether something is true, while the Holy Spirit will always come into agreement with it, as well as confirm a matter according to it.[1]

The written, inspired voice of God is both a hammer that destroys and a sword that divides. If we will allow it to do its work, it can hammer away at all of our wrong concepts. It will cut through all the barriers of our humanity to reveal the spirit that motivates us.[2] 2 Timothy 3:16-17 tells us, "All scripture is given by inspiration of God, and is profitable for doctrine, for reproof, for correction, for instruction in righteousness: That the man of God may be perfect, thoroughly furnished unto all good works."

The Word of God needs to determine our belief system. It must become our instructor, as well as reprove and correct us. The problem is that many Christians decide what they are going to accept in the Word, as well as what they are going to excuse away or ignore. This means that fear or ignorance is often the determining factor behind what people believe when it comes to the Bible. Such an attitude sets the Christian up as the one who corrects the Written Word, while instructing according to personal standards and conclusions. In the end, such treatments often discredit the validity of the complete counsel of Scripture. Handling the Word in this manner is one reason that some Christians fail to overcome.

The Word of God has the ability to cut through the nonsense and get down to the core of the problem. Hebrews 4:12 states, "For the word of God is quick, and powerful, and sharper than any two-edged sword, piercing even to the dividing asunder of soul and spirit, and of the joints and marrow, and is a discerner of the thoughts and intents of the heart." The reason the Bible is capable of exposing our thoughts and motivation is because it is truth.

The written Word is simply the revelation of the Living Word, Jesus Christ. Jesus is truth, and truth is able to make a person free because it

---

[1] 2 Peter 1:20-21
[2] Jeremiah 23:39; Hebrew 4:12

strips away all pretenses and games.[3] It challenges the perspective, and serves as a map to guide people down the right paths. Psalm 119:105 tells us, "Thy word is a lamp unto my feet, and a light unto my path."

This powerful Book is able to sanctify us. Psalm 119:11 gives us this insight about the capability of the written Word in the areas of obedience and sanctification, "Thy word have I hidden in mine heart, that I might not sin against thee."

Jesus said in John 17:17, "Sanctify them through thy truth: thy word is truth."

We know the Word of God is eternal. Psalm 119:89 states, "Forever, O LORD, thy word is settled in heaven."

Jesus made this statement in Luke 21:33, "Heaven and earth shall pass away: but my words shall not pass away." The Word of God is the sure voice of God in our midst. It is eternal and life-changing. It will never let us down.

If the Word of God is His sure voice in the world, why is there so much controversy and confusion over it in the Christian realm? If the Bible is the established voice of God, why do many neglect to read or study it? If the Word is reliable, why is there so much division among the different denominations concerning teachings and doctrines?

The main reason for the conflict over the Word is because one of two ingredients is missing when it comes to properly handling the Word of God. The first ingredient that can be missing is the truth. The truth is summarized in two words: Jesus Christ. Jesus said, "I am the truth" (John 14:6). We are also told in John 1:1 that He is the Living Word.

The whole goal of the written Word is to bring us to the revelation of the Living Word, Jesus Christ. Many Christians make the terrible mistake of searching for the truth in the form of theology and doctrine instead of in terms of a person. When it comes to the kingdom of God, it is not what you know, but whom you know. In other words, do you really know the Jesus of the Bible?

When a person searches for truth in the form of doctrine, he or she will end up mishandling the Word. Instead of becoming caught up with Jesus, such an individual will become a defender of what he or she considers as being true or correct theology. Such a person is usually motivated by intellectual pride and can be aggressive, unteachable, and judgmental in beliefs and attitudes. Such an individual usually uses the Word as a personal hammer to shape people into his or her way of thinking, and as a sword to cut down those who do not agree with him or her. To use the Word in this way will never make disciples of Christ, but casualties.

This is what the Pharisees did with the Law of God. They made men followers of their personal teachings and interpretations, rather than

---

[3] John 1:1-14; 8:32-36; 14:6

followers of Jehovah God. Jesus said this about them in Matthew 23:13 and 15, "For ye shut up the kingdom of heaven against men: for you neither go in yourselves, neither suffer ye them that are entering to go in. ....For ye compass sea and land to make one proselyte; and when he is made, ye make him twofold more the child of hell than yourselves."

The truth is man cannot know the whole truth; therefore, no man has a corner on truth. At best, a man who pursues this form of truth can be the sincerest bigot when it comes to religious beliefs. He can be the most devoted fanatic in his religious activities, the biggest hypocrite in daily living, and a deluded fool in his own conceits. In the end, he will do the unthinkable. He will crucify the truth.

I understand these attitudes quite well because I walked in these very shoes before Jesus broke through my religious pride. He brought me to my knees in brokenness and repentance. I was conceited and a hypocrite, but what showed me the depth of my depravity was when I realized my self-righteousness was actually judging God Almighty. Such a realization can bring powerful fear on a person. I was shaking in my shoes, and rightfully so.

The main goal of Christian leaders, laymen, and devoted saints is not to indoctrinate people to blindly embrace some creed, but to lead them into a loving relationship with the Person of Jesus Christ. This type of leadership does not come by using the Word as a personal hammer or sword, but by personal example of obedience to the Word. Such godly leaders also will trust the Holy Spirit in people's lives to knock down spiritual barriers and expose any unseen opposition in their hearts and lives that may exist towards the truth.

Another cause of mishandling the Word of God is a wrong spirit. Romans 7:6 states, "But now we are delivered from the law, that being dead wherein we were held, that we should serve in newness of spirit, and not in the oldness of the letter."

In his second letter to the Corinthians, Paul reinforced the Scripture in Romans with this statement, "Who also hath made us able ministers of the new testament; not of the letter, but of the spirit: for the letter killeth, but the Spirit gives life" (2 Corinthians 3:6).

The right spirit determines our motivation and perception. We know, according to the Bible that the Holy Spirit is the real teacher of the Word.[4] His main goal is to bring instruction and correction by unveiling the truth to our spirits: the Person of Jesus Christ.

As we can see, the Law without the Spirit is dead. In other words, the Truth, Jesus Christ, simply becomes a concept, belief, or creed. Even though we may be right in our religious beliefs, if the Spirit is not allowed to make those creeds alive and personal to us, they become meaningless text or laws. The Word can only become alive when Jesus

---

[4] John 16:13; 1 John 2:27

becomes real to us; otherwise it is simply a book of history, teachings, and creeds that appears harsh and unobtainable.

Jesus as the Living Word is our mirror, and should be the sole source of our love, devotion, adoration, and worship. We should examine our lives in light of who He is. It is only as the Spirit makes Jesus real to us, that the written Word will become a sword to expose our real spiritual condition. It is within this confine that it will serve as a hammer that will mold us into Jesus' very image.

The Word of God upholds the Spirit, while the Spirit brings life to the Word of God. The two walk hand-in-hand when it comes to discerning the voice of God. If you are mishandling the Word of God, and it becomes void of meaning and life, you are subduing the voice of God. If the Spirit is lacking in your study of the Word of God, you will be quenching the still, small, gentle voice of God that will lead you into all truth in a living, viable way.

Examine what spirit motivates you when it comes to handling the Word of God. A good test is whether reading and studying the Word of God is a duty to you or if it serves as valuable meat to your hungry spirit. Consider if you see it as a book of many rules or as a beautiful, ongoing revelation of Your loving Redeemer.

Let me encourage you that the next time you open your Bible, quit fussing with the dials (Scriptures) and ask the Holy Spirit to take control of them to unveil greater truth to you. Allow Him the freedom to fine-tune you by bringing down any creeds that serve as idols, any beliefs that are etched in stone, or ideas that are founded in pride. You will be amazed at how this spiritual Teacher will bring new life to Scriptures, enlarging your heart and perception. In fact, what the Spirit reveals to you will bring a new song to your heart as you touch the glory of heaven, smell the sweet fragrance of God's anointing, see the wonderful, blessed face of your Lord, and clearly hear the voice of God.

6

THIS IS A TEST

Most of us have heard the emergency signal that radio and TV stations use to test their emergency warning systems. When we hear this signal, we can only be put at ease when the announcer states, "This is a test."

It is amazing to me how many Christians desire to hear the voice of God without realizing that it usually entails a test. Remember the voice of one crying in the wilderness, John the Baptist.[1] John represented the voice of God. He was calling people to repent. His call was both a warning and a requirement. Failure to respond to his warning meant that people failed the test that was set before them.

We see this in the life of the prophets. They represented the voice of God as well. They were sending out many different signals warning Israel of impending judgment. These warnings tested the hearts of every man and woman, and required a response of humility, submission, and repentance. Israel failed to heed the warnings, and tasted the bitter dregs of judgment.

Many centuries ago, people heard the voice of God as Jesus Christ walked this earth. Once again, the voice of God was not always a voice of comfort or encouragement. Keep in mind, during this time the people of Israel were watching for God's visitation that would come through the appearance of their long-awaited Messiah. They were eager to hear God's voice after 400 years of silence. They wanted to see their King in power and glory, but their King came in an unexpected way. As a result, people from every walk of life were challenged.

This is how God works. He comes and speaks to us in surprising ways. Jesus' voice was clearly heard by those around Him, but His words could only penetrate the hearts of those who were lost, hungry, thirsty, and seeking. Although His words brought life, they could only reach those who were poor and sorrowful in spirit. Even though He spoke in simplicity, only those with child-like hearts could understand.[2]

It was another story for those who turned a deaf ear and cold heart to the Son of God. They were tested in ways they would have never imagined. After all, the Messiah was to fit in their religious little world, not challenge it. He was to exalt them, not expose their wickedness. He was

---

[1] Matthew 1:1-3
[2] Matthew 5:2-9

there to honor them, not rebuke them. Nevertheless, His words effectively shook every area of their world. His words threatened their self-righteousness, insulted their complacent ways, and convicted their fearful notions that they harbored towards life. In fact, His voice did more to divide and expose the sin of the rich and famous than any other group. In the end, these people crucified Him to silence Him.[3]

Realize that hearing God's voice may not be a blessing, but a test. When Jesus speaks, He may be revealing your heart condition as He did with the Pharisees. He rebuked the Pharisees because self-righteous pride motivated them instead of the love of God. They were trying to hold on to their own personal kingdom instead of giving way to the sovereign rule of their true King and High Priest.[4]

If God speaks to you, He may ask you to give up something of great importance like He did the rich young ruler. This man called Jesus "good Master." According to Jesus, God alone is good; therefore, this man was actually acknowledging Jesus' true identity. When the young ruler asked Jesus what he had to do to gain eternal life, Jesus told him it began with obedience to the commandments. This young man claimed he obeyed the commandments that were mentioned. Jesus then made the one statement that cut through all his self-sufficient religiosity to expose divided loyalties and idolatry. "If thou wilt be perfect, go and sell that thou hast, and give to the poor, and thou shalt have treasure in heaven: and come and follow me" (Matthew 19:21).

This man's material goods were more important to him than eternal life. He knew he was hearing the voice of God, but it became a curse instead of a blessing. He walked away from eternal life in great sorrow. In His case, God's voice became bitter to the soul rather than a blessing.

If you decide to follow Him, He will require you to give up that which stands in the way of your discipleship. He may ask you to walk away from family, prestige, worldly security, or that which is comfortable and convenient. He may ask you to walk into the unknown, embrace the impossible, and cling to the invisible. And, through it all you may hear only one statement through each testing and challenge: "Trust me."

To continue on this hard, uncertain path you must keep your focus on Him and keep in mind that by being open to lose it all, you will gain it all. This is why Jesus gave this promise, "And every one that hath forsaken houses, or brethren, or sisters, or father, or mother, or wife, or children, or lands, for my name's sake, shall receive a hundredfold, and shall inherit everlasting life" (Matthew 19:29).

Perhaps the voice of God will bring fear to you instead of pleasure like it did the Israelites in the wilderness. Maybe it will pronounce judgment like Jesus did on Jerusalem.[5] Maybe it will bring you to a place

---

[3] Luke 22:2; 23:13-21
[4] John 19:15-16
[5] Exodus 19:16-18; Matthew 23:34-39

of decision like it did the disciples of Jesus in John 6:60-64. Christians need to realize that the voice of God will not make any difference unless they are ready to respond to it in humility and obedience.

Remember what serves as the voice of God among us. It is the Word of God. The Word of God is as bittersweet today as it was when Jesus served as the physical representative of God's voice so many years ago.[6]

Your attitude and response towards the Word of God is a reliable gauge as to your real response to the Living Word, Jesus. After all, we would like to think if we lived during Jesus' day we would not be like the crowd that followed Jesus just because He performed miracles and gave them bread, or like the nine lepers that He healed who never came back to thank and worship Him. We would like to think we would not be part of the crowd that yelled, "Crucify Him, crucify Him!"[7]

Please don't flatter yourself. You and I may very well be part of that crowd today. We may be more interested in the things of the flesh than in the Son of God. We might be motivated to be Christians because of the endless benefits and retirement plan we have been offered by so-called "spiritual leaders" who are nothing more than good salesmen. We may have ungrateful hearts, which means if we are worshipping God, it is with lip service only.[8] And, maybe right now we are crucifying the truth again because we are rejecting it in our hearts.

The blessing of hearing God's voice will only come to those who are truly looking for Jesus like Zacchaeus in Luke 19. Zacchaeus found Him, and so will you if you are diligently seeking Him. As a result, Jesus will invite you to sup with Him like He did Zacchaeus and you will hear Him say, "This day is salvation come to this house" (Luke 19:9).

Like the woman with the issue of blood, you will clearly be able to hear God's voice when you push through all that hinders you, and touch Him in sincere desperation. You will hear Him say, "(Child), be of good comfort; thy faith hath made thee whole" (Mathew 9:22). (Parenthesis added.)

You will hear God's voice when you humble yourself before Him as the woman caught in the sin of adultery. What will you hear Him say? "Neither do I condemn thee; go, and sin no more" (John 8:11).

Maybe you are like the prodigal son in Luke 15. All you need to do is turn around, come home, and ask for forgiveness. You will hear the Father's voice rejoice over you, declaring before the rest, "For this, my brother was dead, and is alive again; and was lost, and is found" (Luke 15:32).

I have heard my Lord's voice many times, but I must admit it comes when I least expect it, and in ways that are humbling. Sometimes it

---

[6] Revelation 10:9-10
[7] Matthew 27:22-26; Luke 17:11-21; John 6:2
[8] Matthew 15:8-9

brings encouragement, while other times reproof. The statement He speaks to me consistently is comprised of two words: "Trust me."

I do not hear the voice of the Lord every day. Sometimes I may not hear it for months on end, but I have His Word, which serves as my main guide. I encounter the voice of God every time I read His Word. Through my pursuit in His Word, the Holy Spirit unveils its truths, and Jesus becomes real.

Let me be honest with you. If you are not impressed with the Word of God, you will probably not be impressed with hearing God's voice. Hearing His voice, if you even recognize it, may cause some excitement, but it will probably be treated as a passing fancy.

The reason I say this is because of what Abraham said to the rich man in hell in Luke 16. He asked Abraham to send someone to his house to warn his brothers about the existence of the horrible place of torment. Abraham's reply needs to serve as a reality check for us. "If they hear not Moses and the prophets, neither will they be persuaded, though one rose from the dead" (Luke 16:31). To confirm this statement, Jesus rose from the grave and people still do not believe.

Hearing God's voice will not change anything unless you have the foundation of faith, and respond in obedience. Believing and applying the Word of God daily to your life establishes that foundation.

Here is another important point to consider: If you are not faithful to respond to the Word of God, why would God bother to speak to you in other ways? If you cannot pass the different tests found in the Word, you certainly will not pass the test that comes from actually hearing His voice.

I have seen this failure in many lives. People assure me if they could only hear God's voice they would know what He wanted them to do, and they would obey. I have watched God give these people clear scriptural instructions, only to see them turn around like the rich young ruler and go their own way.

I remember one such case where a woman was under great oppression and seeking deliverance. She claimed she had asked the Lord into her life and all she needed was direction. The Lord was gracious to show this individual what His heart and mind was for her. She didn't like what He told her, so afterwards she simply reasoned it away and went back to her pigpen. This did not surprise me because she never had made it a goal or habit to obey His written Word.

The next time you want to hear the voice of God, ask yourself if you are obeying His inspired Scriptures. Keep in mind it will involve a test; and faithfulness to His written Word will be a good indicator as to whether you will respond properly if you ever actually heard His voice.

7

WHEN GOD SPEAKS

There used to be a commercial on TV that began with, "When E. F. Hutton speaks, everyone listens." To reiterate the point, they showed people stopping dead in their tracks to hear what this famous person or organization had to say. If only we would do the same when God speaks. If only we would honor God in awe and obedience when we did encounter His voice. If only we would stop. If only we would listen.

Oswald Chambers made this statement, "God never speaks to us in startling ways, but in ways that are easy to understand, and we say, 'I wonder if that is God's voice?'"[1] People have a tendency to spiritualize the works and truths of God. They do not realize that God works in simplicity. God has reminded me of this many times in my life of service to Him to keep it simple.[2]

Religious pride opens well-meaning Christians up to the unrealistic, rather than the practical. I have learned Christianity is a realistic way of living that produces itself in practical ways. For example, I have watched Christians get carried away in their Christian practices. After all, it is so easy to miss God in our spiritual hype and religious nonsense. I test these people's spirit according to the first epistle of John. Usually, I see a common cord among them. They appear to have a religious spirit.

When people have a religious spirit, they tend to live beyond the fundamentals of Christian faith. It is as though they are subjected to something outside of the simplicity of Christ. Although their spiritual influence may appear to be quite spiritual, it falls short of being responsible to the spirit and truth of the Word of God.

A religious spirit spiritualizes everything. It often makes its vessels (the people) appear to be quite noble in their own eyes because they are willing to become the ultimate martyr to prove a point. These individuals may even sense it is not realistic, but they believe God is truly calling them to make these sacrifices.

These individuals point to such people as the prophets. The prophets did some unusual things, but there was a reason for it. God was trying to bring home a point to those who were observing their obedient activities.

---

[1] My Utmost for His Highest, January 30
[2] 2 Corinthians 11:3

Often people with religious spirits are unteachable, and can become quickly insulted when you don't see it their way. Their response usually lacks love. The religious spirit constantly speaks to those who are under its influence. These individuals are not able to discern this voice because they do not know the difference between God and this religious entity. They usually have a faulty foundation because they do not have a balanced understanding of the Word. They have a concept of God, but not a revelation of Him. They do not know God because they have never really entered into an intimate relationship with Him. The tragedy is that they truly believe that the voice of this spirit is God's voice because it is religious and requires sacrifice.

God is not religious, but practical. The main sacrifice He requires is that of love. Sacrifices that come out of God's love are a natural extension of a saint's devotion and worship towards God. Godly sacrifice can never be considered noble, or even sacrificial in light of God's love. In fact, it is a person's reasonable service.[3]

In my years of ministry, I have seen religious spirits come out forcefully in the Church. Certain Christians are vulnerable to this spirit because they are looking for spiritual experiences, rather than the Person of Christ. In much of the Church, leadership is not properly educating or challenging people to beware of religious spirits. Sadly, these spirits serve as a substitution for the Holy Ghost, and will bring confusion and division. Because these types of individuals have a different spirit, it separates them from the Christians who could speak into their lives. Ultimately, the religious spirit succeeds in bringing a reproach on the Gospel by making these individuals look like religious kooks, while they are being set up for disgrace and destruction.

God does speak and is speaking today. His voice is loud and clear, but usually we are not looking in the right places or to the right sources. He speaks in practical ways, but sometimes we are too busy being too spiritual to recognize it. He speaks in simple ways, but we are too full of fake nobility and religious pride to accept His simple and practical words.

Let us now consider some of the practical ways God speaks to us about His character and will for our lives.

The Voice of Creation

God speaks through creation. Romans 1:20 tells us creation declares there is a God. The majesty found in creation gives us valuable insight into our creator's character. We see God's greatness and beauty in light of the world's majestic beauty and vastness. We see His power in the mountains, oceans, rivers, wind, and fire. We witness His unlimited imagination and creativity in the variety of animal life, His incredible care in the beauty of flowers, and His artistic abilities in different landscapes. We see His promises in the rainbow, His heavenly perspective in the

---

[3] Romans 12:1-2

stars and galaxies, and His order in the seasons and makeup of man and earth.

Christians often miss God and His principles when they do not take time to consider the lilies of the fields, the birds of the air, the grass of the field, and the insignificant sparrow. Oswald Chambers observed that Jesus never pointed to man and his activities to prove a principle, but to creation. He goes on to reiterate that our tendency is to consider the ways of the world and successful men, and apply these methods to God's work. Mr. Chambers then points out how Jesus Christ used the things men never look at, such as the beauty and simplicity of creation, to teach us simple but valuable lessons about life.[4]

My co-laborer in the Gospel, Jeannette, found a simple way to put into perspective the obstacles that seem overwhelming. She goes outside and considers God's creation. She looks up into the heavens and ponders the vastness. She remembers that the Lord walks among the stars and names each one.[5] She concludes that God is in control and bigger than all the present obstacles that confront her.

It is in light of creation's declaration that the character of God is truly upheld, and He is glorified. It is in light of creation's vastness that challenges become minor, problems small, and hope arises as God's greatness can be clearly seen and heard.

Obviously, creation is able to point man to the reality of a Creator. It is able to enlarge a finite person to consider the impossible and the magnificent. The tragedy is, instead of "hearing" the earth declares the greatness of God, man, in a corrupted, perverted state, looks at creation as if it is a god or savior. In fact, some worship creation with great fervor. As a result, many have been turned over to delusion. They have exchanged the truth of God for a lie, but in the end, they will stand before the Righteous Judge. As judgment is declared, they will not have an excuse for the blatant disregard and unbelief they showed God in their lifetime. No wonder King David said, "The fool hath said in his heart, There is no God." He not only said this once, but twice.[6]

Creation does call both the unbeliever and idolater fools. It mocks the intellectual skeptic, the humanist, and New Ager. In the end, it will condemn them for rejecting the Master Designer.

Let me ask you a question. When was the last time you listened to the proclamation of creation? When was the last time you considered the many lessons about life and death that our Lord wove into His picturesque design found in His creation? Don't you think it is about time to stop and smell the roses, consider the lilies of the valley and the fowl of the air? Jesus did, and taught many people simple truths in

---

[4] Daily Thoughts For Disciples, March 9
[5] Psalm 147:4
[6] Psalm 14:1; 53:1; Romans 1:20 & 25

relationship to creation that had the ability to change the way they looked at their Creator.

The Voice of Circumstances

Moving God's arm is one of the futile things I have tried to accomplish in the past. I have actually envisioned myself in prayer grabbing a hold of His big arm and trying to get it directed towards changing present, uncomfortable circumstances. In each situation I noticed that I could not begin to budge His arm as circumstances remained unchanged.

Like most people, my life has not always been full of only enjoyable circumstances. As a result, I have found myself clinging to His promises, especially the one found in Romans 8:28, "And we know that all things work together for good to them that love God, to them who are the called according to his purpose."

In understanding this promise I had to consider the conditions for all things to work together for good. I had to first of all love God. I needed to evaluate whether I really loved Him or if I was caught up with religious notions concerning Him. After all, love would allow me to trust Him with my life no matter what was going on.

The second condition depended on me actually allowing His will to be worked out in my life. His ways are perfect; but I must choose to believe Him in all matters no matter how contrary they are to my way of thinking. I must conclude that His ways are right and perfect for me. I realize that loving God and trusting His character means I must know Him and accept the circumstances He allows in my life. In other words, when all else has been said and done in prayer, will I simply stand still and wait to see His deliverance?

Through the years I have come to appreciate the circumstances in my life. They have actually kept me from getting ahead of my Lord. They have disciplined me and created character in me as I have learned to trust and serve Him while in the midst of them. They have directed my paths to the center of His will.

These circumstances have played a major role in my faith walk. I have started most adventures in my walk of faith with an inclination as to the direction I must go, but circumstances have always dictated my actual destination.

I remember when the Lord called the Gentle Shepherd Ministries' team back to Idaho from Houston, Texas. We felt His leading or inclination towards Mackay, Idaho. When we arrived in the vicinity, circumstances placed us around Moore, Idaho, a community located 20 miles from Mackay. God did some incredible intervention on our behalf to get us at this particular place, and He did some wonderful things while we were there.

After almost two years in Moore, the Lord started to lead us to the area around Payette, Idaho. We felt a need to start a Discipleship school. Now note, we felt a need. Sometimes feeling a need and an inclination to do something are linked together, but they are not the same thing. We even had a group of people who volunteered to help us in our endeavors. Circumstances closed the door to Payette, but opened one in New Plymouth, a community that is located close to Payette. The door was closed to a Discipleship school at the time, but opened to a radio ministry for a season.

It is impossible to figure out God, but I have learned to be flexible and not stiff-necked nor opinionated about how God should do things. I have come to recognize that if I am not flexible to move with God, I will miss Him. If I am not willing to allow Him to speak through circumstances, I will miss His best and end up taking detours.

The problem is many Christians have a hard time accepting circumstances that narrow their paths and put them in line with God's will for their lives. They think in terms of what will make them happy, and not what will make them acceptable before God. They are motivated by what serves their purpose, rather than what it means to serve God. They are caught up with what they want, rather than what God needs to do in them before His best can be realized and fulfilled in their life. God always has a better idea. We, therefore, need to trust Him with all of our circumstances. However, we are so self-serving and spoiled it is hard for us to get beyond ourselves and trust His character.

Circumstances also determine what I have already referred to as open or closed doors in our spiritual lives. Jesus said to the Philadelphia Church that He would open doors that no man could shut or shut doors that no man could open.[7] Circumstances are meant to direct each of our steps. As we walk out this life in light of circumstances, we must remember that God is the keeper of every door of circumstances in our life. For instance, open doors become our means of deliverance and escape. They become our avenues to God's greatness and His promises. Closed doors, on the other hand, serve as our protection. They declare, "No trespassing or you will be sorry."

I look back over my life and see many open and closed doors. The open doors have not always been attractive. They have often led me into adversity and persecution. They have opened to great testing and fiery ovens. In Scripture we see these types of doors opening up for God's people. The Israelites walked through the open door of the Red Sea, only to find themselves in the wilderness. David walked through the door of Goliath as an anointed king and victor, only to find himself on the run for years from King Saul. Jesus entered the door of humanity to end up on a cross.

Open doors may not be attractive, but they are the means to reach the Promised Land or your potential in the Lord. They may not be fun, but they are rewarding. They may not be pleasant, but they are necessary.

---

[7] Revelation 3:7

Closed doors are another story. They represent the essence of self, the world, and Satan. Although these doors represent destruction for us, many of us strive to open them because they are attractive and enticing to the eye. These doors appear as the logical way to go. They make sense to our intellectual pride, agree with our fleshly notions, and comply with all of our religious conclusions. Our final evaluation is that these are the right doors, and God is making us pursue our destinies by knocking them down. Notice how He told those at the Philadelphia Church that the doors would be opened by Him and not by human attempts.[8]

To try to open a closed door puts a person in a precarious position. God may allow the door to be opened, and if He does, the individual will pay a high price. This is what happens when a Christian does not trust God's evaluation about the doors that he or she may encounter.

Are you adhering to God's voice in the area of circumstances, and trusting Him in all of your different challenges? Are you avoiding the open doors and trying to open the closed doors? Prayerfully ask the Lord to help you answer these questions. After all, He is speaking to you in various ways. Are you listening regardless of your perception of the circumstances?

The Voice of Chastisement

One of God's goals is to allow enough pressure in our lives to get us to ask Him to speak to us. Oswald Chambers said it best, "Nothing touches our lives but it is God Himself speaking." He instructed us to get into the habit of saying, "Speak Lord," and life will become a romance.[9] Mr. Chambers also goes on to say how God uses chastisement to speak to us. It is His means of discipline, and it is also meant to get us to the place of saying, "Speak Lord."

Hebrews 12:5-11 talks about the chastening of the Lord. This passage tells us the Lord only chastens those He loves. The writer of Hebrews explains that the purpose of chastening is to make us partakers of His holiness; and although it is not pleasant, it yields peaceful fruits of righteousness.

I have felt the chastisement of the Lord many times. In one incident He brought correction to my life over a matter that I had chosen to ignore. I remember this chastisement because it lasted for three whole days. The Lord was making sure I would not forget the lesson. During those three days, He spoke volumes to me. I felt sad that I had failed Him, and I felt reproved because I had ignored some Scriptural warnings and principles, but my spirit was soaring because I knew I was truly His child and He did love me.

A preacher once said he so enjoyed God's chastisement because he realized that during that time, he was very close to the Father's heart. It

---

[8] Ibid

[9] My Utmost For His Highest, (Devotional) January 30

is true, in order for loving parents to chastise a child properly, they must first bring the child close to them. When they bend over to spank the rebellious offspring, the child is placed close to the heart of the parent. When the parent leans over to reprimand the child, they are close to the child's ear that he or she may hear, and eyes that he or she may see how much the parent is fighting for his or her well-being.

Our spiritual well-being is God's priority. He has made a commitment to keep us on the right track with a strong but loving hand. His hand of chastisement may be difficult to accept at first, but when people begin to see the Lord's heart and commitment, they will submit to His rebuke and become broken by their own personal failure.

Chastisement can prove to bring grief for a season, but it is rewarding down the line. As I look back at the discipline I received as a child, I realize I am a responsible adult because of it. It brought the necessary discipline into my life that served as a good foundation in which I could grow and mature as a person.

Are you experiencing some type of chastisement from the Lord? Don't fight it; submit to it. Ask the Lord to speak, and allow His rebuke and instructions to become blessings to you rather than sinking into self-pity or resentment. Thank Him for bringing life-changing chastisement into your life because you know that you belong to Him, and He loves you enough to fight for your spiritual well-being. After all, the purpose of chastisement is to ensure that you will not die, but live.[10]

---

[10] Hebrews 12:9

8

GETTING WITHIN RANGE

Thanks to frequencies and airwaves, we can hear and see the world around us. However, in order to benefit from these incredible mediums, we must be in range of the airwaves. For example, I have lived in places where I could not receive radio or TV. In one place the mountains blocked out the airwaves. In another place I lived in a hole, and in a few places, I simply lived too far from translators.

Today, very few people in technologically advanced countries have to live without TV and radio. We have satellite and cable systems that open us up to a world of endless entertainment. We have radio stations and equipment that allow us the opportunity to tap into various sources of information

What does it take to tap into the right frequencies and airwaves in our spiritual life to hear God? Are there any satellites or equipment that will allow us to overcome the obstacles in front of us? After all, it is not unusual for Christians to have mountains of obstacles standing between them and God. There are Christians who are in holes of depression or despair. Some are far away from their Lord because of sin and spiritual detours. Therefore, what is the solution? Is it simple or complicated? The solution is simple. We have to come in range of God to tap into Him properly.

How do we get within range of God's voice? Depending on circumstances the first sure response for most Christians out of range of God's voice is repentance. You have to be pointing in the right direction to pick up any airwaves. Christians who are giving way to self, the world, or sin are facing in the wrong direction. Such people first have to change their direction before they can establish that line of communication with God. True repentance will always make a person's spirit, will, and mind receptive to God.

There are also other basic Christian virtues that ensure that each of us will not only come within range of the voice of God, but we will be able to remain in the proper position to continue to be receptive. In fact, we hear about these virtues all the time. However, for them to make a difference we must put them into practice daily.

Let us now consider these virtues.

Faith

The second book of Corinthians tells us we must walk by faith and not by sight.[1] Faith is the virtue that keeps us in range of God's voice at all times. In fact, faith serves as the far-reaching spiritual airwave. The problem is that many Christians have a hard time understanding godly faith. They have an improper perspective of it. They are either skeptics operating in unbelief, or they are trying to be super-spiritual, causing them to operate in an unrealistic frame of reference about the subject of faith.

Those who are skeptics limit God. There are reasons for the skepticism. Perhaps these people have stepped out in faith in a certain area, only to fail. They may view God as failing them or not listening to them in crisis situations. Regardless of the reasons, instead of coming to terms with the lesson or instruction behind their failure, they have resorted to trusting their own logic and understanding.

If something does not line up properly to their logic, such as a step of faith, they will become skeptical and critical about it. Their concerns could be legitimate because some people operate out of impulsive feelings and causes, but sometimes these skeptics stand in the way of what God is trying to do in or through one of His servants.

Christians who are skeptical of the working of faith are operating in the sin of unbelief. We are told in Romans 14:23 this shocking truth, "...for whatsoever is not of faith is sin."

Revelation 21:8 gives this warning, "But the fearful, and <u>unbelieving</u>, and the abominable, and murderers, and whoremongers, and sorcerers, and idolaters, and all liars, shall have their part in the lake which burneth with fire and brimstone: which is the second death." (Emphasis added.) If your faith has failed you, do not let Satan win. Allow the Holy Spirit to bring correction in each area of failure. Never resort to logic or human understanding because it will bring you into rebellion against God.

People who operate in an unrealistic way towards faith will put God to a foolish test, and will ultimately fail. These people usually have grandiose ideas about how God operates. Don't get me wrong; God can do the impossible, but God works in the practical. These grandiose ideas usually have nothing to do with real faith, but are motivated by a person's pride. They do not have anything to do with God showing His greatness, but with a person becoming great in his or her own sight at God's expense.

I have had to learn this simple truth. In my initial walk of faith, I was operating out of immaturity. I had a lot to learn about God's character,

---

[1] 1 Corinthians 5:7

which eventually changed my whole perception of faith towards Him.[2] Through the years my grandiose ideas have disappeared, while God's greatness has become a reality. These ideas lost their inflation, and I came down to the practical. The practical eventually turned into the normal. The normal can be described as God stepping on the scene and moving mountains, parting rivers, and solving problems in practical, simple, and unexpected ways.

God does not ask us to jump the Grand Canyon in our initial steps of faith. He simply asks us to take practical, baby steps at first. Each time we take a step of faith, we are being prepared to take bigger steps. Eventually we will come to the place where we will be able to jump the Grand Canyon, without sweat, thereby bringing glory to God.

It is important that we allow God to bring the proper perspective to our faith because it is the airwave that connects us to God, who is our source. The reason that faith serves as our spiritual airwave is because it walks hand in hand with many other spiritual virtues. For example, Romans 10:17 tells us, "Faith cometh by hearing, and hearing by the word of God." Here we see that exposure to the Word of God produces faith.

Faith is associated with righteousness. Philippians 3:9 states, "And be found in him, not having mine own righteousness, which is of the law, but that which is through the faith of Christ, the righteousness which is of God by faith." Righteousness means you are upright before God. This spiritual virtue gives you clout before God.

Real faith includes hope or confidence in God. Hebrews 11:1 tells us, "Now faith is the substance of things hoped for, the evidence of things not seen."

Faith is also associated with overcoming the world. 1 John 5:4 gives us this insight: "For whatsoever is born of God overcometh the world; and this is the victory that overcometh the world, even our faith." This truth is also confirmed in Hebrews 11, the faith chapter.

Hebrews 11:33-35a gives us an incredible testimony about faith overcoming the world and all other obstacles.

> Who through faith subdued kingdoms, wrought righteousness, obtained promises, stopped the mouths of lions, quenched the violence of fire, escaped the edge of the sword, out of weakness were made strong, waxed valiant in fight, turned to flight the armies of the aliens. Women received their dead raised to life again.

Faith helps us get beyond the mountains of obstacles, out of the pits of despair, and brings us close to God in righteousness and hope.

Faith has the ability to bring us into the center of God's will because it walks hand in hand with love. Galatians 5:5-6 gives us this insight, "For

---

[2] If you would like to know about the author's experience with faith, see her book, *In Search of Real Faith.*

we through the Spirit wait for the hope of righteousness by faith. For in Jesus Christ neither circumcision availeth any thing, nor uncircumcision; but faith which worketh by love."

Real faith operates only out of love. This love is first directed towards God. It means that I love God because I know Him. Since I know Him, I can trust Him with my life. Such trust will bring me to seeking and finding God's will for my life. This is genuine faith in action.

Faith totally rests on the character of God. It moves mountains because it trusts in the God who actually moves the mountains. It delivers because it only looks towards the One who delivers. It is overcoming because it believes and hides in the person of Jesus Christ, the One who overcame all.

Faith is also associated with another spiritual ingredient that ensures we are in the range of God. This ingredient is the response of active faith. It is obedience.

Obedience

Obedience can be related to the frequency that is being transmitted. Without the frequency, the airwaves will be useless because there is nothing to channel them properly. Obedience is that connection between our source (God) and our faith. It is what makes our faith alive. James 2:20 and 22b asks us, "But wilt thou know, O vain man, that faith without works (obedience) is dead? ...and by works (obedience) was faith made perfect." (Parenthesis added.)

The prophet Samuel gives us a reality check about obedience in 1 Samuel 15:22. "Behold, to obey is better than sacrifice, and to hearken than the fat of rams."

Every great move of God came after obedience. We see this in the life of Noah, Abraham, Joshua, and Jesus. Philippians 2:8 says this about Jesus, "And being found in fashion as a man, he humbled himself, and became obedient unto death, even the death of the cross."

Hebrews 5:8-9 explains the significance of Christ's obedience: "Though he were a Son, yet learned he obedience by the things which he suffered; And being made perfect, he became the author of eternal salvation unto all them that obey him." Jesus' obedience resulted in man's salvation. Our obedience ensures the completion of His salvation in our lives.

Obedience brings discipline to our spiritual lives. It not only sends out the right message to those around us, but it is also a sign of our love for the One who gave it all on our behalf. John 14:15 confirms this fact. "If ye love me, keep my commandments." We must be obedient to God if we are going to hear His voice. This means we must obey His Word.

So many people desire to know God's will for their lives, and yet they are not obeying what I call the fundamental will of God. The fundamental will of God is found in the Word. For example, there are scriptures, which say, "This is the will of God." Whether Christians realize it or not, many are failing to obey the Lord at these fundamental points or basic commandments of God. For example, God's will is for people to believe upon His Son. Maybe you believe in Jesus, but do you believe Him? The way you show you believe Him is by obeying Him.

It is God's will that His people abstain from fornication. You might be saying, "I am not committing fornication." Are you sure? After all, if you have any idols in your life, you are committing spiritual fornication. Ask the Lord to show you if you are unknowingly committing this sin. If you are committing this spiritual deviation, get rid of your idols and flee from all idolatry.[3]

In 1 Thessalonians 5:18, we are told it is God's will that we give thanks in everything. Are you grateful for what you have, or complaining and moaning about what you don't have? Are you dissatisfied because you feel you are missing out, or are you content because you allow God to fill your life up with Himself? Are you feeling sorry for yourself because you feel like you are a victim, or are you praising God for what He has done for you, and what He is doing in you? It is God's will that His people be thankful, grateful, and joyous.

1 Peter 2:15 tells us it is God's will that we be active in doing good. Are you the type of person who gives that which is convenient, comfortable, and costs you nothing, or do you give sacrificially? Do you do things for personal recognition and religious duty, or because you love God? Test yourself. Do you do good deeds when no one is watching, and give without revealing the source of the gift?[4] These are the types of actions that bring glory to God.

The Apostle John brought doing good into a correct perspective with these words,

> Hereby perceive we the love of God, because he laid down his life for us: and we ought to lay down our lives for the brethren. But whoso hath this world's good, and seeth his brother have need, and shutteth up his bowels of compassion from him, how dwelleth the love of God in him? My little children, let us not love in word, neither in tongue; but in deed and in truth (1 John 3:16-18).

Finally, 2 Peter 3:9 tells us it is God's will that none perish, but that all come to repentance. I have already made reference to this valuable action in our lives. Our Christian life calls for repentance at any point of discrepancy. It calls for repentance when we lack godly qualities, and it calls for repentance when we display ungodly attributes. Repentance gets us in line with God. It is an act of willful obedience. In fact, no one will get to heaven without it. Do you need to repent of something right now?

---

[3] 1 Thessalonians 4:3; 1 Corinthians 10:14
[4] 2 Samuel 24:24; Matthew 6:1-4

John the Baptist told people to bring forth fruits fit for repentance. Test the fruits of your life. How do you treat those around you? Do you honor them? What is your attitude about family, friend, or foe? Do you really love them? Are you blaming everyone else for your rotten attitude, ungodly actions, and unforgiving state?[5]

There are a lot of spiritual benefits in obeying the fundamental will of God. Obedience enlarges and transforms us so we can find the acceptable will of God for our personal lives. It places us in the family of God, and guarantees that we will receive our eternal inheritance in the end.[6]

Revelation 22:14 gives us this special promise concerning obedience to the fundamental will of God. "Blessed are they that do his commandments that they may have right to the tree of life, and may enter in through the gates into the city."

Let me suggest that you take time and find out what other basic commandments can be found in Scripture. Honestly examine yourself and see if you are obeying them with the right motivation (spirit), and that the life of Christ (truth) is being manifested.

What kind of frequency is your life transmitting? Does your life show that you are consistently obeying God? If you are obeying God, obedience will express itself in the next quality, faithfulness.

Faithfulness

Faithfulness is that staying power behind our Christian life. It is the virtue that keeps a person focused and on track. It overcomes despair and depression, and is the ingredient that ensures we will be ready for our Lord Jesus Christ to step on the scene at all times.

Very few understand what real faithfulness is. It is not just loyalty, although it includes loyalty. Loyalty simply holds on, but faithfulness holds on and also serves or occupies at the same time because of faith. Jesus confirmed this when He made this statement in Matthew 24:46, "Blessed is that servant, whom his lord when he cometh shall find so doing."

Faithfulness is the greatest form of devotion because it is anchored down with sobriety, maintained with integrity, and singular in both affection and obedience to the Lord. This level of devotion comes from the heart and reveals itself in practical service. This is why God can entrust a faithful person with both small and great things.

There was a retired woman who declared she wanted to serve God. At the time we were involved with an unbelieving woman who needed some assistance to get to a hospital appointment on a weekly basis. We asked the lady if she would consider helping the unbelieving woman by taking her to her appointment. We saw it was a good opportunity for her

---

[5] Matthew 3:8; 5:38-48; 6:14-15; 7:15-20
[6] Mark 3:35; Romans 12:1; 1 John 2:17

to witness to this woman. When we posed the idea to the zealous, "wannabe" servant, she adamantly refused to participate. She wanted to serve God, but on her terms. Her idea of service put her on a pedestal before others, not at the feet of someone who could not bring glory to her overrated opinion of her Christianity.

Jesus said about those servants who were faithful in all matters, "He that is faithful in that which is least is faithful also in much: and he that is unjust in the least is unjust also in much" (Luke 16:10). Godly faithfulness cannot be faked because it is the byproduct of humility and submission. The humility and submission found in godly faithfulness makes people sensitive to the leading of the Holy Spirit. It makes them watchful concerning the events taking place around them. This quality ensures a person will be in the right place when the Lord speaks.

Many Christians lack this balanced anchor in their life. I have known people who found themselves spiritually bankrupt because they did not possess this staying power. For example, many Christians chase after prophesies and seek ways to make them come true, rather than waiting on God. The secret of the fulfillment of prophecies can only be found in simple faithfulness to God. God will bring forth the prophecy, but it will only happen if the individual shows unwavering devotion and obedience while waiting on God's timing to have His way.

I have had many prophecies, but I have kept them in perspective. I realize a prophecy from God can only come true as long as I am faithful and obedient to Him. Many of my prophecies have come true without my even knowing it. It was only after I reviewed the prophecy that I realized God fulfilled it.

When Christians are busy being faithful, they do not have time to get caught up in the possibilities. They have one mission and priority: To do right by their Lord. All else is immaterial, including prophecies. After all, the impossible is God's problem and obedience is my responsibility. Acceptable obedience comes out of faithfulness.

Faithfulness helps us to maintain the oil in our lamps. Consider the five virgins in Matthew 25 who did not have enough oil. Either they failed to have oil in their lamps or they used it up while waiting for the bridegroom. The five wise virgins were ready. They had faithfully preserved their oil supply until the bridegroom's invitation.

Faithfulness sustains an individual through the waiting process. You cannot learn to wait unless you are learning to be faithful in every area of your life. Learning to wait is another necessary quality in hearing the voice of the Lord.

Silence

We live in a society that is full of noise. It appears as if many Americans do not know what to do with silence. In some cases, the loudest sound to some people is silence. Such people have never really learned to listen or hear in the midst of all the commotion that surrounds them.

I have learned that noise can drown out our fears and problems. It can keep us from coming face-to-face with those things that are painful, as well as the emptiness and failures in our own lives. Often, we hide in the midst of all the noise around us.

Therefore, should it amaze us that God uses silence to speak to us? Oswald Chambers in his book, *Prayer: A Holy Occupation,* reveals how God's silence can serve as a sign of answered prayer, a prelude to a greater revelation of Jesus, or a point where you can display great confidence in what He is doing in your midst. I have discovered these truths about silence in the past. In fact, the silence has appeared to me to be the time that God is speaking the loudest, but I had to stop to listen. These times can be referred to as the "dark night of the soul." They require one to learn how to quietly wait on the Lord.

Waiting on the Lord is the most challenging time to all aspiring ministers and struggling saints. It is a time when some of the greatest light overshadows the dark night of the soul. Oswald Chambers dealt with this subject. He explained how the darkness that our Lord refers to is not darkness caused by sin or disobedience; rather, it is caused by excess light. These times of darkness can cause the disciple to be at a loss for words. However, he or she needs to realize it is a discipline of character. It is also a means to bring him or her into a fuller knowledge of Jesus. In such times one needs to avoid speaking, and simply listen.[7]

These dark times include great testing. We are required to trust the Lord, believe His Word, and be faithful to obey without seeing, hearing, or knowing anything. It is at these places where we finally get out of the way and let God be God. The dark times of waiting often place us in the valley of the shadow of death. There is so much pressing up against us. It is as though we are at the edge of the abyss, ready to fall into the clutches of destruction. Again, by faith we believe He is with us, even though we cannot touch Him. We put our hands over our ears as everything inside of us screams that God is so very far away. We willfully choose to believe He is as close as our very breath, hears our every whisper, and no matter what direction we turn, He is there to catch and embrace us.

This dark time of waiting is a time to collect great treasures. Isaiah 45:3 puts it this way, "And I will give thee the treasures of darkness, and hidden riches of secret places, that thou mayest know that I, the LORD, which call thee by thy name, am the God of Israel." It is in the darkness and waiting that we gain glimpses of our God. These glimpses enrich our lives and give us hope. They allow us to grow in the knowledge of His character and ways as we begin to hear Him in the silence, feel Him in the darkness, and see Him in the midst of our plights. All of this leads us to intimate communion with Him.

---

[7] Daily Thoughts For Disciples, March 15 devotional

Oswald Chambers understood this principle. He shared how there is nothing more trying to the eye than perpetual sunshine. He linked this concept as also being true on a spiritual level. He related how the valley of the shadow is a time of reflection, but it is in this valley that we learn to praise God. It is during this time that our soul can be restored in precious communion with God.[8]

Our souls will be restored during communion because we draw strength in such times. It is important to realize that God so desires to set us apart for Himself. He wants to have personal, intimate fellowship with us. He wants us to know Him so we can enjoy Him and be refreshed in our spirits.

The waiting period also builds godly character. Character can only come out of trials and tribulations. Scriptures such as 2 Corinthians 4:7-17; Hebrews 12:11, and James 1:2-4 confirm this truth, and yet much of the Christian world is preaching to the contrary. Doctrines that tickle fleshly, prideful ears are being given credence over sound Biblical principles. Much of what is being expounded in Christian circles today is nothing more than destructive propaganda.

This propaganda has produced fleshly people, and cheapened the message of grace. It has lowered God to some wimpy character whose love embraces iniquity, tolerates deception, and justifies abominable actions in the name of worldly happiness. What a reproach this has brought on both the character of God and His Gospel!

Since these dark times do build character, Christians must avoid escaping them prematurely. It is not unusual for Christians to become impatient, fearful, and uncertain about their spiritual condition. Believers can be tempted to snatch at anything to break the silence and uncertainty. Sadly, in this vulnerable time, vain imaginations are often accepted as being God's voice.

What about you? Are you in range of God's voice or are you outside of the scriptural peripheral of hearing and seeing Him? Are the airwaves being stifled? Is the frequency failing because the necessary ingredients are missing in your life before Him? Ask the Lord to show you the answers to these questions. He will be faithful to do so because He loves you and desires to be in communion with you.

---

[8] Ibid, March 16 devotional

9

FOLLOWING THE SHEPHERD

"He that hath an ear let him hear what the Spirit saith unto the churches." This was the consistent statement that Jesus made in Revelation 2 and 3 to the seven churches. It was made in light of an absence of love, along with persecution, false doctrine, spiritual fornication, unacceptable works, and complacency. Obviously, Jesus was giving many of these churches an ultimatum: hear or pay dire consequences.

Why is it so important for Christians to hear the voice of their Shepherd? We can give the obvious answers. However, there is one main reason we must hear the voice of the Shepherd. Hearing His voice means we belong to Him and have an intimate relationship with God.[1]

This relationship is why Jesus came. He said He is the way, the truth, and the life and that no one comes to the Father but by Him. In other words, He is the only way to this relationship. He is the truth about this relationship, and out of it will come His life. This is clearly brought out in John 10.

We see Jesus as the Good Shepherd and door to the sheepfold. This door represents protection and the entrance to eternal life. He has proven His heart and intention towards us by giving His life on our behalf. His blood was used as the payment. This makes Him our owner.[2]

As our Good Shepherd, Jesus also takes our well-being seriously. In fact, it is His priority. He does all He can to ensure the best for us. Every time He calls out to us, it is for our benefit. He wants to lead us away from the challenge, temptations, and filth of the world to His green pastures and still waters.

Jesus wants you and me to know He is completely trustworthy; and that we can and must become totally dependent on Him. This is why He stands outside the door of His wayward children's hearts and knocks. He wants to be admitted in order to sup with each of them, as well as show them His gentle nature.[3]

As our committed Shepherd, He wants our hearts to belong to Him, and our minds to be set upon Him in unwavering devotion. He wants us to know Him and His voice so when He calls, we will follow Him into the life He has prepared for us.

---

[1] John 10:4-5

[2] John 10:11-18; 14:6; 1 Corinthians 6:20; 7:23

[3] Revelation 3:20

John 10:3b tells us, "And the sheep hear his voice: and he calleth his own sheep by name, and leadeth them out." In order to know His voice we must first become accustomed to it. We need to know the sound of His voice and associate it with heavenly benefits and satisfaction. In fact, His voice should quickly receive our undivided attention.

Why do we fail to hear our Shepherd's voice? Is it because hearing the voice of Jesus brings us to a place of decision? We must ask ourselves if we really want to hear His voice. If we do hear His voice, we must respond. This place can be uncomfortable to certain believers. Some of them actually run from His voice because of sins and failures. Some ignore His voice because they want to do their own thing. At other times, His voice is muffled, or far away because some of His sheep have allowed things to come between them and their Shepherd. How about you? Are you adhering to the voice of the Shepherd, or are you going in the opposite direction?

John 10:3 also tells us that He calls us by name. Knowing a person's name in our society often implies we may only have knowledge of someone, but knowing and using a name in God's realm implies so much more. Revelation 2:17 gives us this insight into the significance of names: "He that hath an ear, let him hear what the Spirit saith unto the churches; To him that overcometh will I give to eat of the hidden manna, and will give him a white stone, and in the stone a new name written, which no man knoweth saving he that receiveth it."

I once heard the explanation behind this scripture. Apparently, the Romans used stones in their courts to pronounce the verdict. For example, if a person was found guilty, they handed a man a black stone. If they found him not guilty, they handed him a white stone. If this explanation is true, the white stone represents the fact that we will stand justified in the courts of heaven. This justification has come through faith in what Jesus did on the cross. The blood shed on the old rugged cross cleanses us from all unrighteousness; therefore, we have the right to stand before our judge with confidence that we will not be declared guilty.[4] This stone will have our new name on it. The name will prove that our Shepherd has been aware of every intricate detail of our life and activities. It will also be a name that is only known by God and the individual. What intimacy this action implies!

W. Phillip Keller in His book, *A Shepherd Looks at the Good Shepherd and His Sheep*, talks about how a shepherd calls each of his sheep by name as each one walks out of the sheepfold. A good shepherd will also take the opportunity at this time to examine the sheep individually to make sure that the animals are healthy. Not only does a shepherd become familiar with the sheep's well-being, but the sheep also becomes familiar with the voice, touch, smell, and commitment of the shepherd.

---

[4] 1 John 1:7

Scripture shows us God searches our hearts, knows our thoughts, is aware of our heartbreaks, and knows our frame.[5] In essence, we cannot hide anything from Him. What a beautiful picture of Jesus' familiarity with each of us! If only believers acquired the same familiarity with their Shepherd, they could avoid many pitfalls and failures in their lives.

Another important reason for knowing our Shepherd's voice is found in John 10:4-5, "...and the sheep follow him: for they know his voice. And a stranger will they not follow, but will flee from him: for they know not the voice of strangers." As you can see, not only will Jesus' sheep follow Him when He calls, but they will not follow a stranger's voice. I have witnessed this when someone was teaching or preaching heresy. The sheep who belonged to Jesus become agitated and threatened mutiny if the person was allowed to continue in his or her false presentation.

There are many strangers out there vying for the attention of Jesus' flock. They are in total competition with Him. They promote strange doctrines and practices, and they do not care about the spiritual welfare of the sheep. These strangers are only interested in personal gain. They are thieves, wolves, and hireling shepherds.

The Word of God warns us that in the last days these predators of man's souls will flood the sheepfolds and churches with their doctrines of demons and worldly gain. Sadly, many of the Lord's flock will fall prey to them because they do no really know their Shepherd's voice.[6]

This is a serious warning, yet many Christians are totally unaware of their precarious position. I have watched Christians fall into blatant error. I have witnessed unscriptural men being exalted as spiritual gurus. I have witnessed the truth trampled, the Holy Spirit blamed for that which is unholy, the name of Jesus used like a magic wand, and the power of the Gospel demeaned. I have stood in sorrow as people have exhibited faith in faith, calling fleshly worship anointed, and false teachings new revelations of the Holy Spirit.

The sad truth is the wolves no longer have to dress in sheep's clothing to ensure that modern-day Christendom will accept them. They can walk right in and offer their arsenic, and many in the fold will flock to partake of their unholy morsels and muddy water. Why? Are the majority of believers today so spiritually dull that they are unable to discern the holy from the unholy? Are they so full of religious pride they cannot see their vulnerability? Has the delusion of 2 Thessalonians 2:10-11 come upon many because there is no love for the truth? Are those who have been carried away by this false spirituality unreachable?

When I ministered in the Seattle area, I began to understand why few people realized the danger. In Christ we have everything, but I watched many in the Christian fold chase after new experiences,

[5] Psalm 139; Jeremiah 17:8-9
[6] Luke 10:3; Acts 20:29; 1 Timothy 4:1

prophecies, and certain charismatic leaders who told them what they wanted to hear. These teachings stirred up their flesh to emotional fervor and appeased their pride and worldly pursuits. It appeared as if Christ and His Word were not enough. People wanted more, and it was as if Seattle was providing a spiritual smorgasbord. Everything you could imagine was being presented to the sheep, and they could pick and choose according to their liking regardless of the arsenic intertwined in it.

It reminded me of the people of Israel. The manna from heaven was not enough, so they cried to have meat. God sent them a smorgasbord of meat. It appeared to be a blessing for them, but in reality, it was a judgment. Psalm 106:15 tells us, "And he gave them their request; but sent leanness into their soul."

Israel was full, yet they were greatly lacking. A modern-day version of this can be found in Revelation 3:17. The Christians in the church in Laodicea had this opinion of their spiritual condition: "I am rich, and increased with goods, and have need of nothing."

God's evaluation about this church's spiritual condition was contrary, "...thou are wretched, and miserable, and poor, and blind, and naked." Needless to say, His evaluation was the correct one, yet these spiritually bankrupt people could not see it. They were blinded by what they perceived about their spiritual condition.

Christians must never settle for personal opinions concerning their spiritual life. Personal opinions will let people off the hook, and present an unrealistic picture based on fleshly and prideful conclusions. Therefore, saints must strive to understand God's perspective about their lives and agree with His evaluations.

Finally, hearing Jesus' voice and following Him means we are actually abiding in Him. John 15 tells us Jesus is the Vine and we are the branches. As our Vine, we receive all of our nutrition from Jesus. Our well-being and the fruitfulness of our lives are based on our relationship with Him. However, we cannot abide unless we remain in Him by following Him.

Are you abiding in the Vine? The answer to this question will determine if you are truly following Him. If we are hearing our Shepherd's voice, we know the following facts are true: 1) We belong to Him; 2) we are following Him; 3) we know Him in an intimate way; 4) we will not follow a stranger, and 5) we are abiding in Him.

Ask the light of the Holy Spirit to penetrate your life and show you where you stand in Christ. Make sure you are following Him because you are hearing His voice. Once this relationship is correctly established, don't touch that dial! Make sure you always keep within range of His voice. I know you will never regret it, for He is leading you into an abundant, complete life!

Book Four

THE FACE
OF
THANKFULNESS

INTRODUCTION

This book started out as a message for Thanksgiving. The depth of revelation that was being etched in my spirit overwhelmed me as the Lord began to bring insight to my studies. I found myself shocked at its simplicity, inspired by the spirit behind it, and humbled by the example that was brought forth.

Upon hearing about this incredible discovery in God's Word, my co-laborer in the mission field, Jeannette, felt I needed to go one step further and put my information into a pamphlet or book. Because of the amount of information, I chose the latter.

What I am about to share with you may be familiar, but the spiritual depths of this revelation may enlarge your perspective and challenge certain comfortable religious traditions. Some people will rejoice, while others may find themselves being stirred up to respond in a way they have never thought possible.

My prayer is that the message of this book will challenge and change you as it did me. My hope is that you will come out loving Jesus more because your heart is full of thanksgiving for who He is and what He has done for you.

1

A SUMMARY OF THANKFULNESS

Saying, Amen: Blessing, and glory,
and wisdom, and thanksgiving, and
honor, and power, and might, be unto
our God forever and ever. Amen
Revelation 7:12

My journey to discover the incredible revelation I am about to share with you began with a two-part question; "What does it mean to be thankful," and, "how do Christians express it in their lives?"

I knew thankfulness was a disposition and that without the attitude of gratitude, a person could not please, serve, or worship God in a proper manner. In fact, Deuteronomy 28:47-48 would often catch my attention,

> Because thou servedst not the LORD thy God with joyfulness, and with gladness of heart, for the abundance of things; Therefore shalt thou serve thine enemies which the LORD shall send against thee, in hunger, in thirst, and in nakedness, and in want of all things and he shall put a yoke of iron upon thy neck until he have destroyed thee.

I never dreamed that my search to answer this question would lead me on a path that would show me thankfulness outside of my conventional understanding. Amazing discoveries caused me to realize I would never look at Jesus Christ in the same way. Praise God for such a blessing!

My studies first led me to 2 Corinthians 9:11-15. These scriptures paint a clear picture of what inspires thankfulness, the purpose behind it, and the results. According to 2 Corinthians 9:11 thankfulness comes out of abundance. The Apostle Paul put it this way, "Being enriched in every thing to all bountifulness, which causeth through us thanksgiving to God."

The abundance Paul was referring to was not just in regard to material substance, but it was also in reference to spiritual abundance. He confirmed this in Ephesians 1:3, "Blessed be the God and Father of our Lord Jesus Christ, who hath blessed us with all spiritual blessings in heavenly places in Christ."

Paul understood his life was complete in Christ. His soul had been satisfied when he had encountered the fullness of Jesus in His love, mercy, and grace. And, as he continued to gain Christ, he realized what it meant to experience a complete life. This brings us down to a simple truth: It is not what we possess that determines personal wealth, but what possesses us.

If the things of this world hold our heart and control our affections, we are spiritual paupers regardless of how many worldly riches we possess. However, if Jesus holds our hearts and determines our affections, we are the richest of all people.[1]

The Apostle Paul recognized this truth. He knew his life was hid in Christ; therefore, he knew his life was rich with indescribable bounties. He had experienced trouble, but was not distressed. He had been perplexed, but not swallowed by despair. He had been greatly persecuted, but not forsaken. And, he had been cast down, but not destroyed. This apostle had encountered death only to find life. He had experienced suffering, only to find God's glory.[2] Through it all, he knew he was gaining a greater reality of God's unspeakable gift.

Paul was thankful because he knew Jesus, and that this gift of God was the center of his life and focus. He could be confident because he followed this precious gift into the abundant life. Because of his relationship with God through Jesus Christ, he could be excited about the glory that awaited him in eternity.

Paul had an enriched life because he possessed the life of Christ. It was the rich eternal life of Christ in him, which produced incredible thanksgiving in the heart of Paul. As a result, He gladly offered thanksgiving unto God.

Like the Apostle Paul, every Christian possesses this wealth, but few recognize the value of this gift in their lives. As a result, many fail to become thankful.

Are you like Paul? If Christ is in you, you have eternal riches that exceed all the treasures of this present world. If you understand this truth, it will make you thankful. Have you begun to grasp this incredible reality?

Glorifying God

The goal of thankfulness is to bring glory to God. We see this in 2 Corinthians 9:13, "Whiles by the experiment of this ministration they glorify God for your professed subjection unto the gospel of Christ, and for your liberal distribution unto them, and unto all men." This book will reveal that thankfulness and glorifying God walk hand in hand. If you are not thankful, you will not glorify God.

To glorify God means you are honoring Him or magnifying Him either through verbal praise or actions. Honoring God in such a manner can only come from a thankful heart.

---

[1] Luke 12:13-34
[2] 2 Corinthians 4:7-18; Colossians 3:1-3; 2 Timothy 2:11-12

We see that the Corinthians were honoring God because of the Gospel of Christ. This message has the power to change the heart, purpose, and direction of an individual. The Gospel not only changes a person, but also holds an individual responsible to live an obedient, righteous, and victorious life. A changed life makes a difference in this dark world, which will bring recognition and honor to God.

Are you glorifying God because you are thankful for what His Gospel has accomplished in your life? After all, the Gospel is the power of God unto salvation.[3]

Liberal Giving

In 2 Corinthians 9:13, we see where the Corinthians were liberal in helping other saints. Let me make a statement, only a thankful person can be a liberal giver.

Benevolence is a fruit of thankfulness. People who are thankful are also benevolent in actions. However, those who are not thankful have no concept of sacrifice or appreciation.

The ingratitude with which some people approach life is a fruit of utter selfishness. The disposition of selfishness is prevalent in our society. The escalation of its attitude with each generation is reflected by a greater emphasis on self. The more self-centered people become, the more demanding and discontented they grow in their lives. Ultimately, they act as if family, society, and life owe them the best, and since they deserve the best, there is no gratitude when others sacrifice for their well-being. The result is that benevolence is clearly missing from homes, churches, and society. Sadly, when benevolence is missing, so is the reality of God.

God established benevolence. He warned Israel that if they failed to show benevolence in the area of strangers, widows, and the fatherless, that He would greatly judge them. He had, after all, blessed them so they could bless others. Therefore, to fail to be liberal towards others with the blessings of God was a form of neglect and abuse that God would not tolerate from His people.[4]

Liberal giving is distinct from all other forms of giving. Such distinction is found in the fact that it always glorifies God. We see this in the case of the widow in Luke 21:1-4.

After watching many cast great sums into the temple treasury, and then witnessing a widow casting in her last two coins, Jesus said, "Of a truth I say unto you, that this poor widow hath cast in more than they all." The people who gave along with the widow showed what they outwardly possessed, but the widow showed who possessed her heart.[5]

---

[3] Romans 1:16

[4] Exodus 22:21-24; Deuteronomy 24:19-22; 26:12-13; James 1:27

[5] Matthew 6:21

There is nothing that can be as surface and indifferent in our life than giving of our material goods. It can all be for show with the wrong motivation. In the incident of the widow and her mites, many gave for outward show. However, the widow revealed a visible expression of her heart towards God.

As we can see, the eternal worth of a gift is not determined by how much a person gives of their worldly possessions, but how much they give of themselves. Those who gave out of their worldly abundance did not give from their hearts. However, the widow who gave out of both her need and lack gave out of a heart that showed appreciation for the unseen bounties of God.

I once heard a certain pastor say that he could tell a Christian's level of commitment by looking at their checkbook (to see how much that person gave to the church). I do not totally agree with this evaluation. I believe you can tell more about a person's spirituality by finding out what he or she is unwilling to give to God.

It is easier to give money for the cause of Christ, than it is to give all of our heart or life to Him in total abandonment. The rich young ruler in Matthew 19 had probably given beyond the required tithe to the temple treasury, but was unwilling to give it all. Therefore, it is not the amount we give that determines the value God holds in our lives, but what we insist on holding on to when it comes to total abandonment to Him.

This brings us to why people give to God in the first place. Many people give it as a show of their "so-called" piousness. Much like the sacrifice of King Saul in 1 Samuel 15, it serves as a sick substitute for obedience. Others give to silence their religious conscience as a penance for ungodly actions. Some impulsively give after their religious arm has been twisted in order to feel good about themselves. However, real giving never serves as an expression of man's goodness, but of God's goodness.

People should only give because it is a way of sharing God's blessings with others. As the late Ruth Specter Lascelle, Jewish Bible Teacher stated, "Everything that we get from God comes to us freely. Everything that we are to give back to God is to be given generously."[6]

It is easy in our giving to substitute money as a form of commitment and obedience. It is easy to tack God on to our giving as a way to feel good about ourselves. However, giving should never be about us receiving recognition for our "goodness", but about honoring God's goodness to us with all of our hearts.

So much of giving, even in the Church, has a self-serving motivation behind it. Self always has expectations and can become disillusioned quickly when conditions are not met. Such giving is all show and no heart.

---

[6] A Dwelling Place for God; Ruth Specter Lascelle, ©1990 by Hyman Israel Specter, Van Nuys, California, pg. 10

Giving for a liberal giver is the total opposite from those who give out of show. God gave His best when He gave His Son. His benevolent actions are natural because they are motivated by His love. This is true for those who give because of God's goodness. It is natural for them to give without even considering personal cost.

A good definition for liberal giving is thankfulness expressing itself in a selfless way. It is committed, sensitive, and sacrificial. In other words, people who are liberal givers are not looking for appreciation, recognition, or acknowledgment for what they do because of God.

Liberal giving is the ultimate expression of Christianity in action. For this reason. people who claim to be Christians, but are selfish, must examine themselves to see if they are really in the faith.[7] In the end, liberal giving will produce thanksgiving in others who benefit from Christian benevolence, bringing glory to God.

Today, many ministers in the harvest field are finding their work increasingly difficult because many Christians are not liberal givers. Sadly, Christians have to be constantly stirred up to remember those on the mission field. As a result, servants of God have to resort to the marketing methods of the world to keep their name and mission before people to simply function. This ought not to be, for as believers, we are all laborers in the same harvest field.

Each of us must seek the Spirit of God, and find out where we must give, and then make a commitment accordingly. Once He lays someone on our hearts, we must make a commitment to be obedient to what the Lord shows each of us.

As you can see, emotions or promotional schemes do not move liberal givers; therefore, they enjoy immense freedom in their giving. Only the leading of the Holy Spirit moves these people. This is why a liberal giver is a responsible steward, and cannot be easily moved by the ploys that stir up the emotions or cause guilt.

Are you a liberal giver or a self-serving individual? Does your Christianity express itself in thankfulness or in hypocrisy? Is your giving a formality, an outward show, or a matter of the heart?

---

[7] 2 Corinthians 13:5

2

USING THE UNLIKELY

But God hath chosen the foolish things
of the world to confound the wise...
1 Corinthians 1:27a

The Lord reminded me of three incidents in Scripture to start me on the incredible journey to discover thankfulness. Each situation involved three people who had one thing in common—they were Samaritans.

Samaritans have always interested me because they have been considered foolish, weak, base, and despised by the Jewish culture. As I studied the events surrounding these people, I realized the Lord used these individuals to get some very important points across to the "wise," "strong" and "respectable." This reminded me of what the Apostle Paul said in 1 Corinthians 1:27-28 about the types of people God uses for His glory.

God uses the foolish, weak, base, and despised. I used to ponder God's choice until I realized that such people have the ability to reveal prejudice, hypocrisy, and arrogance in others. Such attitudes or responses serve as a test to those who dare call themselves Christians. He also exposes people's level of love, meekness, and devotion to Him by using the unacceptable and the unlikely as the means to reveal the depths of each person's heart. Jeremiah 17:9-10 confirms this, "The heart is deceitful above all things, and desperately wicked: who can know it? I the LORD search the heart, I try the reins, even to give every man according to his ways, and according to the fruit of his doings."

As I observed how Jesus used the example of the Samaritans, I could see how He was stripping away the religious façade of the Jewish people to expose the dead bones of religion.[1] Even though I recognized that Jesus is God Incarnate, I still stood in awe of His wisdom and cleverness to expose the heart of His people.

In my research, I found some conflicting, but interesting, information about Samaritans. The history as to their origins is as controversial as their presence was among the Jews in Jesus' day. Samaritan people were associated with the former capital of Israel, Samaria. This is where they got their name and initial identity as a distinct group of people. The city of Samaria had an ungodly beginning as Israel's capital. A wicked, idolatrous king by the name of Omri was the one who established

---

[1] Matthew 23:24-29

Samaria as the new capital of Israel.[2] He used forced labor to make it into a beautiful city. As with the rest of the cities within the northern tribes of Israel, she was idolatrous in nature.

The Word of God shows that after ignoring various warnings of impending judgment from God to the people of Israel about their evil, idolatrous ways, the Assyrians took the inhabitants, along with most of the other Hebrews within the boundaries that made up the Northern Kingdom of Israel, into captivity in 721 BC. The Assyrians then settled Samaria with captives from other nations. According to my information, these foreign people intermingled with the remaining Israelites.

The lineage of the Samaritans became questionable as these different races intermarried. Because of the various religious and cultural practices coming together, these people developed a mixed bag of beliefs. The Bible tells us that even the Jewish beliefs were accepted and integrated into the various pagan practices. According to 2 Kings 17:23-41, a Jewish priest was sent to Samaria to teach the people about the God of Israel because He slew some of the people for not fearing Him.

The *Smith's Bible Dictionary* gives even more details about the history of the Samaritans. It implies that there was an attempt to separate the Jewish beliefs from other pagan practices. However, even this attempt was a product of a rebellious priest who was dismissed from his position as priest. He was one of the priests who refused to send his foreign wife away in the days of Ezra and Nehemiah. This priest supposedly established worship on Mount Gerizim. His endeavor upheld certain Jewish beliefs, but still changed the face of traditional Jewish practices, developing a religion that was an offshoot of Judaism.

Mount Gerizim began to serve as a religious replacement for Jerusalem to the Samaritans who wanted to capture a semblance of the religious practices of the Orthodox Jews. This was one of the issues that caused major antagonism between the Jews and the Samaritans.

Since the Samaritans had a mixed bag of religious beliefs, the Jews considered them unorthodox. Even though their lineage may have linked some of the Samaritans to the Jewish nation, their belief system made them unacceptable. These people found themselves separated from their distant Jewish relatives by religious prejudices, attitudes of superiority, and rejection.

This must be kept in mind as we study the three Samaritans in this book. Jesus used these three outcasts to answer my question about thankfulness. Without this information about these particular people, much is lost in the revelation and intensity behind the incidents surrounding the Samaritans who were considered outcasts.

I think it is also important to point out that the Samaritans represent humanity in general. Some of the Samaritans' lineage went back to Abraham. But, because it was clouded over with other cultures and

---

[2] 1 Kings 16:22-27

defiled religious practices, these individuals found themselves rejected, isolated, and separated from the blessings and promises given to Abraham by God.

Likewise, man has the potential to reflect the image of God. However, due to his lineage going back to Adam, he now has a questionable lineage that has been clouded by sin. This sin separates him from his Creator and his original potential. His purpose has been lost, his potential marred, and he continually tastes the bitterness of pride, prejudice, and rejection. Because of this bitterness, he knows how life is plagued with unbearable isolation and sorrow.

I am thankful for the example of the Samaritans. These incidents not only show how the grace of God reaches out to the unacceptable, but how such people often respond when touched by the glorious reality of His love, power, and forgiveness. In fact, these Samaritans reveal that thankfulness comes when one's vision, heart, and disposition are changed towards God.

With the history, lineage, and representation of the Samaritans in mind, we are now ready to take our first step in this journey to discover what thankfulness looks like in attitude and action.

Step One

Recognition

3

STANDING AFAR OFF

And came and preached peace
to you which were afar off,
and to them that were nigh.
Ephesians 2:17

The first Samaritan we are going to consider is found in Luke 17:11-19. This Samaritan was a leper. Leprosy was the most dreaded disease in the Bible. According to the *Smith's Bible Dictionary,* this disease started as little specks on the eyelids and on the palms of the hands. It would gradually spread over the whole skin. From the skin, it slowly ate its way to the tissues, bones, joints, and even to the marrow, causing the whole body to rot away, piece by piece.

This disease was considered to be hereditary, contagious, and unclean. As a result, people who suffered from this disease were isolated from the rest of society. Leprosy, therefore, caused greater distress, as it ravaged not only its many victims of their health, but robbed them of family, home, and dignity. I'm sure the idea of death came as a blessed relief to those who were being consumed by this unmerciful monster.

The disease of leprosy is symbolic of sin. Sin is a hereditary problem that finds its origin in the first man, Adam. It is a spiritual disease that starts out small, but spreads quickly to consume a person's life. The Apostle Paul describes it in this manner, "Know ye not, that a little leaven leaveneth the whole lump" (1 Corinthians 5:6b)?

This dreaded spiritual disease perverts our character, blinds our spiritual eyes, and destroys our hearing. It causes great separation in relationships, and ultimately, robs us of real life. Eventually, our lives become a stench to God.

Leprosy caused its victims to stand afar off from the rest of society. Likewise, sin makes a person stand afar off from God.[1] The best eludes a person who is enslaved by sin, and isolates him or her while he or she is consumed in a world of fear, guilt, anger, and hopelessness.

Our first glimpse of this Samaritan shows him standing afar off with nine other lepers. These men were not responsible for their physical plight. They had helplessly become entangled in something that was cruel and beyond their control. Like these men, each of us is born with a

---

[1] Romans 3:23; Colossians 1:21-22

317

selfish condition, and we will find ourselves becoming casualties of something beyond our control.

Like all humanity, the plight of these men was hopeless until that fateful day when they encountered a Man by the name of Jesus. He walked into their midst in the most ordinary way. Even though they could not get close to Him, they still could cry out.

I'm sure these men had probably heard about this man, Jesus. He had made the impossible seem easy, the untouchable seem lovable, the unclean seem acceptable, and the insignificant seem important. They may have even heard the debate over His identity. After all, some claimed He was Elijah or some other prophet, while others boldly declared He was the long-awaited Messiah.[2]

However, would such debates matter to any of these men as they faced the results of their physical prison? These men probably had their own debates secretly going on within their souls. How could they make sense out of life, while facing a hopeless future of suffering and death? Their vision was that of despair. But, maybe in the back of their minds, they silently held on to a glimmer of hope.

Could these unacceptable outcasts of society dare hope that such a Man, as Jesus would ever come their way and take note of them? Their plight was so great. Would He really do something or would He ignore them and turn away from them as outcasts like the rest of society?

Their unspoken hopes were about to be silenced and lost forever by rejection—or realized in a miraculous way as Jesus came into their midst. They would either remain in hopeless despair or discover how true it is that real hope is never out of reach for those who dare to believe.

I'm sure their hearts seemed to stop beating as they cried out to this Man named Jesus, "Jesus, Master, have mercy on us!" Even though Jesus was afar off from the outcasts, surrounded by people and noise, He heard their cries and stopped.

The Word tells us that God is attentive to the cries of those seeking Him.[3] The Apostle Paul goes one step further by giving us this insight about Jesus, "And came and preached peace to you which were afar off, and to them that were nigh" (Ephesians 2:17).

Jesus came down to earth to walk among humanity as the Great Physician. He came to restore man, not necessarily to a society that would shun him because of disease, but to reconcile him back to God for total restoration.

These men did not realize that Jesus came for men such as them. He had come to show sick humanity the way to lasting healing. As He said, "Blessed are the poor in spirit: for theirs is the kingdom of God"

---

[2] Matthew 16:13-16
[3] Psalm 4:1-3; 54; 116

(Matthew 5:3). It was because of their condition that these ten men were likely candidates for a miracle.

Jesus not only heard their cries and stopped, but He looked directly at them and spoke, "Go shew yourselves unto the priests." To the Jews, this command would mean a great deal: But what would it mean to a Samaritan? Did he feel the liberty to submit to a Jewish Priest? After all, how well versed were such people in the Jewish law?

According to the Law of Moses, only the priest could declare a leper clean, resulting in total restoration. We see this truth in Leviticus 14. As you study the procedures surrounding a leper being declared clean, you realize that being healed is a separate act from being declared clean.

Only God could heal a person of this dreaded disease, but the priest was the only one who had the authority to declare the individual clean before he or she could be allowed back into society. This declaration could not take place until the priest had personally examined the person, sacrifices were offered on his or her behalf, and physical consecration had been accomplished.

It struck me that the priest went outside of the camp where the lepers were to do the examination. Hebrews 13:12 tells us that Jesus suffered outside the gate. When you consider how the priest had to go outside the gate to examine a leper, and how Christ, our High Priest, suffered outside the gate on a cross to take care of sin, a wondrous picture emerges.

Jesus, as both the Great Physician and the High Priest, had left the beauty of heaven to meet with man to show him the way of healing. His death on the cross became the very means by which He could declare man to be cleansed. He proved that healing always came from above, and that sin had to be dealt with outside of the religious activities and attempts of man.[4]

The fact that Jesus instructed these men to go to the priest implied one thing--*they were healed.* By faith, each of these men went to the priest. The Scripture tells us they were cleansed on their way to God's representative.

Again, we are reminded that healing and cleansing are two separate acts in the Kingdom of God. Healing may be part of cleansing, but they are not the same. This thought brings a question to mind. How many religious people have been healed, but not cleansed? Obviously, cleansing, not healing, results in restoration. After all, cleansing implies sanctification. Our God is holy, and restoration cannot take place unless there has been cleansing.

It is interesting to see how these men reacted to Jesus' instruction. They merrily went their way without thinking about what had transpired. They had been healed, but how many acknowledged that fact? They had

---

[4] Luke 4:18; Philippians 2:5-8; Hebrews 10:19-22; 1 John 1:7

been products of a miracle, but how many recognized that they were benefactors of something wonderful?

Is this not true for many Christians? How many of us realize what salvation really entails? We run to the altar to say the *"sinner's prayer,"* then go merrily on our way without recognizing the cost. We have been exposed to the greatest miracle known among mankind, *eternal life*, and we don't even skip a beat as we run back into the world, while clothing our fleshly pursuits with a lot of religious terms.

There were ten men who were healed, but how many came back to thank the One who made it possible? Sadly, the percentage represented by this event is very symbolic of how many truly react to the salvation and blessings of God that have been freely provided.

Many unthinking professing "Christians" go merrily on their way, while assuming that all is well. Assumption towards the things of God is nothing more than fruits of arrogant presumption.[5] The origin of this arrogance is self-love. Because of pride, many secretly believe they actually deserve to be healed, and that it has nothing to do with the mercy of God. This type of individual not only fails to recognize God's intervention, but also often demotes a miracle into a logical mental evaluation of something that rightfully happened and nothing more.

All of these men cried out for mercy. "Mercy" means you acknowledge that you do not deserve what you are seeking. In reality, we all deserve our miserable lot in life and eternal damnation. Obviously, most of these men failed to see that Mercy Personified not only heard their cry, but also did the miraculous.

Let us now consider the response of the one who did recognize the source of his healing. His response allows us to see into the attitude that reaches beyond a miracle to find something greater than deliverance from a hopeless disease.

---

[5] 2 Peter 2:9-10

4

THE ONE WHO CAME BACK

Draw nigh to God,
and he will draw nigh to you.
Cleanse your hands, ye sinners;
and purify your hearts, ye double-minded.
James 4:8

Ten lepers cried out for mercy as the Son of God passed through their midst. They were too far away to touch Him, but He was powerful and compassionate enough to touch them all with His healing virtue.

Ten desperate men cried out to a stranger because they were hopeless. This stranger had stepped outside of eternity not only to hear them, but to also meet them in their plight. As a result, their lives would never be the same.

Ten hopeless men cried out, and heaven heard and touched them, changing their devastating plight. These ten men left rejoicing, but only one came back to thank the one Man who took the time to hear, care, and do the incredible.

The man who came back to thank the Man, Jesus, not only understood the isolation his terrible disease had caused him, but most likely, he understood that separation could go deeper than a terrible disease. Such things as beliefs, race, and culture can cause separation. After all, he was a Samaritan who did not fit within any other culture except the one he was born into.

He was the one who in spite of his overwhelming joy realized that joy had an origin. In his case, it could be traced back to the Man named Jesus. He recognized that his newfound healing was an act of mercy because he knew he didn't deserve it.

Thankfulness begins with recognition that any act upon those who are destitute is a display of mercy, kindness, and grace. This man knew the hopelessness of destitution, but in spite of his plight, he had experienced supernatural benevolence. Such an act deserved a proper response.

This Samaritan realized his healing was not only supernatural, but also an act that should not be ignored or taken for granted. Luke 17:15-16 states, "And one of them, when he saw that he was healed, turned back, and with a loud voice glorified God. And fell down on his face at his feet, giving him thanks." We see four distinct responses from this man when he realized he was healed. First, he turned back. In other words, he went back to the source.

It is not unusual to benefit from something and never consciously take note of what really happened. This reminds me of the story of the prodigal son. He never realized what his inheritance cost his father. He took it for granted and contended that it belonged to him regardless of his father's present status; therefore, he had a right to do with it as he desired. In a way, in his own mind, he considered his father as good as dead. Therefore, he had every right to his inheritance. What an affront against his father. But this was the mocking fruit of this son's selfish disposition. Since the origin of his attitude was from selfishness, he ended up foolishly squandering his inheritance because he lusted after it, instead of appreciating what it represented.

When the prodigal son fell on hard times, he began to recognize what he had available in his father's house. At that point, he came back to his senses and returned to the source of his blessings, just like the Samaritan.[1] Coming back is an automatic response of thankfulness that is born in the heart of an individual who finally recognizes that the real treasures are always the products of the sacrifice, mercy, and grace of others.

Much of the time gratitude is missing because man simply fails to comprehend the blessing. This failure is due to man's spiritual blindness to the cost and meaning of such blessings.

Unlike the prodigal son, the Samaritan recognized what had happened before he squandered the opportunity and blessing. It is at the point of recognition that gratitude takes root in a person's heart. It is hard for people to realize that they deserve their despairing lot in life, and any intervention to change it is an act of mercy and grace.

This is the problem where the cross of Christ is concerned. It represents the bountiful eternal riches of God, but many people fail to realize what this point of redemption is all about. They know it is an act of love, but they fail to see the holiness that demanded such drastic actions. This incredible love had to overcome judgment of sin with great mercy and unlimited grace, and silence death with resurrection power. When a person fails to come to a balanced and realistic understanding of the cross of Christ, gratitude is never allowed to take root and produce a heart of thankfulness.

This Samaritan took note and gratitude took root, bringing forth glory to God. In a loud voice, this man began to glorify God. Here is a man who was isolated and shunned, but now he is unhindered in his excitement to bring glory to God. His silent cries turned to joy, and his loud declaration of God's greatness rang out as he received in his spirit the magnificent truth of his healing. God had touched him, and his life would never be the same.

---

[1] Luke 15:11-32

How many in the Church of Christ realize that the cross of Christ is God's way of not only reaching across incredible barriers to reach every man, but is also His way of touching man? People who have truly been touched by Christ's cross know that their lives will never be the same. This realization causes gratitude to take root in their hearts, ultimately bringing glory to God.

The next thing this man did was to fall down at the feet of Jesus. This action shows humility and worship. True worship is a form of thankfulness. You cannot worship God unless you take note of who He is and what He has done on your behalf. Once you begin to glimpse the reality of God and His goodness in your life, there is no way you will be able to restrain yourself from humbly thanking Him.

This was true for the Samaritan. Once he bowed before the Lord of lords, he thanked Him. This is the face of thankfulness. Its source is God, its roots are gratitude, and it responds by glorifying God. It boldly rejoices, visibly worships, and verbally thanks the One who made it all possible.

Have you recently taken note of what God has done for you, beginning with the cross of Christ? Have you turned aside from your activities to go to the One who has changed your eternal destination? Is there evidence of gratitude in your heart? In other words, can people around you now see the face of thankfulness in your worship, service, and life? On the other hand, do you need to go back to the cross of Christ to realize what was made abundantly available to you by His death, in order to establish missing gratitude?

5

MADE WHOLE

And besought him that they might only
touch the hem of his garment:
and as many as touched
were made perfectly whole.
Matthew 14:36

Thankfulness will always bring people back to the source that blessed them. The Samaritan found himself at the feet of Jesus, the One who had healed him. His heart was full of gratitude, his lips full of praise, and his face and knees in the position of adoration and worship.

This man responded to Jesus. Now, Jesus would reciprocate by recognizing the significance of this man's action, "Were there not ten cleansed? But where are the nine" (Luke 17:17)?

People often have the wrong impression of God. They assume He will automatically step on the scene for their convenience. However, Jesus showed that He only responded to the cries and actions of others as they had reached out to Him.

Ten men were crying out to Him when Jesus healed them, but the Samaritan was the only one who came back to personally thank Him. How could Jesus not respond to this man's thankfulness and adoration?

There is a name for Jesus' response. It is called *grace*. Watchman Nee defined God's grace by explaining how it works. It is only when man is at the state where there is no way to solve problems on his own that he is ready to realize love as grace. Therefore, as sinners, we are prime candidates to embrace love that was manifested to us in grace. Mr. Nee went on to explain how grace flows downward; therefore, it can never be realized if we consider ourselves at the same level as God. Granted, love reaches across, but grace reaches downward; therefore, only those who are humbly below God can experience the reality of His grace.[1]

It is vital that Christians remember that we need to make the first step towards God in destitution and humility, and then He will meet us in perfect love that will express itself as grace.[2] It does not take great prayers or deeds to get God's attention. It only takes a desperate plea, a humble spirit, and a grateful heart.

---

[1] The Riches of Watchman Nee; © Living Stream Ministry; pg. 46
[2] Matthew 5:3

Notice Jesus' next statement in verse 18, "There are not found that returned to give glory to God, save this stranger." Since this man was a Samaritan and not of the house of Israel, he was considered a stranger. However, God has always recognized and provided a special place for strangers.

Provision for six refuge cities was made in the Law of Moses. These cities were set aside for the *manslayer, stranger,* and *sojourner.* No doubt God wanted to use these cites to remind the children of Israel that until He laid claim to them, and brought them forth out of Egypt they were also considered strangers in need of a safe haven. These cities also pointed to the ultimate refuge, God. Deuteronomy 33:27a states, "The eternal God is thy refuge, and underneath are the everlasting arms."

Psalm 9:9 tells us, "The LORD also will be a refuge for the oppressed, a refuge in times of trouble."

Jesus had not only come for Israel, but for this Samaritan who would be regarded as a stranger. In fact, this stranger fit the criteria of needing a refuge, and because of his response to Jesus, he was positioned at a place of humility-at Jesus' feet. He was an oppressed stranger in trouble who found the ultimate refuge. Jesus said in Matthew 11:28-30, "Come unto me, all ye that labour and are heavy laden, and I will give you rest. Take my yoke upon you, and learn of me; for I am meek and lowly in heart: And ye shall find rest unto your souls. For my yoke is easy, and my burden light."

The Samaritan had come to Jesus, and now he personally encountered the One who had healed him. He had returned to thank Him, only to receive something much greater than his healing. And, what could be greater than healing? It is something called a new, powerful life.

Jesus told this man that his faith had made him whole or complete. There is an important distinction in this situation. Healing and spiritual wholeness are two different conditions. Healing in this case had to do with the physical condition of a person, while wholeness includes the spirit and soul.

Jesus instructed this man to rise up physically, but He was pointing to a spiritual reality. This man had not only encountered a Man who had the power to heal, but who had the gift of life. Jesus said in John 14:6, "I am...the life."

Today, many people are seeking healing, but how many are seeking life? Healing does not denote real life, but real life implies healing. This man had been healed, but he had not received the spiritual life that comes only from God.

In a sense, this man had been in a spiritual grave. Jesus was telling him to rise up from that grave and its oppression to join the living, and begin to walk in newness of life. The reason Christ could offer the Samaritan greater life is because of this man's faith. He had believed Jesus. Godly faith not only responds in thankfulness and obedience, but it is able to receive. This man not only received his healing, but he was open to receive the fullness of life.

The life that Jesus offers is complete and whole. It brings a spiritual wholeness to the spirit and soul of man. After all, it is in man's spirit and soul that he is plagued by sin, oppressed by bondage, and condemned to death. Jesus' mission had been clear from the very beginning. He did not come to condemn the world, but to save it.[3] In reality, He had come for this man.

Ephesians 2:8 tells us we are saved through faith. The book of Romans talks about how we are justified by faith, and that what is not of faith is sin.[4] The Apostle Paul instructs us in 2 Corinthians 5:7 to walk by faith and not by sight. This walk will always lead a person back to the character, heart, and will of God in obedience. This is why Hebrews 11:6 tells us we cannot please God without faith.

The Samaritan man's action of faith led him back to Jesus. His response of faith not only glorified God, but it pleased Him. As a result, this man would receive the ultimate miracle from Jesus, eternal life.

It is important to note that Jesus healed this man while he was still at a distance. However, this man had to personally encounter, and in a sense, touch, Jesus, at which time he received wholeness of life. You can see this truth throughout people's encounters with Jesus. They had to touch Him before they were made whole.

Many people want the benefits of Jesus' life, but they are not willing to touch the reality of His life, death, and resurrection. They want wholeness, but they don't want to get too involved for it might require something from them that they are unwilling to release. This unwillingness to become identified with Jesus is the sin of unbelief.

This brings us back to an important point. Ten men were healed, but only one was made whole. This shows us that the majority of these men failed to encounter all that Jesus had for them. Sadly, this is a realistic picture of mankind. Jesus will cross many people's paths, but few will encounter His fullness.

This is why we need to heed this one man's example. We must not be part of the majority, but we must be the one who will never settle for less. We must be the Samaritan, who did not take the miracle or the source of it for granted.

The Samaritan's physical condition had made him destitute. Likewise, our fallen, sinful condition makes us destitute. Each person must realize that he or she is most miserable if help is not sought from the only source that can make each of us whole.

The Samaritan took the risk by putting his faith in a stranger by crying out for mercy. The stranger was not just any man; He was and is

---

[3] John 3:17
[4] Romans 14:23; James 2

God Incarnate, the great I AM, who is not only a physician who tends to the needs of the body, but also to the soul and spirit. It is important to realize that Jesus always begins as a stranger to everyone, but there must be a time that each of us cries out to Him for mercy out of desperation and faith. We must take the risk of rejection and disappointment in order to encounter Him.

Jesus heard their cries and stopped. God will always stop to hear the cries of those who are desperately seeking the answer. As a result, this man was healed.

Once the Samaritan realized he was healed, he came back to the source of his blessing. To come back in the spiritual realm means to repent. 2 Peter 3:9 states that God is not willing that any perish, but that all come to repentance. God so desires us to turn back from our present course, and come to the source of real life and eternal blessings. For this reason, we must come back to the source of our salvation and healing to ensure that we receive the complete life God has made available to each of us.

The Samaritan not only came back, but he gave glory to God. When was the last time God was glorified in your life? When was the last time you truly considered what He has done for you?

This outcast fell at the feet of Jesus in thanksgiving and worship. When was the last time you truly thanked God for everything, and worshiped at His feet in Spirit and truth?[5]

As a result, this man was made whole. When was the last time you experienced the power of Jesus' life in you because of faith? Make sure that you have not hid unbelief under the cloak of religiosity. Make sure you have not settled for being a bystander who may benefit from Jesus, but have never personally touched Him in order to embrace the essence of His abundant and everlasting life. In short, examine yourself and find out when you last encountered and touched the great I AM.

---

[5] John 4:23-24

Step Two

THE SEARCHING HEART

6

THE INVITATION

If any man thirst, let him
come unto me, and drink.
John 7:37

In the next encounter, found in John 4, Jesus passed through Samaria, on His way to Galilee. His humanity was evidenced by the weariness that seemed to beset Him. He chose to rest at Jacob's well, while His disciples went to town for food.

Jacob's well is located one-half mile south of Sychar on the high road from Jerusalem. This place symbolizes crossroads; for it is here that the road curves between Mount Gerizim and Mount Ebal.

It was on Mount Ebal that Moses commanded Israel to erect a monument of stones (on which the Law was inscribed) and a stone altar. The children of Israel also stood facing each other at the base of these two mounts as the curses and blessings of the Law were proclaimed.[1] This crossroad represented the choice between life with its blessings and death with it curses. Such a choice hinged on whom a person would ultimately choose to serve. In a way, this crossroad stands between the two covenants: That of the Law, which can do nothing more than curse, and that of grace which brings life and blessings.

This particular place is also situated close to Joseph's tomb, and is one of the most authentic sites in all Biblical lands.[2] Joseph's tomb reminded spiritual sojourners that the eldest son of Jacob and Rachel was not only a great leader, but also a man of great faith. Joseph's faith that God would lead Abraham's descendents into the Promised Land was so immovable that he made his brethren promise to carry his bones with them into the land of blessings.

For over four hundred years, Joseph's bones rested in a foreign land. For over forty years, they were carried in the wilderness because of rebellion. Finally, after hundreds of years of being a stranger in a foreign place, Joseph's bones entered the Promised Land. It is important to note that this great patriarch was only the third person to enter the Promised Land, along with Joshua and Caleb of the older generation. His bones were not left in a foreign land or to the elements in the wilderness like

---

[1] Genesis 50:24-26; Deuteronomy 27:4-26

[2] The Thompson Chain-Reference Bible, © 1988 by the B. B. Kirkbride Bible Company, Inc., Archaeological Supplement; #4388

those who had rebelled, but were brought in by the surviving generation, where they were finally put to rest.

Joseph's bones may have been brought into the Promised Land in a coffin, but both his faith and testimony of God were still very much alive and still live among the many ruins of Palestine today. The tomb of Joseph may represent the promises of God that are not fully realized by the saint in his or her present life, but it boldly declares that God will ultimately keep all of His promises.

This is the place were Jesus chose to rest. He was surrounded by silent, living testimonies of the greatness of God and the unshakable faith of those who chose to believe Him in spite of the insurmountable circumstances that confronted them. However, was Jesus simply passing through? According to John 4:4, He was compelled to take this route. Did He simply stop at this place because He was weary and needed to be refreshed, or did He stop because it represented a crossroad for an unsuspecting individual?

Nothing happens by accident in God's economy. He never wastes time, energy, or lives. He never takes detours. He has a specific plan for every person's life. And, at the proper time, He steps on the scene at the right crossroad, to meet with that person. Jeremiah 29:11 tells us, "For I know the thoughts that I think toward you, saith the LORD, thoughts of peace, and not of evil, to give you an expected end."

Jesus' earthly life verifies this reality. He went out of His way when He came to earth and stepped on the scene of history in the midst of turmoil and struggles for Israel. Even though crowds surrounded Him, He only met and acknowledged hurting and seeking individuals. He always heard the cries of the few, took time to sup with the lonely outcast, and spoke with the isolated rejects.

In each event, it appeared as if Jesus only had a narrow window of time within which to operate. He had come by way of a manger in Bethlehem, during a time of registration and taxation, and left by way of a cross, during the Passover. Each encounter that He had represented a small opening in which to reach into the hearts of men. Knowing that God ordained the timing, He redeemed every minute by walking through these narrow openings, forever changing the lives of the hopeless, lost, and seeking.

Ephesians 5:16 instructs us to redeem the time, for the days are evil. If we are walking in obedience, we must have faith that God ordains all of our encounters. We must also be faithful to take advantage of every window of opportunity to minister the life of Christ to others.

Once again in John 4:7-24, Jesus was about to enter through a window of opportunity. It was in the afternoon, the sixth hour, when He came to the well. This was the time that one lone woman came to the well to draw water.

According to historical teachings, this was unusual because the normal practice of the culture of that day was that the women of the community drew water for their daily needs in the morning when it was cooler. It was a social gathering where the women met and exchanged greetings, news, and the latest gossip.

The fact that this lady came in the heat of the day, and alone, proved that something was amiss in her life. It implied that she was an outcast, and probably at different times, a topic of conversation among the women who socialized at the well.

This woman was not expecting to meet a stranger, especially of Jewish descent. She had come in the heat of the day to probably avoid the crowds, but she could not ignore this man when He asked her for a drink. She was shocked that a Jew would ask her for water, for after all, she was considered unorthodox, a dog.

This is where we begin to see the personality of this woman. She was personal and inquisitive. She was not shy and afraid to speak when it came to asking questions. "How is it that thou, being a Jew, askest drink of me, which am a woman of Samaria? For the Jews have no dealings with the Samaritans" (John 4:9b). Was this man, Jesus ignorant of the maintained cultural practices? Like others who were forced to adhere to such practices, this woman was aware that some practices maintained respect and order within a culture, while other practices hid and condoned prejudices.

She was surprised that this man did not uphold and maintain the practices that had separated her people from the Jewish nation. She did not realize this Man was not subject to the prejudices of finite man that are often marked by pettiness, fear, ignorance, and hatred. He was subject to a higher law that looked beyond race, gender, culture, and beliefs to see the hearts of men and women.[3]

This is when this Jewish stranger responded to her question with an unusual offer, "If thou knewest the gift of God, and who it is that saith to thee, Give me to drink; thou wouldest have asked of him, and he would have given thee living water" (John 4:10b). Obviously, this stranger saw beyond her race and culture something of greater significance--a thirsty soul. After all, why would He offer her living water if she did not have a parched soul?

I'm sure something stirred deep within her soul. This man was offering her something that was not tangible, something that had spiritual meaning and substance. He was offering her something that was living.

No doubt questions flowed as she struggled to understand His invitation, "Sir, thou hast nothing to draw with, and the well is deep: from whence then hast thou that living water? Art thou greater than our father Jacob, which gave us the well, and drank thereof himself, and his children, and his cattle" (John 4:11b)?

She could not see where this stranger had any physical means to change the condition of her thirst. How could He capture water without a

---

[3] Acts 10:34; Galatians 3:28

vessel? She did not realize that she would serve as the vessel that would cradle the waters of the Living God. All this stranger had to do was uncap this water in her soul.

Jesus looked at her, knowing the origin of every question and the struggle of her soul to grasp the invitation. He was also aware of her sincere willingness to receive. "Whosoever drinketh of this water shall thirst again, But whosoever drinketh of the water that I shall give him shall never thirst; but the water that I shall give him shall be in him a well of water springing up into everlasting life" (John 4:13b-14).

For years, Jacob had been the hero of the Samaritans of Sychar because he had provided the well that sustained their life and livelihood for all of their generations. But now a Man stood before her who was offering water that was not only capable of quenching the thirst of a longing soul, but would also bring forth eternal life.

Jacob, the great patriarch, was now fading in the light of this Man. Could this Jewish stranger offer such water? Her soul longed for it. And, there was only one way to find out, and that was to ask for it, "Sir, give me this water, that I thirst not, neither come hither to draw" (John 4:15b).

This Samaritan woman recognized that she was thirsty, but the thirst in question was not of a physical nature, but of a spiritual condition. Her desire to quench it once and for all showed that she was tired of contending with the craving that plagued her soul. She was ready to receive.

This woman's response towards Jesus was that of child-like faith. She believed what He said, and reached out to receive it. There are many people who are spiritually thirsty even in the religious realm. They come to various cisterns provided by man to be refreshed, only to walk away with a greater longing.

It is the heart of Jesus to step on the scene at these broken cisterns and worldly wells, and personally meet with every thirsty soul.[4] All a person has to do is ask for the living water and receive it by faith. It is the refreshing of the thirsty soul that begins to bring forth seeds of thankfulness. After all, nothing is as satisfying as quenching the craving of a longing soul.

Are you thirsty? Jesus' invitation remains the same, "...If any man thirst, let him come unto me, and drink" (John 7:37).

---

[4] Jeremiah 2:13

7

THE SEARCHING HEART

Search me, O God, and know
my heart: try me, and know my
thoughts. And see if there
be any wicked way in me,
and lead me in the way
everlasting.
Psalm 139:23-24

A lone woman stood before Jesus, spiritually ready to receive Living Water. However, before she could receive, He had to set her free to be an open and receptive vessel. Besetting sin oppressed this woman.[1] She was thirsty because leanness had come into her unsatisfied soul. Obviously, she had been searching for something, but it had been in all the wrong places.

Jesus knew this woman's history. He was aware of the lifestyles that had oppressed her and made her an outcast. He also knew something else. This woman had a searching heart. A searching heart is a heart that is weary of dead ends and desires the truth. It is a heart that is ready to grasp that which will fill its emptiness, satisfy its longings, and answer its silent cries.

Jesus turned the searchlight on her life in John 4:16. "Go call thy husband, and come hither." His searchlight was not only about to expose the sin in her life, but also reveal the things she pondered in her heart.

The woman answered, "I have no husband" (John 4:17).

Jesus said unto her, "Thou hast well said, I have no husband: For thou hast had five husbands; and he whom thou now hast is not thy husband: in that saidst thou truly."

It is important to note the significance of this exchange. In a way, Jesus was testing her. She was in sin, but she did not try to justify or make her actions right by dressing them up with excuses or false impressions. Jesus is the truth, and He can only deal with people at the point of truth. If this woman had not been honest, He would have been unable to address the real issues of her life.

Consider the manner in which He exposed her sin. He did not condemn her for her lifestyle. He simply pointed it out, and because of

---

[1] Hebrews 12:1

333

His attitude towards her moral deviance, it became an avenue to confirm something of greater importance to her. Jesus' insight proved to this woman that He was not just an ordinary Jewish man out to condemn her. John 4:19 tells us the woman's reaction to His insight, "Sir, I perceive that thou art a prophet."

Jesus not only had this woman's attention, but now He had her respect. She had started out suspicious of this stranger, but now He was quickly graduating to the status of a prophet who had both spiritual authority and credibility. After all, this stranger knew all about her, implying He was not just a stranger in regards to her life, but that He somehow knew her personally, and He actually cared. This allowed Him to reach into her very being.

Now, this woman could comfortably ask Him questions that had plagued her heart. Obviously, these questions had been there for a while, but now she believed she would receive the correct answer from the Prophet. "Our fathers worshipped in this mountain: and ye say, that in Jerusalem is the place where men ought to worship" (John 4:20).

Are you beginning to see why Jesus came by way of Samaria? Can you begin to understand what Jesus was really after? This woman's heart's desire was to know how to worship God. Most likely, this woman had been searching for the answer without any resolution. Her life tells us she got sidetracked or searched in the wrong places, but her question tells us her heart longed to know how to properly worship God. It also shows us that she had never lost the wonder that surrounded her Creator.

Today, many people are searching for something real and eternal. Their search leads them to many dead ends, on various detours, and occasionally they find themselves in a place where sincere questions become silent cries of the heart. Even though these people may fall into sin, their heart still longs for the reality of the Invisible One who can be gently perceived in the recesses of the heart, and felt in the longing soul by those who are child-like in faith.

These are the people whom Jesus will meet at the crossroads of their life. He will not meet them at the point of their failures. Rather, He will encounter them on the basis of their longing heart. He will go out of His way to answer their questions about the things that are close to the heart of God, but have been silenced by religious traditions and platitudes. After all, God's heart is that we commune with Him, and worship is the place of communion.

Jesus makes four main statements to this woman about worship, which begins to unveil God's heart. His first comment is found in John 4:21, "Woman, believe me, the hour cometh, when ye shall neither in this mountain, nor yet at Jerusalem worship the Father." He is telling this woman that there is going to be a time that worship will not hinge on one place. This is in reference to the Old Testament where God only put His name on one location and that was on the temple in Jerusalem.[2] The Samaritans had established Mount Gerizim as their special worship place. However, to the Jews, Mount Gerizim lacked God's approval for He had not chosen it, nor had He placed His name there.

How many people today feel you can only worship in a religious place? Jesus is trying to prepare this woman to realize that one can worship God anywhere. It is not the place that inspires worship, but the spiritual heart condition of man.

This is Jesus' second statement in John 4:22, "Ye worship ye know not what: we know what we worship: for salvation is of the Jews." Here is a woman who had been part of the religious system of the Samaritans. For years, she has been told the way to worship God. Yet, this Prophet is telling her that she does not even know Who she is worshipping. This would be a hard saying, and would insult any religious person who took pride in his or her particular form of worship or belief.

Surprisingly, this statement did not cause this woman to turn from Jesus. After all, she believed Him to be a true prophet who could rightfully answer her questions. Apparently, she had questions about the form of worship that she had been exposed to. Jesus was telling her that the reason worship was not a reality to her was because she did not know whom she was worshipping.

This woman, like so many in the various religions of the world, had a concept about God, but she did not know the real God. How can a person worship someone he or she does not know personally? Worship of this nature is done in vain.[3]

Jesus' third statement could even be more insulting to those who take pride in their religious roots, "We know what we worship: for salvation is of the Jews" (John 4:22b). Imagine someone telling you that you were wrong about God, and that the group that has greatly opposed your religious beliefs is right. Statements such as these have caused crusades and wars to take place.

He goes on to tell her that the reason the Jews are right is because salvation will come through them. Today, there are many religious groups who claim to have a corner on truth. They imply they know the heart and mind of God. But Jesus is clear here. The Jews know the real God, for salvation was to come through them, and no other race, group, or nation.

We know that Jesus was making reference to the salvation He would provide. God preserved the Jewish Nation to bring forth the Savior of the world. He continues to preserve the Jewish nation in order to fulfill all the promises He had made to Abraham about the future of the King of kings and His chosen nation.

---

[2] Deuteronomy 12:5, 11, 21; 14:23, 24; 16:2, 6, 11
[3] Matthew 15:8-9

This brings us to the fourth statement found in John 4:23, "But the hour cometh, and now is, when the true worshippers shall worship the Father in spirit and in truth: for the Father seeketh such to worship him. God is a Spirit: and they that worship him must worship him in spirit and truth." This is a very powerful declaration not only about worship, but also about the character and heart of God.

Keep in mind, that the Father is seeking those who will worship Him in spirit and truth. Jesus had found this woman—she had not found Him. Her question is about how to properly worship God. Obviously, God Incarnate came by way of Samaria to answer this woman's real heart desire, which was to be a worshipper of the one true God.

The next thing Jesus states is that God is Spirit; therefore, you must worship Him in the right spirit in line with the truth about His character. True worship is not just a matter of paying some kind of homage to something or someone referred to as God. In fact, man cannot properly worship God unless the Holy Spirit is prevalent in his life, for He is the only One who enables a person to properly worship.

The Holy Spirit brings about worship as He unveils the character of God, by revealing Jesus Christ. For in Christ dwells the fullness of the Godhead bodily. Jesus is the truth about the character of God, and as the Holy Spirit leads you to Jesus, He, in turn, will lead you into communion with the Father.[4]

Amazingly, Jesus' hard statements did not insult her. This shows us that she really wanted the truth. Jesus was stating the truth, knowing that not only would His statements answer her questions, but they also would set her free. As John 8:32 tells us, "And ye shall know the truth, and the truth shall make you free."

Each statement of truth was setting this woman free. And, each statement was enlarging her to accept the ultimate truth. Jesus was simply preparing her heart to receive the truth about Him.

Many searching people start out trying to discover answers to those things that press heavily against them. They begin looking inwardly to understand the reasoning behind their discontentment. Eventually, they end up focusing on something that stands on the outside of what they know, ready to answer the questions that have caused inward bondage.

This woman was about to find out whom she must worship. Her discoveries would cause her to rejoice with thanksgiving, as she discovered the true identity of the God of Israel.

This is why true worship finds its basis in thanksgiving. Many people think thanksgiving comes forth because of God's goodness towards them. This is partially true, but real thanksgiving that leads to worship comes when one discovers the true identity of God. It is the reality of God that stirs a searching heart to thankfulness. Such thankfulness automatically leads to worship.

---

[4] 2 Corinthians 13:14; Colossians 2:9

The Samaritan woman at the well was not only learning about worship, but she was being led through the steps that would lead to it. What a loving, committed God we serve. Let us thank Him for His love, grace. and salvation. As we thank Him for what He has done for us, we will begin to praise Him for who He is. This is why the writer of Hebrews penned this inspired scripture, "By him therefore let us offer the sacrifice of praise to God continually, that is, the fruit of our lips giving thanks to his name" (Hebrews 13:15).

Are you at a crossroad in your life because you are searching for a greater reality of God in order to worship Him? If you are, get ready to meet the One who will answer the silent longings of your heart, and lead you into unhindered adoration of your Creator.

8

"I AM HE"

Search the scriptures;
for in them ye think ye have eternal life:
and they are they, which testify of me.
John 5:39

The Samaritan woman was hearing truth about God and worship. The Man who was speaking forth the truth had gone beyond her race and sin-laden past to reach deep into her thirsty soul. In doing so, He had uncovered a longing heart that desired to know the truth about God.

Jesus spoke truths that were simple enough for a child to embrace, but profound enough to change a person's life. Such truths are hard to describe. They are marked with a touch of eternity that is often foreign to the natural ears of the arrogant, but satisfying to the thirsty soul of the humble.

This woman had been searching for truths that would not only silence her longing heart, but also change her life. However, where do spiritual searches take a person when he or she is tired of the religious scene and desires to know the truth?

Her spiritual search had brought her to this place in her life, not by some great religious movement, but by one man. It did not happen in some religious setting, but in the midst of normalcy. This woman was standing at a well that symbolized a spiritual significance to the Samaritans of her village, but served more as an important source of physical water. She was at a physical crossroad between the two mounts that represented the curses and blessings of God; however, the location was part of her every day life.

Everyone stands daily at crossroads where decisions must be made as to the type of life each of us will experience. What was different and significant is that she stood before a Jewish Prophet who knew all about her, and who was answering her questions. He was not giving her platitudes or pat religious answers. He was not rebuking her for her sin or exalting Himself over her ignorance.

The question now is will this encounter satisfy her heart or create more unanswered questions? I am sure she wanted her search to come to an end. But what would actually mark the end of her spiritual journey? In her next statement, she finally revealed what she had really been looking for all along, "I know that the Messiah cometh which is called Christ: when he is come, he will tell us all things" (John 4:25). This woman had many questions about spiritual matters, but she was really looking for someone. She was looking for the long-awaited Messiah who she believed would answer all the questions of her longing heart. By faith, she had not only believed He would come, but that He would put to rest the restlessness of her soul.

Now we are beginning to see the full spectrum of this woman. She was not looking for the right religious group, but she was actually looking for one person, the Jewish Messiah. She was asking questions about God and worship, but she also perceived those answers to such questions were linked to the coming Messiah. In fact, in her mind, this Messiah would be the key or solution to all of the conflicts and confusion that confronted her spiritual world. Because of this silent hope, He alone would mark the end of her long search.

This expectancy shows us the real desire of this woman. She wanted the Messiah to step on the scene and put to rest the doubts, questions, and conflicts plaguing her spiritual world. Many people would consider this woman in light of her past and say to themselves, "The world could do with fewer people like her." I consider this woman and declare the opposite. The world, as well as the Church, could do with more people like her. After all, she was expecting the Messiah to come and make her confusing world right again.

No wonder Jesus came by way of Samaria. He knew in His pre-incarnate state that He would meet this Samaritan woman at the well. He would meet her because she was expecting Him. He would meet her as the Messiah to answer her questions about God and worship. He would meet her to make sense out of her confusing world. He would meet her because she believed, and He would not let her down.

To me, it is amazing that this woman was expecting the Messiah. We have no idea as to how she perceived the Messiah other than that He was expected and would answer all of her questions. No doubt the Samaritans laid claim to the Messiah because of Jewish influences, but to what extent is unknown. The Messiah was to come to the Jewish nation, not to the Samaritans. If half of her lineage really did go back to Abraham, her claim on the Messiah was partial at best. In spite of the debate that was raging over the religious differences between these two religious camps, she was still looking for Him.

The Jews were another story. They had a pure lineage that went back to Abraham and knew that the promises of God surrounded them as a nation. As a result, they had an unhindered claim on the Messiah. Like the Samaritan woman, the Jewish people, too, were looking for the Messiah. They had strict qualifications surrounding the promised Messiah found in the Old Testament. Even though Jesus fit all of these qualifications, many rejected him.[1] They may have been looking for Him, but when He came, they were not ready to receive Him.

---

[1] John 1:10-11

What was the difference between scores of Jewish people and this Samaritan woman? It comes down to the heart condition. Many of the Jewish people were not ready for Him because they had closed hearts towards the truth, and their souls were full of stagnant water drawn from man's traditions. The Samaritan woman was ready for the Messiah because she was searching for the truth.

This reminds me of Jeremiah's words, "And ye shall seek me, and find me, when ye shall search for me with all your heart" (Jeremiah 29:13). It was her searching heart that made her ready for the Messiah to step on the scene, and end her long spiritual journey.

Jesus said this to her: "I that speak unto thee am he." Jesus introduced Himself to her at this point. He was saying, "I am the Messiah." God always introduced Himself. His introduction usually began with the same words, "I AM!" This statement not only ushers a person into the present tense, but also makes God a Living Being who is real and up front. In fact, the term "I AM," brings a person into the only reality that is present, real, significant, and eternal.

Each time God introduced Himself, He would always unveil another characteristic of His unchanging nature. "I am thy shield, I am the Lord, I am the Almighty God, I am the God of Abraham, I am the God of Bethel, I am gracious, I am He." His names are endless and not only unveil His heart, mind, and will, but His infinite character that creates awe in a pure heart, inspiration in a child-like mind, confidence in the fearful, and will humble the most arrogant of individuals.

Jesus, God Incarnate, is no different. He wants to introduce the reality of God to every searching heart. He wants to open up every closed heart, take away the veils from darkened minds, and take the scales away from blind eyes. His major invitation still echoes in the corridors of the Word of God today: "Behold, I stand at the door, and knock: if any man hear my voice, and open the door, I will come in to him, and will sup with him, and he with me" (Revelation 3:20.

True to form, Jesus' introduction often began with "I AM!" "I am meek and lowly, I am the Son of God, I am the bread of life, I am the light, I am the door, I am the good Shepherd, I am the Christ, I am the resurrection and the life, I am the true vine, and before Abraham was, I am."[2]

Jesus' desire to introduce Himself to everyone still remains true today. However, only those who have longing hearts, thirsty souls, and who are seeking the truth will be able to embrace Him as the One who fills every area of their hearts. Jesus is the end to all spiritual searches for He is the One who nourishes people with the bread from heaven and the everlasting water.

Over the centuries, many have heard about Jesus, but He simply remains a historical figure in their minds. Unless He is personally

---

[2] Matthew 11:28-30; John 6:35; 8:58; 10:7, 14, 11:25-26

introduced or unveiled by the Holy Spirit, a person will never be able to personally know Him as the Great I AM, the ever-abiding truth.

Consider, before Jesus introduced Himself to the Samaritan woman, He first answered her questions. It was as though He was verifying His identity by meeting her qualification, that the Messiah alone would answer her heart questions.

Can you imagine how this woman felt? Her long search had finally come to a blissful end as Jesus introduced Himself as the Messiah. She had been looking for Him. Now, He stood before her, and she would not be disappointed.

She must have perceived at one point that this meeting with Jesus did not happen by accident. The Messiah had gone out of His way to meet her. As a result, her thirsty soul was satisfied, her search for truth was completed, and her heart was changed.

However, what do you think replaced the emptiness in this woman's heart? After all, she could not leave this encounter unfeeling or indifferent. It is clear that once weary travelers such as the Samaritan woman reach their spiritual destination, there is an abundance of joy and thankfulness.

I have no doubt that this woman's heart filled with the overflowing waters of joy and thankfulness. In the next chapter, we are actually going to see how these two expressions of a grateful heart manifest themselves in the Samaritan woman.

The question is, are you searching for something that is real? Has your journey made you weary and hopeless? Better yet, when was the last time you personally encountered the great "I AM"? Jesus said it best, "I am the way, the truth and the life: no man cometh unto the Father, but by me" (John 14:6).

9

BOLDNESS

According to the eternal purpose
which he purposed in Christ
Jesus our Lord: In whom we
have boldness and access with
confidence by the faith of him.
Ephesians 3:11-12

Who would have suspected that the long-awaited Messiah would seek out a Samaritan woman, an outcast, to answer her questions? But, He did and now the woman's search finally came to an end. She had encountered the giver of Living Water. Now, she would house the very water she had asked Him for, the water that would bring eternal life.

This not only had to be a miraculous occasion for her, but a humbling one. Can you imagine all the emotions that were stirred up in her? She had to be excited, awed, joyful, and thankful all at once. How would such an array of emotions express themselves?

This encounter between Jesus and the Samaritan woman was suddenly interrupted by the return of His disciples. John 4:27 tells us what transpired, "And upon this came his disciples, and marveled that he talked with the woman: Yet no man said, what seekest thou? or, Why talkest thou with her?"

Jesus' disciples silently expressed the attitude that the Samaritan woman had expected from Him. They were surprised that Jesus had been talking to her. Questions were on the tips of their tongues, but they refrained. After all, their leader seemed to be drawn to the most unlikely people.

The question now was what would this woman do? Her life, as she knew it, had been interrupted. Would she simply go home and keep her meeting with this incredible Man quiet? Or would she say something? What would she do with the Messiah?

John 4:28-29 tells us what her next action was. "The woman then left her water pot, and went her way into the city, and saith to the men, Come see a man, who told me all things that ever I did: is not this the Christ?"

This woman responded to her meeting with Jesus in four distinct ways. First, she left her water pot. The water pot has two representations. Remember she had come to Jacob's well for water;

therefore, this water pot represented the normalcy for the woman. The Messiah had interrupted the normalcy of her life, and now it would never be the same. Her priorities and goals had been turned upside down.

This water pot also represented a daily need. Water was not only vital for life, but it was precious and scarce in that country. This woman had discovered something that went beyond a daily need to embrace an eternal hope: that of salvation. She had tasted something more precious than physical water, for she had discovered the wells of salvation and the joy of its water.[1]

Another thing we must observe is that she did not go home. Instead, she went to the city. Home represented her old life. Keep in mind that she was living in sin with a man. She did not go back to her old life. Her about-face showed that change had occurred, and now something else was compelling her. Obviously, if change had not taken place in her life, she would have simply gone home and thought nothing of it.

However, something did happen! She met the One who sets captives free with truth, heals broken hearts with forgiveness and hope, and brings light to those walking in great darkness. Because of her encounter with Jesus, her life was not only changed, but it would never be the same.

This woman went to the very place that she had probably been shunned, the city. As Isaiah said, she had seen a great light.[2] She was not about to hide it under a bushel. Joy overflowed and thankfulness bubbled forth with excitement. There was newness in her life, and there was only one thing to do, tell others. The Scripture tells us that she went to the men of the city.

In some circles today, her actions would be criticized and condemned. After all, a woman should not go to men, but to other women. Sadly, most women are very suspicious of women of this status. Most likely, the women of her society would not have even listened to her. On the other hand, men are not always leery of such people. This woman not only went to the ones who might listen, but she went to the leaders who would naturally lead others to the Messiah.

It is important to note at this time what was transpiring between Jesus and His disciples. Jesus was talking to them about the harvest field. The disciples had encouraged Him to eat, but He told them that His work was not finished. From this point, Jesus began to talk about the harvest and the urgency to reap while there was time.

This scenario amazes me. While Jesus talked to his disciples about the harvest field, a lone Samaritan woman was actually working in the harvest field. In fact, this woman was serving in the capacity of an evangelist because she was telling others about Jesus.

---

[1] Isaiah 12:3
[2] Isaiah 9:1-2

Many people test an instrument based on gender, status, qualifications, and appearance. However, God used this woman to reinforce an important point—He does not judge according to such surface qualifications, but according to the heart. [3]

God has always looked at the heart, and He judges a person on that basis. It is hard for man to accept God's judgment because his pride and hidden prejudices deceptively set him up to be the ultimate judge in people's lives. And, since man cannot see the heart, he judges according to vile pettiness, vain imaginations, and his own wickedness.

I also believe that at this time, Jesus spoke of the harvest to prepare His disciples to accept another hard truth—that the "unacceptable" Samaritans were part of the harvest as well. As we can see from John 4:39-42, this woman's testimony actually caused the men to come to Jesus to see for themselves. The result is that many believed. At this point, Isaiah's words would ring out, "How beautiful upon the mountains are the feet of him that bringeth good tidings, that publisheth peace; that bringeth good tidings of good, that publisheth salvation; that saith unto Zion, Thy God reigneth" (Isaiah 52:7)! The Samaritan woman's feet became beautiful as she carried the good news to those of her city. This woman who had been rejected by many now possessed the greatest treasure ever known to mankind.

This brings us to this woman's fourth response—she told others about her encounter. The Samaritan woman's willingness to tell others was a bold act. Boldness is another face, or expression of thankfulness.

Think about it. When something great happens to you, isn't it natural to share it? For example, a long-awaited birth of a child makes the parents ready to share the good news with others. Why? The parents are both joyful and thankful about the event.

Such a reaction should be true for a person who encounters the salvation of Jesus Christ. After all, there is a spiritual birth that takes place.[4] Because of this new spiritual birth, this individual has been spiritually healed, placed in an eternal family, filled to overflowing with grace, and restored to spiritual wholeness.

Sadly, many Christians are like the nine lepers who were healed, but never came back to the source of their healing. It amazes me that these same people who remain quiet about Jesus are quick to tell others about the latest diet, best recipe, a good story, or joke. The reason for their silence is usually the same as the nine lepers. They fail to recognize what really took place in their salvation, preventing gratefulness from taking root in their hearts. Such people usually tack Jesus on to their many activities and merrily go back to their old life.

The Samaritan woman understood that something of great significance had taken place in her life, and she was not about to treat it

---

[3] 1 Samuel 16:7
[4] John 1:12; 3:3, 6

lightly. She was not only awed and full of joy, but her bold actions show us that she was indeed thankful.

We do not know the name of this Samaritan woman, but it is not important. As a person, she is meant to decrease. However, what is important was the example she left us. This is why her encounter with the Messiah is in the inspired Word of God.

The example she left us has two major points that we can use to test the type of relationship we have with God through Jesus. First, if a person truly encounters the Messiah and receives His truth, he or she will have a changed life. People who call themselves Christians, but whose lives remain unchanged cause me to question the validity of their salvation experience. Secondly, if Christ has really touched your life, you cannot help but be bold. This boldness is a verbal expression of thankfulness for what He has done.

Right now, you might be saying, "Rayola, I am not verbal about my Christian life, so does that mean I am not thankful?" I realize that fear of failure and rejection plagues many people when it comes to sharing Christ. Even the Apostle Paul asked people to pray for him for boldness.[5]

However, what this woman's life shows me is that because her encounter with Jesus was real, she was quick to share her testimony at the right time. We must make sure that our unwillingness to share is not because we have left our first love. The greatest sign that our love for Jesus has grown cold is that we see no need to share Him with others.

I also realize that evangelism has been made complicated. This woman had no program to follow. She did not have any education or Bible degrees. She was not being led by some intellectual knowledge or training as to what she had to say. She was simply being led by her encounter with the Messiah. Therefore, her proclamation was nothing more than her honest testimony about Jesus Christ.

A testimony about Jesus is nothing more than the honest truth about what He did and is doing on your behalf.[6] It is a way of expressing thankfulness as you verbally acknowledge His intervention. As you grow in a relationship with Jesus, your testimony and level of thankfulness will grow as well. In fact, both will be fresh and exciting, not only to those who are seeking, and find themselves touched by your experience, but also to your own spirit as you proclaim the wondrous truths about the One who secured your salvation on the cross.

Let me leave you with Revelation 12:11, "And they overcame him by the blood of the Lamb, and by the word of their testimony; and they loved not their lives unto the death." (Emphasis added.)

---

[5] Ephesians 6:18-19

[6] If you would like to understand more about your testimony concerning Jesus, see the author's book, *The Power of Our Testimonies* in Volume Six of her foundational series.

Step Three

ETERNAL LIFE

10

RIGHT ANSWER, WRONG WAY

There is a way which seemeth
right unto a man, but the end
thereof are the ways of death.
Proverbs 14:12

The third incident did not directly involve a Samaritan, but as you will see, it is a Samaritan who is ultimately upheld. This Samaritan was the main character in one of Jesus' most popular parables, "The Good Samaritan."

In order to grasp the real theme behind this parable, we must understand what prompted this story. Luke 10:25 begins to set up the scene: "And, behold, a certain lawyer stood up, and tempted him, saying, Master, what shall I do to inherit eternal life?"

It may be hard to believe, but the parable of "The Good Samaritan" is about eternal life. When we think about this story, we remember the extra distance the Samaritan went to help someone, but we never associate his actions with the subject of everlasting life.

It is important to recognize that this lawyer was not asking the question about eternal life for himself. As we will see, he knew the answer, but he was trying to tempt or test Jesus.

Jesus encountered much testing in His three years of ministry. In most cases, He responded in the same manner by turning the test around to expose His challenger's motives. He managed this feat by answering questions with a question, as He did in this case. "What is written in the law? How readest thou?" (Luke 10:26).

The lawyer had tried to put Jesus on the defense, but the Son of God would never stoop to such games as defending Himself. He simply turned the tables on the aggressor, causing the aggressor to be on the defense.

The lawyer found himself answering the question rather than Jesus. He answered it according to the Law of Moses, "Thou shalt love the Lord thy God with all thy heart, and with all thy soul, and with all thy strength, and with all thy mind and thy neighbor as thyself" (Luke 10:27).

Jesus confirmed the lawyer's answer, "Thou hast answered right: this do, and thou shalt live" (Luke 10:28). Cleverly, Jesus caused this man to answer his own question. All he had to do to receive eternal life was to simply love God with everything in his being, and love his neighbor as himself.

This man understood the dynamics of eternal life, but there was a problem in his spiritual life. This brings us to some very important points. Most people know the answer to their spiritual needs; therefore, the problem rarely lies at the feet of ignorance, but in the heart of rebellion. This man knew how to obtain eternal life, but he didn't want to put into practice the dynamics of it by loving his neighbor.

James 1:22-25 gives us this insight,

But be ye doers of the word, and not hearers only, deceiving your own selves. For if any be a hearer of the word, and not a doer, he is like unto a man beholding his natural face in a glass. For he beholdeth himself, and goeth his way, and straightway forgetteth what manner of man he was. But whoso looketh into the perfect law of liberty, and continueth therein, he being not a forgetful hearer, but a doer of the word, this man shall be blessed in his deed.

Jesus was putting up a mirror in front of this lawyer. This man knew the Word of God, but he did not practice it. As a result, he was deceived about the real state of his spiritual condition. His deception kept him from facing the truth, but with the mirror before him, he could not deny the reflection he was seeing.

Consider how the lawyer handled the matter. "But he, willing to justify himself said unto Jesus, and who is my neighbour" (Luke 10:29)? This man saw himself as loving God, but the mirror exposed that he did not really love his neighbor. He actually tried to justify his lack of love for others by redefining his neighbor.

Justification in this way is typical of the human disposition. It is natural for each person to try to justify unloving and ungodly acts in his or her life by redefining the source or meaning of the action. The man was trying to delude himself about his real condition by covering up his rebellion, and justifying his self-righteous pride. It was out of this man's attempt to justify his lack of love that the parable of "The Good Samaritan" was unveiled.

Now, you might wonder what thankfulness has to do with eternal life or the parable of "The Good Samaritan." If you have eternal life, it will produce thankfulness. "The Good Samaritan" simply shows us the dynamics of eternal life. In other words, it shows us how eternal life will express itself. The expression of eternal life is not only that of thankfulness, but it will also inspire thankfulness in others.

Before we go on to unveil the face of thankfulness in "The Good Samaritan," let me summarize the lessons we have been learning about thankfulness in light of John 14:6. "Jesus saith unto him, 'I am the way, the truth, and the life: no man cometh unto the Father but by me."

In the first incident of the ten lepers, we see where Jesus walked in the midst of humanity to show the *way* of healing. In the situation surrounding the Samaritan woman, we see that Jesus went out of His way to show *truth*. Finally, in the third situation, we are going to see how Jesus brings *life*.

This brings us to how these lessons produce thankfulness. The first lesson shows us that it was not enough for Jesus to heal, but that a person must recognize what He has done before he or she can receive a full life. This recognition produces thankfulness.

In the second incident, a woman who was searching for truth found it in Jesus Christ. This truth not only changed her life, but it brought joy that expressed itself in excitement and thankfulness.

Finally, in the third situation, we will see how real life produces thankfulness. The type of thankfulness that comes out of eternal life expresses itself in liberal giving which always brings glory to God.

Now, let us follow Jesus as He begins to expose the heart of the lawyer in light of this priceless parable. At this time, allow the Lord to turn His searchlight on your heart. Make sure you are more than just a hearer of the Word of God.

11

AN EXPRESSION OF LOVE

By this shall all men know
that you are my disciples, if
ye have love one to another.
John 13:35

What started out to be a test of Jesus' spiritual credibility and leadership ended up revealing the spiritual commitment of the one testing Him. Jesus' interaction with the self-righteous lawyer would prove to be the lawyer's unveiling. This man probably believed he was spiritually on the right track. After all, he was a lawyer and had all the answers.

According to *Smith's Bible Dictionary*, the title "lawyer" is generally considered the equivalent to the title "scribe." Scribes were the ones who expounded the Law. They carefully studied the Law, and wrote or translated it for others. In fact, in Jesus' day, they were honored above the Law and considered the final authority. Obviously, this lawyer intellectually knew the Law, but Jesus was about to show that a person must be a doer of the Law for it to make an inward difference in the disposition of man.

The lawyer's arrogance and hypocrisy remind me of what the Apostle Paul said in 1 Corinthians 1:27-29 about the worth of man's intelligence and strength in the Lord's kingdom,

> But God hath chosen the foolish things of the world to confound the wise; and God hath chosen the weak things of the world to confound the things which are mighty; And base things of the world, and things which are despised, hath God chosen, yea, and things which are not, to bring to nought things that are: That no flesh should glory in his presence.

The lawyer's high opinion of himself kept him from being a candidate for God's wisdom, strength, and authority. His religious pride also kept him from being a recipient of eternal life.

Jesus was about to use what appeared to be an "unacceptable" Samaritan to reveal this man's true spiritual condition. He would take what this man considered despised to expose his own despicable heart attitude. He would take that which was abased to show this lawyer the wicked foundation he was operating from. He would take the foolish to unveil the lawyer's hypocrisy.

Even though Jesus told the lawyer he was not far from eternal life, in the end, He would show him that eternal life was far from the lawyer. After all, eternal life stood before this this religious leader. He was close to it, yet so very far from receiving it.

Eternal life was eluding the lawyer because he had deluded himself. When Jesus asked him what was needed to inherit eternal life, he gave Him two requirements: "You have to love God with everything in you, and your neighbor as yourself."

This man apparently saw himself as being obedient to the first commandment, but failing to adhere to the second. Here is where the self-delusion comes into the picture. If you do not love your neighbor as yourself, you do not love God either.

The Word of God is clear about our responsibility to love our neighbor, whether it is our enemy, our spouse, or those in our community. Loving our neighbor is not an option, but a godly responsibility. The reality is we cannot love our neighbor without loving God; and we will never be able to love our neighbor sacrificially unless the love of God abounds in our hearts. The Apostle John makes reference to this, "If a man say, I love God, and hateth his brother, he is a liar: for he that loveth not his brother whom he hath seen, how can he love God whom he hath not seen? And this commandment have we from him, that he who loveth God love his brother also" (1 John 4:20-21).

Obviously, loving one's neighbor is simply the visible expression of loving God. If I love God, I will love my neighbor. If I don't love my neighbor, it simply means I do not possess God and His love. John confirms this in 1 John 4:11-12, "Beloved, if God so loved us, we ought also to love one another. No man hath seen God at any time. If we love one another, God dwelleth in us, and his love is perfected in us."

The Word also tells us that if we love God, we will obey Him. Jesus confirmed this in His own words, "If ye love me, keep my commandments" (John 14:15).

This lawyer did not love God, because he did not obey Him. The type of self-delusion he displayed is a product of a hard heart. This is where the Word of God is written on the stony heart. Therefore, the Word never takes root, causing the person to make the Word of God legalistic, optional, and ineffective.

It is because of the stony heart, God made this statement in Ezekiel 36:26-27,

> A new heart also will I give you, and a new spirit will I put within you: and I will take away the stony heart out of your flesh, and I will give you a heart of flesh. And I will put my spirit within you, and cause you to walk in my statutes, and ye shall keep my judgments, and do them.

Obviously, this lawyer needed a reality check. Jesus will once again show how the matters of the Law were not meant to be a simple mental assent, but a matter of the heart. This man had made the Law a matter of knowledge. His attitudes and actions were verifying how dead the Law had become to him. The lawyer had been testing his own spiritual condition according to his delusion, rather than the fruits of his life. Jesus was about to lay open the fact that this man did not love God. This would not only shatter his delusion, but his comfortable perception of God as well.

Jesus put into practical terms the Law this man took pride in knowing. He described in rich detail how loving one's neighbor is the truest expression of knowing, loving, and obeying God. Jesus could speak about being a good neighbor with experience, authority, and power. After all, He had become a servant, and allowed Himself to be fashioned in the form of a man.[1] This measure not only allowed Him to become identified with man, but it gave Him the opportunity to display the qualities of a loving neighbor.

It is inconceivable for us to realize that God became man's neighbor, but He did. As a neighbor, God Incarnate proved to be caring, benevolent, and sacrificial. He never looked away from the sufferings and needs of others. He dined among sinners, extended his hand to outcasts, and met the lost and hopeless.

As man's neighbor, Jesus never did anything that personally benefited Him. He came down from glory to be man's neighbor. He gave His best, His all, and He did it for the glory of the Father and the benefit of man. His final act on the cross revealed His ultimate commitment as the neighbor to all mankind.

The example of Jesus as a neighbor is a tall order to fill. However, the truth is, for a Christian to be any less of a neighbor is to display irresponsibility and hypocrisy.

Keep in mind, Jesus told the lawyer if he would love God and his neighbor, he would inherit eternal life. Therefore, loving one's neighbor is the visible evidence that one loves God and has inherited everlasting life.[2]

What kind of neighbor are you? Don't deceive yourself about your spiritual condition. Would your actions display a stony heart towards your neighbor or a loving heart that cannot be indifferent to the plight of those around you? Do you close your eyes and ears to the needs of those around you or do you open your arms wide to embrace them as Jesus did each of us on the cross?

---

[1] Philippians 2:6-8
[2] 1 John 3:15-18; 4:7-14

12

THE COUNTERFEITS

This people draweth nigh unto me with their mouth,
and honoureth me with their lips;
but their heart is far from me.
Matthew 15:8

The lawyer who knew the Law asked Jesus who constituted his neighbor. This man was not asking out of innocence or ignorance for he knew the answer, but because he was trying to justify his lack of love for his neighbor. Without godly love, one will not properly respond to others.

It is at this point that Jesus answers his question with a parable. Parables were simple stories that had hidden nuggets of truth. Those with a pure heart would glean the nuggets, but those with hard hearts would pass over them, failing to recognize their real value and purpose.

Jesus began the parable by describing the one who would serve as an example of the neighbor. He refers to this potential neighbor as a "certain" man. According to *Strong's Exhaustive Concordance*, the word "certain" in this text can mean anybody. Right away, Jesus is establishing the fact that anyone regardless of race, culture, gender, religious preferences, or age is not to be exempt from neighborly kindness.

This certain man went down from Jerusalem to Jericho. It is amazing how Jesus threw this small detail into the story. This small bit of information about the man coming from Jerusalem would only tantalize the hearer's ears. This man could have been Jewish, which would definitely require a response from someone in the lawyer's position.

Such a detail also allowed for speculation as Jesus cleverly stretched the lawyer's mind to embrace unknown possibilities. The truth is no one knew this man's nationality or religious affiliation. However, in the recesses of many minds, such a detail allowed one to draw a conclusion about this man's nationality. In other words, this small bit of information had the potential of stirring up the imagination to fill in the blank spaces. As the possibilities started to take root, Jesus expertly painted a greater picture, crowding out this detail to encompass all possibilities. After all, a person's neighbor can be anyone.

On the way to Jericho, this certain man fell among thieves who stripped him of his clothes, wounded him, and left him for dead on the road. Now, Jesus is setting up a more uncomfortable scenario. This man who could be Jewish was now in a precarious position. He was requiring more than a neighborly "hello." He was in need of personal attention.

It just so happened that a certain priest was traveling down the same road. Once again, we encounter the word "certain." This priest could have been any one of the priests that served in the temple. He could be one of the lawyer's friends.

Priests had a very important position in the Jewish religion. They actually served as an intercessor or mediator between Jehovah God and the Jewish nation. As mediators, the priests would not only be concerned about reaching God, but about touching man.

The Law of Moses called for a proper response from those who represented it in the Jewish society. But, look at the priest's response to the wounded man. He pretended he did not see the man. His actions stated that the wounded man did not really exist, even though the priest had to walk over to the other side of the road to avoid coming too close to him. Obviously, the priest concluded that if he pretended to be blind or unaware of this man's plight, it would alleviate his responsibility towards him. His philosophy was simple, "Out of sight, out of mind."

The priest's response is symbolic of the ways and attitudes of the dead religion of man. Such religion is so often like the symbol of America's justice system, the blindfolded woman holding the balances. This symbol is to represent the fact that justice is blind to everything until the facts are weighed. The problem is that the balances are often lopsided, making justice not only blind when it serves its purpose, but ignorant as well.

Religion is different in the fact that it chooses to put on the blindfold to remain in blissful ignorance to basic responsibilities. Even though it may give the appearance of righteousness, it continues to deny the power that results in godly action as it travels in the ways of indifference and wickedness.[1]

The next person who came on the scene was a Levite. A Levite is a teacher of the Law. In Joshua's day, the Levites were disbursed throughout all Israel. It is interesting how the Levite responded to the beaten man.[2] Unlike the priest, he actually looked upon him, but afterwards, passed to the other side to avoid the truth concerning his responsibility.

Why did the Levite look at the man? He was probably determining if this man was important or worth saving. Remember, the Levite is the teacher of the law. Teachers evaluate and separate facts in order to teach them. This man was evaluating the situation and apparently deemed this man not significant enough to save, creating his own concept of truth or reality.

---

[1] 2 Timothy 3:5
[2] Joshua 21

Like the Levite, many people intellectualize Christ's words to apply them as they will, instead of applying them according to the Spirit of God. Such people act solely on the basis of what will serve their purpose. This form of evaluation is extremely sinister because it covers prejudices, justifies selfishness, and is highly judgmental.

The priest's reactions represent those of dead religion that chooses to be blind towards the ways of godly fundamental responsibilities. The Levite, on the other hand, represents the response of the dead letter of the Law towards the real spirit and truth behind it. A person who operates within the dead letter of the Law is unable to experience any real life because he or she has no heart. The Levite represents the Law that becomes a matter of the mind, rather than the heart. It lacks the very spirit, which could give it life and purpose.

In the case of the priest, he avoided looking at the wounded man to keep his conscience at bay. However, in the situation of the Levite, it actually showed he lacked a conscience that could be aroused to act in a compassionate manner. Both responses are unacceptable, but the second one is frightening.

The third person to encounter the victim was a certain Samaritan. It is important at this time to consider what kind of attitude would be invoked in this lawyer towards the identity of the third person in the parable. A Samaritan was an unacceptable individual especially to a pious man such as he was. He would avoid having any association with the likes of such a person. As we can begin to see, Jesus was probing past this man's religious veneer and self-righteous pride to expose his lack of love for his neighbors as nothing more than the sins of prejudice and self-righteousness, which are fruits of hatred.

This Samaritan who was passing through saw the wounded man and had compassion on him. As a Samaritan, he was not responsible to the Law of the Jews; therefore, he did not possess the burden of responsibility as the priest and the Levite. Yet, this man, who would have been looked down upon by a pious Jew, did not pretend the man did not exist. He did not ignore his plight. Rather, he took compassion on him.

"Compassion" in this text means to yearn in the bowels or be compelled to respond.[3] There are different ways to describe the response of compassion. First, real compassion not only takes responsibility for the hurting, but it becomes identified with the person. It actually enters into a person's sufferings. The Samaritan bound up the man's wounds, poured oil and wine on his wounds, and set him on his own beast to bring him to the inn where he took care of him.

The second type of compassionate response is that it will go the extra mile.[4] Not only did the Samaritan take responsibility to take care of

---

[3] Strong's Exhaustive Concordance of the Bible, #4697
[4] Matthew 5:39-44

this man, but he also went an extra mile to provide for all of his care until he was healed.

Finally, real compassion requires personal cost. The Samaritan's compassion cost him time, energy, and plenty of money. However, there is no indication that the Samaritan gave any thought to the expenses that his compassion incurred. His main concern was to make sure the man was properly cared for.

As Jesus came to the end of the parable, He asked, "Which now of these three thinkest thou was a neighbour unto him that fell among the thieves?" (Luke 10:36).

The lawyer could do nothing but respond in a correct fashion, "He that showed mercy on him" (Luke 10:37a). Notice how he did not directly accredit the Samaritan as being the good neighbor. It must have been a bitter pill for him to digest. An unacceptable man had proved to be godlier than a priest, a Levite, and even a lawyer.

In Jesus' description of who constituted a true neighbor, we begin to see that our neighbor is anyone we cross paths with in our journey on earth. It is easy to pretend or to ignore moral responsibilities, but in the end, God's probe will reveal the real condition of our hearts.

Let us now bring this down to a personal level. To be a good neighbor, we must not be blind to the needs of others, ignore the lost, nor disregard the unacceptable. If such people cross our path, we must reach out and touch them in their need. If we don't, we are no different than the hypocritical lawyer, the complacent priest, and the merciless Levite. All three lacked the love of God.

It is important to make sure that we are not justifying our lack of love by hiding behind position, religion, or the letter of the Law. We must have a religion that can be compelled to move with compassion, and a conscience that is not seared by intellectual pride. We must be willing to enter into the sufferings of others, and go the extra distance to make sure that such people's needs are taken care of to the best of our abilities.

Here is an important question to answer. If you were that man lying on the road, who would you want to come alongside of you, the priest, the Levite or the Samaritan? The answer is easy and so is the challenge, "Love your neighbor as yourself."

Finally, what kind of neighbor are you? Are you simply religious about such matters or are you compelled by the love of God? Are you shrewd about who you help or do you have real compassion? On judgment day, would God consider you a good neighbor? You are the only one who can honestly evaluate if you would be deemed a "Good Samaritan".

13

WILL THE REAL SAMARITAN PLEASE STAND UP?

In whom are hid all the treasures
of wisdom and knowledge.
Colossians 2:3

Jesus had lifted up to the lawyer the real example of what it meant to be a good neighbor. This lawyer had justified his lack of love, but now the parable of "The Good Samaritan" was not only revealing his lack of love, but also exposing the hypocrisy and prejudice he silently justified. In fact, the mirror Jesus held up before him clearly exposed his false piousness.

A study of the rich picture Jesus painted in this parable brings the realization that there is a lot involved with being a good neighbor. We must recognize that to be such a neighbor will greatly cost us. We can always delude ourselves about the type of neighbor we are, but there is always a day of reckoning when we have to face up to the truth, that it is impossible to be a "Good Samaritan."

The idea of "The Good Samaritan" requires something that is beyond man's best, exceeds the righteousness of the most pious, and is utterly sacrificial in nature. When we finally realize that being a good neighbor is beyond our ability, it dawns on us how hopeless our plight is. Keep in mind that a person must love his or her neighbor to inherit eternal life.

This reminds me of the Apostle Peter's words, "And if the righteous scarcely be saved, where shall the ungodly and the sinner appear" (1 Peter 4:18)? (Emphasis added.) One must conclude that no matter how religious we are, we are in trouble.

The only consolation we might have is that those in our religious world are probably failing the "good neighbor" test as well. Like most of us, they are "good neighbors" when they get a notion to look around to see the needs of others or when it fits into their time frame. Their response is not really sacrificial, but an attempt to make themselves feel good about their deeds or silence their nagging conscience.

When individuals are honest, they begin to realize that real giving is a struggle because the flesh hates inconvenience and sacrifice. Contention is created when hearts ignore that which does not serve one's personal purpose, while pride tries to take the credit for any benevolence.

Let's face it, the world encourages us to live totally for self, heaping things upon ourselves, and getting the most out of life and this world. It is a philosophy that is readily accepted, but it has also caused people to become selfish, arrogant, hard-hearted, and self-serving. This is why Jesus gave this warning in Luke 12:15, "Take heed, and beware of covetousness: for a man's life consisteth not in the abundance of the things which he possesseth."

Religion is often used as a veneer that covers up the vanity and covetousness of man. It actually hides in the shadow of an appearance of righteousness, so that the real light is never allowed to expose its hypocrisy. Every day, people walk the road between religion (Jerusalem) and the enticing fragrance of the world. (Jericho means place of fragrance.)

Along this road, it is not unusual to encounter victims that require more than a nod or a greeting. They are in need of personal involvement and investment. In the end, they serve as a test to show how real a person's religion is. Sadly, many religious people are no different than the world they look down upon. In fact, they are worse, for the world is quick to show more compassion than they do. This is why James made this statement, "Pure religion and undefiled before God and the Father is this, to visit the fatherless and widows in their affliction, and to keep himself unspotted from the world" (James 1:27).

As I began to meditate on the spirit and example of "The Good Samaritan," I searched the recesses of my mind to see if I have ever met such a person. After all, if I did, I knew I would never forget him or her, for such a person is bound to make a lasting impression on anyone. As I searched to see if I had encountered such an inspirational hero, to my surprise and awe, I discovered such a person. His name is the Lord Jesus Christ.

Jesus used the term "a certain Samaritan." Again, the word "certain" implies that it could be anyone. However, as you check out the character of "The Good Samaritan," there is no doubt that Jesus fits all of the qualifications. Like the Samaritans, Jesus' lineage would have been considered questionable because of Joseph not being His biological father. Surprisingly, He was referred to as a Samaritan in John 8:48.

Like the Samaritans, the Jewish leaders considered Jesus unorthodox in such areas as the Sabbath. They not only viewed His life as unacceptable, but they were jealous of Him because He was a threat to their religious kingdom. As a result, His own people rejected him.[1] Jesus was eventually isolated from many of His own, especially on the cross.

Jesus had been fashioned in the form of a man in order to become man's neighbor.[2] He challenged, touched, and changed the lives of

---

[1] Matthew 12: 1-14; John 1:11

[2] Philippians 2:7-9

everyone who crossed His path. What is incredible about Jesus becoming man's neighbor is that He did so to become his Redeemer.

The Son of Man had to walk the same dusty roads of humanity in order to walk up the path of Calvary. He walked many times on the road between the world's influence and man's religion to meet and minister to each victim He encountered along the way. Each person automatically became His neighbor when he or she crossed His path.

It is easy to take for granted what Jesus did as Man, but when you catch a glimpse of Him as "The Good Samaritan," it takes on greater meaning. As "The Good Samaritan," Jesus did a great deal more than we can comprehend.

For example, we have no idea what it really cost "The Good Samaritan" in the parable to take care of the wounded man. Likewise, we have no idea what it cost Jesus to redeem us. We catch an occasional glimpse, develop a general idea, and even try to put an amount on it, but in the end, all we can say is there is no way we can repay Him for His actions.

God did put a price on man's sin, and it was too great for us to personally pay. This is why Jesus came to pay the ultimate price for our souls.

This brings us to the "certain" man that fell prey to thieves in the parable. Can you guess whom he represents? He represents you and me. We have all fallen prey to the greatest thief of all, Satan. He not only robs, but he leaves his victims for dead, knowing that destruction will soon follow.[3] This destruction usually occurs, not because of more abuse, but because of neglect.

Keep in mind; it was the neglect of the priest and the Levite that could have ultimately cost this man his life. Satan knows the uncaring hard heartedness of man, and trusts that what he does not finish off with his attacks, man will with neglect.

This is why the example of "The Good Samaritan" is rich with meaning. Jesus was not responsible for man's plight, but like the Samaritan, He became responsible. This responsibility was not in adherence to any Law, but a response of love, mercy, and compassion. In the end, Jesus fulfilled or completed the spirit or intent of the Law.[4]

It is important to recognize that Jesus did not do something because He had to, but because He chose to. This is the nature of mercy. This truth was even acknowledged by the lawyer when he called the actions of the Samaritan merciful, and not religious or obedient.

Jesus showed mercy for hopeless man when He took compassion on him. In fact, He entered into man's sufferings. He allowed Himself to experience all that man experiences. He drank the bitter cups of

---

[3] John 10:10
[4] Matthew 5: 17-18; Romans 10:4

temptation, rejection, suffering, betrayal, and even death, partaking of every last drop of each cup. Hebrews 4:14-15 confirms this, "Seeing then that we have a great high priest, that is passed into the heavens, Jesus the Son of God, let us hold fast our profession. For we have not an high priest which cannot be touched with the feeling of our infirmities; but was in all points tempted like as we are, yet without sin."

Jesus also went the extra mile when He went to the cross of Calvary, then to the grave.[5] What an incredible price to pay for people who were spiritual strangers and enemies to Him. The Apostle Paul summarized it best in Colossians 1:21, "And you, that were sometime alienated and enemies in your mind by wicked works, yet now hath he reconciled."

Not only did Jesus Christ go the extra mile, but He also left provision for us in our weak and frightful state, just as the Samaritan did the wounded man. "And behold, I send the promise of my Father upon you: but tarry ye in the city of Jerusalem, until ye be endued with power from on high" (Luke 24:49).

The Holy Spirit is the provision given to every believer to sustain and hold him or her until he or she reaches the heavenly city. The Apostle Paul made this statement in reference to this provision,

> In whom ye also trusted, after that ye heard the word of truth, the gospel of your salvation: in whom also after that ye believed, ye were sealed with that Holy Spirit of promise, Which is the earnest of our inheritance until the redemption of the purchased possession, unto the praise of his glory (Ephesians 1:13-14).

In the parable of "The Good Samaritan," we have been given diverse contrasts between the genuine and the hypocrite, a compassionate heart and a hard heart, and a hearer only of the Word from a doer of it. These contrasts can clearly be seen between the religious lawyer and the One accused of being a Samaritan and of the devil, Jesus. Where the lawyer was failing to properly love his neighbor, Jesus so loved that He took action and responsibility to love His neighbor to the very depths of death and the grave to bring forth eternal life.

Where the priest failed in the parable to act as a caring mediator, Jesus succeeded as our High Priest. He not only intercedes for us to God as He sits on the right hand of the Father, but He became identified with us, so He could bring restoration to our lives.[6]

Unlike the Levite that operated in the dead letter of the Law, Jesus became the Living Word that fulfilled the written Word through example and sacrifice.[7] Both His example and sacrifice lead to spiritual healing, freedom, and life.

---

[5] Matthew 5:38-44: Luke 9:52-56

[6] Hebrews 7:25; 8:1

[7] John 1:1

Obviously, Jesus was and is the ultimate "Good Samaritan" and the wounded man who had been left for dead represents each one of us. If you have received Jesus into your life as Lord and Savior, you have personally experienced the compassion and tremendous sacrifice of the ultimate "Good Samaritan." You have also been provided for until you reach your final destination. With this in mind, what should your attitude and response be towards the One who gave everything up for you to bring you life, healing, and restoration?

14

GO AND DO THOU LIKEWISE

And David said to Solomon his son,
Be strong and of good courage and do it.
1 Chronicles 28:20

Jesus had finished the parable of "The Good Samaritan" and now the lawyer had to acknowledge what it meant to be a "godly neighbor." Obviously, it entailed more than he was willing to do, especially for someone to whom he had no personal or emotional attachment.

The whole situation began when the lawyer attempted to test Jesus. He quickly lost control of the situation. Instead, he found himself being tested. He was forced to face the harsh reality that he had miserably failed to be upright in his actions throughout his lifetime.

Imagine if you will, how this all began because the lawyer asked Jesus what he could do to inherit eternal life. He discovered that to embrace everlasting life he had to do more than put on a religious cloak, look pious, and talk like a religious expert. He had to love and obey God by actually loving his neighbor. Jesus forced him to face a harsh reality. His neighbor wasn't just anyone—it was <u>everyone</u> who crossed his path.

It was only after he had to face the hypocrisy of his own piousness that Jesus said these words: "Go and do thou likewise." Jesus' instructions were not optional, but a command. After all, if the lawyer wanted to inherit eternal life, he must love his neighbor.

It is important at this time to point out that Jesus' command was not intended to give the lawyer the key to eternal life, but to bring him down to His feet to seek the key. The lawyer's problem was not a matter of disobedience, but one of a disposition that needed to be changed. The solution to this problem was not in trying outwardly to clothe him with attempts to be a "Good Samaritan," but to recognize the fact that only God's intervention could make him a "Good Samaritan" at heart. This change could not occur unless he fell humbly at the feet of Jesus, confessing his rebellion, and his inability to comply. This is true for every person.

Man does not have the type of love within his being that would inspire him to be spent and spilled out for a stranger as a sacrifice. In fact, the person who displays the greatest form of man's love pales in comparison to the love of God. Man's love is limited, self-serving, temperamental, and miserably fails when faced with rejection, hatred, and persecution.

Obviously, to be a "Good Samaritan" is a monumental task too great for any of us in our natural power. It would be like the building of the temple without any help. King David realized it would be a great feat for anyone to accomplish. He did all the preliminary planning for his son, Solomon. God gave Solomon wisdom and favor with man, but Solomon needed to be strong and of good courage to build the temple. David's instruction to Solomon was simply, <u>do it</u>.[1] As a result, the most beautiful temple ever constructed was erected in God's name.

Jesus' instruction to the lawyer is intended for each of us. To be a "godly neighbor" is not up for debate. We are being told through teaching and example to <u>do it</u>, to be a "Good Samaritan."

This brings us to the place where we must come to terms with the harsh reality that we are already doomed to fail in this area. We may have the best intentions, but we are incapable of loving and showing true compassion. It is only from this humble perspective that we can begin the journey that will make us a "Good Samaritan" in spirit and truth.

This spiritual poverty that plagues each of us is designed to help us recognize our need for God, not on the basis of religious merits or duty, but on the grounds of mercy, grace, and a growing relationship with God. As we mourn our spiritual plight and reach heavenward, God will reach downward through His Son to meet us. When God reaches us through Jesus, it means another humble soul is delivered from the road of destruction into greater life.

Such commands as the one Jesus gave the lawyer bring an individual to the reality that they are indeed poor in spirit.[2] To be a true "neighbor" as described in the parable would mean living a life that is constantly being spent and spilled out on behalf of others. This is personally impossible, but yet the responsibility to do so remains because Jesus, who is our example, responded in like manner, and as His followers we can do no less.

As Jesus walked this earth and died on the cross, He revealed something about the nature of God that cannot be ignored. He demonstrated that His incredible love is always expressed in sacrificial giving, "For God so loved the world that He gave His only begotten Son" (John 3:16). This sacrificial and godly giving is not only an expression of God's eternal love, mercy, and grace, but it serves as a mark (or label of eternity) that brings value and purpose to everything that is done in this world on Jesus' behalf.

The Word of God is clear that those who love Him will be generous. Ruth Specter Lascelle made this statement in one of her books: "The children of Israel under the law were <u>restrained</u> from giving for they

---

[1] 1 Chronicles 28
[2] Matthew 5:3

brought too much. The church today under grace must be <u>constrained</u> to give, for they give too little."[3] She then challenges the Church to recognize that because of the work of Christ, Christians should be compelled to hilariously and cheerfully give not only their offerings, but themselves as well.[4]

The question is how can a person be a "Good Samaritan"? Jesus answered that question in the parable. Godly and acceptable giving can only come out of God's love and sacrifice.

When God reaches an individual with His love, hard hearts melt into grateful hearts. In the daily devotional, *"Our Daily Bread,"* October 9, 2000, Hebert Vanger Lugt wrote these words: "Gratitude is what spoils life when it is left out." Gratitude comes from a benevolent disposition. It is expressed in thankfulness that is based on the character of God. And, as Mr. Lugt noted, such people who possess this type of gratitude may be poor in worldly goods, but are truly rich in other ways.

Christians should always be giving out of their spiritual abundance regardless of their financial status. However, the level of gratitude towards God determines the spiritual riches a person possesses. Once individuals recognize what God has accomplished through His Son, they will begin to love Him more and more. Out of this love, which is of God and from God, a desire to reach out to others will grow with each new revelation of Jesus along with each step of faith and obedience.

The love of God will bring us to the place of sacrifice. "I beseech you therefore brethren, by the mercies of God, that ye present your bodies a living sacrifice, holy, acceptable unto God, which is your reasonable service" (Romans 12:1). Since people do not have the ability to be a "good neighbor" according to God's standard, they must offer their lives to God and allow the Holy Spirit to shed the love of God abroad in their hearts.[5] As a person submits to the precious working of the Holy Spirit, the life of Jesus will become a reality in the person, enabling him or her to reach out to others through sacrificial love.

Once again, we see it is not our lives that are being spent and spilled out, but rather the precious life of Christ. We have nothing of ourselves that can make a lasting difference. As we allow the life of Jesus to be offered to others, our inner man will become refreshed by His presence and example.

As the true neighbor of humanity, Jesus Christ touches and rescues others through us as the heart of God is realized in practical ways. This is why each believer must not justify away the responsibility of being a "good neighbor." It is the actions of a godly neighbor that serve as a living testimony of God's goodness, inspiring thankfulness and gratitude

---

[3] Exodus 36:3-7

[4] A Dwelling Place for God; © 1990 by Hyman Israel Specter, pg. 10

[5] Romans 5:5

in the hearts of others. This not only pleases God, but it brings Him much glory.

As one can see, thankfulness can only be inspired in the hearts of the recipients when Jesus' followers manifest His life to others out of a grateful heart. It is when the life of Jesus is openly expressed that His people are able to display the face of thankfulness to a lost, desperate world.

Do you possess the face of religion or of thankfulness? Keep in mind; the face that is being expressed in your life is the truest reflection of your heart condition.

15

THE CHALLENGE

In everything give thanks;
for this is the will of God in
Christ Jesus concerning you.
1 Thessalonians 5:18

Thankfulness is a matter of God's will. It is part of the sacrifice of praise and leads to true worship. It lies at the heart of benevolence, and produces the response of liberal giving for the glory of God.

Over the years, I have found that being thankful is the greatest challenge for many Christians, including myself. When I became a Christian, I was a typical spoiled American. I have been conditioned to consider the value of my life based on what I did not have, rather than what I possessed. I considered happiness in light of present circumstances and possible future expectations, rather than present blessings and a secure hope in Jesus.

This attitude followed me into my Christian life. I found myself being discontent in my Christian walk when life was not going my way. Even though I knew what Paul said about contentment, I found myself valuing my life in light of the conditioning I had received in my culture.[1] I knew discontentment was a product of ingratitude, but I could not conjure contentment up no matter what I did. As a result, I often overlooked God's blessings, and lived according to future possibilities, rather than present reality. Eventually, I found myself walking in unbelief, for my reliance was upon the world. This reliance constantly robbed me of the virtue of faithfulness as I failed to see that which was in front of me.

Personally, I have had to come to terms with the challenge of thankfulness. After all, it is not an option in the kingdom of God. I had to realize that my focus, disposition. and heart condition have been greatly influenced by the culture I was raised in. Ingratitude at any level is unacceptable to God; therefore, I had to wade through this influence. Once I waded through this influence, I had to obey the instruction the Apostle Paul commanded, which was to follow after righteousness, godliness, faith, love, patience, and meekness.[2]

---

[1] Philippians 4:11; 1 Timothy 6:6-12
[2] 1 Timothy 6:11

Through the years, I began to see how I was influenced by the unholy value system of the world. This allowed me to identify what I needed to overcome in the disposition of my heart. In my struggle to develop the Christian life, I started to realize that it is hard to be a Christian in America because of the influence of the culture. In countries where Christians are persecuted, they must decide to die for the sake of the Gospel. However, in America, the country of abundance, one must decide to live for the sake of the Gospel in spite of the abundance. The reason for this is because abundance gives a false illusion. For example, many people who enjoy the riches of this country see themselves as self-made or self-sufficient. They accredit their worldly wealth to their personal attempts, rather than to God's blessing upon this nation. This has created the self-serving attitude that people have a right to squander these blessings however they choose. Such an attitude has created tremendous abuses of resources, energy, and time.

As a result, America is a nation of waste. We see this waste all around us. Personal strength, wealth, or success is no longer based on character, but on what one possesses outwardly. Unborn babies are constantly being sacrificed on the altars of selfishness. People are negated or considered insignificant in the scheme of things in the name of personal security, money, success, and happiness. Morality is adjusted according to hypocritical, perverted preferences or concepts such as political correctness. Relationships are sacrificed in the name of material wealth. Pleasure is now the desired god, while the worship of money is the normal way of life.

This culture has also influenced the Church as it has invaded many Christians' perception of what constitutes the Christian life. As a result, this same waste in America is prevalent in the Church. It has wasted valuable resources in the name of success, happiness, and prosperity that could have been used to bless others. It has wasted talent as it strives to build "bigger barns," rather than further the kingdom of God.[3] It pursues after worldly security over establishing people by faith on the eternal Rock of Ages. It is storing up treasures on earth, rather than treasures in heaven. In fact, it has become so earth-bound and worldly-minded that it no longer possesses a vision of heaven. As a result, it has a perverted sense of righteousness and morality.

Sadly, so much of the Church has become so worldly in its philosophies and pursuits that it no longer stands distinct. The thankfulness that is often displayed in the Church is not genuine benevolence, but fleshly and conditional. It is determined according to personal purposes or agendas, rather than whether something is working a greater eternal glory for the sake of Christ.

This has caused a division to take place. Christians who have an understanding of real Christianity are becoming more disillusioned with this system. They are dissatisfied because they know something of

---

[3] Luke 12:16-21

importance is missing. Therefore, they are being forced to come out from its influence to discover their real life and place in Christ.[4]

The challenge of thankfulness brings us back to the three Samaritans. Their examples show every Christian that thankfulness should be their response. If thankfulness is missing, it identifies three possible problems.

The first problem has to do with vision. Sin blinds people to not only the plight of their condition, but to the solution. Like the ten lepers, Christians claim they personally encountered Jesus. However, how many Christians are like the nine who went on their way without even considering the mercy and grace that was extended to them? How many Christians are like the Samaritan who came back and began to worship Jesus?

When Christians fail to recognize or lose sight of what Jesus did for them, it is because they have the wrong focus. Essentially, they have lost sight of the cross and the healing virtues that flow from the grace of God.[5] They have substituted the redemption of Christ with personal righteousness. Such a misdirected focus will prevent the life of Jesus from being established and manifesting itself. This forgetfulness means they have forgotten their humble beginnings and how God came out of the way to secure for them a new life.

One of the reasons Christians forget their humble beginnings is because they never realize their spiritual plight in the first place. It is hard to forget a deed that met one at his or her desperate need.

For example, the one act that stood out in my mind happened when I was in the fourth grade. My parents were divorced and we lived in what was considered an upper-class community. Needless to say, my family did not financially fit in this neighborhood. I will never forget the mocking, isolation, and struggle I endured at my grade school. But, through it all, one kind deed from one of my teachers reached into the darkness of my life and still remains bright in my mind.

The sole of my left shoe was falling off. I often felt the sidewalk under my stocking foot in the morning as I walked to school. I wondered how my mother could afford shoes, even though at that moment, it appeared as if there was no other option. Sometime during the day, my fourth-grade teacher pulled me aside into another room and handed me a brand new pair of tennis shoes. She quietly did other small, kind acts for me throughout the school year. Today, her name and deeds are branded into my heart. In a way, I carry a personal memorial in my heart to her.

Jesus' death on the cross went beyond any mere deed of man. His act needs to be branded into the hearts of those who claim to know Him. Their lives should serve as an ongoing living memorial to His incredible sacrifice.

---

[4] 2 Corinthians 6:14-18
[5] 2 Peter 1:8-9

The second problem points to the heart condition. Ingratitude produces a hard heart. Like the Samaritan woman, Christians must keep their heart open and seeking. They must never lose their desire to know the truth, or the faith to recognize that the Messiah can address all issues and silence the secret cries of the heart according to that which is eternal. Once an open, receptive heart receives from Jesus, it cannot help but manifest itself in bold declarations.

The problem is that many Christians do not have an open, trusting heart to receive from Jesus. They are closed to Him because they do not possess the faith. Without the faith, many fail to seek Him in regards to their many challenges or problems. Therefore, if He came their way, they could not receive because of their unbelief.[6]

This brings us to the final aspect of thankfulness. It is a disposition that expresses itself through sacrificial benevolence. This sacrificial benevolence is not only capable of producing thankfulness in the hearts of others, but it will bring glory to God. We witnessed this in the parable of "The Good Samaritan."

Most people appreciate benevolence. Even in societies such as America where many are quick to reject Christ, they still uphold some of His principles and examples, such as in the case of "The Good Samaritan." In America, there are "The Good Sam Club" and "The Good Samaritan Law" that protect people from legal action when they unsuccessfully try to help others. And, people who show neighborly actions beyond the norm are affectionately referred to as a "Good Samaritan."

It amazes me that societies that have been kicking God out at every level of life would promote anything that is associated with Him. I realize that before I was a Christian, I had no concept as to the origins of "The Good Samaritan." However, as I think about how the godless world picks and chooses the things of God, while negating His very existence, it reminds me of the hypocritical lawyer in Luke 10, but only on a bigger scale.

The one thing that this nation and the Church should be expressing is thankfulness to God. We should be expressing it in godly benevolence, instead of squandering it to defy, ignore, or discredit God. In fact, so much of the abundance in the lives of Americans has been exploited, used, and abused in the name of freedom or happiness. This has made a mockery out of the blessings Americans have enjoyed.

If the spirit of "The Good Samaritan" really existed in this society and in the Church today, the face of both would drastically change at every level of function. Sadly, as our society and Church fall further away from an attitude of gratitude and godly giving, the mirror of "The Good Samaritan" is being slowly raised up, not as a standard, but as a judgment to show the hard heartedness of men in both realms.

---

[6] Mark 6:4-6

If you are a Christian, test your heart and life today. Make sure you have not stifled the spirit behind "The Good Samaritan." Make sure your life is openly displaying the face of thankfulness, and not covering ingratitude and a hard heart with a religious cloak. If your life truly displays the face of thankfulness, it will manifest itself as it did in the Apostle Paul's life in 2 Corinthians 9:15 when he made this declaration about Jesus Christ, "Thanks be unto God for his unspeakable gift."

Book Five

ABC's
FOR THE
CHRISTIAN
LIFE

(DISCOVERING NUGGETS OF WISDOM)

INTRODUCTION

As a high school graduate, I appreciated the nuggets of wisdom that occasionally flowed down to me. Even though I was at an age where I found my arrogance in regard to my intelligence and capabilities at a peak, I still was able to recognize wisdom in spite of my overrated zealousness and inexperience in the matters of life.

In order to advance in grades each of us had to learn the ABCs associated with education. These ABCs included the rules in regard to language, the basic principles surrounding the functions of the world around us, and the formulas and equations that govern mathematics.

We know that the purest goal of any responsible educational institution would be to prepare the students to function as adults in society. It is supposed to give them tools to continue to make advancements on a personal level that will prove to be beneficial to their life.

As I was considering the Christian life, I began to see how believers must also graduate from one level of Christian experience to the next. The Bible refers to it as being "...changed into the same image from glory to glory, even as by the Spirit of God" (2 Corinthians 3:18c).

In order to make advancements in our spiritual lives, we must not only experience the reality of it, but we also must gain the spiritual nuggets to properly mature. Like all new graduates, we must also face the different terrains of life. These terrains will expose and challenge our character and resolve along the way. Such times can prove to be frightening, yet wondrous as we discover different aspects about life.

This small book about the ABC's of the Christian life is designed to help Christians to consider what it means to advance to greater spiritual heights, while they maneuver through the terrain that will be facing them as they sojourn through this present age.

Philippians 3:12-13

A is for **adventure**

People *approach* life from different angles. Depending on their *attitude* towards life, it will seem like a grave burden, endless drudgery, on-going competition, or an overwhelming battle. However, life is a teacher. Its main responsibility is to bring us to an understanding as to what really constitutes our very being. For example, we are told life is a matter of education, success, happiness, having families, or possessing material possessions. Such concepts about life come from the world's philosophies, but God's wisdom puts this in perspective when Jesus asked what does a man profit if he gains the whole world but loses his soul?

The question we must answer is what constitutes life? Life serves as a teacher, but it is also an *adventure* we must take to discover the answer to this question. Over twenty centuries ago, a person took such a venture. He gave up the glories of His heavenly home, took on the form of a servant, and was fashioned as a man in the womb of a virgin. He grew up in the barren wilderness of humanity. The reason He did this was to secure life for each of us on an old wooden cross. It is this brutal instrument of death that now serves as the believer's *altar*. The man's name is Jesus Christ. He not only answers this question, but also offers us the means to find this life as we venture through this world.

As we consider the example of Jesus, we can begin to see how life is indeed an *adventure* that brings us to discovering its real meaning. Sadly, people can miss the real meaning of life. They can take moral detours in the name of happiness, pursue vanity in the name of wealth, delusion in the name of education, and remain complacent towards all challenging possibilities in light of *avoiding* any possible failure.

We must be willing to risk what we consider to be life to discover lasting life in the midst of what stands doomed. Many people live what they call life, when in reality they are living in some type of existence, but life cannot be found in any of it. What people often taste are the temporary pleasures of the world, and the endless fruits of sin and death, such as turmoil, uncertainties, sorrow, and despair. In the end most people despair over life or rage against it, but they rarely find it.

The Apostle Paul put this *adventure* called life in perspective when he talked about *apprehending* and being *apprehended*. The apostle wanted to *attain* something that was beyond this present world to possess the heights of this life. Obviously, he understood that it came from *above*. Even though he could not really comprehend the infinite aspects of it, he knew that he wanted to find it to obtain it for himself. He knew that whatever it required to secure this life, it would be worth the price of knowing and *abiding* in the presence and power of God.

The life that Paul wanted to *apprehend* could only be found in the revelation of Jesus Christ. He wanted to *apprehend* Jesus on a personal level and be completely *apprehended* by Him in consecration and devotion as His *apostle* to the Church and His *ambassador* in this dark world. Obviously, Paul knew what he was after, and he wanted to have the *assurance* that he would possess this life. Therefore, he would not let anything deter him from his goal as he pursued his high calling and life in Jesus.

Assurance comes out of knowing our God. We are *assured* that He will never change. It is within this environment that we can learn how to prove what is that good, *acceptable,* and perfect will of God.

As we follow the great saints of the Bible, we can begin to see that their pursuit for life started with them taking an *adventure* into the unknown. Abraham sought for a city made by God, and the people of Israel ventured to the Promised Land to find the life God had promised them. As believers, we seek Jesus to ensure that all the promises of God are fulfilled in our lives. As we *accept* the need to take this incredible *adventure* to *apprehend* the *assurance* of this life, our *attitude* towards God will develop and mature as we embrace the life of His Son. In our embrace of Jesus, we will begin to please our God by presenting Him with those things that are considered *acceptable* to Him.

Although this *adventure* can seem overwhelming and frightening, know that God's guidance is there to see you through each lesson, failure, and discovery. Jesus is the *Alpha* and Omega in every matter regarding God and life. We must begin with who He is and end with who He must become to us. Therefore, *always* consider the perspective of the Bible. It started with God and ended with a revelation of Jesus. Clearly, this life is discovered between these eternal perspectives. It is time to get your map and weapon ready (Bible), your clothing prepared (humility), and your compass tested (Holy Spirit) in response to beginning this venture. Make sure your *adventure* will be enriching as you make a commitment to *always* discover the secret of a lasting, true, and satisfying life that can only be *apprehended* in Christ.

John 14:6

B is for bridges

You might wonder why the "b" in the ABC's for spiritual graduates point to *bridges*, especially since *bridges* are not mentioned in the Bible. *Bridges* point to connections. That which connects us to the reality of life is relationships with others.

People were designed to interact in relationships. Relationships are meant to give people a reality check about personal character, social skills, work habits, and attitudes towards life. In fact, there will not be any aspect of our inner being that will not be exposed by our association with others.

As we consider relationships, we realize that some *bridges* will fall in disrepair due to neglect; others have to be *burned* because of different paths that must be chosen; some have to be repaired because of separation, and the rest have to be *built* and maintained through personal investment.

Clearly, one of the biggest aspects of our lives that we truly need discernment in is our relationship with others. We know that *bad company* corrupts good morals. We also know that when we follow Christ, we have to leave worldly relationships *behind*. These relationships could include our family and close friends. After all, as followers of Jesus we cannot carry anyone down the narrow path of self-denial and the cross. As the sword of truth comes down, there will definitely be a separation between those who belong to the ways of the world and those who belong to Jesus Christ.

This brings us to the one relationship that we must seek after, and that is a relationship with God through Jesus Christ. Jesus Christ is the only *bridge* that can connect us to a relationship with God. We are told that Jesus Christ is the point of reconciliation for all who are alienated from God by sin. Clearly, Jesus serves as the *bridge* that closes the gap between man and his Creator.

In John 14:6 Jesus talks about being this bridge. He said He was the way, the truth, and the life. But what is He as the way, the truth, and the life about? He goes on to say that no one can come to the Father but by Him. He is a *bridge* back to a relationship with the Father. Such a relationship points to reconciliation and communion. It is out of this relationship that life comes.

The Bible tells us what we must do to cross this bridge. We must begin by *believing* what the Word of God tells us about Jesus. He is the way because of who He is and what He did on the cross for us. We must travel this way with child-like *belief* that originates in the heart. This *belief* means I am simply persuaded that all that is said about God and salvation in His Word is true.

Clearly, *believing* means I receive such matters as being true in my heart. Once I receive these simple truths as being absolute and pure, I will be *born again* from above. Jesus said it best, unless a man is *born again*, he will never see the kingdom of God.

To be *born again* from above means I have been given a new heart and spirit. The life I now possess is a heavenly life, the life of the Son. My new heart will be inclined towards God, and I will walk according to a new spirit. As Paul stated, I have become a new creature, the old will pass away and all things will become new.

This new life opens the way for me to experience the many *blessings* of God. These *blessings* are eternal. However, the greatest *blessing* is that I will *behold* the Son through revelation, wisdom, and understanding. Granted, we initially *behold* the Son on the cross, but we must also *behold* Him in His glory as God in the flesh. As we *behold* the Son in greater ways, we will fall in love with Him. This love will produce *benevolence* in us. Such *benevolence* will express itself in consecration to God and sacrifice towards others.

Sadly, many will miss Jesus as the *bridge*. There is only one such *bridge* and the *broad* way that leads to destruction is more attractive and less challenging than the narrow *bridge* that leads to the unseen and uncertain walk of faith that will lead us into unfamiliar territories.

This is why we must become as the *Bereans* were in Acts 17:10-12 in our spiritual journey. They studied the Scriptures to make sure that a matter or *belief* upheld the intent of God's counsel and Spirit. These individuals knew that this was the only way they could avoid taking unhealthy and destructive detours away from the entrance and hope of the *bridge* sent forth by God, formed in a womb, designated to be nailed to a cross, and lifted up on a cross as our only hope of salvation and life.

Deuteronomy 30:19-20

C is for crossroads

Crossroads represent *choices*. At the points of *choices*, we must *choose* which bridge, path, or road we will travel. Jesus clearly talked about a broad road that will lead to destruction, and a *constricted* or narrow path that will lead to life. As we consider this *constricted* path, we must recognize that it is not attractive. Unlike the broad path that can include many ways, paths, or *choices*, there is only one way that leads to life. This way will *challenge* any independence to live according to personal preferences. It will cause discomfort in the inner being as *character* is exposed. In fact, this path is *constricted* by a *call* to pick up a personal *cross* that requires self-denial to fulfill a heavenly *commission*.

For the children of Israel, the *choices* were made clear. They had to *choose* between life and death. Life pointed to blessings and death pointed to a *cursed* life. Obviously, God was not only making the *choices* clear, but He was showing that these *choices* were a personal matter. If they *chose* life, it meant they would have to live a *consecrated* life unto Him, separated for His purpose and glory. If they *chose* the various ways of self, the flesh, and the world, they would be *choosing* the broad path that would prove to be the ways of death that ultimately would lead to spiritual ruin.

Today, many people operate from the premise of the blame game. In other words, the quality of their life is blamed on the people, environment, or *circumstances* in their life. They refuse to take responsibility for the quality of their inner being. After all, they are the ones who are making the decisions as to how they are responding to a situation. However, in our selfish culture, the blame game always allows such people to avoid taking responsibility for their *choices* and their *character.*

People do not automatically possess *character. Character* is formed when people go against their natural preferences. Their natural preferences are towards the ways of darkness. They prefer to give in to that which is selfish and self-serving, rather than go against the grain of what is natural to produce an excellence in the type of person they are becoming. Such excellence points to being honorable in *conduct,* pure in motives, benevolent in actions, and *compassionate* in service.

A life that is not *content* to settle for inferior ways will develop an excellent spirit. Daniel had such a spirit. He refused to *compromise* with his present, worldly, and idolatrous environment. He maintained his ways in righteousness. Although thrown into a lion's den because he would not *compromise* his life before God, he was not only willing, but also *content* to allow his God to determine the length of his life. He simply stood in *confidence* of his great God's power to deliver him according to His eternal plan.

To walk this narrow path takes *courage. Courage* is not a matter of *character*, but one of *choice*. In fact, *courage* is what develops *character. Character* that finds its origins in *courageous* decisions will eventually manifest itself in *courage*: the *courage* to make the right decisions, to stand for truth, and to not be afraid to regard one's life in light of death.

The Bible talks about such *courage*. Saints are *commanded* to be of good *courage*. Such good *courage* is beneficial to others. Consider the *courage* of Moses, Joshua, Caleb and even our Lord Jesus Christ in His humanity. These men became examples and leaders to others. The key to their *courage* was that they found their strength in God. Their *confidence* in God was sure, thereby, they obeyed His *commandments*. As a result, great things were accomplished in and through their lives. Moses led the people of Israel out of Egypt through the wilderness. Joshua brought them into the Promised Land, Caleb gained the best of the inheritance that was designated for his tribe, and the Lord Jesus Christ overcame the world, thereby, redeeming us from the slavery of sin and its consequence of death.

As you face your life, you must keep in mind that it will take *courage* to face the unknown at each *crossroad* in your life. It will take *character* to make the right *choices*. It will take *confidence* in God and obedience to His *commandments* to live a *consecrated* life that will bring Him glory, and to be *counted* worthy of all acceptance. Such a life will mean that we are *crucified* to the influence of the world. Death to the influence of the world will assure each of us as believers that we will realize our high *calling* in Christ as we line up to Him as our *cornerstone*, as well as carry out our *commission*. Such a walk will ultimately reflect the *countenance* of our Lord's glory in this dark world of doom and *chaos*.

Hebrews 11:6

D is for diligence

As a Christian, I have come to realize a very important aspect about the Christian life, it must be *discovered*. The Bible tells us we are strangers and pilgrims in this world. As a stranger we do not belong to this world. We are simply passing through to get to our final *destination*. Although we may hold *dual* citizenships, the one that we must guard and maintain at all times is our citizenship involving the kingdom of God. In fact, we are in this world serving as ambassadors of Christ, officially representing our King and His unseen kingdom.

As spiritual pilgrims, we are in search of a place in which we can freely worship our God. We are fleeing the oppression of the different aspects of this present world that hinders us in our *devotion* and worship of the one true God of heaven and earth. We must search for this unseen life with the intent of *discovering* it no matter the cost.

The cost might prove to be two-fold, but it will include the process of *dying*. As a pilgrim I must *die* to the present life in order to *discover* a new life of *devotion* to God. In my search I will not only lose my present life as I know it, but I might also lose my physical life. Many pilgrims have lost their lives in their search, but they were willing to pay any price to have that glorious liberty of *discovering* the satisfying life that awaited them.

Our search for this life will take *diligence* on our part. *"Diligence"* means to investigate, crave, *demand*, and to seek after in a careful manner *(SC, #1567)*. As you consider the meaning of this word, you can see where there is a powerful *desire* to endeavor to find the purpose or source of your search. You will not just be casual in your journey; you will be steadfast in your exploration. You will develop a *determination* to find your life no matter how *dark, discouraging,* and *despairing* the circumstances or terrain may be around you. As Christians, our goal must be to seek out and find this life in the midst of that which is *dead, doomed,* useless, and lost.

Obviously, we must *dare* to find this life. It will take courage and faith to seek out such a life in the midst of that which has no life. However, this existence can be found when we finally *discover* God. God is the source and essence of the life we seek. Jesus summarized what we are seeking when He stated that He was the *door* to life. It is hard to recognize this *door*. At times we become lost looking for it. However, God is not lost, but He is unseen to the fleshly eye, the hard heart, the selfish *disposition*, and the worldly mindset.

This brings us to the subject of *disposition*. Jesus spoke of His *disposition* in regard to His humanity. He was lowly in spirit and meek in attitude. In Philippians 2:5, we are instructed to have the mind of Christ. The mind of Christ points to attitude.

Attitude serves as a reflection of our true *disposition. Disposition* is made up of inclinations and tendencies. By being lowly in spirit, our inclinations will be towards seeking, knowing, and pleasing God. By ensuring that all of our personal strength is under the control of the Holy Spirit, our tendencies will change as the old gives way to the new life, or way of being that is being established in us. Such practices or applications point to the *disciplined* life of a Christian. As a *disciple* of Jesus, we will walk in His same steps, follow His examples, and *declare* His teachings.

As we have considered the letter "d" in our presentation of the Christian walk, much appears negative. There is *death, darkness, damnation, division, discord, discouragement, despair,* and *destruction.* These words truly point to the type of life we will experience when self is reigning, the flesh is demanding satisfaction, and the world is demanding the price of one's soul to experience its forbidden fruits.

However, the Christian has the promise of the *dawning* of a new *day* in the person of Jesus Christ. In the midst of great *darkness* shines the bright morning star upon the lives of those who have received the promise of eternal life. As Christians, we need to make a *determination* to let this star shine brightly in our hearts. In order to ensure this life shines, we must make a *determination* to know nothing except Christ and Him crucified. He must become our life if His light is going to shine in our souls and through our countenances.

As the light of Christ fills our soul, we will know the *delight* that comes from tasting of His sweetness and partaking of His greatness. In order to partake of Jesus' *divine* nature, we must first of all *draw* near to Him in complete assurance and confidence.

In considering that we live in a *dispensation* of grace, we must realize we have been given the gift of time to *discover* what it means to live this glorious life of Christ. Obviously, we must hold to pure *doctrine,* but we must also realize it is not *doctrine* alone that leads us to revelation, but the reality that we have free access to abide in our Lord. Abiding points to the fact that our Lord *dwells* in us through His Spirit and we *dwell* positionally in Him as our only place of refuge, as well as the *door* to, and the source of our life and hope. But, as the writer of *Hebrews* reminds us, we must *diligently* seek the One who is able to reward us for the faith that is steadfast towards God.

Matthew 24:13

E is for endurance.

The Christian life, in many cases, has been reduced to some sort of pleasant walk in the park. However, this picture is far from the realities of this adventure. The Christian life is a very challenging walk. We must walk through the barren wilderness of sin, the dark influences of the world, and contend with the fruits that follow the ways of death to complete our course. One of Jesus' instructions was that we must *endure* to the end if we are going to be saved.

It is vital that we face our limitations so that we can *embrace* the means God has provided to *endure* the challenges this spiritual journey will pose along the way. It is clear that we must properly *experience* the different aspects of the eternal life in us if we are going to be *edified* or built up in our Christian faith.

The challenge for most Christians is to realize that we are *earthbound* by our flesh and greatly inspired by the world in our way of thinking. Since we are of the *elect* that have been given a heavenly inheritance, we must learn to soar like an *eagle* on the wind of the Holy Spirit above fleshly and worldly influences. This is necessary if we are going to have a heavenly perspective. It is from a heavenly perspective that we will develop our spiritual *ears* so we can hear what the Spirit is saying.

Another challenge is that most Christians think that the sum total of their spiritual life was *experienced* at their initial salvation. Such thinking is incorrect. What we received upon salvation was a new life. This new life must be worked in us, through us, and out of us in obedience. The Apostle Paul actually instructs us to "...work out your own salvation with fear and trembling" (Philippians 2:12c). Salvation is free, but the life it imparts must become a reality that penetrates every aspect of our disposition, attitude, and conduct. People must be able to see this life clearly in operation within us as a living testimony of our Lord. Clearly, the very life of Jesus must be worked in us to *ensure* that we will become the living *epistles* that Paul made reference to in 2 Corinthians 3:1-3.

Jesus gave us insight into what we must do to *experience* this life. He made this statement in Luke 13:24, "Strive to enter in at the strait gate; for many, I say unto you, will seek to enter in, and shall not be able." At our initial salvation we have received life from above, but we must *enter* into the ways of this life. According to this Scripture, we must actually strive to *enter* in. Obviously, there are obstacles that would prevent us from *entering* into the door that leads to this heavenly, victorious existence.

The biggest obstacle has to do with the fact that there is only one *entryway*. It is the person and work of Jesus Christ. The Apostle John tells us that we must walk as Jesus walked if we are to abide in Him. Jesus went by way of Calvary. Obviously, the obstacle that looms in front of us is the cross of Christ. It represents a total death to the old life. As a result, the initial striving has to do with the temptation of trying to figure out some other way to *enter* into this life. We may try religion or good deeds, but all such attempts do not serve as the door. Jesus stated He was the door, and that only those who were hirelings or thieves would strive to *enter* in through other means. Such attempts remind us that many will not be able to *enter* into this straight way.

As Christians, we must learn to seek our Lord *early* in the day. We must always start with Him as our focus and maintain that perspective in each decision we make and in the way we conduct our lives. After all, we must first make an *exchange* of that which is *earthbound* with the heavenly. This is what we do when we come to the cross. We come to make the great *exchange* of the old with the new. We must also make this *exchange* on a daily basis to change our focus.

Changing our focus is vital if we are going to *exercise* unto godliness. The Christian life is clearly an *exercise* in the ways of righteousness. After all, we have *escaped* the corruption of this world. Therefore, we must *exercise* by always going forward in our life with God. It takes much discipline, but this is the only way we can *earnestly* contend for our faith in the midst of this present age of darkness.

There is a great struggle to come into the place of life and fellowship with God. As we travel the narrow way, we will recognize our need to *endure* to the end. We need to become like King David in 1 Samuel 30. His town had been burned and all of the soldier's families had been taken into captivity. The despair was so great that David's own soldiers were speaking of stoning him. It was bleak for David. However, David *encouraged* himself in the LORD his God. Victory came out of that *encouragement*.

David's source of *encouragement* reminds us that God is the Rock. As long as we cling to Him in faith, we will *endure* the challenges of our life and the adversities of this present world.

Matthew 4:19

F is for follow.

Regardless of whether we are aware of it or not, we are *following* something or someone. We may be *following* signs along the way, or perhaps even our dreams to experience and accomplish certain *feats*. Needless to say, whatever we are *following* is actually determining the direction we are walking.

In this Scripture, Jesus is calling men to *follow* Him. Such a call seems simple enough, but the problem is what does it truly mean to *follow* Jesus? We cannot see Him like the first disciples. Therefore, how do we *follow* Him without becoming *fearful* in our walk or giving up in despair due to *failure* because of the unknown?

The Apostle Paul gives us insight into what it means to *follow* Jesus in 1 Timothy 6:11: "But thou, O man of God, flee these things, and follow after righteousness, godliness, faith, love, patience, meekness." The first thing we must do is *flee* the influences of evil in our life. These influences could be the things of this world, the lusts of the flesh, and the desires for the riches of this present age. Most things that entangle us are not necessarily bad, but it comes down to the type of emphasis we may put on them. Our emphasis can make them idolatrous, obsessive, and destructive.

It is not enough to cease from doing something unless you *fill* that area of your life with the things of God. Therefore, we are called to *follow* that which is righteous or just. We must pursue after godliness or that which is virtuous. We must seek after those things that will enlarge our *faith* towards God. This is what will please God. Our greatest desire must be to possess the love of God, which will prove to be honorable. We must allow the character of patience to be established in us as we become *faithful* in our walk. In the end, we must have the discipline of meekness reigning over our attitude and conduct.

The Apostle Paul goes on to say "Fight the good fight of faith, lay hold on eternal life, unto which thou are also called and hast professed a good profession before many witnesses (1 Timothy 6:12). Clearly, there is a battle over our *faith*. Satan wants to undermine our confidence in God. Therefore, there is a battle we must *fight* to ensure that we will remain steadfast in what we know is true if we are going to *finish* this course.

One of the biggest battles has to do with the war between the Spirit and the *flesh*. We are told that the *foolishness* of our selfish disposition is bound in our hearts. Such *foolishness* will demand to have life on its terms. It is *fiercely* independent. It does not mind religious matters as long as such religion does not require it to go against its self-serving ways. Once it is challenged it will raise its head to reveal the character and ways of a *fool*.

The *flesh* must be crucified so that a person can give way to the work of the Spirit. However, it is a battle to put the *flesh* on the cross. It will prove to be a coward. It will cry, scream, and yell *foul* all the way to the cross. It will try to *flatter*, accuse, and make it appear that you are crucifying the very means by which you can discover the *fullness* of life. However, the *flesh* is a liar. It represents nothing more than the *filthy* rags of the old life. This is why we must *forsake* all that is attached to this life. If it is left to reign, it will ultimately keep us from coming into *fellowship* with our Lord, knowing the *fullness* of the life He has prepared for us, and possibly *facing* the *future* judgment of the tormenting *fires* of damnation.

The Bible also tells us that the way is narrow and *few* will *find* it. The word *"few"* is used in relationship to the harsh reality that not many will truly discover their life in Christ. We often think of Christians in the majority because people who are associated with Jesus often surround us. Granted, there are many that call themselves Christians, but how many of them are simply wearing a label or some type of religious cloak? Jesus stated that many are called but *few* are chosen. In other words, *few find* the essence of their life in Him, discover their place in the Body, and reach their potential in His kingdom.

It is important to realize that the Lord has *foreordained* our lives before the *foundation* of the world. Obviously, we must *find* the way to this life. We must keep in mind that we are *foreigners* in this present world, and we are traveling to a place that is *foreign* to us. This is why we must *follow* the ways, examples, and instructions of our Lord.

To embrace and *flourish* in our spiritual life during our journey through this present world we must always seek *forgiveness* for our sins, as well as walk in it towards others. We will *find* such pardon because of the redemption of Jesus Christ. Once we receive salvation through the *forgiveness* for our sins, we must establish our lives on the only true *foundation* of Jesus Christ. As we become rooted in our spiritual *foundation,* we can experience Jesus as our all in all. His life will *fill* up every corner of who we are, and are destined to become in His kingdom.

2 Peter 1:3

G is for godliness.

When we think of the letter *"g"*, we cannot help but remember that our life and journey through this world must begin and end with *God*. It is from the premise of *God* as our Creator, the only One who serves as the essence of our life, hope, and substance, that we can begin to explore the different aspects of our Christian life according to who He is.

One of the first words that I am reminded of when I come to this letter is the word, *"grace."* What a *glorious* word. *Grace* reminds us that *God* manifested His *glory* when Jesus Christ took on flesh to redeem us. We know we are saved by *grace* through our faith. *God's grace* is His way of showing us undeserved favor. After all, He did not have to solve the problem of our sinful plight. He could have let us die in our sins. However, the motivating factor was His love. He had the means and power to provide a way out of our plight by offering the *gift* of eternal life. His actions to provide the solution spoke of His incredible *grace*. This is why we are told that Jesus is full of *grace* and truth. He is truly the manifestation of how *God's grace* would work on our behalf to bring forth the mercy of forgiveness and the *gift* of life. As the Lord's *grace* is unveiled in His work of redemption, the power of His *Gospel* will take on *greater* meaning and purpose. We will know what it means to no longer stand *guilty* before the righteous Judge, but to stand justified.

This brings us to how *God's* intervention on our behalf will actually express itself in our lives. It will express itself in *godliness, goodness, gentleness,* and *glory. Godliness* points to our conduct. Something cannot be considered *godly* unless it finds its origins in *God*. Therefore, if our conduct, as to the affairs of our life, cannot be traced back to *God* as its very source or inspiration, it cannot be considered *godly*. The Apostle Peter brings this out in his epistle. He tells us that *God* has given us everything that pertains unto life and *godliness*. Clearly, there will be no excuse as to why we fail to walk out our life in Christ in a *godly* way.

It is not unusual to hear people refer to others as being *good*. However, the Bible is clear that there is no *"good"* thing in the flesh. In fact, only *God* is *good*. This may seem confusing when one of the virtues of the fruit of the Spirit is *goodness*. Therefore, it is important to understand what constitutes *goodness*.

"Goodness" points to what is beneficial. Such benefits can actually bring delight to God and others. Clearly, there is nothing beneficial in the flesh. However, everything that comes from *God* is beneficial because it is eternal. Obviously, if a person's conduct exhibits *godliness,* it will clearly benefit others around him or her.

Goodness also means to be morally upright. However, it is important to keep in mind that *God* is the One who established what is considered morally upright. When a person is being *"good"* in this area, it is not because they are *"good."* It simply means the individual is morally in line with what is considered acceptable to *God*. This is important to understand. A person may be morally acceptable in light of wicked practices, but this does not mean he or she is truly good or saved.

There are many religions in the world that promote moral accountability, but they do not possess the true Jesus. These religious people may impress others with their moral practices, but they are still dead in their sins, condemned by unbelief towards the Son of *God*.

"Gentleness" reminds us that we must be kind. To be kind, we must be meek in attitude, benevolent in our actions, and quick to honor others over our own self-interests and needs. *Gentleness* makes us pliable in God's hands, and considerate of others in their plight. As a result, *gentleness* reveals itself in the ways of excellence. It shows tremendous strength in its actions, revealing the *greatness* of its character.

The conduct of *godliness,* the moral accountability established by the *goodness* of *God,* and the kind acts of *gentleness* will ultimately reflect His *glory*. Our potential as Christians is to reflect the *glory* of Christ. This *glory* has to do with the light that is present in our inner man. In other words, it actually points to our understanding that will determine the type of light or life that will manifest itself through our disposition. Sin actually marred our disposition or understanding. Therefore, we all start out reflecting the old man or the world, instead of our Creator.

We must now consider what it will take to develop *godliness* that will ensure the *goodness* of *God* that will manifest itself in the *glory* of Christ. First of all, we must *grow* in the knowledge of Christ. As we *grow* in our awareness of Christ, we will begin to *gain* more of His life. As His life *grows* in our inner man, our hearts will become tender and fruitful *gardens* of communion. We will learn how to *gird* up our mind, put on the *garment* of praise and humility, and take on the *gentle* disposition of a servant who is pure and without *guile*. In our servitude, we will learn what it truly means to be *great* in His kingdom. After all, true servants of *God* are considered the *greatest* in His kingdom.

As we *grow* in the knowledge of His *glory* and *greatness*, we will experience the purifying fires of adversity. This is when our faith in Him will be tested. Faith must be enlarged in its capacity to receive, in order to be brought forth in maturity. Of course, the adversity, will cause our faith to become more precious than *gold*. This is the beauty about *growing* into the *godly* ways of *God's goodness* and *glory*.

It is vital that you always *grow* in your spiritual life. Without such *growth,* you will never display *godliness, goodness* and *gentleness* in your life. Ultimately, your life will fail to fulfill its purpose, which is to bring *glory* to your Creator.

Matthew 5:3

H is for heaven or hell.

The letter "*h*" reminds us that we are on a path that leads us to one of two places: *heaven* or *hell*. Our goal on this earth should be to make sure that we are living in such a way that we are preparing for *heaven*. After all, earth is a classroom where we are being prepared for our future destination. The choices we make will determine if we are becoming children of *heaven* or children of *hell*.

Sadly, most people think that just by saying a certain prayer, it will change their destination. However, what will determine each of our destinations is how we live. How we live will establish the path we walk. As Christians, we must make sure we are living the life that will put us on the narrow path to *heaven.*

The first aspect of our life is that we need to realize we are a *habitation* for the life we are and will be living. What we posses or pursue will determine what type of *habitation* we will become. We know that we must operate in a *holy* state. Our state is determined by what we allow to influence us. If we allow the things of *hell,* such as *hatred* with its roots of bitterness, unforgiveness, *haughtiness,* and idolatry to influence us, we will become *hardened* towards the truth. We will also become spiritual *harlots* as we pursue the things of this world to fill our lives with so-called "meaning" and "purpose." We will become prone to the seductive doctrines of demons and the *heretical* presentations of others.

Habitation comes down to your *heart* condition. The Bible clearly tells us that out of the *heart* come the issues of life. The *heart* serves as the mainspring for who we are and who we become. In its unregenerate state, it is full of deception and wickedness. This is why when God spoke of a new covenant, He stated that He would give man a new *heart* and spirit. In other words, He would give man a new disposition. In this new disposition or *habitation,* man would actually know how to properly respond to God in obedience.

As we begin to consider the new condition that God wants to establish in our inner being, we must recognize the *healing* that will occur. So many people are walking around with broken *hearts.* They have been wounded and devastated by the sin and darkness of this present world. They have become lost in the maze of despair and *hopelessness.* They have nowhere to turn.

For some, the light of the world will begin to penetrate their *hopelessness.* That light is Jesus. His warmth and compassion begin to bring *hope* to these devastated souls. As they walk towards this light and embrace it as God's provision for their lost state, He will quicken the inner man with a new *heart* and spirit.

The beauty about a state of brokenness is that it causes us to be *humble* towards our Creator. God has mentioned this broken state of *humility* in the Scriptures. He refers to it as a broken *heart* and a contrite spirit. In this condition, God is able to draw near to such a person to minister His life and *hope* to him or her.

In this new state or condition that man is given, he would begin to grow up into the *head* of the Body. We know the *head* to be Jesus. Man would begin to *hallow* or set apart God in His thinking. He would feel the *hand* of God upon his life as he began to actually *hear* what the Spirit is saying. Because of this new state, he would find himself more inclined to *heed* the Spirit's instructions and warnings. He would develop *honest* practices as he learned to *honor* others above his personal desires and pursuits.

This new state would allow these individuals to become *holy* temples, *habitations* or *homes* for the *Holy Spirit*. They would understand what it means to be *happy*. True *happiness* can only occur when Jesus has taken His rightful place in each of our lives. As He takes His rightful place, each believer will begin to understand what it means to be seated in *high* places in Christ, as well as *hiding* in Him as his or her ark.

In this place with Christ, the *hunger* that was present in each of our souls will give way to that satisfaction of knowing our life is complete in Him and because of Him. We will now cling to the Rock as we *hold* tightly to it with our faith.

The question is what kind of *habitation* are you becoming? It will determine if you are prepared to enjoy the beauty of *heaven* or whether you are prepared to taste the bitter, tormenting dregs of *hell.*

Ephesians 1:13-14

I is for inheritance.

Inheritance points to *identity.* You cannot claim your *inheritance* unless you can first become *identified* to it. The *inheritance* for Christians is spiritual. In fact, an earnest payment of the Holy Spirit has been given to every Christian to *identify* him or her to this eternal *inheritance.* Obviously, such an *identity* comes from the presence, *intervention,* and work of the great *"I AM"* in a believer's life.

We know that God is the *"I AM."* In His *immutable* attributes He is ever present. Since He is *infinite* there is no real time frame in which He operates. For example, there is no real past to Him for He was present. There is no real future in the spiritual realm for Him because He will be present. Granted, He desires that the past will *instruct* us in the ways of His wisdom. He wishes the present to be *inspired* by the leading of His Spirit in the ways of righteousness, as well as His people living in the Spirit according to His work of sanctification. His desire is for us to take these matters to heart so that we will avoid the judgment that will take place in the future upon all those who are disobedient. To ensure that His abiding presence is realized and is *increased* in our lives, He must be our reality, hope, and purpose in the present. This is the only way that we are going to *inherit* His kingdom.

For God to be our *"I AM"* we must avoid that which would undermine His authority, power, and *intervention.* The greatest affront against Him as the *"I AM"* is *ignorance.* The prophet Hosea warned that people would perish because they lacked knowledge about God. The Apostle Paul stated that God would no longer wink at *ignorance.* The reason is clear, people can truly know Him, but they choose not too. They like their *ignorance* because they do not have to become responsible for the foolish ways of their life.

Sadly, many people claim they know Him as God, but in reality He is missing. They do not know who they are worshipping. When God is missing, the darkness of *ignorance* fills the void. *Ignorance* points to superstition. Superstition is associated with pagan practices. It reveals that these individuals have erected *images* within the secret corridors of their vain *imaginations.* These *imaginations* point to *idolatry.* Wherever there is *idolatry* there is a divided heart. *Idolatry* serves as a breeding ground for *iniquity* or moral deviation to operate within the inner being. Affections will become *inordinate* as they become caught up with the attractions of the present world. The more fleshly people become, the more their practices become *immoral.*

Another breeding ground for *idolatry* is *idleness*. America is a good example of a nation where people have become *idle*. When people are not busy in a constructive way, they can become lost in their vain *imaginations*. They take on an attitude of *ingratitude* as their fleshly appetites enlarge in their pursuits. It is from this platform that *imaginations* begin to explore the possibilities of evilness. As these individuals allow their vain *imaginations* to become their reality, they become desensitized or *indifferent* towards what is real and holy. This state will cause them to become more *insensitive* to their conscience. Their love will grow cold towards that which fails to stir up their sensual appetites. As the conscience is seared, the mind becomes reprobate in its way of thinking. In the end, such individuals will eventually lose all sense of God in their conscience.

The Word of God is clear that if we give way to the works of the flesh, we will not *inherit* the kingdom of God. The main way we can ensure our spiritual *inheritance* is to have *integrity*. It is said of King David that he walked in the *integrity* of his heart. *Integrity* points to honesty that has been established in upright character. Because of his *integrity*, David possessed humility. When in doubt about a matter, he would *inquire* of the Lord. When wrong, he would repent after being *instructed*, warned, or chastised.

Our *inheritance* also reminds us of the *impossible* that can be turned into the possible. The plight of man started when Adam fell from an *innocent* state into a doomed state of death. Because of the *independent* attitude and actions of disobedience, all were born into a corruptible state that caused separation from God. In fact, there was no hope for any of us to put off the corruptible so that the *incorruptible* could be put on without some miraculous *intervention*. This *intervention* would clearly have to come from outside of the human race. The disciples asked Jesus, "Who then can be saved?" Jesus answered them in this way, "With men this is impossible, but with God all things are possible" (Matthew 19:25b & 26b).

This brings us back to our heavenly *inheritance*. It has been allotted to us because of the miraculous work of redemption. This work came from above, outside of man's various attempts. At a result, we are reminded that our faith connects us to the possibilities of God as we choose to believe the work of Jesus on the cross.

Our *inheritance* also reminds us of our place in the kingdom of God. This place is often described by one little word that we often take for granted, and that is the word *"in."* The word *"in"* is found throughout Paul's epistles as a means to describe our place and *inheritance* in God. It implies *inclusion*.

We are told that we have been placed *in* Christ, and He has been placed *in* us. In other words, we find everything we have need of *in* Christ and because of Him. *In* Him all is complete. Nothing can be added that will bring value to our lives, and if anything is taken away in regard to our life *in* Him, there will be a loss of order and purpose. Because our life is hidden *in* Christ, and His life is being unveiled *in* us, God cannot look down without seeing His Son. It is from this premise that an *intimacy* in a relationship with God is established.

It is Jesus' life *in* us that becomes that *incense* or fragrance that reaches heaven and brings God pleasure and honor. Obviously, there is no meaning or purpose in regard to our life outside of the life of Christ that is *in* us. As we consider Jesus, we must recognize that He is our real portion or *inheritance*. Such a reality reveals that we must be *identified* to, as well as posses this *inheritance* now so that it can be fully realized in heaven. The challenge for each believer is obvious. We must become *increasingly* aware that Jesus is indeed our all *in* all.

Romans 3:28

J is for **justification.**

What does it mean to be *justified?* Someone told me that *justification* means "just as if I never sinned." In other words, in such *justification* I can stand *justified* in my present state in spite of my past. *Justification* is necessary to ensure salvation, as well as necessary to finish our spiritual *journey.*

We are on a *journey.* We are passing through this world. However, without the means to be pardoned from our sins, there is no way that we can finish this course in a beneficial way. Obviously, we could not stand *justified* before God without the issue of sin being resolved. Clearly, sins have to be taken care of before any of us can stand acceptable before our holy God. This requires establishing a means by which the Law could be satisfied so that we could be pardoned from the required *judgment.* The *judgment* upon all sin was death. God provided a pardon. However, it takes faith on our part to receive the pardon. When a person receives the pardon, he or she is able to stand *justified* before God in his or her present state.

Since our sins had to be remitted, our Lord's redemption became necessary. He remitted our sins on the cross. However, we must receive this redemption by faith. Faith reminds us that the *just* shall live by it.

The concept of *"just"* reminds us of the type of life that will express itself when the state of *justification* has truly been established. Being *"just"* points to being righteous, upright, or in right standing with God. If you are *just*, you will be honorable in your conduct, making you upright towards others. If you maintain inward integrity, which is a manifestation of being *just*, then you will be in right standing with God. If you do what is right by obeying God, you will be considered righteous before God.

Clearly, *justification* does not mean you have a ticket to live any old way. It simply means you are starting from a clean slate. A clean slate allows you the opportunity to live a different life and establish new ways, relationships, and practices. You will no longer be accused, condemned, or haunted by the old ways. Clearly, we must do everything in our power to maintain a pure and acceptable slate before our Lord.

God has different references made about Him. One is that He is a *jealous* God. *Jealousy* is very much associated with the flesh and condemned. However, God's jealousy is not fleshly but holy. As God, He alone deserves our worship and service. As a result, He becomes *jealous* when people worship other gods. His *jealousy* righteously guards and demands His preeminent, rightful position in people's lives.

This brings us to the covenant that was established. God is also referred to as *Jehovah. "Jehovah"* points to God as Lord. The word *"Jehovah"* reminds His people that He is a covenant God. Covenant involves becoming *joined* in or party to an agreement. Such agreement points to identification. In other words, we come into agreement at the place of the covenant. From this agreement, we can become identified to the promises of God.

God showed His intention towards His people by establishing covenants. It is on the basis of His covenant that we approach Him. Throughout Scripture, we as believers are given insight into the promises and blessings that are attached to His covenant. For instance, God, who is known as *Jehovah-Jireh,* serves as our provider due to His covenant. We also know from the premise of *Jehovah* that He is our banner, healer, righteousness, shepherd, and peace to name a few benefits. In the end, we will know the fullness of His promises as He takes His ultimate place as *Judge.* He will bring *justice* to this world by righting all that has been made wrong by sin, rebellion, and Satan. Of course, all of these benefits will be realized because of the covenant He has made with His people.

As Christians, we have an everlasting covenant, established on the basis of God's redemption. The one who is the author of this redemption is the Lord *Jesus* Christ. *"Jesus"* is the Greek word for the Hebrew name *Joshua. "Joshua"* means, "*Jehovah* saves" or "*Jehovah* is our salvation." The word "the" means He alone holds this name, title, and position. As our Lord, we are reminded that He is our owner who has established an everlasting covenant with us through His blood. As the Christ, He is the Anointed or Promised One of God. Since the name of *"Jesus"* stands in the middle of this title, we are reminded that salvation connects man to the one and only true God in light of the work of redemption that would be brought forth by the Anointed or Promised One. The prophet Isaiah actually described the Messiah in this way: "For unto us a child is born, unto us a son is given, and the government shall be upon his shoulder; and his name shall be called Wonderful, Counselor, The Mighty God, The Everlasting Father, The Prince of Peace" (Isaiah 9:6).

We can know the abiding confidence of this covenant. Such an abiding confidence points to a very important anchor in our soul. This anchor is *joy.* Jesus stated that certain things were written so that our *joy* could be full. This *joy* is not happiness, but a realization that all that was said is true. As believers, we can rest in the certainty of His Words. We can rejoice in them because they have the assurance of heaven behind them.

Are you living according to a *justified* state? This means your Lord does not have to display *jealousy* because you have received His pardon and know Him as *Jehovah.* You possess the anchor of *joy,* and rest in the assurance that you will not meet Him as your *judge,* but as your Redeemer.

John 18:36

K is for **kingdom.**

As Christians travel through this world, they must remember that their citizenship is elsewhere. There are two *kingdoms* in operation in this world. One is the *kingdom* of darkness and the other one is the *kingdom* of light. Christians belong to the *kingdom* of God, but they must remember that they have been translated into this *kingdom* of light because of Jesus Christ.

It seems that Christians either ignore that they have been translated into a different kingdom, or they are riding high on misconceptions and heresies concerning their place and part in God's *kingdom*. Self-serving leaders are often promoting these misconceptions. Some are claiming that the Church will usher this *kingdom* in. However, the *kingdom* of God is already here and in operation in the lives of people. In fact, some of these misguided and heretical individuals seem like they are pursuing the concept of a personal *kingdom* in the name of Christ. These people are not seeking out the *King of kings* to serve Him properly in this unseen *kingdom*. The truth is Jesus, not man, will establish the physical *kingdom* that has been promised in His thousand-year reign on earth.

Jesus said of His *kingdom* that it is not of this world. His words do not mean that the *kingdom* of God is not in operation in this world; rather, it has not been established, nor does it operate according to this world. His *kingdom* has no agreement with it. The *kingdom* of God is unseen, while the world operates in the fleshly realm. The *kingdom* of God begins as a small, insignificant seed in the hearts of those who believe the Gospel, and begins to slowly spread out like a tree to embrace the impossible and the eternal. On the other hand, the world's kingdoms shine in a false glory that lacks substance and will one day cease to exist.

Jesus gives us insight into God's *kingdom*. It is God's good pleasure to give it to us. We are also told that we have been appointed to it. This makes sense when you realize that as believers we serve in an official capacity in this *kingdom* as an ambassador. We are not only citizens of this *kingdom*, but we officially represent its interests in this world. The main interest of this realm is the salvation of souls. It is true, as representatives of the *King of kings,* we are after others to become part of this unseen monarchy, but the reasons are not self-serving or to make it a powerful *kingdom*. The *kingdom* of God already has all authority and power behind it.

We are to seek this *kingdom* for we must inherit it. Jesus is the one who holds the *key* to this realm. He serves as the door, and only faith will allow that key to unlock the fullness of life that is on the other side of this incredible door. Obviously, we must truly become citizens of the *kingdom* of God. However, as loyal subjects of Jesus, we are to seek to live according to the righteous ways of this incredible realm. Clearly, the *kingdom* of God must first be established in hearts, and then it will be made known to others.

One of the manifestations of this *kingdom* is *kindness*. People are not attracted to tyranny. Jesus is not a harsh *king* or master. He is a *kinsman*. Like Boaz showing honorable responsibility towards Ruth, Jesus accepted the responsibility to establish our allotted inheritance as children of God. This opened the way for an intimate relationship between God and His people.

Giving Jesus as our payment showed the extent of God's *kindness* towards those who were His. Jesus becoming identified with each of us in our plight revealed the sacrificial love that motivates the grace and benevolence that is often extended through *kindness*. The meekness in *kindness* serves as a source of power and strength often shown through compassion and consideration.

It is in a relationship with God through Christ that we can begin to *know* Him. The Apostle Paul talked about growing in the *knowledge* of Jesus. *Knowledge* means to perceive, resolve, and understand. *Knowledge* alone can feed our pride and become destructive. However, *knowledge* that is motivated to properly perceive Jesus with the intent of resolving issues that are spiritually oppressive and destructive, can bring us to an understanding about the character and ways of our Lord.

In John's first epistle he stipulates that we can, must, and should *know* Jesus. *Knowing* points to the ability to properly stand and discern the matters of life based on the *knowledge* of Christ. Everything that is said, thought, or done is considered within the confines of this *knowledge*. As a result, a person can truly *know* what is right and acceptable. Therefore, on judgment day there will be no excuse for not *knowing* the truth.

Since we, as Christians, should *know* what is true, we must be responsible to *keep* it in integrity and purity. *Keeping* a matter, points to regarding it in a right way and obeying it. We need to *keep* Jesus' sayings, but *keep* or refrain ourselves from coming into agreement and practices with that which is evil.

The beauty about the word *"keep"* is that it reminds us that God is our *keeper*. He is the One who maintains our lives. He watches over us and ensures our well-being. Such a position should also remind us that God is our shepherd and husbandman. However, to ensure His protection, we need to *keep* our relationship with Him at the forefront of all that we do. We need to value this relationship and regard it as our most prized possession to ensure the necessary *knowledge* that we will need to inherit His *kingdom*.

Ephesians 5:8

L is for **light.**

Jesus is the *light* of the world. We know that we walk according to what we can see. Seeing is not a matter of what we can see with the eye, but what we can actually perceive or understand. Clearly, we walk according to physical light, but we also walk according to the *light* of our personal understanding.

This is why the Bible tells us that the *light* of Jesus is actually His *life*. As Christians, we walk according to our understanding of Jesus. We cannot see Him, but we can experience the essence of His *life* in us. Since we possess the *light* or *life* of Jesus, we will reflect Him in our *lives*.

To possess the *light* of Jesus as our very *life*, we must *learn* of Him. We are actually instructed to *learn* of His *lowly* disposition and His meek attitude. The truth is we must un*learn* the behaviors from that which has influenced and conditioned in us in the *lustful* ways of the flesh and the destructive ways of the world. Ultimately, we must take on the mind of Christ. This means we will become *likeminded* with Him.

To be *likeminded* means we will have agreement with Jesus. Agreement is so important to our Christian *lives*. It points to intimate fellowship. We will know His will and come into submission to His work within us. As a result, we can also come into agreement with those who are *likeminded* in their Christian faith. When there is such agreement between God's people, much can be accomplished. However, many of God's people remain independent in their way of thinking and doing. Independence is a wonderful tool of Satan because he can always divide and conquer.

Sadly, many people are *lost* because they do not possess the *light* of Jesus. In fact, the glorious *light* of the Gospel has never been able to penetrate their dull understanding with their need to be saved. They have failed to see Jesus as the glorious Passover *Lamb* of God that is able to take away the mark of death upon their *lives*. As a result, these people will fail to discover the power of salvation that came forth when the *lion* of Judah died on the cross. As the *lion*, Jesus took on the *lowly* disposition of the *Lamb* to become our personal sacrifice and substitute on the altar of the cross. Those who are lost walk according to the *lies* of Satan, the *lust* of the flesh, and *love* for this present world. As a result, the *leaven* of sin has consumed their understanding with darkness. This is why Jesus warns that even the *light* in us may be great darkness. He also exhorted us to take heed as to how we hear or understand a matter.

As children of the *light,* we do not have fellowship with darkness. In fact, the *light* we walk according to is like a candlestick or a *lamp* that will guide each step through the darkness of this world. We know there is the *light* of Jesus' *life,* the powerful flame of the Spirit, and the *illumination* of the eternal Word of God.

The Bible talks about how the Word *illuminates* the way for us. Psalm 119:105 reminds us that it is a *lamp* unto our feet and a *light* unto our path. It cleanses as water, it exposes like a sharp sword, breaks down like a hammer, and is a fire that can purify and consume. The beauty about the different *lights* of God is that they allow us to *leave* the ways of darkness and death behind us.

The *light* Christians are to walk according to will bring them to *liberty* in the Spirit. In fact, this is the hope found in the *light* that comes from above. *Light* represents the glory of something. For the *light* from above reminds us of the Father of *lights.* All perfect gifts come from Him and there is no variableness, or shadow of change and uncertainty in Him. For His glory will never change. But, in God's kingdom we must have the *liberty* to discover this incredible *life* that has been freely given to us. We must actually *labor* to truly possess it.

Jesus put it in this perspective in John 6:26b-27,

> Ye seek me, not because ye saw the miracles, but because ye did eat of the loaves, and were filled. Labor not for the meat which perisheth, but for that meat which endureth unto everlasting life, which the Son of man shall give unto you; for him hath God the Father sealed.

The people asked Jesus what it meant to labor for the meat that would not perish. He answered in this way, "…This is the work of God, that ye believe on him who he hath sent" (John 6:29b).

Labor in this text means struggling through the temptations of the flesh, the attractions of the world, and the personal dreams and pursuits of self in order to come into a place of belief and total reliance upon Jesus Christ as *Lord* and Savior. *Liberty* in the Spirit can be found once a person is able to get past this war in the soul. It is in such *liberty* that the real *labor* in our Christian faith can be summarized in *loving* the *Lord* with all of our heart, soul, might, and mind. Such *love* will cease to be a *labor* when one truly makes Jesus Christ *Lord of* his or her *life.*

Titus 3:2-3

M is for **meekness.**

Living the Christian life requires a right attitude. Jesus revealed His attitude in Matthew 11:29, that of *meekness.* In our culture, *meekness* is considered weakness. However, in Christianity it is a point of strength. It points to a person's strength actually being channeled or disciplined through the Holy Spirit for God's use and glory. Strength that is not properly disciplined is destructive, and can prove to be used in abusive ways.

Jesus was a revelation of a powerful *mystery* that had been veiled in Scripture. This *mystery* would result in the redemption of souls. However, it required Jesus to give up His capacity as God (His authority and power) to become *man.* As the Son of *man,* Jesus took on a lowly disposition and a *meek* attitude to serve as an example as to what God initially intended when He formed *man* in His image.

As our *Maker,* God knows what will bring satisfaction to our spirit, and enable us to reach our potential. It is only through *meekness* that *man* is able to reach his potential, and properly *minister* to others. A *meek* attitude allows the Spirit to work the disposition and life of Christ into every believer. Ultimately, it will *manifest* the very light of Jesus as His *majesty* or glory is unveiled through the disposition and attitude of those who truly have embraced His attitude by faith.

Obviously, as Christians we must develop this *meek* attitude. In order to do this we must begin to partake of the *manna* or bread that came down from heaven. Partaking means that we must believe to the point that we apply or assimilate the truth about Jesus into our way of thinking, being, and doing. This will cause His pure *milk* (doctrine) to establish us on the right foundation, and His *meat* (revelation) to line us up to the cornerstone of His ways. As we *meditate* upon the purity of His *milk* and the discerning qualities of His *meat,* we can begin to see how *marvelous* He is. Such a revelation will transform our *minds.* The more our *minds* are transformed, the more we will be able to see the *manner* in which our Lord's love, *mercy*, grace, and *mighty* power work on our behalf.

Today, Jesus serves as our *Master.* He truly *mastered* the righteous life in His humanity. As a result, He is our great teacher. As His followers, students, or disciples, we must be willing to abandon all that we know in order to follow Him. Such abandonment reminds us that we must become *martyrs. Martyrs* are people who are already dead, but serve as living testimonies or *memorials* of the One whom they now serve.

When we think of *memorials,* we are reminded that when we encounter one, we must remember. To remember, points to *meditating* on an event, lesson, or instruction that is associated with such a *marker.* As believers, we are to recall the *measures* God took to bring about eternal life. Out of this eventful time in history, Jesus established a *memorial* to bring to remembrance what was actually brought forth. We know that *memorial* to be communion. Every time we partake of communion, we remember that our redemption cost God in ways that could never be *measured* by human calculations.

During His crucifixion, Jesus experienced the *malice* of man's darkness and hatred that he possessed towards his *Maker.* On the cross He *mourned* the destruction of sin upon humanity, knowing that many will remain dead in their sins, even after the gift of life has been secured and offered to them. However, a *miracle* would take place in spite of death and destruction. Jesus would rise from the grave and prove victorious over death. He would then become our *Mediator.*

As our *Mediator,* Jesus would serve in the capacity of High Priest. He would *minister* on our behalf. He would stand before heaven as the One who became sin for us so that He could satisfy the demands of the Law. As our advocate, He would be quick to stand in defense of us in our times of struggle and failure, reminding all of heaven that no accusation can be brought against us for we have been pardoned. This pardon was accomplished because He became our substitution on the cross.

As believers, we are called to be *ministers* of the Gospel. We must remember that we are part of the greatest *miracle* that ever took place. Because of our born-again experience, we now possess a new life that is *marked* by eternity and resurrection power. As believers, we make up a lively priesthood that must offer up spiritual sacrifices of praise and service. We must always remain lowly so that we can *mourn* that which breaks the heart of God. In *meekness,* we must always *mix* unfeigned faith with all we do to avoid walking in unbelief, indifference, and disobedience towards our spiritual responsibilities. Such a life will prove to be fruitful as God adds to His kingdom and *multiplies* His blessings in our lives and among His people.

Deuteronomy 15:7-11

N is for **needy.**

Through the years I have often mentioned to God and others that we are a *needy* people. The pride of man wants to convince him that he is self-sufficient, not *needy*. However, God cannot meet us unless we realize that we are indeed in *need* of His intervention. To be *needy* reminds us that we do not have all of the answers to the matters of life. We are not in control of our lives; therefore, we are at the mercy of that which is unseen.

Being *needy* points to being poor in spirit. We are literally cringing beggars before God. And, without His intervention, we will find ourselves miserable and lost. In fact, we depend upon His blessings to have all of our *needs* met, and upon His long-suffering to see us through times of temptation, failure, and despair. We must remember at all times that the poor in spirit are the ones who will inherit the kingdom of God.

The Bible guarantees us that God will take care of our basic *needs*; therefore, we do not *need* to be anxious about them being met on a daily basis. This brings us to a very important subject, and that is the difference between *needs* and wants. Most materialistic Americans cannot distinguish between that which is *necessary* from their selfish desires. They often perceive their wants as something they must have in order to live. However, wants feed the lusts of the flesh, while *needs* maintain the physical aspects of life. In fact, we have three basic *needs:* they are food, water, and clothing. Sadly, most people take for granted God supplying their *needs* as they pursue temporary wants in an attitude of ingratitude. Needless to say, these wants will not add any value or real substance to their present life.

In the Old Testament, God revealed His attitude towards those who were *needy*. We see where He regarded, or took note, of those who were poor. He had blessed His people so that they could properly minister to those who were *needy*. Such ministry would involve benevolence and compassion. As you study God's concerns for those who were less fortunate, you begin to realize that such people served as a test to His people. Do His people possess the benevolence to recognize the *needs* of others, and the compassion to enter in with another person in his or her plight regardless of the cost?

Every time we meet the *needs* of others, we are recognizing our humble or small beginnings. We all start out *needy* before God. In His mercy and grace He meets us so that in turn we can serve as the extension of His heart, hands, and voice as we meet the *needs* of others as a testimony of our Lord's love and commitment.

A good example of our spiritual plight can be found in the parable of "The Good Samaritan." This parable is about what it means to truly love your *neighbor*. Any time you live in a *neighborhood,* community, and even a *nation*, you must realize you are indeed a *neighbor* to whosoever you encounter. The man that was beaten and left for dead represents each of us before we encountered Jesus Christ. Keep in mind Jesus took on humanity so that He could become our *neighbor.* As our *neighbor,* He regarded our miserable plight and set out to do something about it. The cost for being our good *neighbor* is beyond our comprehension, but the result is that we now have a second chance at a *new* life.

In the parable of "The Good Samaritan," the Samaritan took the wounded man and *nurtured* him back to health. This act may have appeared *noble*, but in reality, it was a point of reasonable service. When love is motivating you, and compassion is your daily companion, entering into someone's plight is your reasonable service. This good *neighbor* was doing what was honorable and *necessary.* The truth is genuine character would *never* allow a person to forsake another person in his or her plight. Likewise, Jesus could not abandon us to our miserable plight.

The problem with some Christians is that they maintain a *nominal* life before the Lord. In other words, they have established their own comfortable *nest* of indifference in regard to Jesus. They do enough to be considered Christian, but they *never* develop a true passion for lost souls. Such people may draw *near* to God with lip service, but their hearts are far from Him. They may appear *noble,* but they are not honorable in their actions towards others. They may give the appearance that they are walking according to the light of Jesus, but *nothing* has changed in their disposition or attitude. There is no indication of a *new* life.

These people may feed themselves with the things of religion and the world, but they do not care to *nurture* others with the *nourishing* morsels of God's Word. The soul of these individuals eventually becomes tormented by its own darkness. After all, their vanity, despair, and hopelessness represent the dark *night* of the soul. *Nothing* makes sense as they wrestle with the emptiness of their own life.

As Christians, we must take on a *needy* disposition in order to learn how to be a good *neighbor* to those we encounter. Granted, they may not appreciate the concern we have for their souls, and they may resent the truth. However, we cannot forsake them until we know that we have done all we can for them to discover the *new* life that awaits those who will believe upon the Lord Jesus Christ.

Hebrews 5:8-9

O is for **obedience.**

Christians have a hard time separating the gift of life that comes through salvation, and *obedience* that is a natural response of unfeigned faith that results in good works. When Christians talk about the need to *obey,* people confuse it with works. *Obedience* done out of love for our Lord is not a matter of working for or earning salvation. Rather, it is a natural response that comes from one who is truly saved. Jesus put it in this way: "If you love me, keep my commandments" (John 14:15).

In the Book of Hebrews, we learn that Jesus was actually brought to perfection in His humanity through *obedience. Obedience* is a discipline. However, you must first *observe* what is right before you can truly *obey* according to the spirit or intent behind it. In fact, people could keep the technical aspect of the Law, but fail to maintain its integrity by failing to *obey* it according to the intent or attitude of it. This is why Jesus stated that as His servants we must teach His disciples (followers) to *observe* all things that He had commanded. They must see it according to the spirit or intent to maintain the integrity of it in their own personal applications and practices.

One of the main ways that we can learn to *obey* is by picking up our personal cross. Of course, we must deny ourselves the luxury to have life on our terms before we apply the real discipline of the cross. The cross is what disciplines our walk. In fact, it brings us into step with Jesus, as we come under his yoke. It is through such discipline that we truly learn what it means to *obey.* After all, there can be no *obedience* without the proper discipline and attitude.

Discipline points to *order.* God is not a God of confusion, but of *order.* The opposite of *order* is chaos. Many people's lives are chaotic. Without proper *order,* people will not be *open* to the *opportunities* available to discover their life in God. They will not know how to properly *occupy* in the way that is edifying to them. In fact, they may become *offended* by the intrusion that the Christian life, with its responsibilities, will require.

This is why we must first deny ourselves to bring the proper *order* to our lives. Once self is out of the way, we are now able to give way to the work of the cross and the Spirit. *Obedience* to the work of the cross allows us to *obtain* the prize. The Apostle Paul talked about this prize in relationship to becoming identified with Christ in His death, burial, and resurrection. The prize is the life of Jesus being realized in us.

The work of the Spirit points to the concept of *oil*. God *ordained* the making of special pure *oil* in the *Old* Testament. This *oil* pointed to the Holy Spirit. Such *oil* was used to stipulate what God was *ordaining* in relationship to His character and work among His people. The *oil* was used to anoint His prophets, priests, and kings. These people were actually set apart by the *oil* to do God's bidding. The anointing represented a point of calling, recognition, and service.

Every Christian has the anointing of the *oil* of the Holy Spirit upon their life. We know that each believer is called. This means as Christians, we have a calling upon our lives. Each Christian makes up part of a lively priesthood. This means that we have been *ordained* to serve both God and man. As Christians, we must first *offer* up our bodies and lives as a living sacrifice for God to use for His purpose and will. As priests, we *offer* up spiritual sacrifices of praise, as well as practice good works on behalf of God in ministry to others.

The Christian life reminds us that we have put off the *old*. We cannot expect to carry the *old* ways into the new. The *old* will defile the new, and the new will destroy the *old*. The ways of the *old* will continue to serve as *obstacles* that will cause confusion and hinder our spiritual growth. As a result, we will never learn what it means to *overcome*.

Scripture is clear that we must *overcome* the flesh, the world, and Satan to ensure our candlestick is not removed. Remember, a candlestick means nothing if the *oil* is missing. It will have no ability to serve as a light or a reflection in this present world.

As *overcomers,* we will know the victorious ways of the Christian life. We will understand that God has made an *oath* with us by way of an everlasting covenant. This covenant gives us the *opportunity* to become *one* in spirit, mind, heart, and will with our Lord. It will bring us into a place of total agreement. However, to come into this place of agreement, we must realize that unless He has *ordained* a matter, it will prove to be useless in light of eternity.

This brings us to His *ordinances*. Jesus gave the Church two such *ordinances*. They are water baptism and communion. Water baptism points to identification and communion points to establishing that *oneness* or agreement with Him and among each other.

Obviously, we must clearly decide to *obey* His *oracles*. They have been *ordained* by Him and inspired by His Spirit. We must knock on all doors, but only walk through the ones He *opens*. After all, each *open* door represents a new *opportunity* to discover the life that God has clearly *ordained* for each of us.

1 Peter 2:9

P is for **peculiar.**

God has always referred to His *people* as being *peculiar.* This has a couple of meanings. It points to *people* who belong to Him. In fact, He has actually *paid* for or *purchased* these *people* for Himself. This *payment* is referred to as redemption. Since His *people* belong to Him, they are set apart for His good *purpose* and *pleasure.* It is by faith in Him that He is able to *perform* a good work in His people until His eternal *plan* of salvation is fully realized in their lives, and His *promises* are brought to fulfillment.

Peculiar also points to God's people being special. As for Christians, they are considered saints. As saints, we have actually been placed in a lively *priesthood.* As New Testament *priests,* we must learn to follow the *pattern* set forth for the *priests* of the Old Testament. This *pattern* included acts of consecration, sacrifice, anointing, and wearing of special clothing that clearly set them apart in *purpose.*

For New Testament *priests*, they must come to terms with what it means to be in this *position.* They must understand that they were indeed *poor* in spirit because of their fallen state of sin and death. Out of grace, they have been *pardoned* for *past* sins. This *pardon* is to remind them that they are not to live life for the *pleasure* of self in this *present* world, but to live unto God for His *purpose*, ensuring that they are *part* of His kingdom. They must *ponder* God's Word in order to *partake* of the divine nature of Christ. This ensures that by faith they will grow up in the knowledge of their Lord. As they grow in a relationship with the Lord, they will know *peace* of mind, as well as come to a *place* of *perfection* or maturity in their Christian life.

The main goal of every *priest* is to serve God in such a way that He will be honored and glorified. The *priests* of God were to be single focused. For example, the Old Testament *priests* were not given land. The reason for this was clear: God was to be their portion or inheritance. Likewise, the *priests* of the New Testament have not been *promised* earthly blessings, but spiritual, heavenly blessings. Such blessings remind each of us as Christians that our real *prize* is to *possess* Jesus Christ.

In the Old Testament, the obedient ministry of the *priests* was capable of ensuring the very *presence* of God in the midst of His *people.* After all, it was God's desire to dwell and walk among His *people.* His Spirit served as the *pillar* of fire that *protected* the children of Israel during the night, as well as served as the cloud that guided them during the day. When God was among His *people* in the wilderness, He also *provided* them with manna from heaven and water from the Rock.

Once again, as believers, we are reminded that God's Spirit dwells within us. We are, therefore, to walk according to the Spirit. As a result, we have the same guidance and *protection* as the children of Israel. Likewise, all of our needs and blessings come from the great *Provider*, for it is His good *pleasure* to give us His kingdom. The Lord so desires His *people* to *prosper* in ways that would allow them the freedom to invest back into His kingdom for His glory.

As New Testament *priests*, we must insist on personal *prudence*, *purity*, and *piety* in our lives. This will require us to separate ourselves from the *pollutions* of the world. Such separation points to *purging* ourselves from the influences of that which is unholy. When people *purge* themselves in this way, they will separate themselves from the *perverse* ways of the world.

Keep in mind that the world *permits pride* to reign, and the flesh to *pursue* that which will make a person into a child of *perdition*, rather than a child of God. This will cause such *people* to walk a *path* that will cause them to *perish* in their sins. Even though God's wrath rests upon such *people*, He continues to be long-suffering or *patient* towards them in the hope that they will come to repentance before they taste of His anger. However, people who insist on the *perverted* ways of self and the world will *prove* to be foolish, rather than *prudent*.

As God's *priests*, we must offer the spiritual sacrifices of *praise*, as well as intercede in *prayer* for others. In adverse times the sacrifice of *praise* will show unfeigned faith. It is true that unfeigned faith connects believers to the very *power* of heaven. Such a connection will ensure the effectiveness of our *prayers*. After all, faith is counted as righteousness. And, the *prayers* of the righteous avail much.

Obviously, as believers who walk by faith, we will become *peculiar* to those who do not understand the ways of God. To stand distinct or special can end in *persecution*. The Scripture is clear. Those who live godly lives will suffer *persecution*. This brings us back to the need to be *prepared* to stand for truth, in order to withstand any opposition against it, so that in the end we will stand and *prevail* because of it. It is in such times that we must become *pillars* that are firmly *planted* upon the Rock of Ages, Jesus Christ. No matter what opposes our life in Christ, we will not be moved from this incredible foundation, making us overcomers.

Another aspect that will make believers *peculiar* is their commission to *preach* the Gospel. As servants of God, we as believers do carry the most important message. The Gospel is the *power* of God unto salvation. We must *proclaim* it to every creature. However, it will take the *power* and *preparation* of the Spirit for people to hear, believe, and receive it as truth.

The question is, are you willing to become *peculiar?* If not, you cannot expect to be an effective *priest, prepared* by God unto every good work for His *purpose* and glory.

1 Peter 3:18

Q is for **quicken.**

Christians must realize that the Holy Spirit has *quickened* them. In other words, the Spirit has made them alive. As Scripture states, we all start out dead in our sins; therefore, we must be *quickened* in the spirit by the very life of Christ. This takes place when we are born again from above. However, to maintain this spiritual awakening is another matter altogether.

The Apostle Paul instructs Christians to awake, to stir themselves up. Since our Lord would ask *questions* to reveal the motives of the heart, we must ask ourselves *questions* to consider where we might be spiritually. It is important to realize that there is much that can dull our spiritual discernment or put us to sleep spiritually. This is why we must constantly stir ourselves up to examine ourselves at different times. We are going to examine some of these conditions that will put us to sleep on a spiritual level.

Compromise with sin will rob us of our spiritual awareness. Justification or *qualification* of sin in our conscience will blind us as to how sin is affecting our lives. Instead of the senses being alive to cause us to see the error of our ways, they become sensitive towards the outward environment. In a way, it is like putting a cloak on our sins so we do not have to face the hypocrisy of our own lives. This allows us to turn a critical, judgmental eye towards those who might be struggling in some type of sin. Such compromise will make us indifferent to reality, which will make us hard, critical, and unreasonable towards others. Keep in mind, where sin reigns, death is its constant companion. People in this state need to be *quickened* to see their own sin so that they can repent and overcome.

Associations with the world will make us, as believers, spiritually dull. In fact, it will desensitize us to the fact that we are not awake to what may be happening around us. This is when destructive seeds can be sown into the way we look at or perceive a matter. Destructive tentacles can begin to find their way into our ability to properly discern what is going on in our own lives. Death will flow through these tentacles.

Unbelief is another condition that will close us down in our spiritual lives. The Word of God has the power to stir us up to the truth of a matter. But, if we are skeptical towards the matters of God, the Word will have no real impact. It will not have the power to penetrate the inner man to reveal an indifferent attitude towards God. Indifference simply means a person really has failed to choose to not only believe God, but to truly love Him. After all, if he or she loves Him, he or she will also believe and obey Him.

This brings us to what it means to be made alive. It simply means to become alive to the Spirit. When we compromise with sin, we grieve the Holy Spirit. When we come into agreement with the world, we are coming under the influence of another spirit. Such influence will *quench* His work. As a result, the Spirit cannot convict, warn, or instruct us. If the Spirit cannot convict us, we will not be able to follow after Him. If the Spirit is not able to warn us, we will not be led by Him. If the Spirit cannot instruct us, we will be unable to walk in Him. Therefore, we will be subject to the flesh, which will serve as the only means by which we judge matters.

We know according to the Scriptures that the natural man is unable to properly discern the things of God. In fact, the flesh will *quarrel,* debate, and mock the Spirit in His wisdom, ways, and reasoning. Ultimately, the ways of the flesh become a *quagmire* to it subjects, as such people become increasingly embedded in its destruction, and begin to drown in its darkness of unbelief and delusion.

Sadly, instead of seeing the destructive ways of the flesh, people tend to clothe themselves with some type of religious cloak. In a sense, they take on a *quasi* state. This means they can be involved with various religious activities, but there is no real *quality* behind any of it. They will accept the outward *quantity* of their activities as reality, instead of seeing that there is no life in any of their religious activities. Such individuals have become basically dead, dull, or indifferent to the life and truth of the Spirit.

In this *quasi* or partial state of religion, the heart is missing. God has often contended with His people over such a state. As recorded, they had their sacrifices, but there was no obedience. They had their rituals, but there was no real worship. They had their religious disciplines, but there was no life in such unrealistic burdens. At one point God made this statement, "For thus saith the Lord GOD, the Holy One of Israel: In returning and rest shall ye be saved; in quietness and in confidence shall be your strength: and ye would not" (Isaiah 30:15).

The people of Israel had strayed from God. It was His desire for them to return to Him, and come to a place of rest in Him through reconciliation, thereby, ensuring salvation. This salvation would be realized in the *quietness* of a soul that was no longer restless because it was at peace with God. It would be illuminated in the light of confidence based on genuine faith as these wayward people repented and returned back to Him from their backsliding ways. However, these foolish people would not return to Him in repentance. They continued to walk in the ways of death, rather than become *quickened* in the spirit to once again experience unbroken fellowship with God.

As Christians, we must make sure that we maintain the life of the Spirit in all we do. It is the Spirit that will *quicken* us daily to the matters of God. Therefore, we must avoid substituting the inner life of the Spirit with outward religion in the attempt to cover up a spiritually dull state.

2 Corinthians 5:18-19

R is for **reconciliation.**

The tendency for most Christians is to think of Christianity in terms of being saved from the consequences of death brought on by sin. This is partially true. Jesus had to *redeem* us from the consequences of sin so that our sins could be *remitted* through the act of pardon. This meant He actually *ransomed* our souls back from the slavery, claims and *ruin* of sin. However, the initial consequence of the *rebellion* of sin in the Garden of Eden was the breaking of fellowship between God and man. Therefore, the real goal of Jesus was to *restore* man back into a *relationship* with God through *reconciliation.*

We are clearly told in these Scriptures that God has *reconciled* the world (people) unto Himself through Jesus' *redemption. Reconciliation* points to peace with God, giving each of us the *right* to boldly enter into the throne of grace. When we come seeking God's mercy, Jesus will actually serve as the place of *refuge* for us. When God considers us, He will see the wisdom, *righteousness,* sanctification, and *redemption* of His Son. As a result, He can *receive* us unto Himself in sweet communion. In the place of communion, we will find *rest* for our souls.

The invitation from Jesus is clear; we must come to Him to partake of the *rivers* of Living Water. Every person needs to experience true *revival.* Whether we are being *raised* up with a new life, or *renewed* in the inner man because we have become dull or spiritually asleep, *revival* must occur. This process begins when we come to a place of *repentance* where we turn back to face God to *reason* with Him over our sin.

Sin needs to be exposed and *rebuked.* Once we come to an understanding and agreement about our sin with our Lord, we need to make a decision to *return* back to the *Rock* of ages, where we will find pardon, *reconciliation, restoration,* and *rest.*

In order to *return* to God from a lost or *rebellious* state to experience such *revival,* we must *repent* of our sins. In *repentance,* we will put on the *raiment* of humility. We will come seeking the Lord's mercy to be *released* from the slavery of our sin and *rebellion.* Then, we will *reckon* that the *record* established by the work of *redemption* is true. It is by faith we will *reckon* that we are indeed dead in Christ to the influence, work, and activities of sin upon our life. Such *reckoning* will allow us to be *raised* up in newness of life.

The newness of life *reminds* us that we have the same *resurrection* power that *raised* Christ up actually pulsating through this new life. As we put off the old to walk in the new, we will experience the power of the

Spirit. As we are established in the distinct and *royal* status as priests and kings, we will sense a new freedom that will cause us to *rejoice* in the glorious work that is being done on our behalf. As a result, we will begin to *reap* everlasting life, as that which is fleshly loses its *rights* and hold on our lives.

We must *remember* our humble beginnings. As believers, we found our identity at the foot of Jesus' cross. The cross *reminds* us that we brought *reproach* upon the *reputation* and character of our Creator. We were *reprobates* in our ways, maintaining our *rights* according to the *roots* of *rebellion,* unbelief, and bitterness. Instead of *resisting* the darkness of Satan, we *resisted* the Holy Spirit's *reproof.* We failed to *render* good for evil. Rather, we called evil good and good evil because it served our selfish purpose. Ultimately, we showed contempt towards God as we *rejected* the *record* that He gave concerning His Son and our need for salvation.

However, God is long-suffering towards us so that we can come to *repentance.* The Father draws us to the Son, the Son invites us to partake of the Living Water, and the Holy Spirit *reproves* or convicts us of our need to be forgiven and saved. As we come to God in need, the *revelation* of His love and provision He showed forth through His Son will be unveiled to our hearts. Upon *receiving* His provision, we will start to sense the *rain* of His Spirit coming forth in our thirsty souls, the *rod* of the Word taking hold of our hearts, and the gentle *reins* of the Son pulling us towards the bountiful *riches* that He has made available to us through His *redemption.*

This brings us to *real religion.* So much that man does in the name of religious activity does not constitute *real religion.* It is man's *religion.* Instead of being *ruled* by the Lord of lords and King of kings, man is being *ruled* by *religious* leaders, systems, or *rituals.* Such *rule* points to dead letter *regulations* that are devoid of life. There is no *reality* of God's Spirit or life in any of it. Because of the tendency to substitute *religion* for practical Christianity, the book of *James* describes *real religion,* "Pure religion and undefiled before God and the Father is this: to visit the fatherless and widows in their affliction, and to keep oneself unspotted from the world" (James 1:27).

The fact that we have been *reconciled* back to God *reminds* us that *redemption* has provided a way for us in which we can come into the fullness of the life that was established on our behalf. However, to possess this life, we must *run* the *race* that is set before us. Most of the Christian life is preparation so that we as believers can be *ready* to face the various terrains this *race* will bring us to. As a result, the Apostle Paul talked about the preparation, discipline, and goal of this *race.* Ultimately, we will receive the prize of Jesus, and the *reward* of a crown of *righteousness.*

Are you enjoying the benefits of being *reconciled* back to God? Such *reconciliation* points to a place of *rest,* the fruit of peace, and the endurance to *run* the *race* until one finishes the course.

Jeremiah 29:11-13

S is for **seeking.**

Most people perceive that the greatest challenge in their present life is to live it. As Christians, we have discovered that the greatest challenge for us is to *seek* out the life that has been ordained for us. Our purpose for *seeking* out this life is to actually find it. In the fifth chapter of the book of Amos, we are told to *seek* the Lord and we shall live. Clearly, our life is found in the Lord.

The question that we must ask ourselves is does this *spiritual search* ever cease? The truth is that we must *seek* God daily as long as we are in these bodies. The flesh actually serves as a very dark curtain that causes God to become obscure to us. Therefore, we must wade through the obstacles of the flesh to find Jesus. Every day is new, along with God's mercies and compassions. Such newness allows us to *seek* God in every test, challenge, temptation, and tribulation in order to find Him.

How do we find God? It depends on what capacity we need to *see* Him in. After all, we must *see* Jesus. If we are *seeking* God to find mercy, we need to approach Him in *sackcloth,* which points to a contrite *spirit.* If we are *searching* for God to obtain *salvation* or deliverance, we must come to Him in meekness of attitude and *submission* of *spirit.* Ultimately, if we find Him, we will come away with a greater revelation of the *Son* of God who truly is our Redeemer and Deliverer. If we are *seeking* His will, we must recognize the authority of the *Scripture* and the leading and revelation of the *Spirit. Scripture* serves as His *spoken* oracles. The *Spirit* of God will always confirm *Scripture,* uphold God's character, and ensure the integrity of what is honorable and acceptable to God.

There are various obstacles that will cause us to take detours in our *search. Sin* will cause the biggest obstacle in our Christian lives. It will cause us to live according to the dictates of our *selfish* flesh and the *self-serving* ways of the world. The devil uses *sin* as a *snare* to entrap us into the tentacles of death, ruin, and despair. *Sin's shame* will cause us to go into *self-justification* or delusion. We must *separate* ourselves from the influences of *sin,* the compromise of *self,* and any agreement with the world. In fact, as Christians, we must become *saints* who are truly *set apart* in our attitudes, conduct, and lifestyles from the world.

Sin reminds us that we need to be *saved.* The Bible talks about how we have been *saved* from the dictates of *sin,* we are being *saved* from the influences of *sin,* and we will be *saved* from the consequences of *sin* in the future. We are instructed to work out our *salvation* in fear and trembling. To work out our *salvation* points to us giving way to the work of *sanctification.*

Being *saints* always points to a *sanctified* life. Only God can *sanctify* us. This means that we have been *set* apart unto God for His *sake.* As you *study sanctification,* you will realize that God puts us in a place of *sanctification.* This place is in Jesus Christ. It is the *Spirit* who actually *sanctifies* or does the work on the inward man to *set* us apart for God's use.

In order to ensure *sanctification,* we as believers must consecrate ourselves. This involves *self-denial* as we abandon our former life. Such abandonment would require us to *sell* out to *secure* the life that has been foreordained by God. In order to abandon all, we must apply the cross to every aspect of our *self-life.* This means *sacrificing* the hopes and dreams of our former life to take on the will, mind, and life of our Lord and *Savior.* Such *sacrifice* points to personal *suffering,* but it also ensures us that we will be glorified with our Lord.

As we apply the cross to the *self-life,* we will become living *sacrifices* that can be offered up for God's glory. In this process we will become the *salt* of the earth. To be the *salt* means that we will bring flavor, as well as contrast by *standing* for the truth. Truth always serves as the *salt.* For those who have an open wound due to *sin,* it can bring healing. However, for those who want to maintain their rebellion, truth will serve as a *sharp sword* that will expose their foolishness and unbelief.

We are also told that the Holy *Spirit* has *sealed* us until the fullness of redemption can be realized in our lives. The *Spirit* empowers us to live the life of a *saint.* However, a *saint* is also a *sojourner* or a *stranger* in this present world. In our status as *strangers,* we, as Christians, must always *seek* for the place of *safety* as we confront the different challenges of this world. We know that our true *safe* haven is Jesus. Our life is hid in Him as we have been positionally *seated* in high places with Him. We take comfort in knowing that our journey through this world will only last for a *season* in light of eternity. However, we must be *steadfast* to keep our eyes upon our heavenly destination in order to avoid detours wrought by *sin* and the false *signs* of this world and man's religion.

Saints also must become *sheep* in disposition. Such a disposition points to *sincerity* and *submission.* Godly *submission* is the source of real *strength* in the character of a *saint.* Such *submission* knows how to be discrete and disciplined in its conduct and *service* to God. In such *submission,* the life of Christ will be emitted as an acceptable *savor* to God. This *savor* edifies believers, while it brings the harsh reality of the judgment of death to those who are still lost in their *sin.*

We must always *seek* to *see* Jesus in all matters, as well as *submit* to the work of *sanctification.* This will ensure our *status* as *strangers* in this world and as children of God. Ultimately, we will be able to come home without bringing *shame* to our Lord and *Savior,* Jesus Christ.

2 Corinthians 5:1

T is for **tabernacle.**

It is important to understand our relationship to God. We know we must seek to be in a right relationship with Him. We must come into a place of communion to enjoy who He is. This brings us to the subject of what we must become to God. God desires to dwell among His people. In the Old Testament, He established a *tabernacle* for Himself. The *tabernacle* was nothing more than a *tent.* Since it was a *tent,* it could be packed up and moved from place to place. We are told that a cloud led this *tabernacle* by day, and a pillar of fire protected it by night.

For the children of Israel this *tabernacle* became the center of activity for them. They did not move without it or according to it. We know that the cloud and the fire represented the Holy Spirit. Later, when the children of Israel were settled in the Promised Land, a *temple* was built. This *temple* was established in a place designated by God, and was to be identified by the name, presence, and glory of God.

In Acts 17:24 this statement was made in the midst of the beautiful temples of Athens, "God, who made the world and all things in it, seeing that he is Lord of heaven and earth, dwelleth not in temples made with hands." This seems to be contradictory since it is God's desire to dwell among His people. How would God resolve this issue? It is simple. He would take the *tent* or body of man, establish it as a *temple* on the one foundation of His Son, and *tabernacle* or dwell in this individual.

Today, many people fail to see the simple *truth of* how God used the old to point to the new. When the curtain was *torn* in the *temple* upon Jesus' finished work on the cross, it was declaring the old was now giving way to something glorious. Common man was no longer separated from coming into the midst of the *temple.* He now would serve as the *temple* of the Spirit. God's presence, power, and glory would dwell in him. Wherever he went God was sure to be in his midst.

Christians serve as a walking *testimony* of God's name, character, and ways in the midst of this dark world. As *temples* of God, they must remember that they were brought forth by the *travail* of Jesus on the cross. Before they came to the liberation of Christ, they served harsh *taskmasters* of sin, self, the world, and Satan. They were nothing more than *tares* in the harvest field of humanity, ready to be separated, plucked up, and judged in the fires of hell.

Praise God, the *truth* of Jesus' redemption on the cross penetrated the dark, hopeless *thoughts* of the minds of those who proved to be heirs of God's kingdom. They begin to see a way out of their *terrible* state of doom. As their minds began to grasp the *thread* of redemption that ran through the Bible from the first promise of redemption in Genesis 3:15 to its appearance in the case of the harlot Rahab down to the Apostle Paul's escape from his enemies because of his newfound *testimony* of Jesus Christ, they would grab a hold of it by faith. In essence, they chose to *trust* the character of God and put confidence in His Word. At that point they were *translated* from the kingdom of darkness into the kingdom of God's dear Son. The *truth* not only set them free to discover God, but it began to *transform* their minds. In this inward *transformation,* they would become the *temples* of the Holy Spirit, as well as lively stones that would make up a precious priesthood. They would not only stand distinct as His people, but they would be part of His royal, heavenly family. The Lord would *tabernacle* among them as Emmanuel, God with His people.

The *translation* into the kingdom of light would change these people's *taskmasters* and their plight. Before, they were subject and always in compliance to the *thief* of this world who robbed, killed, and destroyed all hope. They found themselves falling into the *traps* of *temptation*. They experienced *tribulation* without hope. But, when they discovered the *true treasure* of heaven, Jesus, instead of standing condemned and hopeless by the *transgressions* they had committed against God's Law and covenant, they found forgiveness. The philosophies and *traditions* of the world that had greatly influenced them gave way to the living Spirit and the glorious truth of God's intervention through His Son. What seemed to be the endless *trials* of life could now be used to fine-tune their faith, *temptations* could be turned into godly patience, the *thirst* of their once empty souls could be satisfied by righteousness, and their *tears* of sorrow could be turned into *tears* of rejoicing. Instead of their *tongues* cursing the destructive ways of life, they could now praise and *thank* God for His love and faithfulness to do an incredible work in their life.

As Christians, we must remember that we are now part of a New *Testament* or covenant. We have a new *teacher,* the Spirit who will lead us into all *truth* about Jesus and the ways of righteousness. However, we must guard ourselves against the *temptations* of our former life and the world. In order to maintain our spiritual edge, we must choose to love *truth* and reject the compromise of worldly *tolerance*. We must *tremble* at the Word of God, rather than situate it according to our religious *traditions* and personal righteousness. We must remain *tender* to the gentle impressions of the Holy Spirit instead of pursuing the ways of the flesh. We must not *think* too highly of ourselves, but remember that the vainglory of this present life is like the grass and the flowers that will fade with the changing of seasons and *times*. The only *thing* that will remain sure is that which belongs to God.

As *tabernacles,* we must have the presence of God within us to set us apart. We must be *touched* by His life and empowered by His Spirit to serve as living *testaments* of His greatness. As believers, we must adhere to our commission to bring the *tidings* of good news to the rest of the world. And, we must constantly live in light of that glorious hope that one day in the *twinkling* of an eye, we will put off all that is corruptible in order to put on that which is incorruptible. Therefore, we must strive to ensure that all corruption loses its power in our lives, as we embrace that which is eternal and *trustworthy* of all praise, honor and glory, the Lord Jesus Christ.

Ephesians 4:13

U is for **unity.**

There is much discussion about *unity*. Most people see the concept of *unity* as the means by which to solve the problem of conflicts brought on by differences between people. Such a concept is not far from the truth, but the problem is few *understand* what it actually takes for people to come into true *unity*.

There are different types of *unity*. There is *unity* that is present when people agree about a matter, but such agreement is fragile due to the fact that people will eventually disagree about an issue. People's level of character or maturity will determine how people handle such disagreement. In fact, people can like you one minute and turn on you the next, proving that they are *unreasonable*. In such a state people can prove to be *unmanageable, undisciplined, unyielding,* and *unruly*.

To walk according to such an *unreasonable* disposition will cause such individuals to become an *unwalled* city. An *unwalled* city simply means a person is *unprotected*. Consistent with the lack of inward restraint, these people will demonstrate that they are *untrustworthy* in their intentions. They may also prove to be *unlawful* in their dealings, *unfaithful* in their commitment, *unfruitful* in their accomplishments, *unthankful* in their attitude, and *unjust* in their practices.

Another type of *unity* is based on spirit. The Bible tells us that deep calls to deep. In other words, we are going to be attracted to people who are motivated by the same spirit. The agreement we have may be healthy or *unprofitable,* or acceptable or *unholy* depending on the influence of the spirit. For Christians, there is only one spirit in which they can come into *unity*, and that is the Holy Spirit. To come to the place of *unity,* as Christians, we can only find our agreement at the point of the person, character, and work of *Jesus Christ*. It is at the point of Jesus that we partake together of the *unleavened* bread from heaven.

Christians may prove to have problems in the area of agreement because they operate in a mixture of spirits. This usually means they have not applied *unfeigned* faith in certain areas of their Christian walk. They may put their faith or confidence in doctrine or good works, but not in God and His Word. Without pure faith, a person will bring him or herself under another spirit. This will cause him or her to become *unstable* in his or her thinking and ways.

The Holy Spirit is the one who brings the Body of Christ into *unity*. He serves as the essence of every Christian's *unction* or spiritual endowment *(SC, #5545)*. The Spirit is the One who will *uncover unknown* mysteries and revelations, bringing believers to an *understanding* about the will and ways of God. He will enable each of us, as believers, to be *upright,* as He establishes us in a life that will be considered *undefiled* and *unblemished* to our Creator.

The third type of *unity* is established at the place of communion. It is this third type of *unity* that points to the state of oneness. The Godhead possesses this oneness. This is where there is total agreement between the three Persons of the Godhead. Each one comes into submission to that which has been established. For example, all three Persons of the Godhead have come into agreement concerning salvation, and now work in total agreement towards the goal of bringing all heirs of salvation into the kingdom of God. There is no inconsistency in their purpose, desire, or work. They work not as an efficient team, but as one complete *unit.*

Jesus made this important statement about this type of *unity* in John 17:21: "That they all may be one, as thou, Father, art in me, and I in thee, that they also may be one in us; that the world may believe that thou hast sent me." He also stated that He gave us the glory that was bestowed upon Him in His humanity by the Father, that we may become one. And, in this oneness we will be brought to perfection so that the world can know that the Father sent Him.

It is obvious that the *unity* established through example of the oneness that existed between the Father and Son cannot be faked or improved upon. For Christians, it involves agreement in the right spirit according to the truth of God, which has been clearly expressed in the Son of God. This type of *unity* was established in love, and serves as evidence that we, as believers, are indeed one in spirit and truth with the Son. From this premise, we must admit that such *unity* goes deeper than intellectual agreements, titles, doctrines, personal beliefs, and causes. It reaches into the heart, where there is truly identification to the person, character, and work of Jesus Christ.

It is important to *understand* what our part is in the Christian life to ensure true *unity* with God and one another. We already have established that we must walk by faith towards God and His Word. The problem today for many Christians is that they are very *unskillful* when it comes to the Word of God. As a result, they are often *unprepared* to come into agreement with that which might challenge or insult their fleshly pride and ways. In their ignorance towards the ways of God, they often fail to obey His Word. Failure in this way means that they will remain ignorant and *unrighteous* towards the will and ways of God. Instead of keeping themselves *unspotted* from the world, they will find themselves giving way to the *ungodly* attitudes and practices of the world. Such practices point to agreement with the world, where a battle between the Spirit and the flesh will incur.

In this *unproductive* state, these carnal or immature Christians will be *unable* to discover the *utmost* for their lives. These individuals will not know what it means to *uphold* God in His rightful place in their lives.

They will never experience in their present life the fullness, joy, and beauty of the *unspeakable* gift that God has made available to everyone who truly believes upon the Son of God.

1 Corinthians 15:55-57

V is for **victory.**

One of the greatest benefits that the Christian life offers us is *victory.* People who are subject to the bondage of sin, the oppression of this world, and the torment of Satan, are nothing more than *victims.* Eventually, they will be offered up as sacrifices on one of the many altars of the world as the kingdom of darkness mocks them in their foolishness.

Twenty centuries ago, Jesus Christ allowed Himself to be offered up on the altar of the cross. His life and ministry appeared to be in *vain.* In His *vexed* state of suffering, death, and despair, people openly mocked Him. It was as if they were trying to strip away the last *vestige* of *value* that His life and teachings had brought to the seeking souls that had been forever touched and changed by Him.

However, His life, along with His *voluntary* sacrifice, His death, and His burial would not prove to be a point of *vanity.* It is true His body had been torn like a *veil.* However, this was symbolic of the work that He was doing on the cross. He was providing a way into the place of reconciliation and communion with God. To confirm this, the *veil* in the temple was ripped by God from top to bottom. Because of the work of Jesus' redemption on the cross, mere man could now enter into the Most Holy Place in the status of a priest.

As we travel this present world, most of our activities will prove to be *vain* if they do not have the mark of eternity upon them. Even though we start out with what appears to be our whole life in front of us, we must remember that our present life on this earth is nothing more than a *vapor* in light of eternity. We must remind ourselves that it is not our present life that stands in front of us; rather, it is our eternal destination that lies before us. To reach this destination, we must learn how to overcome in the present to ensure *victory* throughout our lives.

We must be realistic about the extent of our physical life. We are nothing but clay *vessels* that must experience the fires of adversity, the poundings of tribulation, the separation of sorrow, and even taste death to become pliable in the hands of our Potter. Keep in mind, only our Potter can bring forth our *value* as *vessels* in His kingdom.

In order to come to such a place, we must become a *voluntary* offering. Sacrifice may seem like a *valiant* thing to do, but in reality, it is our reasonable service. It is from the point of our reasonable service that we will embark on our real *vocation* as servants of God. As believers, our life does not belong to ourselves, but to Jesus. He is our *Vine.* Therefore, our life, activities, and fruits will become an extension of His life, influence, and character upon our lives. We will not exist or move outside of Him.

This is a point of encouragement. After all, there is no *variableness* in our Lord. He is the same today as He was yesterday and will be tomorrow. As a result, we can know Him. As we discover who He is, we will be able to recognize His *voice*. As we follow Him, we will gain a *vision* of that which is eternal. This is the essence of true *victory* for the believer.

We must recognize that since we are residing in corruptible flesh, much of God's ways are *veiled* from us. Like Jesus, one day this *veil* of flesh will part, and we will behold the unhindered glory of our Lord. We will realize that the ultimate *victory* will be realized at the end of our journey. For this reason, we must keep our *vision* clear and heavenly directed.

In my Christian journey I have discovered that there are two perspectives, which must discipline my *vision*. They are Jesus' cross and eternity. The cross will cause me to be *vexed* over the present condition of this world, while eternity will enable me to be *valiant* in my stand for truth and righteousness, regardless of what it might cost me. By being *vexed* in my spirit towards the world, it will keep me from returning to its *vomit* and stench. By taking courage in my life in God, I can be assured that my life will never be *void* of purpose and meaning.

As we consider the full picture of the *victorious* life of a Christian, we can take courage. The truth is, we may be simple clay *vessels* carrying around a precious cargo (the life of Jesus), but one day we will come home. At that time, the *veil* of our flesh will part, and we will hear the precious *voice* of our Lord as He welcomes us home. As the Apostle Paul stated, "O death, where is thy sting? O grave where is thy victory" (1 Corinthians 15:55)?

Deuteronomy 8:1-3

W is for **wilderness.**

There are a lot of words that begin with *"w."* You might be *wondering* why I would choose the word *"wilderness."* Keep in mind life is a journey. You will see a variety of terrains as you sojourn through this present *world*. Different terrains point to different aspects of our Christian life. One of the terrains that Christians will face many times in their Christian life is the *wilderness*.

We already know that the children of Israel *wandered* through the *wilderness* for forty years until the rebellious generation died out. To *wander* means you do not really have any real destination. The children of Israel had been on their way to the Promised Land, but because of unbelief, they could not enter into their destination. This made them *wanderers* in the *wilderness*.

Wanderers often indicate those who are fugitives before God. They have no purpose in light of eternity or a real destination that has any real meaning. As Christians, we are not *wanderers* in this present age, but strangers in the *world* and pilgrims that will have no agreement or place in the present age. As we travel the byways of this present *world*, there is no *way* that we can avoid the spiritual *wildernesses* in our journey. In fact, they are necessary. Every great saint of God, including Jesus, went into the *wilderness*. As you study the purpose of *wildernesses* in a saint's life, you will realize this is where believers are separated, tested, prepared, and established in their spiritual lives.

Consider the children of Israel. They were separated from Egypt by being led into the *wilderness*. This separation proved to be a hard *way,* but it was necessary so that they could *worship* their God and serve Him. It was in the *wilderness* that the tabernacle, the center of their spiritual life, was prepared. It was in this barren *wasteland*, that their faith was tested as God provided their food and *water*. Sadly, these people missed the opportunity to enter into all that God had for them because they *wallowed* in the memories of their past lives that were attached to the *world*. Even though they tasted the bondage of their slavery, they remembered only that which fed their fleshly *wants*. This fleshly preference simply showed they were fleshly, poverty stricken, and *weak* in their faith.

In the case of Moses, he learned to be a shepherd in this *wasteland*. John the Baptist came out of the *wilderness* as the Voice that would prepare the way for the Messiah. The Spirit led Jesus into the *wilderness* where Satan tested him.

This brings us to the importance of these *wildernesses*. For every person who is naturally born into the Adamic race, he or she will discover that his or her soul represents the inner *wilderness* caused by sin. According to the *Word* of God, the *ways* of the Adamic disposition are *wicked,* and will place people under the *wrath* of God. Such people will ultimately experience the *whirlwind* of judgment, as the *walls* that have been established by all of their fleshly attempts, fall upon them in utter ruin.

As Christians, we know that the *wicked ways* of the Adamic disposition are the essence of sin that separates people from God. Those who maintain this fallen disposition live according to its darkness, ignorance, and rebellion. We also know that the *wages* of sin is death. As lost people *walk* according to the leanness of their souls, they will automatically seek out *wells* that they hope will sustain them. If these *wells* have any *water* in them, they will discover that the *water* is deadly, stagnant, and has no ability to sustain life.

In their search for meaning and purpose, these individuals will also *walk* in the *ways* of the *world,* only to find vanity. Such poor souls will become *weary* with the emptiness that plagues them. They may *wrestle* with what appears to be nothing more than mockery towards the *waste* that follows their life, but these individuals often hold onto the bleak *winter* that resonates through the barren darkness of their souls.

Some people seek purpose in *worldly wealth.* These individuals believe that if they can fill the emptiness of their lives with things, they will not taste the bitterness of their loneliness and vanity. However, *worldly wealth* simply enlarges fleshly appetites. These people will eventually find themselves in an endless *whirlwind* that will take them down into utter despair. As they become more entangled with the tentacles of the *world*, they become more tormented by the *wants* that are becoming insatiable, as well as always proving to be temporary.

As Christians, we have been delivered out of the slavery of sin and death by coming to the *wells* of salvation. As the *written Word* reveals, Jesus Christ serves as that glorious *well.* The *Living Word,* Jesus, died on the cross so that His blood could *wash* away our sins, making us as *white* (pure) as snow before God. He became our point of *wisdom,* righteousness, sanctification, and redemption so that we could be victorious in our *walk.* He offered the Living *Water* that would bring forth eternal life. He became poor so that we could become spiritually rich with the *wealth* of heaven. He sent the precious *wind* of the Holy Spirit to remove the *winter* from our souls by bringing forth regeneration in our inner man. Now our Lord serves as our *way* to life, reconciliation, restoration, *worship,* and communion with the Father. Clearly, He is *worthy* of all honor and praise.

Jesus serves as the Living *Word,* but we now must become His *witnesses.* This requires us to become *watchmen* over our lives. We must not *wink* at sin, ignorance, or rebellious independence in our lives.

We must *wait* on His leadership and instruction. We must recognize our *weaknesses* to allow His grace to become sufficient. We must *withstand* with His truth, *withhold* any agreement with the *world*, and become *workmen* that will rightly divide the *Word* of truth and do the *will* of the Father to avoid standing before Him in shame. This will ensure that we will be able to properly discern when and how to use the sword of the *Word* as a *weapon* against all of Satan's advances.

As His *workmen*, we must do the *work* and bidding of our Lord. We must not *waste* time *warring* against the Spirit because we refuse to become *weak* and poor in humility due to obstinacy of the flesh, and *wrong* because of worldly influences. We must know that if there is any *worth* in our lives it is because God has *wrought* it.

Remember, when you come to the *wilderness* in your spiritual *walk*, do not *war* against it; rather embrace it. Know it is a time of purifying your faith, establishing your life, and developing your spiritual character so that you can enter into all that God has for you.

Ezekiel 14:14-20

X is for the e<u>x</u>cellence found in the ways of God.

The letter "x" is a vital part of our alphabet, but it does not take up a very big section of the dictionary. It often serves as a symbol. It has been used as a signature by those who could not read or write, as well as in algebra equations. It is used as a means to rate questionable movies, and points to a specific chromosome that determines our gender. It is used to take a short cut when writing out the word of Christmas. However, it is simply *Xing* Christ out of the equation of what should be the real purpose for celebration.

Some words begin with "x." There is a *xanthippe,* an ill-tempered woman; *xebec,* a Mediterranean sail ship; *xylophone,* a percussion instrument; and of course the popular word "x-ray" (WD). Such words remind us that an ill-tempered woman will tear her house down; Jesus taught from a boat; believers should have a song in their hearts; and, the Christian life must cause us to become transparent in our personal e<u>x</u>aminations.

When you study how the letter "x" affects our alphabet, you can begin to understand that it will "mark the box" or highlight an emphasis to the right answer (or presentation) to bring significance or clarity to a matter; or, it will cross out a matter altogether. When we consider how this letter affects our presentation of something, and apply it to our Christian life, it will either highlight a matter as being significant due to its relationship to God; or, cross it out because it is associated with the works of the flesh. For example, e<u>x</u>alting or highlighting something to a place of importance must be based on the type of presentation of God, His truth, and message. From that point, the spirit behind it must be tested, the character proved, and the motives e<u>x</u>posed to ensure that it will be counted e<u>x</u>cellent as being worthy and acceptable to God.

On the other hand, the works of the flesh and the influence of the world must be e<u>x</u>tinguished from our lives. John the Baptist stated that God was going to take an a<u>x</u>e to the root of the old religious system to bring forth the new. To take an a<u>x</u>e to the old for us means that we must mortify the works of the flesh and separate from the influences that the world has upon our mind, will, and affections.

This does bring us to the word *"xeno."* It comes from the Greek form *"xenos"* which means stranger, guest, or foreigner *(WD).* Here is one word that points to the Christian in relationship to the present world. We do not belong to this world; therefore, we must be and will be separate from its influences and importance in our lives as we simply pass through as strangers.

When we consider our life in God, we must realize how much of it is beyond description. It is unseen, but it is eternal and holy, pointing to its *exceptional* worth that it brings to all who will possess it. Since it is beyond description and even comprehension by our limited minds, we may have to use the means of symbols to point to something that holds the answer, but must always be *examined* in light of God's character, as well as His ways and Scriptural principles.

The choices that have to do with the Christian life and the world always bring us to the crossroads of life. It seems like we come to the spiritual "X" crossings many times during the day. We must decide if we are going to ignore these different crossings, or become cautious that a decision must be made as to what we must do at each spiritual warning or caution sign.

In many cases we must be prepared to make an *exchange*. We must always be willing to leave the old way of ignoring, rebelling against, or sliding through these different points of decision. To ignore, rebel, or slide through these crossings simply means that we will go with the natural preference of the selfish disposition. However, at each intersection of life, we must consider whether we will *exceed* the fleshly desires of our base inclinations and tendencies in order to do what is honorable, or *excuse* away our rebellion as we risk our spiritual well-being. Sadly, there are those who see the caution signs as an opportunity to beat the odds. The result is that many have foolishly lost their lives.

It is important to make the right decisions in order to ensure that we are found to be *excellent* in our character and conduct before God. Judgment was about to come down upon the people of Jerusalem for the third and final time. God clearly showed Ezekiel that He would individually deliver three men—Noah, Daniel, and Job, but not the families or citizens of Judah. When you consider Noah, he was *excellent* in his faith because he refused to come into agreement with the wickedness of the world. Instead, he walked with God and found grace. His life was used to bring judgment upon the rest of the world.

Daniel by faith developed an *excellent* spirit because he would not come into agreement with the ways of the world. He remained separate, and as a result was able to intercede on behalf of Israel so that the people could return to Jerusalem.

Finally, there was Job who maintained his faith before God in the midst of being attacked by Satan. As a result, he saw God in a way that forever humbled him, enabling God to bless him. Obviously, since our God is *excellent* in all that He does, we must become *excellent* in our spirit, life, and conduct. The working of unfeigned faith towards God will highlight such a life.

This brings us to another important aspect of our life in God. Life is a teacher. There are some who want to figure life out before they embark on it. In other words, they want to step into life with all of the answers to avoid failures. There are some that only want to know life from the angle of what is pleasurable or positive before they will accept it. There are individuals who what to situate their environment to what they consider to be perfect before they will commit to the different aspects of life. Then, there are those who try to line life up to their reality before they will concede to life's unpredictable challenges. Clearly, people are trying to *exercise* their will upon life to bring about their particular *expectations* in regards to their take on what constitutes personal meaning and happiness. Obviously, such people are trying to determine the essence of their own life. However, life is never discovered on such terms. Life can only be discovered when it is actually *experienced. Experience* involves tasting the good, bad, and indifferent aspects of life. These *experiences* will *expose* the quality of one's character.

Jesus took on humanity to *experience* every aspect of life, including death. He did not shy away from it, or accept only what was pleasurable. He did not try to situate it to some perfection, or control it. He tasted every aspect of life, *except* sin. As a result, He serves as our *example.* His *example* allows us to live in *expectation* of His promises, as we *exercise* godliness. As we adhere to the *exhortation* of His Word, we will be able to be strong and do *exploits.* As a result, the life that comes from Jesus will *excel* all of our *expectations* in this present world.

However, we must also beware of operating in a *mixed* spirit. Wherever there is a *mixture* in our spiritual life it is because we have not added faith to a situation. Such a *mixture* will *tax* our resolve as our love begins to *wax* cold toward that which will challenge our attitude. If we fail to repent, we will begin to walk contrary to the truth of God, as we become indifferent to His Word and ways. To be contrary in this way will end with us eventually *Xing* Christ out as the center of our commitment, love, and service, thereby, losing our way in this present darkness.

Matthew 11:28-30

Y is for **yoke.**

When you consider the Christian life, you realize there is a *yoke*. Most of us know what a *yoke* is and what it is used for. It is a wooden bar or frame by which two creatures (such as oxen) of like status and abilities are joined at the heads or necks for working together *(WD)*. We also know there are *yokes* that are carried by one person to transport goods.

Jesus spoke of a *yoke*. This *yoke* implies a couple of possibilities for Christians. First, we are to be *yoked* with Jesus in our walk and work in the harvest field. Over the *years*, I have discovered different things about this *yoke*. It first started out as a cross that I had to learn to bear. As I allowed the cross to discipline my walk through obedience, it became a *yoke*.

This brings me to the second aspect of the *yoke*. Jesus is carrying the heaviest part of it, making it easy for us to endure. Jesus stated that we needed to take His *yoke* upon ourselves in order to learn of Him. Without the proper discipline in our spiritual walk, we will fail to learn of Him because we will never really become identified with Him. Without identification, we cannot walk as He walked, which means we are walking in step with Him according to His *yoke*.

Sadly, many Christians are not walking according to Jesus' *yoke*. To understand the essence of this *yoke* as believers, we must recognize that it has to do with identification that is established through obedience. His *yoke* actually points to His lordship. This obedience comes out of a lowly disposition and a meek attitude. What we will discover as Christians is that Jesus carried the same *yoke* of obedience when it came to the Father.

The *yoke* allows us the means to come under the burden. Jesus stated that His burden is light. When considering what enabled Jesus to endure His *yoke* of obedience when He went to the cross, you will realize that it was due to the burden of love. Love makes *yokes* easy to bear.

The problem with many Christians is that they may display zeal in their Christian devotion, but they are still *young* in their Christian life. They often run ahead of God, instead of learning what it means to come under His *yoke* to carry the burden of love. They have not yet learned how to consider the lessons of *yesterday* to establish a viable relationship with *Yahweh,* the God of Israel for today. *Youthful* lusts continue to influence their lives. Because of their *youthful* ways, they have not come to the place where they truly *yearn* for a life that is pleasing to *Yahweh.*

430

To come to a place of being properly *yoked* with Jesus, believers must truly learn what it means to *yield* to the Lordship of Jesus. We can talk about loving God, but love will express itself in obedience. We can talk about commitment, but commitment involves self-denial and coming under the *yoke* to lift the burden of slavery and death that plagues others.

It is important to keep in mind that we all will *yield* to some type of *yoke*. It may be tormenting and oppressive such as the *yokes* of sin, the flesh, and the world. Or, we can choose to submit to the liberating *yoke* of Jesus. However, it will come down to who we decide to serve. There are only two masters in this world, Jesus and Satan. Satan's *yoke* may give people a sense of independence or freedom, but eventually it will bring them to spiritual ruin. Jesus' *yoke* will end in discipline that will set a Christian free to discover his or her life in God.

Which *yoke* are you coming under?

Hebrews 12:22-24

Z is for **Zion.**

We are coming to the conclusion of this small book of our spiritual search for nuggets of wisdom that will prepare us to face the rigorous challenges and trials of life. We started with Jesus as our Alpha, the beginning of all matters, but He also serves as our Omega, the end of all matters. This brings us to the matter of what will mark the end of the journey.

We know that when we see Him in all of His glory, we will know that we are home. However, there is a name for this destination. It has been referred to as heaven and Paradise. However, there is another name for it, and that is *Zion*. *Zion* points to the perfect homeland, paradise, or utopia. We know that the source that ensures such perfection is the abiding presence of God in our midst. In fact, if we do not stray in our journey, we can taste a bit of *Zion* in our travels.

In order to taste a bit of heaven on earth, we must avoid a few traps. We must stay away from becoming *zealots*. These are people that operate according to fleshly *zeal*. The Bible is clear that people can have a *zeal* for God, but do not really know Him. *Zeal* can cause us to get ahead of God's plan, rather than carrying it out. In the end, we will put God to a foolish test in our ignorance and lose sight of Him. Ultimately, we will end up with a big *zero* for all of our *zealous* activities.

Another trap we must avoid is insisting on staying in our comfort *zones* about God. There is a tendency of wanting to put God into a nice comfortable box. From this premise we can rest on our so-called "laurels" since we believe that we have our Christian life all figured out. This state simply points to a false security of trying to maintain what we have managed to establish about Jesus. However, such familiarity will breed contempt when it is challenged. Jesus is eternal, and there is no way that any person can put Him in some understandable box. Along the way He will challenge such comfort *zones* to bring about maturity.

The other trap that we must beware of during our spiritual journey is the one set by the world. The world opposes any real love and devotion to God. As a result, it will set up detours that will cause us to *zigzag* in and out of our Christian life. In other words, we will end up with a mixture of a worldly religion that will cause life to appear as a *zoo*. As we *zip* in and out of worldly activities, while trying to adjust our responsibilities as citizens of the kingdom of heaven to the demands of life, we will eventually become *zombies* who will end up suffering from total burnout. Out of the burnout will come anger against God because He, along with His righteous ways, will not adjust to the world's perverted practices.

As Christians, we must finish the course if we are going to receive the crown of righteousness. Finishing the course means experiencing the glory of *Zion*. This reminds me of the wilderness called *Zin*. The children of Israel passed through five wildernesses before they entered the Promised Land. They were to pass from the fourth wilderness of Paran into the Promised Land. However, they rebelled in unbelief and had to spend the next forty years wandering in this wilderness.

After forty years of wandering, the children of Israel came into the wilderness of *Zin*. They were so close, yet they found the way to be hard. Due to their attitude of ingratitude, God sent fiery serpents into their midst to chastise them in their obstinacy. They humbled themselves in repentance. A bronze serpent was lifted up in the wilderness as a solution to their plight. All they had to do was look at it, thereby, stopping the deadly bite from claiming them as its victim.

Twenty centuries ago, the Son of God was lifted up on the cross to take the sting out of death. His death on the cross reminds us that the way is hard, and that the last wilderness of this present world may prove to be the hardest to endure. We do not know what our wilderness of *Zin* is going to look like. We do not know what tests or trials we might have to face before we reach *Zion*, but the one promise we can hold on to is that it will be glorious. And, as those who have gone before us, we will have to admit that the bridges, crossroads, wildernesses, and the yoke of this present life, amounted to nothing more than a light affliction, which lasted for a moment, but worked in each spiritual traveler a far more exceeding and eternal weight of glory.

Obviously, we cannot let up in our Christian walk. We must possess the eternal inheritance secured for us. We must daily seek out the prize of heaven, sell whatever it takes to buy truth, insist on integrity and righteousness in our own lives, and dig deep to find the nuggets of wisdom in the midst of darkness and deception. We must never settle for less from ourselves. Rather, we must strive to reach our potential of reflecting the light and beauty of heaven, Jesus Christ. This is the essence of our victory. After all, it is His kingdom, His power, and His glory that awaits us, as well as the promise of living in our spiritual *Zion* in the light of His glorious presence forever.

BIBLIOGRAPHY

Strong's Exhaustive Concordance of the Bible, © 1890 by James Strong; © 1980, 1986 assigned to World Bible Publishers, Inc.

Webster's New Collegiate Dictionary, © 1976 by G. & C. Merriam Co.

Smith's Bible Dictionary

So Send I You/Workman of God; Oswald Chambers, © 1993 by Oswald Chambers Publications Association Limited

A Dwelling Place for God, Ruth Specter Lascelle, © 1990 by Hyman Israel Specter

Jewish Faith and the New Covenant, Ruth Specter Lascelle © 1980

The Seeking Heart, Fenelon, © 1992 by Christian Book Publishing House

Becoming a Fool, Os Hillman, February 11, 2006

Born After Midnight, A.W. Tozer; © 1989 by Christian Publications

Tozer On Worship And Entertainment, Compiled by James L. Snyder; © 1997 by Christian Publications

Whatever Happened to Worship?, A. W. Tozer; © 1985 by Christian Publications

My Utmost for His Highest; Oswald Chambers; © 1963 by Oswald Chambers Publications Association, Ltd.

Daily Thoughts for Disciples; by Oswald Chambers;© 1990 by Oswald Chambers Publications Association 1976

Wings of the Morning; Video; © 1992 by A.C.E, Inc.

Prayer: A Holy Occupation; Oswald Chambers; © 1992 by Oswald Chambers Publications Association, Limited

A Shepherd Looks at The Good Shepherd And His Sheep; Phillip Keller; © 1978 by W. Phillip Keller

The Riches of Watchman Nee, © 1999 by Living Stream Ministry.

Our Daily Bread, October 9, 2000

The Thompson Chain-Reference Bible, © 1988 by the B. B. Kirkbridge Bible Co. Inc.

ABOUT THE AUTHOR

Rayola Kelley, an ordained minister of the Gospel, was born again and saved out of a cult in 1976 while serving in the U.S. Navy. Her spiritual journey continued through extensive discipleship, before following the Lord's call upon her life into full-time ministry 35 years ago, when, with Jeannette Haley, founded Gentle Shepherd Ministries.

Through the years, Rayola's gift of teaching the Word has opened many doors for her to teach adult Sunday school, oversee a fellowship for over 15 years, hold evangelistic meetings in churches, conduct seminars, and speak at retreats. She has served in jail ministry, and is well known for her gift of spiritual insight and counseling. Upon being called to be a missionary in America, Rayola, along with Jeannette Haley established different fellowships where intense Bible Studies and discipleship training were conducted to equip believers for the ministry. These different mission fields in America entailed working in various churches as well as working with other cultures such as Korean and Hispanic nationalities.

Rayola, along with co-laborer Jeannette Haley, (professional artist, author of Christian novels, Bible Studies and stories for children) began sending out a monthly newsletter containing articles for the Body of Christ in 1997 which continues to grow. Ms. Kelley has authored over 55 books, and numerous Bible Studies including an advanced Discipleship Course (available in both English and Spanish) that is being used in countries such as Africa, Bulgaria, Israel, Ireland, India, Cuba, and Pakistan. Among her many books is *"Hidden Manna"* which deals with destructive cycles in people and relationships, and *"Battle for the Soul"* which presents a clear picture of the battle that rages in the soul. She has written six in-depth devotional books, including both the Old Testament and New Testament devotional study which takes the reader through the entire Bible in one year. All of her books are hard-hitting, bottom-line spiritual food for the hungry and thirsty soul to "chew" upon in order to *"grow strong in the Lord, and in the power of His might."*

Rayola currently resides in Oldtown, ID where she continues to fulfill Christ's commission to make disciples through teaching, spiritual counseling, and writing.

Please visit Gentle Shepherd Ministries Web Site at: www.gentleshepherd.com for further information, and to access her challenging and informative audio sermons.

Other books by Rayola Kelley:

Hidden Manna (Original)
Battle for the Soul
Stories of the Heart
Transforming Love & Beyond
The Great Debate
Post to Post: (1) Establishing the Way
Post to Post: (2) Walking in the Way
Post to Post: (3) Meditations Along the Way

Volume One: Establishing Our Life in Christ
My Words are Spirit and Life
The Anatomy of Sin
The Principles of the Abundant Life
The Place of Covenant
Unmasking the Cult Mentality

Volume Two: Putting on the Life of Christ
He Actually Thought It Not Robbery
Revelation of the Cross
In Search of Real Faith
Think on These Things
Follow the Pattern

Volume Four: Issues of the Heart
Hidden Manna (Revised)
Bring Down the Sacred Cows
The Manual for the Single Christian Life
Parents are People Too

Volume Five: Challenging the Christian Life
The Issues of Life
Presentation of the Gospel
For the Purpose of Edification
Whatever Happened to the Church?
Women's Place in the Kingdom of God

Volume Six: Developing Our Christian Life
The Many Faces of Christianity
Possessing Our Souls
Experiencing the Christian Life
The Power of Our Testimonies
The Victorious Journey

Volume Seven: Discovering True Ministry
From Prisons and Dots to Christianity
So You Want To Be In Ministry?

Devotions
Devotions of the Heart: Books One and Two
Daily Food for the Soul: Books One and Two

Gentle Shepherd Ministries Devotion Series:
Being a Child of God
Disciplining the Strength of our Youth
Coming to Full Age

Nugget Books:
Nuggets From Heaven
More Nuggets From Heaven
Heavenly Gems
More Heavenly Gems
Heavenly Treasures

Gentle Shepherd Ministries Series:

The Christian Life Series
What Matter Is This?
The Challenge of It
The Reality of It

The Leadership Series
Overcoming
A Matter of Authority and Power
The Dynamics of True Leadership

Books By
Jeannette Haley
Books co-authored with Rayola Kelley:
Hidden Manna (Original)
The Many Faces of Christianity (Volume 6)
Post to Post 3: Meditations Along the Way

Other Books:
Rose of Light, Thorn of Darkness (Volume 7)
Interview in Hell (Volume 7)
Interview on Earth (Volume 7)
The Pig and I
Reflections of Wonder (Devotional)

Children Books:
Little Stories for Little People
Traveler's Tales
The Adventures of Zack and Mira
The Adventures of Paul and Dana
(A House on the Beach)
The Monster of Mystery Valley